A History of Italian Economic Thought

This book provides the non-Italian scholar with an extensive picture of the development of Italian economics, from the sixteenth century to the present. The thread of the narrative is the dialectics between economic theory and political action, where the former attempts to enlighten the latter, but at the same time receives from politics the main stimulus to enlarge its field of reflection. This is particularly clear during the Enlightenment. Inside, this book insists on stressing that Galiani, Verri and Beccaria were economists quite sensitive to practical issues, but who also were willing to attain generally valid conclusions. In this sense, 'pure economics' was never performed in Italy. Even Pareto used economics (and sociology) in order to interpret and possibly steer the course of political action.

During the Restoration period (1815–48) there was a slowdown of the economists' engagement, due to an adverse political situation, that prompted them to prefer less dangerous subjects, such as the relationship between economics, morals and law (the main interpreter of this attitude was Romagnosi). After 1848 and up to 1890, however, in parallel with the *Risorgimento* cultural climate, a new vision of the economists' task was eventually manifested. Between economics and political Liberalism a sort of alliance was established, whose prophet was F. Ferrara. While the Historical school of economics of German origin played a minor role, pure economics (1890–1940 approx.) enjoyed considerable success with regard to both economic equilibrium and the theory of public finance. Consequently, the introduction of Keynes's ideas was rather laborious. Instead, Hayek had an immediate success.

This book concludes with a chapter devoted to the intense relationships between economic theories, economic programmes and political action after 1945. Here, the Sraffa debate played an important role in stimulating Italian economists to reflect upon the patterns of Italian economy and the possibilities of transforming Italy's economic and social structure.

Riccardo Faucci is Full Professor of the History of Economic Thought, Pisa University, Italy. He is co-editor of *History of Economic Ideas*.

Routledge history of economic thought

Edited by Mark Blaug

Co-Director, Erasmus Center for History in Management and Economics, Erasmus University, the Netherlands.

A History of Italian Economic Thought

Riccardo Faucci

Routledge
Taylor & Francis Group

LONDON AND NEW YORK

First published 2014 by Routledge

2 Park Square, Milton Park, Abingdon, Oxfordshire OX14 4RN
52 Vanderbilt Avenue, New York, NY 10017

Routledge is an imprint of the Taylor & Francis Group, an informa business

First issued in paperback 2019

British Library Cataloguing in Publication Data
A catalogue record for this book is available from the British Library

Library of Congress Cataloging in Publication Data
Faucci, Riccardo.
[Economia politica in Italia. English]
A history of Italian economic thought / Riccardo Faucci.
  pages cm. – (The Routledge history of economic thought)
  1. Economics–Italy–History. I. Title.
  HB109.A2F37713 2014
  330.0945–dc23

                                          2013040608

ISBN: 978-0-415-51983-0 (hbk)
ISBN: 978-0-367-86702-7 (pbk)

Typeset in Times New Roman
by Wearset Ltd, Boldon, Tyne and Wear

Contents

Acknowledgements

I would like to thank Mrs Rachel Costa née Barritt, PhD for her professional revising of this book.

1 General problems of interpretation

Schumpeter's lesson

This profile of the history of Italian economic thought aims to illustrate, through comprehensive reference to texts, the contribution provided by Italian economists to the development of economics over the last five centuries. Their achievements were not confined to *analysis*, i.e. to the complex of specialist techniques of enquiry into economic phenomena, but also embraced *vision*, namely, the political and ideological (pre)conceptions that shaped the common ground of the economists' profession through the centuries. Both aspects are deemed here to be important in the formation of economics. Economists never limited themselves to such issues as the effect a tax on consumption goods might exert on the level of prices, or the impact of money expansion on employment; economists were and are implicitly or explicitly inspired by some design of an ideal society in which a meaningful role is assigned to the economic measures they advocate. In short, vision in this book corresponds to German *Weltanschauung*. It includes both value judgements on what *is*, and on what *is to be* (Schumpeter 1994 [1954], Chapter 4; Dobb 1973, Introductory).

A comparison with Schumpeter is of interest. Despite the fact that he considered science and ideology as two conceptually distinct moments, it should not be disregarded that they represented focal points of his attention throughout his entire experience as a thinker, and were often closely interlaced. For instance, his entrepreneur is also a sociological *Idealtypus*, his analysis of 'socialism' is strongly ideological and paves the way for his pessimistic forecast with regard to the future of a 'free' society. Moreover, glancing at another leading character among twentieth-century economists, it can hardly be overlooked that Keynes's analysis of uncertainty, speculation and the inducement to invest heavily depends on his scepticism concerning the possibility of spontaneous reform of historical capitalism, and on his strong conviction that economic collaboration among countries was vital to provide the necessary support for recovery from the economic collapse of the 1930s.

These commonsense considerations may justify the present writer's opinion that no clear-cut demarcation can be made between a merely *internal* (theoretical) approach, and a so-called *external* approach focusing on the intellectual and material context in which economic ideas arose. Paraphrasing Kant, pure theory separated from its historical context is empty, while descriptive history without theory is blind.

For these reasons, one cannot be fully content with a history of economics of the 'economic theory in retrospect'-type (here, reference to Mark Blaug's textbook is almost compulsory), which searches for continuity of theorizing throughout the various phases of the history of economic thought – starting from the present state of economics – and then seeks antecedents in the past, to be reshaped in a modern guise for the sake of rendering it more familiar or appealing to a present-day reader. Of course, in endeavouring to reconstruct the evolution of some crucial and specific economic concepts, such as the theory of interest, or control of the money supply, the measurement of 'utility', and so forth, such an approach could be highly fruitful. But if the intention is to give a general account of the evolution of economic thought in a specific nation or culture, the 'economics in retrospect' approach may not be the optimal solution.

Moreover, the category of 'economic thought' is broader than that of 'economic analysis'. Far from being a mere aggregate of pieces of theory, the concept of economic thought transcends each individual stage; it aims at a comprehensive picture of the role and outcomes of a highly complex phenomenon, namely the construction of a twofold science which is not only a 'box of tools', but also an agenda for political choice, a pedagogy for the ruling (and ruled!) classes. In a nutshell, 'economic thought' represents a crucial moment of a nation's autobiography.

This unique dual nature of economics, which constitutes its special feature in the domain of the social sciences, should always be kept in mind. Throughout its history, economics has fought to establish a demarcation line that would set it apart from morals and theology. In modern terms, economics has become less and less normative in the sense of *ought to be*, and more and more positive, in the sense of *to be*. This movement towards scientific autonomy has led to the formation of a special language and methodology that is increasingly 'scientific' and theoretically based.

While this may be the expected evolution from a normative complex to a science in the proper sense, there can be no doubt that since the beginning of the modern age many Italian economists have shown a special interest in theoretical concepts, in accordance with their ambition to build up an entirely value-free discipline. These remarkable efforts, which to some extent parallel those carried out by Galileo Galilei in the physical sciences, represent a distinctive feature of Italian economics, and prompt interesting comparisons with the enquiries pursued by English and French economists in the same years.

It should be made clear that in drawing a contrast between 'positive' and 'normative', we are referring to the historical evolution of economics as a science and its emancipation from subjection to morals and religion. It is not a question of the differentiation between positive and normative economics in a modern sense; that is, in the sense that the Pareto optimum is a normative, non-positive concept. Such a distinction is absolutely internal to economics, and, although it may imply a reconsideration of the influence of value judgements in economics, it by no means calls for a rethinking the foundations of economics itself.

While this conclusion can be considered as acceptable to all contemporary economists, it cannot be disputed that the evolution of economic science over the five centuries of our review coincides with the emancipation of economics from non-economics; namely, from religion, morals, philosophy and kindred spheres of reflection. Even more significantly, it can be observed that economists have singled out from the terrain of these doctrines only what was of use for the improvement of their own theories – for instance, the progress of physics and mathematics influenced many theoretical economists of the twentieth century. Naturally, this is not in contrast with the idea of the growth of economics as an autonomous discipline – it is a validation of this process, tending to enrich economics in its tools and scope.

Below, we will describe the normative prescriptions which, although springing from outside the terrain of economics *stricto sensu*, belong to the closely related field of politics and inevitably contribute to influencing the economist's choices.

Two versions of economic liberalism

From the mid-eighteenth century onwards, Italian economic thought – following the evolution of the general course of economic ideas in Europe – gradually abandoned its primitive positions favourable to political absolutism, and manifested an increasingly sympathetic attitude towards liberalism. It is undeniable that the doctrine of political liberalism – taken as a doctrine of the limits of state power over individuals – is the current of thought that most profoundly permeated the European economists, especially in the Enlightenment, to such an extent that some of the major figures, from Locke to Smith, are considered as classics in both fields. The nexus between *political* liberalism and *economic* liberalism (in Italian, the latter concept is expressed with the term *liberismo*, which corresponds to libertarianism and, in the last analysis, to *laissez faire*) has become entangled over the course of time.

Early liberalism was imbued with the concept of 'natural laws'. According to the physiocrat Mercier de la Rivière, the sovereign himself was subject to the 'natural' laws of the economy, and had neither the power nor the right to violate such laws; indeed, should he have the audacity to do so, damage would occur. In Italy, owing to the political fragmentation of the peninsula, divided up as it was among small regional states, this general conclusion did not come to the fore so clearly. Nevertheless, such writers as Ferdinando Galiani – himself an adversary of the Physiocrats, as we will see – reveal a clearly perceptible awareness that the market, insofar as it presupposed impersonal yet necessary relations, constituted a mechanism independent of the individual will of the statesman. Thus it was imperative for political reforms to be in accordance with economic laws; failure to fulfil this requirement would spell doom for such reforms. The cogency of economic laws therefore seemed to validate Horace's line in his *Epistulae*: '*Natura furca expellas, tamen usque recurret.*' In fact, as we will see, Galiani adopted an approach to economics – and to politics as well – which approximated methodological individualism. Subsequently, from Joseph A. Schumpeter through to Karl R. Popper, the latter concept became a cornerstone of modern liberal thought.

As is well known, the existence of so many currents of liberalism flourishing in Europe during the nineteenth century, demonstrates that what was at stake was not a drastic alternative between 'omnipotent government' and absolute *laissez faire*, but rather a reasonable balance between the prerogatives of the government and fundamental individual rights. Naturally, the demarcation line was subject to variations, due to changes both in the structure of the economy and in the degree of social consciousness. Reasonably, the liberal jurist and economist Giandomenico Romagnosi, claimed that economic freedom should not be left 'unbridled', but should be subordinated to equity and justice. Similar conclusions were reached by the *Risorgimento* statesman Marco Minghetti in his 1859 book on the relationship between economics and morals (see Chapter 4 below).

These criteria may nevertheless appear somewhat generic. More pragmatically, in his action as a statesman, Count Camillo Cavour embodied a liberalism open to British liberal-reformist influences, and awarded a prominent role to state expenditure – especially in public works such as railways – as an engine of economic growth.

Among the *Risorgimento* economists, Francesco Ferrara alone professed an extreme libertarianism, with tones that anticipate Murray Rothbard: 'Government, claiming to represent all people, represents nobody' (Ferrara 1992 [1858]: 235). But as we will see below (Chapter 5), his was a lone case.

This overview of the positions in the field would not be complete if one were to disregard the fact that several economists active in politics were imbued with the principles of Catholic social thought, which they attempted to reconcile with those of liberalism. The current of Catholic liberals featured many important leaders, including Manzoni, Gioberti, Rosmini and Lambruschini in the spheres of literature, philosophy and educational sciences, and Messedaglia, together with Lampertico, in the realm of economics and statistics. Despite Pius IX's severe condemnation of Catholic liberalism in his *Syllabus* (1864), this stream of thought actively contributed to the *Risorgimento*, and to the post-Unity intellectual movement.

A watershed between 'old' and 'new' liberalism can be located around 1890, when a new version of pure economic liberalism arose, mainly owing to the influence of Austrian thought. This school, which set the rational consumer at the centre of the economic scene, posited that all operators were endowed with perfect knowledge and assumed full competition between all sellers as well as an absence of institutional barriers. Economic individualism and political individualism were seen as two sides of the same coin. Maffeo Pantaleoni's 1889 book *Principii di economia pura* was the main product of this particular kind of subjectivism, where political theory and economic theory converged (see Chapter 6).

After 1900, however, Pantaleoni abandoned his faith in the symmetry between economic and political theory and his belief that they were governed by the same static, maximizing rules. Instead, he became more and more attracted by dynamics, an approach he considered to be more appropriate for an evaluation of the impact of the various social systems on the whole structure of society. Pantaleoni admitted the existence of different kinds of dynamics, varying according to the type of social organization. Thus, he acknowledged a 'first type' dynamics corresponding to an absolutely free society, and a 'second type' dynamics corresponding to a society hampered by artificial constraints (such as monopolies and paternalist government). Overall, Pantaleoni lost faith in political liberalism – more properly, in democratic liberalism that he considered as a degeneration from pure liberalism – which, he now felt, not only failed to confirm economic liberalism, but paved the way to socialism and therefore was destined to bring about its own downfall. For these reasons he opted to embrace authoritarian – and, in the last analysis, Fascist – positions in politics, believing that such positions were by no means incompatible with economic freedom.

Vilfredo Pareto also contrasted economic liberalism with political liberalism, although in different terms. Economic liberalism, on which general economic equilibrium was based, was to lead to the so-called Pareto optimum, and to the two theorems of Welfare Economics, a mathematical translation of the Verri–Helvétius–Bentham 'maximum of happiness' principle. But political liberalism, Pareto argued, had degenerated into an unstable regime, leaning towards 'demagogic plutocracy', a perverse alliance between monopoly capitalists and protected workers. Economics and (political) sociology were an expression of two different spheres of human conduct that could never go hand in hand.

The complexity of these issues was solved, so to speak, by another Italian economist who discussed at length the relationship between *laissez-faire* and political liberalism: Luigi Einaudi. Unlike most previous writers, Einaudi represented economic and political liberalism not only as pure theoretical abstractions, but also as convergent and connected systems which had sometimes found their full accomplishment in the course of history – e.g. in ancient Greece or in Italian medieval towns – and in more modern times whenever strong self-regulating social institutions were interposed between the State and the individual. In this sense Einaudi, himself an advocate of secularism, praised the Catholic Church as a voluntary organization of worshippers in a context of small enterprises scattered throughout a district characterized by a number of workers' unions interacting in mutual, constructive, competition. He viewed such a situation as allowing both economic and political liberalism to reach their optimal equilibrium. The late medieval and early humanist rhetoric of the civic virtues – summarized in Ambrogio Lorenzetti's famous fresco of 'Buongoverno' in Sienna – was relaunched in a more persuasive form (see Silvestri 2008).

An opportunity for fruitful cooperation between political and economic liberalism was provided by the Italian theory of public finance. Reflection on the nature of the relationship between state and its citizens in order to make a comparative assessment of the cost of the tax burden versus the benefit of the public expenditure was a peculiarity of the Italian school of public finance during the 90-year period between 1850 and 1940, a school whose merits have been acknowledged by such distinguished scholars as J. M. Buchanan and R. E. Wagner (see De Bonis and Fausto 2003).

In the vision of this school, the nature of either 'monopolist' or 'democratic' state can influence the tax system and hence the degree of freedom that citizens can enjoy (see Chapter 6).

The political engagement of Italian economists in the *Risorgimento*

The economists *qua* intellectuals who took an active interest in the crucial political issues of their time exerted a generally positive role in Italy. Not only did they fulfil the function of enlightening the ruling class as to the most suitable manner of addressing the complex aspects of governance and of avoiding mistaken procedures, they also often played a challenging – and frequently successful – substitutive role in the many situations in which the traditional political forces proved unable to master situations involving economic crises and/or social unrest. This feature, probably shared by all countries where democracy was not solidly established, was recurrent in Italian history.

At the origin of this phenomenon there lay a process of class diversification. Throughout the eighteenth century and up to 1848 the 'economists' *qua* social group mainly belonged to the class of landowners or gentlemen farmers. The standard economist was typically a *rentier*, often an aristocrat, whose traditional training prescribed a private education, a *grand tour* throughout Europe, and the publication of economic writings dictated by his experience in managing his own farms or consisting of official reports and memoranda if he held public positions. In 1848, during the very short time when all Italian states enjoyed a constitution, most of these figures actively collaborated with their sovereigns. The case of Pellegrino Rossi, formerly professor of political economy at the Collège de France, who was Prime Minister under Pius IX and who was assassinated by a revolutionary, is an extreme manifestation of the overlap between the role of the economist and that of a prominent politician.

After the 1849 reaction, several economists, mostly from Naples and Palermo, sought refuge in the Kingdom of Sardinia, the only one to retain the constitutional charter. Living in Turin or in Genoa, these exiles earned their living as civil servants, professors or journalists, thereby making a major contribution to the intellectual progress of civil society. The extent of their achievements can be measured by the increase in daily newspapers and journals that published articles on economics, and by the launching of editorial projects. All this contributed to 'modernizing' the profile of the economist as a social figure.

The economists inside the new state's institutions

After 1861, and above all after 1876, when the so-called *Sinistra storica* (Historical Left) succeeded to the *Destra storica* (Historical Right), the process of formation of a body of public servants with special training in law and economics was gradually completed. The growing importance of the middle class employed in the civil service led to a specialized demand for economics – more precisely, for broader economic-administrative knowledge – and to an increase in the university faculties where economics was taught.

The examples of economists occupying high-ranking positions in the Parliament, in various branches of the administration, and/or in Italian cabinets, are countless. Let us recall just a few names. Angelo Messedaglia, professor of economics and statistics in Padua and Rome, was at the head of the committee that drew up the new cadastre of the Kingdom of Italy. Salvatore Majorana Calatabiano, professor of political economy and of public finance in Messina and Catania, was Minister of Agriculture, Industry and Commerce in 1878 and was instrumental in the passing of the first Italian law on forestry. Many economists, such as Antonio Scialoja, Francesco Ferrara and Agostino Magliani, were appointed as members of the *Corte dei conti* (Court of audit) from its establishment in 1862. All three held the post of Finance Minister. It is noteworthy that all the above-mentioned personalities had been appointed life-long senators.

Among the post-*Risorgimento* generation, two outstanding economic experts can be cited. Luigi Luzzatti, professor of commercial and constitutional law in Padua and Rome, and Vittorio Ellena, the powerful general secretary to the Ministry of Agriculture, were the authors of the tariff reforms of 1878 and 1887, both of which were protective. Luzzatti was also Treasury Minister for almost a decade and on this occasion he carried out the conversion of Italian bonds in 1906. In 1910–11 he became Prime Minister.

During the severe mid-1890s economic crisis another competent politician-economist entered the scene. Sidney Sonnino, a half-English Tuscan landowner, translator of such authors as J. E. Cairnes and W. Thornton, was a pioneer of research on the 'Southern question', namely the quest underlying the economic and social backwardness of the south of Italy, from an innovative socio-economic viewpoint. A liberal belonging to the Right, he was appointed as Finance and Treasury Minister in 1893–94. He distinguished himself for his severe budgetary policy and supported the foundation of the Bank of Italy. He subsequently became Prime Minister in 1906 and 1909–10, and Foreign Minister in 1917–1919.

Another important name is that of Carlo F. Ferraris, professor of finance and public administration in Padua and a follower of the German school of *Kathedersozialisten*. Ferraris's greatest achievement was the 1905 railway nationalization he accomplished as Public Works Minister.

In the first two decades of the new century, Francesco Saverio Nitti, an economist-sociologist who had a chair of public finance at Naples, was Agriculture Minister in 1911–14, when he created the powerful INA (National Insurance

Institute); and Treasury Minister in 1917–18, when he successfully managed the war finances. He became Prime Minister in 1919–20.

Another economist, Vincenzo Tangorra, professor of public finance in Pisa, was appointed as Treasury Minister in the Mussolini 1922 coalition government as a representative of the Popular (Catholic) Party. His premature death forestalled his possible contribution to political affairs.

Several chaired economists also served under the Fascist regime, among whom one may cite Alberto De' Stefani, Arrigo Serpieri, Giacomo Acerbo, and Giuseppe Tassinari (the latter three being professors of agricultural economics). They held key positions in the Mussolini cabinet, and played a role in several important, though controversial, economic events, such as *Quota Novanta* (appreciation of the Italian currency in order to reach the rate of 90 lira per pound sterling in 1926), the *Bonifica integrale* (land reclamation, mainly of the Latium Marsh) and the *Battaglia del grano* (an effort both to extend wheat production and to increase land productivity mainly for the purposes of autarky) in the late 1920s and early 1930s.

Numerous examples of intensive participation of economists in political developments can also be found after the fall of the *Commissione economica per la Costituente* (Economic Commission for the Constituent Assembly, 1945–46). The Commission mapped an extensive picture of the economic situation of Italy and its perspectives for reconstruction. In 1947–48, Budget Minister Luigi Einaudi, who had been appointed Governor of the Bank of Italy two years earlier, successfully brought inflation down thanks to an energetic restrictive monetary policy in accordance with classical (quantitative) monetary theory. In 1955 Budget Minister Ezio Vanoni, professor of financial law in Pavia, presented the first draft of a national five-year economic plan, the so-called *schema Vanoni*, based on the Harrod model which, at that time, was considered very modern. A significant feature of the Vanoni plan was its encouragement of the introduction of Keynesianism into Italian political debate (see Chapter 8).

In subsequent decades, the phenomenon of the committed action of prestigious economists in high-level political affairs received a further impetus from the European unification process. In 1993–94, Premier Carlo Azeglio Ciampi, formerly Governor of the Bank of Italy, was praised for achieving Italy's entry into the European Economic Union, a merit he shared with Giuliano Amato, professor of comparative constitutional law in Rome but also well-trained in economics – he in turn was Premier in 1992 and 2000. A special political role was covered by Romano Prodi, professor of industrial economics at Bologna, formerly IRI President and EU commissary, who led as Premier the Centre-Left coalition of *Ulivo/Democratici* in 1996–98 and 2006–08. On the opposite side of the political spectrum, the Berlusconi cabinets (1993–94, 2001–06 and 2008–11) included professional economists such as Antonio Martino, Antonio Marzano and Renato Brunetta, along with Giulio Tremonti, a chaired financial law jurist.

In November 2011 Bocconi University economist Mario Monti, former European Anti-Trust Commissioner, shouldered the heavy legacy of the previous Berlusconi cabinet, during which the Italian economy had suffered both an income recession and an increasing burden of public debt. Immediately dubbed *'governo dei professori'*, the Monti cabinet was in fact composed not only of university teachers but also of prominent bankers, leading entrepreneurs and top civil servants.

The Monti solution was justified by the apparent inability of the previous majority to adopt the measures suggested by the EU in order to offset the economic/financial crisis. There was a classical extraordinary situation that required an extraordinary solution, such as a *'governo del Presidente'* (of the Republic) entitled to carry out those unpopular measures that the parties were not ready to take. This feature is not to be considered as a radical novelty in post-war Italian constitutional history, where temporary cabinets, mainly headed by an independent personality, have occasionally been appointed to allow political crises to be resolved. At least two quite recent cabinets have been considered by historians as 'technical' – the above-mentioned Ciampi cabinet; and that led by the former general director of the Bank of Italy, Lamberto Dini (1994–96), who was appointed after the crisis of the first Berlusconi Centre-Right coalition.

The sudden conclusion of the Monti experience (ended 2012) may also be explained by the Premier's political ambition to no longer act as a technocrat 'lent' to politics, but rather more directly as a political and party leader in his own right, thereby implicitly rejecting the role the President of the Republic had assigned him.

To sum up, the subtitle of Robert Skidelski's second volume of his biography of John Maynard Keynes, *The Economist as Saviour*, may be extended to many Italian economists who have been engaged in politics at the highest levels throughout the last 150 years. Nevertheless, co-optation of 'technicians' in politics should not be too frequently performed in a normal democracy. There are two specular risks. The first is that any organic programme based on sound economic principles, and suggested by economists, might conflict with a merely opportunistic 'calculus of consent' expressed by political parties, and would be therefore nullified. The second is that these programmes, mainly centred on severe, rather than on accommodating, policies, could be hard to swallow for public opinion, thereby contributing towards a climate of tension. To sum up, our present-day political system appears condemned to oscillate schizophrenically between both resistance to change and attraction towards change whatever it may be.

'Militant' versus 'functionary' economists

The above reference to Italian economists' interaction with political power prompts reflection on a crucial distinction, made by Antonio Gramsci in his *Prison Notebooks*, between the 'great Italian intellectual militants' (Gramsci's favourite example was that of Benedetto Croce) and the 'intellectual-functionaries', called upon to execute the projects put forward by the former. According to Gramsci, the 'militant' intellectuals were involved in creating the national (bourgeois) ideology, while the 'functionaries' were, rather, a product of the social division of labour in a capitalist society and were assigned to the comparatively more obscure but no less crucial work of disseminating and executing the designs of the former group. Gramsci exemplified his argument with reference mainly to literature and philosophy, undoubtedly his favourite topics (see Isnenghi 1979), but his intuitions may also be of use for our research.

It should be noted that in Gramsci's terminology a 'militant' is by no means a revolutionary, but rather an intellectual leader who produces ideas that are mainly designed with the ruling class in mind; and 'functionary' has nothing to do with a bureaucratic profession but generally embodies a figure springing from an organizational background (a journalist, a publisher, a teacher) who contributes to spreading and popularizing the militants' ideas and therefore to moulding public opinion.

In Italy, there existed no economist whose influence could be compared to that enjoyed by Benedetto Croce – a thinker who throughout half a century acted as a veritable intellectual dictator. To some extent, however, Luigi Einaudi's role among the economists closely approximated the model of a militant intellectual. Gramsci himself attended Einaudi's lectures in Turin and always respected him, though this respect did not stop him criticisizing Einaudi's extreme *laissez-faire* views. Einaudi's teaching, moral and political as well as economic, was based on a unique mix of scholarly learning and sound commonsense, and undoubtedly helped to form a modern economically oriented public opinion in Italy. But even as a scientist Einaudi liked to accompany the reader with the aid of a brilliant and compelling illustration of economic phenomena. Rhetoric in the original meaning of the art of persuasion was his strong point. However, Einaudi's main economic ideas about taxation were not shared by the majority of his colleagues (see Chapter 7). This feature highlights a significant difference between Einaudi and Croce, the latter having produced a host of faithful disciples in the fields of philosophy, literary criticism and historiography. In conclusion, there was never an 'Einaudi school'.

Naturally, the Einaudi case doesn't exhaust all examples of a militant economist. Numerous other economic writers exerted a considerable impact on public opinion through their successful action as freelance journalists and economic commentators. In Italy, as elsewhere, the growth of public opinion in a modern sense owes much to the economics profession. As early as 1900, all leading newspapers had their 'own' economics columnist. Between the economic commentators we can find both 'militants' and 'functionaries'. Liberal-conservative *Corriere della sera*, where Einaudi wrote for 25 years, had its counterpart at *La Stampa* of Turin (liberal on the left) in the form of Attilio Cabiati, who previously collaborated with the socialist *Avanti!*. The Turin-based *La gazzetta del popolo* (die-hard Right) presented articles by Giuseppe Prato. *Il mattino* of Naples (Centre) expressed its economic opinion through Nitti.

Some perplexities arise from the cases of Pareto and Pantaleoni, who around 1900 frequently wrote for *Il secolo* of Milan (leaning towards democratic radicalism). Their teaching transcends the strict Gramsci category. Both were too aristocratic to bow to the exigencies of public opinion; rather, they proudly cast themselves in the role of 'preachers in the wilderness'. Yet there can be no doubt that Pantaleoni, moreso than Pareto (or De Viti de Marco), approximated Gramsci's 'militant' model.

From courtiers to independent thinkers

The reflection on 'militant' and 'functionary' economists prompts enquiry into certain aspects of the position of economists in Italian society. An international comparison may be of help. Unquestionably, in Britain and to a lesser extent in France, economists had enjoyed an autonomous role since the age of Enlightenment. Both Hume and Smith were independent thinkers (only after he had already written the *Wealth of Nations* did Smith become a public servant at the head of the Custom House). Quesnay was a courtier, but the king's protection allowed him to benefit from a position of comparative independence. Turgot became minister after gaining success as an *Encyclopédie* writer; Ricardo was a wealthy broker, and later on became an MP, and so forth.

In Italy, after Machiavelli and Botero – the very first two 'economists' considered in our survey – the perspective broadens to include merchants like Davanzati and scientists like Montanari, whose position in society was quite similar to that assumed by many seventeenth-century British authors like Mun, Petty and others. In the eighteenth century a number of public servants, mainly of aristocratic origin (Carli and Verri were counts, Beccaria a marquis, Galiani the youngest son of a marquis, Filangieri a member of a princely family), were actively engaged in promoting economic reforms both in Northern and Southern Italy. Finally, many of the early economists were churchmen. The most 'modern' – in the sense of internationally oriented – was Abbot Galiani, who served as embassy attaché in Paris in the 1760s and as a public official in Naples in the 1780s.

The 1796–99 revolutionary *Triennium* had a dramatic impact on the frame of mind that had theretofore been the hallmark of intellectuals. Their attitudes could not fail to be affected by the new patriotic spirit that influenced literature, philosophy and even economic thought. Consequently, many economists found themselves in conflict with absolutism, and several prominent figures suffered from the consequences of their political choices (see Chapter 3). In the Restoration period a similar situation befell many economists (see Chapter 4).

The post-Unity model: France, Germany or Britain?

The *Risorgimento* saw a considerable participation of economists in the struggle for unification. The increasingly widespread acknowledgement of the work of economists in Turin during the 1849–59 *decennio di preparazione* ('decade of preparation', that is, preparation for the subsequent Unity) enabled them to play a crucial role in the process of political unification. This brought about a remarkable osmosis between economics, politics and administration.

A more specific explanation for the massive presence of economists in Parliament during the Liberal age of 1861–1922 (witnessed by Augello and

Guidi 2002–03) is to be found in the commitment to *laissez-faire* shared by all leading political and intellectual forces. In accordance with the teachings of Cavour, and also with the British model, it was felt to be vital for politics and economics to engage in concerted action. In this context, the 1863 Scialoja–Chevalier treaty of commerce between Italy and France was modelled on the 1860 Cobden–Chevalier ultra-Liberalist treaty.

However, after 1880, faced with the unexpected difficulties Italy was experiencing in the industrialization process, a new vision gradually emerged which was less favourable to free trade and *laissez-faire*. The orientation of economists and politicians shifted towards much-admired Bismarckian Germany, which – in alliance with Italy – had achieved victory over Austria in 1866 and – completely on its own – had defeated France in 1870. The year 1882 saw the Triple Alliance between Germany, Austria and Italy, destined to last until 1915. The year 1887, on the other hand, marked the start of the new Italian commercial tariff, which supported the domestic production of wheat and cotton (the representatives of agricultural and textile interests were numerous in Parliament) through a system of high import duties, and also protected the 'infant' (iron and steel) industries for self-evident military reasons.

In contrast, the other aspect of the German economic model, namely Germany's progressive labour legislation – a cornerstone of Bismarck's strategy that aimed to provide a strong basis of popular consensus for his political action – was never introduced in Italy, although many economists who had studied in Berlin under such teachers as Schmoller and Wagner were inclined towards the 'Germanic' school of state intervention (see Chapter 5).

At the opening of the twentieth century the new Premier, Giovanni Giolitti, abandoned the authoritarian style of government of his predecessor Francesco Crispi. However, while on the one hand Giolitti was more open-minded as far as the right to strike and recognition of the trade unions were concerned, on the other he did not reject the protective tariff system and hesitated to introduce courageous liberal measures in the economy – primarily a reform of indirect taxation (both the duty on wheat and local consumption rates were particularly unpopular). But a committed group of economic experts, led by Nitti, supported Giolitti in creating an embryonic Welfare State through a public system of life insurance and through a *Banca del lavoro* designed to collect the emigrants' remittances, without jeopardizing the lira's international solidity.

Giolitti's political and economic culture had a strong German imprint. He knew the language very well, he admired the German Reich, and in 1915 he shared a neutralist position that exposed him to violent attacks from the Nationalist side.

After the 20-year Fascist dictatorship, post-1945 Italy was sensitive to the strong appeal of the United States' social and economic model (as well as of its economics), while the appeal of the Soviet Union's experiment was mainly confined to PCI militants and sympathizers.

Italy and the international context of economic theories

In terms of the reception of foreign economic doctrines, the economists were conversant with the main currents of thought that were dominant in their day, although they attempted to modify them according to their vision of Italian reality. Thus, they followed mercantilist ideas in the seventeenth and early eighteenth century; they broadened their views to encompass the more up-to-date international currents of thought (Locke, Hume, the French schools) in the mid-eighteenth century; and they were more sympathetic to Malthus, Sismondi, Senior and (above all) Say – rather than Ricardo – in the early 1800s. After Unity they received input from the German, and later the Austrian school, and – from 1900 onwards – from the Lausanne school (see Chapters 4, 5 and 6). An interesting further aspect of Italian economics is the 'discovery' of Marxian thought between 1890 and 1910.

It is worth touching here on the troubled reception of Keynes in Italy. There was resistance to introducing Keynes's *General Theory*, either owing to the influence of liberal pre-Fascist economists like Einaudi, or, more reasonably, due to the fact that Italy was a backward country with problems of accumulation of capital rather than of idle resources (see Chapter 8). From 1950 onwards, Keynes became increasingly popular among economists, especially those who shared the political views expressed by Democrazia Cristiana (DC), the strongest party in the country and the pivot of any government coalition. There was a significant effort to translate Keynes's economics into the social doctrine of the Church.

A quite different situation is found with regard to Piero Sraffa's influence over the more theoretically trained Italian economists – an influence that lasts to today but one that reached its apogee in the 1960s and 1970s.

In more recent years, in line with the success of the new 'classical' macroeconomics, as well as in parallel with the many constraints caused by the severe slowdown in the pace of the Italian economy, most economists appear more sensitive to fiscal and monetary orthodoxy – although their views are often tempered by prudent and politically opportune appeals to fairness in income distribution. This reflects a pronounced change in macroeconomics from Keynesianism to New Orthodoxy (or Washington Consensus), which became pervasive throughout Europe as well as America and, even more significantly, in the EU governing bodies.

Styles and schools

In the Italian tradition of economics two main 'styles of thought' can be discerned – not only two different ways of presenting economic concepts, but two different conceptions of the aims and tasks of economic research. These two styles are, per se, alternative to each other, although some authors may have indulged in one or in the other at different times of their scientific production. A few examples are given below.

The first may be defined as 'thinking-for-acting economics' style. It implies a pragmatic view of economic research as the task of defining (and circumscribing) problems and indicating the ways to solve them. In this approach, both economic analysis and empirical research are regarded as necessary, with the proviso that a fairly good knowledge of the economic situation is an obvious prerequisite for any reform. The final goal is nevertheless decided by political considerations. Overall, this perspective can be regarded as closer to the British and American tradition.

The second approach could be defined as 'economics of the common good'. Such an approach holds that economists cannot remain indifferent to the realm of ought-to-be – their action should be underpinned by a strong sense of involvement in determining the actual goals of economics. Incontrovertibly, economic analysis is necessary, as in the first style, but both its scope and aim are quite different – economics must be at the service of the ideal of improving social relations, establishing better interpersonal confidence, reaffirming the importance of reciprocity in exchange, and so forth.[1]

Sure, the *pubblica felicità* [public happiness] expression, often accompanied by the companion expression *economia civile* [civil or civic economics], appears in the majority of eighteenth- and early nineteenth-century economists. Such thinkers as Muratori, Genovesi, Palmieri and Romagnosi – where *economia civile* is transformed into *incivilimento* [civilization], thereby to some extent broadening its spectrum – were frequently inclined to use this terminology as a means of bridging the gap between the means and the goals of economic action. It must be stressed, however, that this approach did not represent a genuine alternative to the 'Robbinsian' majority approach, implicitly shared by most economists (of course, including those before Robbins!). In this perspective, the 'civil/civic economics' approach takes on the more plausible character of a rhetorical device with the function of enabling economics to march hand-in-hand with morals and religion.

Admittedly, the Enlightenment discussion on happiness was relaunched during the nineteenth century by several liberal-Catholic economists, as in the case of Minghetti, and above all by the Church through Pope Leo XIII's social encyclical *Rerum novarum* (1891), the path-breaking manifesto of the new Catholic attitude towards modern society and its economy (including economics) after a century of an overall negative attitude.

Yet in spite of this flowering of literature, and work in the sphere of 'economics of the common good', the most renowned Italian economists of the last three centuries can be classed as an expression of the first of the two styles mentioned above. From Galiani to Ferrara, from Beccaria to Pareto, from Pantaleoni to De Viti de Marco, from Caffè to Sylos Labini, one can trace a long sequence of leading thinkers who were comparatively indifferent to defining 'ends' as separated from 'means'. They devoted their main efforts to elaborating theoretical schemes in order to interpret reality and, if necessary, to change it, but shied away from becoming entangled in the question of the relationship of economics with the realm of ought-to-be.

In contrast, a figure who certainly cannot be classified among members of the latter group, is Piero Sraffa – undoubtedly the most 'abstract' of the major Italian scholars of economics, a true descendant from the classics and above all from Ricardo. In the Italian tradition at least two interesting, yet isolated, economists who showed an ideal affinity with Sraffa's approach can be singled out, namely Ortes and Fuoco (see Chapters 3 and 4).

The essential focus of Sraffa's interest lay in determining the invariant properties of a timeless system, rather than indicating its applications to historical reality. Did Sraffa (and his forerunners) belong to a 'third school'? Be this as it may, in the eighth chapter of this book we will recall that Sraffa's theory of 'wage as independent variable' paved the way for a struggle for higher wages independently of labour productivity, an assumption that was part of a strategy of the left-wing forces in the 1970s.

It is precisely for these reasons that this book draws inspiration from a celebrated article by Luigi Einaudi, *Conoscere per deliberare* (Einaudi 1974c [1959] in Einaudi 2006). The Turin economist stated that most political issues have an economic content and cannot be examined without regard for the tools of economics. The example chosen by Einaudi was a trifling one – a comparison between the pay levels and career opportunities of university teachers in Britain and in Italy. Einaudi demonstrated that the many platitudes about the better economic treatment of British teachers when compared to their Italian colleagues were devoid of truth. But the underlying thrust of Einaudi's argument was to bring attention to the fact that whenever politicians are involved in making decisions about matters that have economic implications – even when exercised only by way of a simple parliamentary vote – it is crucially important to take into consideration the scientific nature of the problems concerned and to evaluate the issues with proper methodological rigour. Note, however, that Einaudi didn't believe that the economist had to reason as a *doctrinaire* or, still worse, as a prophet. On the contrary, both the character of the *doctrinaire* and that of the *amateur* must be expelled from public discussion.

Of course, this by no means implies that all 'happiness economists' disregard the maxim *conoscere per deliberare* [literally, 'knowing for deciding']. Luigi Einaudi himself shared both viewpoints at different times of his life (see Chapter 7). Furthermore, the moral-economic approach deserves greater attention today, given the severe difficulties of the national and international economy. Such issues as poverty, social and gender discrimination, unjustified overstatement of GDP due to neglecting negative externalities, and neglect of equality in favour of mere efficiency, can no longer be considered as mere 'heterodox' queries, or, still worse, as pointless questions. They touch each of us in our everyday life.

What we are trying to stress is that the economists of the 'second style' mentioned earlier – more exactly, both the ancient and present-day economists who were, or are, followers of this line of thought – did (do) not conceive of political economy as an entirely autonomous science. Consequently, it is important for economics to be set in relation to some external doctrine or system of values. This crucial feature, dominant in a Catholic country like Italy, can by no means be underrated. Of course, a basic question is to be raised. Why and how is a special high authority entitled to fix such supreme aims? And why should a common researcher in economics mould his/her thoughts to this authority?

This book

Before concluding this introduction we wish to stress that this book is mainly based on primary sources. This does not imply that an updated secondary bibliography has been sacrificed. In the last 20 years or so, interest in Italian economic thought has been addressed in considerable depth by numerous scholars, both from a philological and from an analytical point of view – thanks to such initiatives as national and international research groups, conferences, reprints of classics, editions of annotated correspondence, and similar projects. Italy presents the unique case in the world of two formally separate, but effectively converging associations for the history of economic thought. Moreover, Italy boasts at least three professional journals covering the history of economics. Twenty years ago, one such journal started its issues with a 247-page long review covering the historiography of Italian economic thought, spanning the period 1700 to 1950 (see VV. AA. 1993a). If a new issue on the same topic were to be arranged today the number of pages that would need devoting to such an enterprise would be at least double.

Finally, the reader should also bear in mind that in the eighteenth and nineteenth centuries especially, various works of the most important Italian economists crossed the Alps and received consistent attention – and in many cases were translated, especially in the Mediterranean area of Europe (see Asso 2001). One should also not forget that, equally, all the works of the most renowned *foreign* economists were translated, learned, and commented upon by many Italian scholars.[2] The case of John Maynard Keynes is perhaps best known, for reasons that will be illustrated below (see Chapters 7 and 8). But the cases of Smith, Malthus, Ricardo, Say, Sismondi, List and Marx also bear witness to the profound involvement of Italian economists in interpreting and 'importing' foreign ideas into the Italian tradition of thought (see Barucci 2003).

We hope that the main issues in economic theory that have been successfully (or unsuccessfully) carried on by Italian economists can be quite clearly detected from our narrative. However, it is indisputable that the present author feels a special attraction for the *intellectual* adventure of Italian economics – from its early steps in the sixteenth century, through its vicissitudes between the seventeen and early nineteenth centuries, to its 'high theory' years between 1890 and 1920, right up to its conclusive merging with the international scientific movement after the Second World War. Today, when an 'Italian way to economics' in the proper sense doesn't exist any more, a calm balance of this ultra-centennial experience can be drawn.

An antecedent of this book was *L'economia politica in Italia dal Cinquecento ai nostri giorni* (Faucci 2000), a much thicker volume written for an Italian audience and replete with minor and less well-known names. As the reader can easily acknowledge, the secondary literature issued since 2000 is abundant, and it is important for a foreign reader to understand the great interest Italian economists of today still feel for their predecessors. A list of colleagues to whom I feel myself indebted is impossible to write down. The reader can easily infer my gratitude towards the authors more frequently cited, those whose works have improved my knowledge, a knowledge which is, alas, very far from exhaustive. Anyway, two exceptions have to be made: Pier Luigi Porta and Duccio Cavalieri have stimulated my self-critical spirit with their very kind comments throughout the last 20 years.

Finally, this book is dedicated to my grandson Niccolò.

Notes

1 For a theoretical account see Sacco and Zamagni (eds) 2002; for an application to the history of economic ideas in Italy, see Zamagni 2012 and Bruni 2012.
2 At the same time as we were completing this book, an international conference entitled 'Translations of Economic Texts into and from European Languages' took place in Pisa (12–14 September, 2013).

2 Machiavelli to Genovesi

When did Italian economics start?

In seeking to determine an appropriate point of departure for this journey through the history of Italian economics, the decision was made to leave medieval economics outside our horizon, not because it is undeserving of further study, but for two – we hope – justifiable reasons. First, medieval economic thought coincides, to a large extent, with the teaching of the Church, whose language was Latin, the *lingua franca* throughout Europe for many centuries. Another source of medieval economics can be detected in the documents written in vulgar Italian by merchants and bankers in various regions, particularly Tuscany and Lombardy. The historian Oscar Nuccio devoted many hundreds of pages to arguing that the birth of modern economics should not be sought in the teachings of the Franciscan and/or Dominican Fathers, but (predominantly or exclusively?) in the merchants' bills and accounts together with the *glossae* written by jurists, above all those concentrating on usury.[1]

Certainly, the merchants' accounts do have an undeniably fascinating economic content, and reveal the technical perfection reached by Italian business in the Middle Ages; but this documentary material is more a source for reconstructing the concrete life of the time than a body of writings that illuminate its economic thought.

Additionally, one should not overlook that it was only with the advent of the Modern Age that the conditions arose for the birth of political economy as a science composed of observation or theorization. Markets could no longer be considered as exceptions to a self-consuming economy. A monetary economy displaced what the nineteenth-century German Historical school paradoxically labelled as 'natural' economy. There was an increasing process of division of labour, if not within the factory itself, as Adam Smith would depict it in his *Wealth of Nations*, but rather on the level of the whole of society.[2]

Above all, a new middle class of citizens earning variable incomes, the amount of which depended on the general state of the economy, was beginning to occupy an increasingly prominent position between, on the one hand, the old landed aristocracy and, on the other, the wage earners (*'popolo minuto'*) living in the towns.

As a consequence of the decline of the medieval dualism between Church and Empire, national states were formed, under the impetus of the need to organize a secular structure of government. This meant, *inter alia*, assessing the amount of wealth to be taxed, establishing the amount of expenditure for wars and public works, encouraging certain productive sectors and discouraging others, and regulating the value of the monetary standard. The complex dialectics between the market and the State marked the first step towards the birth of the Western economy, and consciousness of this dialectic began to emerge at the dawn of the modern era.

Economic 'democracy' versus political absolutism: Machiavelli and Botero

Town and country in Machiavelli

In Italy, even though political unification was not achieved until as late as 1861 owing to the persisting hegemony of a foreign power and to the existence of the territorial domain of the Church, political writers' reflections began at a much earlier date to concentrate on the economic factors of the greatness of nations.

Niccolò Machiavelli (1469–1527) is perhaps the first of the modern political thinkers to have taken an interest not only in the best form of government – a typical Aristotelian theme – but also in the material factors of the greatness of a state. Even more so than his celebrated *Principe* (1513), his *Discorsi* (1519) were concerned with the relationship between economics and politics, offering some observations on the inverse correlation between the power of the State and the concentration of private wealth in just a few hands. The history of Rome, he argued, showed that the less a state's citizens are eager to accumulate wealth, the more powerful that state would become. A growing polarization of wealth tended to increase the struggle among the classes and was a serious factor behind instability; 'civil inequality' would therefore manifest itself when ownership of property was inordinately concentrated, as political power would thus come to coincide with economic power. Machiavelli pointed out that when landed property prevails, as in the domains of the King of Naples (he was writing shortly before the accession of Naples to the monarchy of Spain) no republican (in the sense of popular) regime can have been formed. In his *Istorie fiorentine* (1520–25) he noted that in Florence the landed classes strongly opposed the introduction of the cadastre, claiming that this reform would worsen their position since their incomes were easy to ascertain, whereas the condition of merchants with varying incomes and no visible property would be comparatively improved. Moreover, in their view such treatment would be unjust for the further reason that the landed class was traditionally the ruling class and therefore merited more lenient fiscal treatment. Machiavelli impartially lays out the pros and cons, but reveals his conviction that all ruling classes – whose fortunes could usually be ascribed to past episodes of brutal violence – insist that their own private interests should be considered as general ones.

In his life-long research into the factors leading to the greatness of a state, Machiavelli argued in favour of population increase but expressed his fear that the population could become concentrated in too few sites. He therefore advocated a uniform territorial distribution: 'And since nature cannot offset this kind of disorder [that of uneven distribution of population in the territory] it is necessary that industry stands in for her' (quoted   by Arias 1934 [1928]: 6).

Leaving 'nature' alone would risk creating an excess of population in some lands, and a shortfall in others. Machiavelli therefore welcomed internal migration with the aim of improving the productivity of wastelands, by means of land reclamation using hard-working manpower.[3]

Population and political power in Botero

La ragion di stato (1589) by Giovanni Botero (1544–1617), the Jesuit, is the product of the Catholic Reformation (or rather Counter Reformation) established after the Council of Trent. It is a work that reveals the transition from a Renaissance conception of the State as 'a work of art' to a conception of power that can be defined as coldly administrative. Appearance becomes more important than reality: the rulers' true intents must be masked from their subjects' view, if necessary.

Botero's economic ideas are concentrated in a few pages of Books 7 and 8 of his work. He emphasized that the prince must hoard gold in state coffers for military necessity, but must save his reputation in the eyes of his subjects and, above all, avoid conveying any impression of greed (Botero 1997 [1589]: 140–2).

However, Botero pointed out, a rule for distributive justice in taxation should be observed. Real taxes on landed property were to be preferred to personal taxes, since capitation or poll taxes were likely to be uneven. Industry must be taxed, but industrial activity exerted by non-natives should be subject to higher taxation. Only in cases of extreme necessity should the prince resort to public loans, the interest burden of which often proved ruinous to the State.

Like Machiavelli, Botero believed that a state's greatness was a function of the number of its inhabitants, there being a positive relationship between population, income and tax revenue. In another work, *Delle cause della grandezza e magnificenza delle città* (1588), Botero observed that there was a limit to the expansion of towns, owing to the increasing difficulty in feeding their populations, with the consequent danger of famine. This approach seems to prefigure Malthus's two contrasting forces of procreation and food production, as well as 'positive checks' that counter overpopulation (in fact, Botero was translated into English as early as 1609). In Botero's vision, equilibrium between population and resources could be reached through adequate mercantilist policies.

Early reflections on money: Davanzati and Montanari

Metallists and cartalists

Schumpeter wrote that the Italian literature on money in the seventeenth and eighteenth century 'kept a higher level than any other' (Schumpeter 1994: 292). This feature can be partially explained by the existence of many different currencies in the numerous separate states, leading to severe difficulties in determining their relative value. In this context, two distinct streams of thought can be identified: the 'theoretical metallists', namely scholars who assigned to money the quality of a commodity possessing an intrinsic value linked to the value of the metal (either gold or silver); and the 'theoretical cartalists', who rejected this idea. But one may also speak of 'practical metallists' and 'practical cartalists' (Schumpeter 1994: 288–91) who, even when respectively disclaiming or claiming the commodity character of money, acknowledged that policy reasons might dictate a compromise. Thus there was a growing realization that in order to maintain public trust in the standard of value, or to offset the necessity of government to manage money, it would be helpful to find a middle way between the need to use metal for money, and the need to distinguish the value of money from that of metal. Denying that money is a commodity is in fact the necessary step towards the quantitative theory of money.

Italian economists were, in the main, theoretical metallists. This can be explained partly by the still-extant memory of the metallic coinages of Venice, Florence and Milan in the Middle Ages – which had led to a high demand for Italian coin throughout Europe – but above all by the lack of confidence in government, which was regarded as incapable of ensuring 'healthy' fiduciary circulation. However, they were also practical cartalists, insofar as they acknowledged that the sovereign should govern the money supply through the State mints and therefore should fix the legal exchange rate 'outside of the market'.

Davanzati: money between market and law

There is no evidence that Italian economists participated to any great extent in the great debate on the sixteenth-century 'price revolution' caused by the enormous influx of precious metal from the Spanish colonies to Europe, a debate which prompted Bodin, Malestroit and others to formulate the quantitative theory of money (Schumpeter 1994: 311–17). The only exception is Bernardo Davanzati (1529–1606), the Florentine merchant and historian of the English Schism that occurred under the reign of Henry VIII. Among Davanzati's merits, he formulated a correct theory of the origin of money as arising from the difficulties engendered by barter exchanges, and put forward the view that the exchange value of commodities was attributable to the intensity of demand in the presence of a limited supply, as exemplified by the high price of a mouse during a siege (on account of its value as food).

Davanzati has bequeathed to posterity two economic booklets, *Lezione delle monete* (1588, translated by poet John Toland in 1696, in Hutchison 1988: 18); and *Notizia de' cambi* (1580s, exact date unknown). In the former of these two essays Davanzati fixes three points:

1   If the market exchange rate between gold and silver differs from the legal rate, this will lead to withdrawal of the undervalued metal.
2   *Tosatura* [coin clipping] is not only morally wrong, it also serves no purpose since the prince who commands it will receive smaller revenues from taxation.
3   The Mint should not obtain revenue from coinage, since coinage is a public function.

Moreover, the essay treats the question of the division of labour as based on specialization and on climatic characteristics (see Perrotta 2012: 320).

The second booklet contains a brilliant definition of the merits of *cambiavalute* [money-brokers], arguing that their work leads to free competition: 'although their individual intent is not so good, the universal outcome of their action is entirely good' (Davanzati 1804: 55). This can be seen as an important anticedent of Adam Smith's 'invisible hand' principle.

Montanari: two criteria for 'small' and 'big' coins

Geminiano Montanari (1633–87), a university professor of mathematics and astronomy, can be regarded as a modern scientist, more interested in rigorous demarcation of the terrain of investigation than in metaphysical diatribes on the 'essence' of phenomena (Bianchini 2012: 372).

In his *Trattato mercantile della moneta* (1683) Montanari showed awareness of the change in the relative value of gold and silver arising from the discovery of new mines. He thus stressed the need to find a principle that would be independent of this source of fluctuation.

Montanari observed that the value of coin was determined differently in the case of 'big' coin (cast from gold or silver) when compared to 'small' coin (cast from an alloy of different metals). The value of big coin, he suggested, sprang from the general principles that give value to all things; namely, want and rarity, and in the last resort from the intensity of demand for such coin; the demand, in turn, was a function of the available wealth (namely, income) of those who sought to acquire it. Here Montanari precisely anticipates Adam Smith's 'early' theory of price, as it appears in the *Glasgow lectures* (see Smith 1978 [1763–64]: 495–6).

The value of small coin, on the other hand, depended on the prince's will. Therefore, Montanari was a metallist with regard to big money, which was coined exclusively for the sake of international trade; while he was a cartalist regarding all money that circulated within national borders.

In his conception, this double circuit was capable of functioning in a satis-factory way if, and only if, the two circulations worked independently from one another. There could, however, be cases where the prince might perhaps order the Mint to issue an excessive quantity of small coin. Since small money had a value given by a fixed ratio to an 'imaginary' money – the latter being a money of account for the sake of international payments – it followed that when the quantity of small money was too abundant while its ratio to the imaginary standard remained the same, the small money could become overvalued. Con-sequently, big money would be withdrawn from the market. 'Bad money expels good money', Montanari repeated, along with Gresham. The realignment between the two types of money would require a new par. Montanari's obvious advice to the prince was that the issue of small coin should be carefully control-led, and, above all, clipping should be strictly forbidden.

As has been noted, the concept of 'bad money' is not limited to counterfeit currency, but extends to overvalued money as compared to undervalued money. If the sovereign privileges some kind of money, as it has been coined in one metal rather than in another (in bimetallist systems), the result will be that the undervalued money will be exported abroad (where it is not undervalued) and will disappear at home (see G. Ferri 1983: 154).

In all other respects, Montanari followed Jean Bodin as a committed sup-porter of the quantitative theory of money. He argued that *alzamento* [monetary devaluation] was dependent on the influx of gold and silver into Europe. Spain was in net debt to the rest of Europe owing to her lack of industry at home and her inability to employ the metal inflow productively.[4]

Towards an almost 'complete' theory of international exchanges: Antonio Serra

Schumpeter credits the mysterious writer from Cosenza, Antonio Serra (15?–16? complete dates unknown), as holding a key position among the founders of the 'quasi-systems' as mental constructs, blended with economic theory and policy recommendations (Schumpeter 1994: 194). Serra's work *Breve trattato delle cause che possono far abbondare li regni d'oro e d'argento dove non sono miniere*[5] was presented to the Neapolitan Viceroy when the author was in prison. No information is available that explains why he wrote the text (whether upon the Viceroy's request, or as a device to obtain his pardon), or why he was impris-oned in the first place (whether as a punishment for counterfeiting or involve-ment in a revolt against Spanish rule: see Reinert 2011: 10). All that is known is that the Viceroy did not free him and Serra died in prison. Despite his unfortu-nate personal destiny, Serra has been never been forgotten, as testified by numer-ous reprints of his work (see Roncaglia 2012a: 413).

Serra observed that the reasons why some countries might produce larger quantities of precious metal than others could be natural (existence of mines) or accidental. The latter category could be further split into two causes: (1) 'proper', namely the existence of a surplus of agricultural products for export, and other natural advantages, and; (2) 'common', namely (a) non-agricultural, technologically advanced 'artifices'; (b) an enterprising population; (c) extensive trade, and; (d) a favourable policy, including stability of government. This was a typical mercantilist agenda.

The Vice-Kingdom of Naples, ruled under the Spanish crown and governed by a Madrid representative, suffered from a scarcity of metallic currency. What remedies could be indicated? Another writer on economics, Marc'Antonio De Santis, proposed forbidding all Neapolitan importers from paying in metallic currency, and requiring foreign importers pay by means of letters of exchange. The consequence, De Santis asserted, would be a revaluation of the exchange rate between metallic money and the value of the letters of exchange, which were to be equated to paper money.

Serra objected that the Kingdom's monetary problems could not be solved by sheer technical devices, but only by coherent action on the economic structure of the country. He claimed that the country was suffering from a deficit of foreign trade, owing to the different elasticity of international demand for Neapolitan commodities in comparison to those produced in Venice or Genoa. Serra was no bullionist, unlike most early mercantilist writers who considered importing precious metal as an aim in itself. He believed that management of the currency would not be a valid remedy unless it had been accompanied by an energetic industrial policy based on import substitution. Serra had a clear perception that *artifici* [manufactured goods], in contrast to agricultural products, could enjoy disproportionate returns (on this see Roncaglia 1999: 3, 421–38). He was thus firmly convinced that Naples should specialize in production that would accrue a higher return, taking into account the availability of skilled workers and the favourable localization of industries. If productive factors were to become superabundant, then emigration – at least temporary – could be conceded.

Serra cannot be considered as a forerunner of David Hume's automatic equilibrium mechanism. He failed to grasp that a permanent outflow of metal was impossible owing to its effects on the level of internal prices, which would fall until the outflow came to an end (see De Viti de Marco 1890: 125).

Consequently, instead of a lowering of domestic prices, as would be the case in an automatic equilibrium model, Serra assumed that the most likely effect of a metal outflow from Naples would be bankruptcy among the Neapolitan merchants, and large-scale emigration or a rise in the rate of interest, with a consequent increase in the phenomenon of usury (see Benini 1892: 222–48; Rosselli 2000: 61–82).

The *Buongoverno* in Broggia and Muratori

At the origins of the 'Southern question'

At the dawn of the eighteenth century, Neapolitan economists realized that the role of the capital city was increasingly that of a mere centre of consumption to which all resources of the region had to be sacrificed. In the interpretation of

Paolo Mattia Doria (1667–1746), a descendant of the Genoese family who moved to the South, this was considered an outcome of the (failed) Masaniello revolt against the Spaniards (1647), which had the effect of persuading the foreign rulers to feed the idle populace of the town (the so-called *lazzaroni*) in order to quell popular unrest and maintain peace and order (Doria 1973 [c.1713, exact date ounknown]: 65).

Doria's meditations could rightly be considered as lying at the origin of the 'Southern question' debate.

Carlo Antonio Broggia (1683–1763) wrote a *Trattato de' tributi* (1743; the complete title is longer), which was intensively read both in Italy and abroad. In the Preface he praised Machiavelli's method, insofar as it highlighted the difference between actual reality and the distorted image the ruling class was eager to inculcate in the minds of subjects. Broggia's study of the tax system represents a vantage point for detecting the manner in which taxpayers are deceived as to the final amount of the tax burden. Here he may be considered one of the early ancestors of the 'fiscal illusion' doctrine that was subsequently developed by authors such as Ferrara, de Viti de Marco and Puviani (see below, Chapter 6); his aim being to illustrate the lack of transparency in the State's economic actions when no democratic controls exist. But despite this, as Broggia stated in his conclusion, the *raison d'état* teaches that a necessary tax must be paid without excessive objection.

As far as money is considered, Broggia was a forerunner of the function of money (as identified with the State's Treasury) as a store of value, although this feature is shared by many other mercantilist economists. The money surplus to be generated by a favourable balance of trade was regarded as crucial in order to trigger domestic economic expansion (see Graziani 2004 in Broggia 2004: xx); further, it was vital that this surplus not be employed in importing luxury goods from abroad, but rather to favour domestic production. Here, Serra's teachings are particularly evident.

Broggia condemned luxury, partly because it caused a division of the population between master and servant and was therefore not conducive to creating a civic spirit (see Broggia 2004, Chapter 8). On the other hand he showed sympathy towards poor peasants who were unjustly weighed down and exploited. Commenting on their wretched condition, he quoted the Virgilian line '*Sic vos non vobis mellificate apes/sic vos non vobis fertis aratria boves.*'[6] Broggia believed the peasants' work should not be penalized by unjust or arbitrary charges; in general the tax system should be inspired by principles of efficiency as well as equity. The former goal was to be reached by reducing the costs of tax collection (an anticipation of Smith's fourth principle); the latter, by taxing material things rather than persons, and respecting the proportionality criterion (Smith's first principle). Taxation should be applied to fixed incomes assessed through the cadastre, not to variable incomes. Consequently, the extra income deriving from special abilities should be exempted. Industrial and entrepreneurial incomes, including profits, should likewise be exempted. Indirect taxes should be comparatively light and preferably assessed on consumption.

Muratori's happiness principle

In comparison to Broggia, Abbot Ludovico Antonio Muratori (of Vignola near Modena, 1672–1750) represents the second of the two 'styles' of economics outlined in the introductory chapter. His *Riflessioni sulla pubblica felicità* (1749) enjoyed high circulation and was translated into French in 1772 and Spanish in 1790.

A churchman, Muratori took special care to distinguish between the 'private good', which depends on nature itself, and the 'public good', which depends on customs and civilization. Interestingly, Muratori made the point that the private good, if not corrected by the notion of the public good, would degenerate into vice. In contrast, the synthesis of private and public good would lead to virtue. The interest of a well-ordered state thus corresponded to the public good based on a well-intentioned private good. This concept would later be developed by Romagnosi (see Chapter 4).

On policy matters Muratori was remarkably far-sighted. He advocated measures of state intervention in order to increase the 'human capital' of the country, such as technical schools, laboratories and agrarian institutes. Furthermore, he proposed a reform of university courses through a reduction in the teaching of metaphysics and an increase in mathematics and logic. A few years later Genovesi raised precisely the same issues.

A committed mercantilist, Muratori assigned to the State the task of developing domestic production and encouraging infant industries. Public works were also crucial (see Boldizzoni 2012: 377). Exports were to be regulated according to a mechanism that anticipates Smith's vent-for-surplus scheme. Muratori also contemplated the importing of luxury goods, which in his view should be allowed since prohibitive 'sumptuary laws' had never succeeded.

In his comments on public debt, Muratori offered some observations to distinguish between perpetual and temporary debt, asserting that the former was an evil, whereas the latter was not – provided that the State was able to defend itself from creditors eager to obtain a rate of interest greater than the average profit achievable through commerce.

A further distinction made by Muratori concerned the contrast between the 'extrinsic' (nominal) price of commodities, and the 'intrinsic' price (corresponding to the quantity of precious metal contained). The rule, he maintained, was to keep the two prices in equilibrium as far as possible. Moreover, in order to discourage those who exported coin merely with the intention of melting it down and profiting from the difference between the two prices, he suggested keeping the extrinsic price somewhat higher than the intrinsic. Muratori also pointed out that the phenomenon of increasing and decreasing extrinsic prices (i.e. inflation and deflation) was not symmetrical; during periods of inflation all commodity prices tended to rise, yet against a backdrop of deflation many prices showed resistance to falling. A phenomenon that modern macroeconomics has defined as 'stickiness' (mainly of wages) was clearly envisaged by this eighteenth-century churchman.

Late mercantilist writers' views on commerce and agriculture

After the seventeenth-century economic and political crisis, the eighteenth century witnessed a number of efforts to modernize the economy. Even in the Pope's domains, there was turmoil. New *Congregazioni* [ministries] were established in order to employ idle labour forces and promote public works. Even so, the overwhelming deadweight of the mortmain – landed property of the Church which could not be alienated and was left unexploited – hindered any programme of mobilizing available resources. Another problem sprang from the grain trade. Faced with recurrent shortages of wheat, many writers queried whether the edicts against wheat export were the most effective way to ensure the necessary domestic supply and whether such measures were self-defeating. A free grain trade, in their view, could have positive repercussions on the peasants' standard of living. In 1748 Pope Benedict XIV allowed freedom of the wheat trade domestically, with the exception of the territory of Rome which continued to be subject to *Annona*, a system of public compulsory grain hoarding at non-market prices.

Two Roman writers on economics, both of whom were late mercantilists, are of some interest. Abbot Lione Pascoli (1674–1744) cherished the dream that a modern stock exchange could be established on the Capitoline hill. Another idea he entertained was that the River Tiber should be made genuinely navigable (a recurrent aspiration, also shared by Garibaldi during the *Risorgimento*). On other matters, Pascoli advocated freedom of wheat exports. Another Roman economist, the banker Marquis Gerolamo Belloni (1688–1760), whose *Dissertazione sopra il commercio* (various editions from 1750–57) achieved great popularity abroad and was translated into English, French, German and Dutch (see Belloni 1803 [1757]: 8–22; Reinert 2012: 272), explained the abundance of money in a state as the consequence of the favourable balance of trade with scarcity resulting from an unfavourable balance. Belloni also noted that while Europe's balance of trade with the West Indies was favourable, with the East Indies it was unfavourable; the net balance was negative. This phenomenon had been signalled a century earlier by Thomas Mun, whose work Belloni had probably read. On the other hand, there is no evidence that Belloni was acquainted with Hume's automatic mechanism.

Money, Belloni argued, had two prices – the 'intrinsic', which was based on the quantity of metal contained, and the 'extrinsic', based on public esteem. The exchange was in equilibrium when the two values coincided. This seems to embody an interesting analogy with the concept of 'imaginary money'; that is to say, money with an invariable metallic content serving as money of account in conditions of frequent devaluations of the currency. Two centuries later, Luigi Einaudi – although not referring to Belloni, for whom he had few words of praise[7] – returned to this topic with a not altogether hostile appraisal of the concept (see Einaudi 2006 [1936]: 153–81).

Belloni's 'Colbertism' is apparent in his claim that when the balance of trade was passive, a country would lose its metal, and the only remedy would be a severe restriction on trade in order to stem the outflow (Belloni 1803: 70).

The more advanced Grand Duchy of Tuscany was home to writers who had freed themselves from many mercantilist preconceptions. Archdeacon Sallustio Bandini (1677–1760), in his *Discorso sopra la Maremma di Siena* (1737), proposed the introduction of a system based on a single land rent tax – the *decima* [tithe] – and the abolition of all indirect taxes on exchanges and consumption. However, despite contending that the price of wheat should be freely tradeable, Bandini was not in favour of free imports of grain.

On the other hand, neither did he look approvingly on large-scale estates that employed both fixed and circulating capital. Rather, he made the case for small-sized farms and the maintenance of sharecropping. This approach differentiates Bandini from the more advanced Physiocrats.

Bandini had a wide-ranging economic background. He was familiar with Boisguilbert, from whom he drew the concept of agents' expectations as well as the concept of the velocity of circulation of money (Baker 1978: 129–31; see the original, Bandini 1978 [1737]: 233–5).

Bandini defined money as the *vile ministro* of commerce – an almost literal translation of Boisguilbert's concept of money as *le valet du commerce* (see Béraud and Faccarello 1992: 168), thereby clarifying that in the normal state of the economy, money served the sole purpose of facilitating transactions and had no other function. On the other hand, there is no evidence that he had read Locke, whose essays on money and interest were translated in 1751 by two Tuscan economists: Gian Francesco Pagnini and Angelo Tavanti (Baker 1978: 137).

In conclusion, Bandini is probably the best product of a regional stream of thought whose peculiarities cannot be exclusively ascribed either to mercantilism or to Physiocracy, but are certainly more akin to the latter school (of which Bandini can be considered one of the forerunners).

Two *grands-commis* in Austrian Lombardy: Neri and Carli

Abbot Pompeo Neri (1706–76), and above all Count Gianrinaldo Carli (1720–95), mark the transition into the subsequent period. Neri spent the first part of his life under the Grand Duke of Tuscany before moving to Milan; Carli, a Dalmatian astronomer, came from Venice. Both men served under Empress Maria Theresa, but neither of these two experts on applied law and economics went beyond their duty of 'consultant administrators' in the Schumpeterian sense, and both were assigned subordinate tasks. To the extent to which they had the opportunity to express their opinions, both Neri and Carli manifested quite conservative ideas, as was frequently the case among public servants in contact with the Crown and the Court.

Their 'philosophy' was straightforward. According to Neri there were two kinds of nobility – one based on blood and birth, and another composed of the ruling administrative class. It is evident that Neri was prompted by the distinction between *noblesse d'épée* and *noblesse de robe* that arose in seventeenth-century France under Louis XIV. But Neri's argument went further. Not only did he maintain that a balance must be achieved between these two types of aristocracy, he also emphasized that their natural leadership must be carefully safeguarded in any political regime – including 'democracy' – because it was only thanks to their mutual cooperation that political stability (the supreme goal of the State) could be assured.

In Carli's writings virtually the same statements are reiterated, in order to reject, on the one hand, Rousseau's ideas of absolute equality, and on the other, Hobbes's theory of the necessary subjection to an absolute power. Carli's objection, advanced against both Rousseau and Hobbes, was based on his conviction that inequality was a natural condition of mankind, but that this condition could be mitigated if power was tempered by law (an echo of Montesquieu).

Carli was also the author of an article on *La patria degli Italiani* (1765), which has been often considered as an anticipation of the *Risorgimento*. In actual fact, however, Carli's primary aim was to deny that the idea of the fatherland could erase differences between one town and another, or distinctions between noblemen from different family backgrounds – in short, the divergences among the various aspects of the multi-faceted Italian situation. In his assessment, 'love for the fatherland' was merely a generic cultural sentiment that could not – and should not – be translated into political terms.

In 1751 Neri participated in the bilateral commission between Piedmont and Lombardy in order to regulate the coinage of their own currencies. Naturally, the preliminary step involved ascertaining the price and quantity of precious metal necessary for the 'noble' coinage. Here Neri, following Belloni, had recourse to the concept of imaginary money, assigning it the value of 1 oz of fine silver.

In the same year Carli wrote a dissertation *Dell'origine e del commercio della moneta e dei disordini che accadono nelle alterazioni di essa* [On the origin and commerce of money and on the troubles that arise when its value is altered], in which he added further technical considerations. He observed that relying on the weight of coin was no longer possible, since alloy money had become increasingly widespread. Furthermore, the prince should not alter the value of money, as the loss of metallic content had a disastrous effect on prices and on public confidence.

Carli pointed out that when the standard was double (gold and silver), if one metal diminished in market value while the legal parity between the two types of coin remained unaltered, the owners of the metal that had diminished in value would run to the Mint to coin the metal and gain the difference between the value of the coined and uncoined metal. The opposite movement – fusion of coins in order to transform the metal into bullion – would be observed in the reverse case.

After hazarding a guess as to the amount of metal present in the currencies of the various states of Italy, Carli came to the conclusion that it was necessary to melt the main currencies down, so that the correspondence between intrinsic value, market value and legal value could be ensured. In particular, Carli proposed to remelt the Milanese silver *ecu*. This was achieved, after considerable difficulties, in 1778, and led to a marked revaluation (see Vianello 1939).

Carli and Neri also contributed to a major undertaking, the setting up of the cadastre (the census of land produce), in order to reassess the land tax. As is well known, at the basis of the census there lay the concept of 'normal' income. Taxing this ideal income, rather than actual one, allowed Milanese agriculture to prosper throughout the following century, thanks to the enterprising spirit of those farmers who felt encouraged to introduce the greatest possible number of improvements and thereby gained from the difference between their effective income and the normal income that was taxed.

Genovesi between 'civil philosophy' and economic reformism

Genovesi's personality and general vision

Let us conclude this chapter by looking at a figure who represents a bridge between a conception of economics as an art of the statesman, and a more mature conception of economics as a science of civil society. Abbot Antonio Genovesi (1713–69) was one of the most celebrated Neapolitan economists of his century. Professor of metaphysics and ethics at the university, it was through the good offices of his mentor, the *provveditore* [minister] for education Celestino Galiani, that he was able to escape the ecclesiastical tribunal. A few years afterwards, in 1754, he was offered the first chair of economics in Italy ('of commerce and mechanics') – the second in absolute terms in Europe – established by the Tuscan businessman Bartolomeo Intieri. Genovesi's main work on economics – *Lezioni di economia civile* (1765–67) – was placed on the *Index librorum prohibitorum* by the Santo Uffizio, along with all his philosophical writings.

As a thinker, Genovesi was an empiricist with strong leanings towards Materialism. He opposed the old-fashioned metaphysics and scholastic dialectics by appealing to a frankly materialist anthropology: 'The source of every appreciation and value is man, the man who toils, eats, drinks, dresses, inhabits, consumes' (Genovesi 1963: 493). Thus, man should be studied principally as a social animal; a 'man of nature', *à la* Rousseau, he reasoned, does not exist.

In his writings, Genovesi observed that the increasing polarization between luxury and misery – already noted by Broggia as we have seen – was the most striking feature of modern societies, alongside a plague of ignorance and, above all, illiteracy. In order to overcome this state of affairs, he argued, reforms should be imposed from above by an indisputable authority, as had been successfully achieved by Louis XIV of France and Peter the Great of Russia. Although Genovesi was neither a liberal nor a democrat in the modern sense, he was, in many respects, a committed reformer.

His analysis of human behaviour was based on the dialectics between two forces that ran symmetrical to the forces of gravity – the '*concentriva*', which could be compared to a centripetal force and corresponded to self-love, and the '*diffusiva*', comparable to a centrifugal force and corresponding to altruism. Harmony, he believed, arose from equilibrium between these two forces. Genovesi argued, however, that the '*concentriva*' dominated in barbarian populations, while the '*diffusiva*' prevailed among civilized peoples (Genovesi 1977: 227).

Genovesi also touched on a subject of crucial importance in eighteenth-century moral (and economic) thought, namely the issue of how interests can derive from human passions, a subject Albert Hirschman highlighted in his 1977 classical book. Genovesi suggested that the latter were spurred by the dialectics between pleasure and pain. More precisely, the principal moving force was 'pain, uneasiness, unsatisfied desire and everything that produces boredom and unpleasant irritation' (Genovesi 2005 [1765]: 297). Hence, 'if relieving pain and troubles can be defined as interest, it is clear that man naturally does not act if not for interest' (ibid., p. 300). In particular, the specific interest of each nation was 'a sympathetic principle, spring of the three quarters of human actions' (ibid.).

In his vision, certain common features could be discerned in a survey of the economic history of each nation. Mankind, he noted, had passed through different stages of civilization; all nations were, at the outset, 'wild and wandering', then 'barbarian and stably settled', and subsequently 'cultivated but not commercial', and finally 'cultivated commercial' (ibid., p. 311). These steps were seen as corresponding to the stages in which the predominant activities were hunting, fishing, pasturage, agriculture and metal-working.

It is interesting to note that such a sequence shows affinities with the theory of economic stages delineated by the Scottish Historical School of Ferguson, Robertson and Smith, although Genovesi was probably directly influenced by one of his teachers, Giambattista Vico, whose lectures he attended at the University of Naples (see Pesciarelli 1978: 597–607). In addition, Genovesi was very familiar with Hume's *Political Discourses*, but in 1757–58 he also translated, jointly with his brother Pietro, John Cary's *History of British commerce, completed by a translation of Thomas Mun's English treasure*.[8]

One of the predominant features of modern society, Genovesi reasoned, was luxury. In the chapter 'On the arts of luxury', he assumed an intermediate position between Mandeville – who in the *Fable of the bees* praised luxury, even though he defined it as a vice – and Rousseau, who, in the two discourses *On the origin of inequality* and *On letters and arts* denounced luxury as the worst outcome of modern civilization. Genovesi's approach distinguished expenditures according to their subservience to 'necessary, comfortable and uniquely delightful objects'. He admitted, however, that such a distinction was not easy to define. Rather, analysis should be performed on the basis of a sociological and anthropological approach, endeavouring to pinpoint the economic impulses to consumption. In a class-structured society, the main drive was the desire to distinguish oneself from others – a total absence of luxury would mean a uniform, classless society. Genovesi the churchman did not refrain from morally condemning 'mad', uncontrolled, luxury, but Genovesi the economist admitted that luxury may trigger a positive emulation process which favoured frequent social mobility, both upwards and downwards. There are interesting prefigurations of Veblen here. Moreover, Genovesi did not neglect to recall his mercantilist inclinations in advising that luxury should never be allowed when it meant importing luxury products from abroad.

His attitude towards those that he defined, in a very modern stance, as the 'labouring classes', was somewhat contradictory. On the one hand he extolled them as the backbone of the nation; on the other, he suggested they should not be remunerated excessively since high wages would induce men to laziness. It is likely that rather than a backward-bending individual labour supply, what he had in mind was a macroeconomic strategy for economic development – a cheap labour force could increase both output and employment without leading to an increase in prices.

Genovesi also addressed the question of 'non-mechanical' jobs, or, in the language of classical economists, the unproductive labourers. The military profession should, in his view, obey the 'minimum possible' criterion; that is to say, the strictest correspondence of their total number to the nation's needs. Such a restriction did not affect the legal profession, which, Genovesi pointed out, was subject to a feedback process – an increase in the number of legal cases generated a greater number of lawyers, and vice versa. Genovesi's explanation for the increasing number of medical doctors is striking. He claimed that a life of excessive luxury – which he evidently considered an imminent danger for the masses – caused greater sickness among the population.

The Lezioni

The structure of *Lezioni* presents several remarkable aspects. The first part deals with matters of economic and social history from antiquity to modern times, by illustrating the main factors of the progress of humanity, namely population growth, the expansion of commerce, and so forth. In the second part Genovesi's analysis focuses on value, price, money, interest, public debt (here Hume is frequently quoted), foreign trade and the economic content of contracts. The final part of *Lezioni* is devoted to the discussion on happiness, virtue and wealth.

Although the range of subjects addressed in *Lezioni* is imposing, an original treatment of the more specific economic topics is lacking. Genovesi followed Galiani's *Della moneta* (see Chapter 3 below) in arguing that want endows things with value, and that differing wants follow a decreasing order of relevance (from necessity to luxury), durability, and intensity. Furthermore, he noted that if wants are decreasing while the quantity of goods pertaining to such wants remains unchanged, then the value attributed to those things that satisfy it will fall accordingly. In his posthumously published lecture notes, known as *Elementi del commercio* (1757–58), Genovesi (2005: 136) stated: 'The prices of things are in direct reason according to the want of them and in inverse reason according to their physical quantity.' More complex is a definition given in his published *Lezioni*:

price is a compound ratio, directly of the wants and of their heaviness and duration, as well as the ability of things to satisfy these wants, the durability of these things and of the efficiency in producing them; and reciprocal [i.e. inversely] of the quantity available and of the toils in producing them.

(Genovesi 2005: 665)

Here, Genovesi was clearly alluding to commodities produced using unskilled labour only, without the aid of capital. The repeated mention of '*fatiche*' [toils] appears to foreshadow the Marxian concept of 'socially necessary labour'.

His treatment of price distinguished between a real and a monetary price. He considered money as having an intrinsic price determined by the value of the metal, as well as a legal value, and, finally, a value given through its utilization for the sake of commerce, by lending it at interest.

Genovesi also examined the phenomenon of '*alzamento*', i.e. the reduction of the quantity of metal contained in the currency while maintaining the same nominal value. This device, which the prince might introduce in order to gain from the difference when a currency was brought to the Mint for exchange with gold or silver, was useless at an international level because all foreign payments would be accepted with good money only. Genovesi was unacquainted with the idea that a depreciation of the domestic currency could help exports, at least temporarily.

Development and underdevelopment

Genovesi has always been considered as a forerunner of development and underdevelopment theories (see VV. AA. 1956b). Depicting the South of Italy as a backward area, he suggested a programme of interventions which tend to prefigure Adam Smith's opening to Book IV of the *Wealth of Nations*; claiming that such a programme had the aim of enriching both the nation and the sovereign.

Some considerations on population dynamics can also be found in Genovesi's works. He argued that the most negative effect of depopulation – a typical eighteenth-century concern – was that when manpower was lacking in agriculture, lands could not be adequately cultivated. Genovesi calculated that the 'optimal population' of the Kingdom of Naples was six million, double what it was at the time he was writing. In this context the term 'optimal population' was taken to mean that, given the available resources, such a population could adequately cultivate the whole of the available land, while the term 'population' referred to the *productive* population (see Villari 1959: 86).

However, a population increase was not, in his view, the only way to boost production. Inspired by his mentor Bartolomeo Intieri, a skilful inventor as well as a successful merchant, Genovesi maintained that improvements in techniques must go hand-in-hand with education and training of the labour force. Overall, his model may be defined as a land-cum-labour theory of production, to some extent akin to that of William Petty. Moreover, arguing that only countries enjoying an advanced agriculture could expand their industry and trade, his ideas foreshadowed the conclusions that would be reached by Smith concerning the 'natural course of things' in *The Wealth of Nations*, Book III. Yet Genovesi had no physiocratic leanings. In his vision, agriculture was not alone in acting as a 'productive' sector, indeed agriculture itself had no special merits in determining the general surplus of society. Rather, he believed that a strong agricultural sector played a key role in allowing a country to obtain a surplus from exports which would then become available for expanding non-agricultural trade as well.

The Neapolitan thinker died seven years before the publication of *The Wealth of Nations*. It would not appear that Smith had any knowledge of Genovesi's thoughts. This notwithstanding, some affinities between the two authors can be noted, as briefly mentioned above. On the economic advantages of education, both Genovesi and Smith displayed keen concern and awareness of its important role, although Smith saw primary education above all as a remedy against the intellectual torpor induced by the exaggerated heavy division of labour, while Genovesi believed that education – and particularly literacy – was a powerful tool for improving the workers' capabilities. As far as higher education was concerned, while Smith treated it as a free market where the students (as buyers) demanded (and judged the quality of) the 'good' defined as education, and the teachers (as sellers) competed in supplying it, Genovesi primarily insisted on the need to produce education from the point of view of the interest of the State. Under this perspective Genovesi would probably have defined education as a public good.

Thus, while sharing a belief in the significance of education, considerable differences in their approach to educational questions can be traced. This was due mainly to the very evident imbalance in the levels of growth between mid-eighteenth-century Scotland (a 'young' and dynamic society where new topics such as sociology and comparative law were being introduced into the course syllabuses), and the South of Italy (an 'old' society where rhetoric and eloquence – the discipline taught by Vico, one of Genovesi's masters – were still considered as the cornerstones of a humanist/legal education built on a long-standing tradition). Overall, the opinion of Southern mid-eighteenth-century thinkers was that the historical backwardness of the South could be overcome only through an energetic initiative led by the State as a substitutive factor.

Notes

1 See Nuccio (1984–87); and the posthumous Nuccio (2009). For a different interpretation see Barile (2012): 59–65.
2 See the classical reconstruction by Dobb (1946, Italian translation 1958).
3 Antonio Gramsci was attracted by Machiavelli's economic thought. Through his sister-in-law Tania, he asked his friend Piero Sraffa whether Machiavelli's economic ideas could be assimilated to the mercantilists or rather to the Physiocrats. In his reply, Sraffa suggested that Machiavelli could more properly be likened to William Petty. See Gramsci (1996), vol. II: 548–9, 569.
4 See Montanari (1683), reprinted in A. Graziani (Sr) (ed.) (1913): 239–379. See also VV. AA. (1993b).

5   See Serra (2011) [1613], edited with an introduction by S. A. Reinert, who provides the Italian text as well.
6   Broggia (1804) IV: 141; see also the anthology of Neapolitan economists by Tagliacozzo (1937): 83.
7   See the negative assessment of Belloni's work in Einaudi (1953) [1938]: 119–51.
8   The late mercantilist Cary was a source of inspiration for Genovesi's main textbook on economics. See Venturi (1969), Chapter 8. More recently, see Reinert (2007): 155–92.

3 The heyday of eighteenth-century Italian economics

Economic reforms and 'high theory'

The 44-year period 1748–92 was a time of peace in Italy and, if one excludes the Seven Years' War, also a time of peace in the rest of Europe. It coincided with the great development of economics, as well as of economic and institutional reforms – although still within the framework of absolutism. Naples, Lombardy and Tuscany, and even more so the isolated Venice and Piedmont, were active centres of theoretical debate and policy proposals. Efforts directed towards the secularization of society – culminating in the (temporary) abolition of the Jesuits by Pope Clement XIV in 1773 – together with the reflection on individual rights and on the limits of state power, all constituted manifestations of the alignment of Italian culture and society with the general Enlightenment climate. In particular, a significant step in this direction was represented by the penal law reforms culminating in the abolition of the death penalty and judicial torture in Tuscany in 1786.

The decade 1760–70 was crucial for the flourishing of French physiocracy. It is worth recalling that the original message of physiocracy did not concern the primacy of agriculture – had this been so the overwhelming majority of eighteenth-century writers should be considered Physiocrats. Rather, it involved their special conception of the 'natural order of things', regarded as the underlying inspiration on which positive laws should be based. The physiocratic insistence on education assumed the objective of enlightening public opinion on the actual working of natural laws (see Albertone 1979: 27).

In Italy this message was also received, although in a narrower sense. For most Italian economists of the time, education did not pursue the aim of converting the public to the *a priori* principles of natural law, but rather, and much more pragmatically, the task of narrowing the space traditionally occupied by the Church's teaching. This goal was part of Genovesi's programme.

On the other hand, policy proposals put forward by the Italian economists gained a wider audience within Italy than did those of the Physiocrats in France, despite the fact that France was a broad, centralized, state, while Italy was – with the single exception of the Kingdom of Naples – a patchwork of small regional entities. In effect, despite the French Court's encouragement, the Physiocrats achieved only two political successes – the 1764 liberalization of the wheat trade and the 1774–76 anti-corporative edicts passed by Minister Turgot. In comparison to the scanty results achieved by the reform movement in France, the 'enlightened' Italian economists succeeded in promoting numerous reforms covering taxation, money and commerce (see Pecchio 1849 [1829]: 261–79).

Another feature of Italian economics in the second half of the eighteenth century was its receptiveness to the stream of economic ideas from abroad. These were generally ideas originating from French rather than British sources, as knowledge of English was not yet sufficiently widespread in Italian cultural circles. In particular, the Scottish school of economics and sociology, better known as the Scottish Historical school, had no special impact in Italy, with the exception of David Hume's *Political discourses*, translated as early as 1774. It may seem surprising that the first Italian translation of the *Wealth of Nations* appeared as late as 1790 in Naples – it was translated in Germany in 1776–78, and in France in 1781. As a consequence, 'Smithianism', as a mode of economic thinking, arrived in Italy relatively late.

According to recent reassessments there are significant analogies between late eighteenth-century Italian economic thought and some currents of present-day economics which consider economic phenomena not only from a quantitative, but also from a qualitative and institutional perspective – based on such concepts as *felicità pubblica* (public happiness) and 'civic values'.

The insistence of eighteenth-century Italian economists on public happiness prompts interesting speculations. Nevertheless, fundamental differences on this matter can be discerned between eighteenth-century Italian economists and their modern-day counterparts. One should not disregard the profound difference between the economic problems associated with the Italian Enlightenment and those encountered by the followers of the 'happiness' approach today. Eighteenth-century Italian economists found themselves grappling with a number of serious challenges: the problem of development from backwardness (rather than that of opulence and distortions in consumption), the need to create new resources (rather than ensure efficient management of already-existing resources), as well as the challenge of employing the idle populations in agriculture and manufacturing (rather than of creating new services leading to a 'happier' humankind). In other words, eighteenth-century Italian Enlightenment economists were dealing with a pre-industrial economy and not a post-industrial one.

Moreover, it must not be forgotten that eighteenth-century reflection on happiness represented a necessary passage towards a non-religious conception of human behaviour, and required a compromise with the tradition that was still dominant. Two economists, Verri and above all Beccaria, paved the way for the subsequent accomplishment introduced by Bentham; namely, the extension of the felicific calculus to all scopes of human activity.

With all its imperfections, and even naiveties, it cannot be doubted that Utilitarianism constituted the basis for modern economics. Its message (extendible in itself to other branches of human sciences, first and foremost law) was that of emancipating economic reasoning from moral and religious values. It is no coincidence that Bentham started his work on economics with his *Defence of Usury* (1787), which at first glance may appear to have been written in order to criticize Adam Smith's idea of fixing a maximum rate of interest. But principally it was an attack on the still-extant religious doctrines that condemned 'usury' – namely, lending according to the current interest rate – as unjust and/or immoral.

Italian economists, on the other hand, were concerned with the impact of law and institutions on the (good) working of the economy. In doing so, they had to tackle the weight of ancient laws and customs that protected the abstract rights of owners but without encouraging the economic exploitation of those rights. Feudalism had encumbered landed property with such a vast array of burdens – barriers to selling and exploiting vast lands that were weighed down by prohibitions on alienation, such as *fidei-commissa*, rights to primogeniture, and, last but not least, the enormous Church estate – that any rescue of the economic condition of the country seemed impossible without significant legal reform. Legislators thus had to become economists in their own right, and had to carefully consider the economic impact – in terms of both costs and benefits – of legislative reforms.

Thus there was a growing realization that a more efficient working of the market could enhance not only growth, but also better income distribution. A proposed move towards greater freedom of trade in wheat was prompted by an intention to provide higher incomes for peasants and tenants. Quite a different policy goal inspired Richard Cobden's Anti-Corn Law League in the 1840s. Cobden's action aimed to raise the real wage rate by reducing the price of bread and consequently lightening the production costs of manufacturing, England's crucial economic sector. In contrast, Italian eighteenth-century economists, who lived in a backward environment, aimed to increase *all* land incomes (including rents) in order to attract more capital to agriculture, the crucial sector of the economy in Italy.

But a programme of freeing all productive forces, expanding all markets, simplifying the existing economic legislation, and transforming the existing fiscal system into a less oppressive means of collecting tax revenue, did not imply an absolute *laissez-faire* approach; rather it advocated an agenda of public action. The degree of interventionism depended on the degree of backwardness. The aim was always the same; namely, overcoming underdevelopment but using means that differed according to local situations.

Ferdinando Galiani: money, value and methodology

Galiani's conservative realism

The label 'unaccomplished genius' has always been attached to Ferdinando Galiani (of Chieti, 1728–87). He, it is said, had a mind endowed with extraordinary subtlety but lacking the inclination to expand such intuitions in an organic and systematic manner. Galiani's interests ranged from Latin literature to Neapolitan dialect, from archaeology to international law, from comedy to economics. Highly praised by the adepts of the French Enlightenment, disputed yet respected by Ferrara, favourably cited by Marx, and extolled by Einaudi, Galiani has attracted the attention of many outstanding readers throughout the centuries (see Faucci and Giocoli 2001: 9–20).

Unlike his compatriot Genovesi, Galiani was no admirer of Montesquieu, who he deemed an abstract thinker, unable to distinguish between what 'is' and what 'ought to be', and, more specifically, between real social forces and the unreal constructs of law. This attitude toward Montesquieu can be explained by the fact that Galiani was a follower of the absolute state and did not share Montesquieu's 'mixed government' model, which closely prefigured the liberal model. Still more radically, Galiani rejected Rousseau's utopianism and doctrinarism. Sceptical as he was about the possibility of defining a 'common good', Galiani was dubbed *Machiavellino* [little Machiavelli], a nickname which may have alluded either to his very small stature or to his endorsement of the Florentine writer's unprejudiced approach to politics, the lens through which Galiani sought to study the interplay between economic and social forces. Writing in 1773 to his friend Madame d'Epinay, Galiani cynically argued:

> Monarchy is founded mainly on the inequality of economic conditions; this economic inequality is based on the low price of food; the low price of food on the existence of restrictions to trade. The absolute freedom of trade leads to increasing prices of food and therefore to the peasants' enrichment. The increasing prosperity of peasants leads to the republican form of rule and this latter to the equality of fortunes, the destruction of which has cost us six thousand years.... Everybody speaks in favour of the good of others. Damn the others! The others do not exist. Say what benefits you most. Or keep your mouth shut.[1]

Galiani's study of the complex nature of economic phenomena prompted him to inquire into a method of crystallizing such phenomena into their constituent parts and then recomposing each of them. Substantially, he was a forerunner of the so-called compositive method – in Schumpeter's terms, methodological individualism – introduced by the Austrian school of economics. To our knowledge, no Menger specialist has recalled the latter's parallel with Galiani's approach to economics.

However, Galiani also foreshadowed the *ceteris paribus* approach that would later become famous with Alfred Marshall. The two methods, which he probably considered as converging, were in his view most useful in matters of economic policy. In his 1770 *Dialogues sur le commerce des bleds*, Chevalier Zanobi – Galiani himself – explains to his adversary, the pro-physiocratic Marquis de Rocquemaure, that 'a single change determines an enormous difference' (Galiani (1958) [1770]: 25). Consequently, policy measures must always refer to the present and never pertain to a timeframe that also encompasses the future: 'There is always time to change the law, if the situation changes' (ibid., p. 181).

Economic theory, he argued, is in all cases a guide for economic policy, but one must keep in mind the different logical steps before applying it to reality. Here the so-called 'method of subsequent approximations' is clearly prefigured.[2]

Passions, wants and value in 'Della moneta'

Galiani's acknowledged masterpiece, *Della moneta* (1751), was published anonymously when the author was only 23. In his preface to the definitive 1780 version, Galiani states it to be 'a fruit of my youth', composed 'with no help from men and almost without any help from books'.[3] Yet this feature appears to have had no negative impact on the work, which is not only rich in theoretical reasoning, but also fully of its time as far as awareness of contemporary economic literature was concerned. For instance, Galiani discussed, among others, not only Oresme, Davanzati, Serra, Jacques Bernouilli, Petty and Locke, but also the more recent Law, Broggia, Muratori, Dutot and Melon.[4]

At the origin of any economic behaviour, Galiani proclaimed, there lies 'passion', which renders humankind perpetually unsatisfied with its present situation and constantly thirsting for change. Moreover, the things most ardently desired (note that Galiani used the term *cosa* [thing] rather than *bene* [good], while Serra used the term *roba* [stuff], insisting on the material aspect of the commodities that are exchanged) are those that allow us to obtain satisfaction, not only economic, but of status or of social prestige as well.

His approach to value is altogether subjectivist. Value is a human judgement that compares utility with rarity. Utility is a thing's capacity to procure happiness for its owner. Commenting on Davanzati's observation that 'a natural lamb [in the original: *vitello*, calf] is nobler than one of gold, but how much is it valued?' (Galiani, English translation: 25), Galiani solved what Adam Smith, 25 years later, would be unable to solve – the so-called paradox of value which dictates that goods endowed with a high use value have a low exchange value, and vice versa (see Einaudi 1953 [1945]: 285). Galiani rightly observed that utility is always relative, and that increased intensity of demand (for instance, owing to scarcity) will cause an increase in the exchange value of things that usually have no value at all – such as mice, which acquire value during a siege owing to the lack of food. In more modern terms, it is marginal utility, not total utility, that determines value.

Rarità [scarcity] is also a relative concept: 'a proportion between the quantity of a thing and the use which is made of it' (Galiani, English translation: 28). In order to define the effort expended in obtaining a thing, he introduced the concept of *fatica* (a Neapolitan dialect word for labour, in the sense of toil), namely the production cost in terms of labour (without the assistance of capital): 'Labour alone gives things value' (ibid., p. 29). This idea gained the favour of Marx in his *Critique of Political Economy* (1859). However, labour in Galiani's framework requires more elements that in Marx's. Since it is by no means homogeneous, labour is not entirely measurable with a single yardstick, because natural and acquired talents are not uniformly distributed. Its value implies three variables: (1) 'the number of people' employed in production; (2) the time necessary for production; and (3) 'the different price of those who work' (Galiani, English translation: 29).

When rarity (namely supply) is the same in the above-considered cases, value is directly proportional to wants, and therefore to demand. There are both natural and artificial wants, the latter of which includes those induced by fashion and which has the effect of making utility coincide with novelty even when there is no real improvement 'of the arts or the comforts of life' (ibid., p. 33). Both the uniqueness and monopoly of a thing have an effect upon price, which in these cases 'forms a compound ratio' of the buyer's needs and the seller's esteem. Therefore, if both judgements are 0, the price will also be 0, and the good in question will be not brought to the market at all.

In general, price influences the quantity that is demanded, and vice versa – there is a reciprocal dependence. 'Consumption [namely, demand] increases price; and high price leads to the reduction of consumption' (ibid., p. 35). An interesting and clearly presented solution to this vicious circle is given through the example of a Mohammedan population suddenly converting to Christianity. New vines will be planted and more wine will be imported; people will adjust the wine supply to meet the new level of want. Here Galiani shows his under-standing of the difference between a shift in the demand curve due to an exogenous factor variation (consumers' habits) and a shift along the same demand curve due to a variation in price (*ceteris paribus*).

Origin and role of money

Galiani was sarcastic about theories which assumed that, once upon a time, humankind subscribed to a covenant to accept 'money' as a means of payment.

> Where are these meetings, these conventions of all the human race; in what century did they occur – at what place? What place, what ambassadors ... decided so firmly to that extent that, many centuries afterwards, even when one people ignored the existence of another, they did not change their mind?
> (Galiani, English translation: 48)

If all peoples at one time or another have resorted to money, this demonstrates that money has always been considered as belonging to 'the intrinsic constitution of things' (ibid.).

Money must therefore be considered an entirely spontaneous institution. In the same way, more than a century later, Menger and his disciples of the Austrian school developed a theory concerning the unreflecting origin of the main social institutions which conflicted with the theory put forward by the German Historical school of economics. The latter school stressed the importance of 'organization', and, more generally, of planned action directed towards a specific goal (constructivism). Nevertheless, Menger's *Grundsätze* (1871) cites Galiani, altogether generically, for his subjectivist theory of value.

It should be underscored, however, that the representatives of the Scottish Historical school (mentioned earlier) shared a similar view on the spontaneity of social institutions. The difference lay in the Scottish school's insistence that the process of the formation of institutions does not arise by chance, but follows the natural development of the productive forces – a sort of *ante litteram* materialist conception of history (see Pascal 1938; Meek 1967). But this version of historical Materialism appears to be extraneous to the Neapolitan economist.

Money, in Galiani's view, serves two functions: (1) that of a universal measure of value, and; (2) that of a 'pawn' and general equivalent. It has been observed that Galiani does not assign money the function of a store of value, something envisaged by several mercantilist economists (see Cesarano 1976, 1990). After illustrating the role of money, in Book 2 Galiani presents a sort of 'conjectural history' concerning the way through which money has acquired its main functions. T. W. Hutchison (1988: 260) defines Galiani's method as based on 'decreasing abstractions', somewhat similar to the subsequent approximations method, which is not altogether incompatible with that of conjectural history.

Galiani describes the working of a centralized economy, where producers deposit their commodities in public warehouses, receiving some *bullettini* [certificates, notes] in return, which represent the value of goods in terms of 'toil' and allow the owners to withdraw an amount of commodities of equivalent value from the warehouse. In short, the certificates are like credit instruments. A further 'portion of toil' has to be left to the warehouse to allow for the cost of the operation: this 'portion' representing the duties and taxes that are due to the prince. If a large amount of commodities are to be brought to the warehouse and exchanged, the notes become an obstacle to speedy circulation and are therefore replaced with metal money, whose value is guaranteed by the prince himself. Hence, it is clear that an intrinsic value of money does not exist at all. Following Schumpeter's distinction, Galiani can be called a theoretical cartalist.

Galiani then addresses the problem of an invariable measure of value, starting from the concept of 'imaginary money', which did not circulate but was used as money of account. It was divided into 12 *denarii*, each of them divided into 20 pence. But even the imaginary money must be compared to the existing currencies, which, in turn, are of variable value owing to the changing value of the various coined metals, and/or of the changing metallic content of the various currencies. In the long run, Galiani rightly observed, the ratio between the imaginary money of account and the actual currency is inevitably subject to change; consequently the former cannot be considered as a reliable standard of value. What should be done, then? Galiani concluded that the commodity most closely approaching the definition of an invariable standard is man himself – 'easy to compute, when one values ... only in terms of the qualities of the body' (Galiani, English translation: 78). Here he draws inspiration from the Guinea slave market, but he extends his argument to the market of free workers whose price is calculated by their subsistence wages. Thus, Galiani foreshadowed Smith's concept of commanded labour – namely, the fact that the lower the price of commodities representing the fixed amount of the worker's subsistence wages, the richer the worker's employer would be.

Galiani argued that a country's welfare does not depend on the plentiful supply of precious metals, but on the plentiful availability of commodities. Nevertheless, some kind of currency is necessary; not in order to produce wealth but to enable wealth to circulate. An easy way to increase wealth in a country is to export commodities; an exporting country becomes a creditor towards foreign nations. By attracting money from abroad the country's domestic prices will increase, but higher prices at home need not be cause for alarm if this comes as a result of developing industry and welfare, as shown by a comparison between the low prices in a backward region as such Abruzzi – Galiani's birthplace – and the high prices in a flourishing city such as Paris. Moreover, when there is plenty of money there is the potential advantage of being able to set aside a portion of this for speculative purposes.

Effects of devaluations per factum principis

Not only did Galiani speak out against the prince's frequent recourse to altering the ratio between the value of money and that of commodities, he also provided an economist's appraisal of the effects of such action. The *alzamento* (literally, 'raising the coin', in fact, devaluation of money) *'denotes a profit, which the prince and the state enjoy because of the slowness with which the multitudes change [their mind on] the relationship between the prices of things and of money'* (Galiani, English translation: 166; original italics). This is a very 'modern' definition, and one which refers to the different ways in which the public is affected by a loss in the purchasing power of money and how they adapt their behaviour accordingly. Galiani underlines that there is always a certain time period during which 'the real variables of the economic system (incomes and their distribution) gradually react to the changes in monetary variables' (Di Nardi 1987: xv).

Primarily, the phenomenon of *alzamento*, decided by the prince, had the aim of lightening the burden of public expenditure. However, Galiani observed, fixed income earners, who are indeed the first to be affected by such a measure, though they will at first maintain the same expenditure habits will subsequently ask their employer (the prince himself) for a pay increase. If they are successful in obtaining this then the original aim of the measure will be frustrated. Merchants, on the other hand, will be damaged by the worsening of the exchange rate as far as imports are concerned, but by the same token will be encouraged in their exports. Moreover, they will benefit from higher domestic prices for their products and from a reduction in the real weight of their domestic debts. *Rentiers*, Galiani also pointed out, would be the hardest hit, but they merited no special safeguard since they belonged to the unproductive layers of society.

To sum up, in Galiani's account the effects of *alzamento* are not unequivocally bad. Defining the measure as 'iniquitous' simply because it redistributes income from creditors to debtors is therefore unwise. If those creditors are idle persons who are forced to actually work after *alzamento*, then the economic outcome can be considered positive.

Della moneta's fourth book deals with circulation. Even without formally endorsing the quantity theory of money he had learned from Locke, Galiani showed he had grasped its meaning. He writes that 'the circulation of money is ... an effect, not a cause of wealth' (p. 203). He attempts to calculate the yearly income produced in a country, the money that circulates, and the average velocity of circulation, implicitly using the $V = PQ/M$ formula. In particular, he analyses the different payment intervals within the group of the 'large merchants' and that of the 'small shopkeepers' (p. 205). Among the factors that may increase the velocity of circulation, the issuing of paper money should be considered. Galiani also adds interesting observations on the different payment intervals within and among the social classes.

Interest, probability and risk

With regard to interest, explored in Book 5, Galiani borrowed from Jacques Bernouilli the application of probability calculus to economics, and this allowed him to develop important reflections on forecasting and expectations.

> The intrinsic value always varies, according to the degrees of probability which might or might not be enjoyed from a thing.... 100 future ducats with 90 degrees of probability [the English translation erroneously reports '100 degrees' (p. 261)] of not being lost and 10 degrees of being lost, become 90 present ducats and should be valued as 90 for any contract, game, or exchange.
>
> (Galiani, English translation: 261)

The interest due becomes a price to be paid for insurance. Galiani terms this 'the price of heartbeats' (p. 263) that derives from the risk (hence, the fear) of not recovering the sum. In any case, interest is not the reward for the productivity of money in the form of capital. Moreover, as Umberto Ricci observed, interest in Galiani does not depend on abstinence, as in the post-classical nineteenth-century economists like Senior and the Austrians, but on risk (see Ricci 1999: 10).

Hence, interest is not a net reward, but rather an illusory surplus income calculated only in order to balance the present value of money with the future one. The difference between interest and usury is therefore that the latter is only a reward 'beyond chance'. It is difficult to find in Galiani a theory that genuinely foreshadows the 'subjectivist' theories of interest, as based on the temporal preference of agents.[5]

In dealing with the long-standing problem of usury, Galiani favourably commented on Pope Benedict XIV's *Vix pervenit* (1745) which distinguished between interest as a component of a loan's price, and usury as a sum above this price. But Galiani added that in order to repress usury it is above all necessary to ensure 'mildness of government, a certain justice, industry and frugality of the people', so that the yield of money will represent merely 'the price of insurance' (p. 265). Consequently, he opposed all legal fixing of the rate of interest. In fact the interest on a loan, its insurance price, depends on so many variables that it cannot be defined by the government. Here Galiani prefigures the well-known position held in Jeremy Bentham's *Defence of Usury* (1787) – the market alone must be the judge.

The 'Dialogues': a plea for differentiated grain policies

The *Dialogues sur le commerce des bleds* (1770) were composed in Paris soon before Galiani's forced return to Naples owing to a diplomatic incident. Galiani's French was checked by his friend Denis Diderot.

According to some commentators, the *Dialogues* could be seen as expressing the economist's transition from his original *laissez-faire* position to a protectionist and interventionist one dictated by the experience of the 1764 famine in Naples. But even if these circumstances may have played a role in his decision to compose the book, both the *Dialogues* and *Della moneta* give insight into Galiani's tendency to theorize; namely, towards looking for the 'first causes' of events. The interpretation of *Dialogues* as a conversion to some kind of empirical approach, or worse still as an anticipation of the German Historical school's method (see Cesarano 1986) is erroneous.

The *Dialogues* structure draws inspiration from Galileo's *Dialogo dei massimi sistemi*, with three *dramatis personae*: Chevalier Zanobi (Galiani himself), the Marquis de Rocquemaure (a pro-Physiocrat and therefore an adversary of Galiani), and a third figure, the President, officially equidistant from both of them but actually mildly favourable to Galiani. All these fictitious names concealed historical personalities (see Galiani 1958 [1770]: 9–10).

The *Dialogues* are above all a treatise on the *theory and method* of economic policy, based on the idea that it is impossible to establish uniform guidelines for the entire range of problems involving economic structure. With impeccable methodology, Galiani proceeded to examine the structural features of four countries – the republic of Geneva, Holland, France and England – in order to evaluate the policies that each of them should adopt. Galiani concluded that public wheat trade controls were necessary in Geneva (a small state that was not a grain producer), but unnecessary in Holland (a medium-sized state of manufacturers and seamen that would never find itself facing the risk of a shortage of wheat). With regard to France, a wheat-producing nation with a large population and considerable wealth differences between regions, Galiani argued that domestic free trade in wheat, with substantial limitations on export, would have been much more successful in averting the danger of a famine than the 1764 physiocracy-inspired edict on unlimited free export. Last but not least, England, a producer of wheat mainly for export, based its flourishing wheat trade on its highly developed shipping industry. As a consequence, the earnings gained by England (and Holland) from the wheat trade were much greater than in monocultural countries such as Turkey, Sicily and Poland, which were unable to sustain export using their own fleets and whose gains from the wheat trade remained very low.[6] (Incidentally, Galiani would not have recommended mono-culture as a development strategy, in contrast to the policies advocated by the many underdevelopment economists in the 1950s.)

Turning to France, Galiani was sceptical with regard to this country's capacity to improve cultivation for export. If all the land was cultivated and the population was still growing, as it was in France, there would be no potential for additional export of agricultural products. On the implicit assumption that marginal returns in agriculture were decreasing, Galiani believed that France's main economic interest should be oriented towards an improvement in commerce and manufacturing.

The subsequent pages of *Dialogues* examine the microeconomics of the wheat market – the type of demand, which, Galiani realized, was inelastic to price, and the various phases of production as well as the number of producers. He suggested the wheat trade should be regulated by a system of differentiated import duties (possibly inspired by the British Corn Laws), and he also proposed completely free domestic trade. Like Smith six years later, Galiani was definitely hostile to bounties.

From Naples to Milan: the *Caffè* experience

It has been observed that prior to the Austrian occupation of Lombardy, Milan had no remarkable economists, indeed no economists at all (Vianello 1942: vii). The new Austrian rule that succeeded Spanish dominion, stimulated a demand for services of a technocratic nature as a result of Austria's strong tradition in the field of administration. This direct demand for administrative services encouraged the best minds to reflect upon the foundations of economics as a guide to action. This was, in turn, conducive to further indirect demand for pure theory. The propitious dialectics between theory and action gave birth to a high season for Milanese economics; in no more than a few decades Lombardy became the most active centre of ideas, mainly concerning economic policy.

The previous chapter examined two forerunners of the Milanese Golden Age in economics: Neri and Carli. Here we will present the two main representatives of this age: Verri and Beccaria.

Il Caffè (1764–66) was a journal founded by a group of learned noblemen gathered together in the quite informal *Accademia dei pugni* [Academy of Fists] (see Francioni and Romagnoli 1993). This group of noblemen included mathematicians, *literati* and economists. *Il caffè* was the first Italian periodical that aimed at treating, in brilliant literary style, such challenging topics as the role of commerce, the definition of luxury and the meaning of happiness. Polemic against the pedantic and rhetorical tradition in literature, as well as against the burdensome legacy of Roman and medieval law, provided the main threads for the journal's discourse.

Political economy had a not insignificant role in this modernization project. *Il Caffè* exerted a ceaseless pedagogical impulse against leisure in favour of industry and workmanship. Further, in order to be effective, this pedagogy needed to offer exemplary models of behaviour to men and women who desired to occupy distinguished positions in society. Accordingly, in addition to indications as to the most suitable types of economic behaviour to adopt, the journal hosted studies on good manners, and descriptions of social virtues and vices, with the aim of illustrating a phenomenology of social conduct that simplified the more elaborate treatments of moral psychology drawn up by Shaftesbury, Hutcheson, Hume and Smith.

In particular, the nexus between moral sentiment and economic interest plays a recurring theme in many articles. Alessandro Verri, Pietro's younger brother, championed – in opposition to the stoic moral of duty – the moral of persuasion, whose aim was to enlighten all people on questions pertaining to their own well-intended interest and to its affinity with the interests of others (see A. Verri 1993 [1765–66]). Alessandro Verri was not acquainted with Smith's *Theory of Moral Sentiments*, which was published a few years earlier, but it is evident that his idea of *compassione* as the supreme virtue – provided it is combined with *amor proprio* [self-love] – is very close to Smith's 'sympathy'.

However, if the journal's social thoughts were up-to-date, its economic reflections were still placed in old mercantilist ideology. Pietro Verri, writing on the meaning of 'luxury' in its proper sense, argued that there must be some productive luxury (an apparent oxymoron!) which leads to greater employment and higher income for the leading sectors of the economy, and consequently higher receipts for the State through taxation. But while conceding that there existed another kind of luxury which proved destructive of families' assets, Verri maintained that even this latter form of luxury was not altogether negative, for the State would be allowed to confiscate idle property through taxation.

A rather different subject is addressed in the two-page contribution by Cesare Beccaria, entitled *Tentativo analitico su i contrabbandi* [Analytical attempt about smuggling] (1764). The subject seeks to determine the value of smuggled goods at which a smuggler can reach his break-even point even if his remaining goods are confiscated by the police. It is evident that once this equilibrium point has been determined, the symmetrical problem of determining a duty rate that allows the revenue authority to equalize its receipts against losses, is resolved. Beyond this specific issue, the article intended to illustrate the logic of economic choice, which consists of solving cost and benefit problems. Economic equilibrium depends upon balance between the two.

Pietro Verri: a theory for action

The passionate and quick-tempered Count Pietro Verri (of Milan, 1728–97), son of a member of the Milanese Senate, was for almost 30 years a faithful servant to Empress Maria Theresa and her two sons Joseph II and Leopold II; but in the last few years of his life he opted to support the republican government of Milan and to become 'citizen Verri'. Judging by his letters, Verri appears to have approached political economy in the early 1760s during the

Seven Years' War, when he stumbled upon such authors as Forbonnais, Melon, Dutot and Hume.[7] He then entered into an acquaintance with a noteworthy character from a military-economic background – Henry Lloyd, author of an *Essay on the Theory of Money* that came out in 1771 (the same year in which Verri published his *Meditazioni sull'economia politica*).[8] But despite his sincere reform-oriented stance, Verri remained an aristocrat – insistent that his rights of primogeniture be respected by his younger brothers. Indeed he did not hesitate to engage in a legal action against them that poisoned their relations for some decades.[9]

It has been observed that Verri was by far the most important *political* thinker in mid-eighteenth-century Italy (Salvatorelli 1935: 52). More recently it has been said that Verri's view of 'civil society' was a direct antecedent of Romagnosi's *incivilimento*: namely, a vision of an integrated system of moral, economic and legal norms intended to promote the pursuit of happiness (Porta, Scazzieri 1999: 813–52).

The life and works of Romagnosi will be presented in the following chapter, but it should be stated straightaway that it is hard to discern a similar organic (and Romantic!) programme in Verri's writings. Verri and his group of friends in the *Accademia dei pugni* intended to build a *political* theory built upon strictly utilitarian-individualist premises. His strongly held belief that individual preferences must be clearly manifested and, consequently, that all political decisions must be publicly expressed, marked him out as a forerunner of liberal-individualist, rather than traditional paternalistic or Jacobin egalitarianist, ideology. To his mind, only by open competition between alternative issues could the antinomy between individual and general interests be settled. Any reference to a 'common good' independent of individual choice was absolutely extraneous to the Milanese writer.

Verri's two short philosophical writings, *Meditazioni sulla felicità* (1763), and *Discorso sull'indole del piacere e del dolore* (1773) should be read in combination with his major economic work, the *Meditazioni sull'economia politica* (1771). In the former, centred on the contrast between moral duty and individual interest, there are implicit references to political economy, inasmuch as 'the goal of the social pact is the well-being of all people who contribute to moulding society; the result is public happiness, namely, the greatest possible happiness, *ripartita* [shared out] among all citizens with the greatest equality possible' (Verri 1964a [1763]: 100; see also the reprint of the original Verri 2002 [1781]).

Verri clarified that it is only under an enlightened rule that all subjects can satisfy their wants without interfering with others. This is the essence of a civil society, where 'every human being surrenders his own independence to gain liberty' (Verri 1964a [1763]: 99).

A more ambitious goal lay behind Verri's *Discorso sull'indole del piacere e del dolore*, a work that earned praise from Immanuel Kant (see Papini 1929: 7). Here one also finds some points in common with the *Theory of Moral Sentiments* (published by Smith 14 years earlier), but it should be kept in mind that many of these ideas were freely circulating throughout Europe.

Verri, like Smith, believed that pleasure and pain were conditioned by our relationships with our neighbours. Verri speaks of 'fear and hope' (Verri 1964b [1773]: 12); the sentiments each of us feels towards a judgement that is expected to be given by an ideal (social) spectator. Experience of the reaction of others towards one's own conduct strongly affects the experiencer's moral sense. In comparison to Smith, however, Verri embraced a straightforward sensualist option. He argued that pain is the main wellspring of human action, one through which humankind is expected to improve itself. Consequently, all efforts are made in order to avert pain, and this effort, in the form of disutility, is the proper yardstick for measuring the value of goods. The balance between pleasure and pain is the basis for the rationality of any action, not only 'economic' ones. 'Each act of ours,' he states, 'is like a purchase' (Verri 1964c [1773]: 67).

Verri's 'Meditazioni': utilitarianism and sensualism

The *Meditazioni sull'economia politica* is a very hastily written book, composed with the intention of teaching Beccaria a lesson (his more junior friend had suc-ceeded in securing an appointment as professor of economics in Milan, much to Verri's dismay). Despite this less-than-altruistic intent, the *Meditazioni* proved a success, and the book was translated into French, Dutch and German. In Adam Smith's library there were two copies of the 1772 Livorno/Leghorn edition (see Einaudi 1953 [1933]: 74). However, Verri was never quoted by Smith, and those similarities that do exist can be explained by the 'spirit of the times' (see Groenewegen 1986: x).

The book's standpoint is sensualist. Verri opens with an analysis of wants, springing from the dialectics of pain and pleasure, as a prelude to a verdict upon happiness. Savages do not feel 'unhappy', because, slaves to their habits as they are, they do not perceive new wants. Similarly to Galiani (nowhere cited), Verri adhered to a subjectivist theory of value. Such concepts as utility, plenty and want were always discussed as phenomena affecting individual persons, and were to be understood as ratios. Utility and rarity, in Verri's view, are the deter-minants of price, and must stand together because things that are rare but not useful, and things that are useful but not rare, have no price.

The equilibrium between production and consumption

Verri presented macroeconomic equilibrium as the situation whereby, in a country, the annual 'reproduction' (aggregate supply) matches the annual 'con-sumption' (aggregate demand). If the former exceeds the latter, there will be development; in the reverse case, there will be decline.

The crucial factor of production is labour. Here Verri distanced himself from the Physiocrats, arguing that 'sterile' labour is not only just as productive as agricultural work, but is indeed even more productive since it produces value for both the worker and his employer, and the worker's wage is not necessarily at subsistence level.

The marketplace is where sellers and buyers face each other directly. Verri contended that the monopoly price is the highest price possible. Smith put forward a similar argument (Smith 1979 [1776], vol. I: 78), but Verri's analysis looked more deeply at the question. He asserted that the monopolist brings to the market only a part of his merchandise, taking advantage of the buyer's state of need – in modern terms, the monopolist appropriates a part of the consumer's surplus.

Moreover, Verri indicated an important consequence of free competition: 'When the number of the sellers is increased in this manner, naturally enough the more they are, the more difficult it is for them to agree among themselves, and the more the increased sales make up for the decrease in price' (Groenewegen translation, 1986: 17; Italian edition, Verri 1964a: 144). Again, Verri reasoned in terms of negatively sloped demand curves, and realized that if elasticity is high, total expenditure (corresponding to the seller's revenue) will increase even in presence of lower prices.

Unluckily, Verri identified the equilibrium price with the equation $P = C/V$, where C is the number of consumers and V is the number of sellers. The so-called Verri–Frisi formula – from Paolo Frisi, a mathematician acquainted with the *Società dei pugni* – obscured the correct intuition that demand and supply are not absolute quantities, but respectively a decreasing and an increasing function of price. This formula, which has been extensively discussed (see Luini 1995: 127–45), survived the death of both the writers and was reproposed by several nineteenth-century authors.

With regard to the question of equilibrium between consumption and production, Verri was ambiguous. On the one hand he declared that in order to reach equilibrium, it is necessary to ensure 'the greatest possible increase in sellers of each commodity, and the greatest possible reduction in buyers' (Groenewegen translation 1986: 19; Verri 1964a: 148, a viewpoint that can be seen as reminiscent of old mercantilist ideas about monopoly. But it has also been observed that Verri understood the concept of effective supply (see Porta and Scazzieri 2000: 92) as a situation of perfect equilibrium with effective demand. In this case, no problem of disequilibrium will arise since in a normal situation 'every *seller* of a commodity is, and must be, a *buyer* of the commodities he consumes; indeed, it follows that every man is a *seller*, because he must be a *buyer* as well' (Groenewegen 1986 translation: 20; Verri 1964a: 148). This was an apparent prefiguring of Say's Law (on this see Tiran 1993: 445–71).

In policy matters Verri was a committed free trader. Prohibitions and trade restrictions should, he maintained, be gradually reduced, and he suggested that the government should adopt a line of 'inviting and guiding', rather than of 'forcing and prescribing'.

Money and public finance

Verri observed that normally prices are high when the quantity of commodities is low, and the quantity of money in circulation is high. But, he added, a further increase in the quantity of circulating money could lead to some increase in the quantity of commodities as well since sellers would have expectations of higher profits.

Interest is the price for money granted as a loan, and grows with the growth of the loans, diminishing with their diminution. If the interest on loans decreases, money-lenders will be induced to look for alternative forms of investment, such as real-estate or manufacturing. Incidentally, it may be observed that Verri neglected the question of investment in land improvement, and his biography shows that, although a landlord, he never showed a great interest in farming (Verri 1984).

Like Galiani, Verri addressed the question involving the velocity of circulation of money, which he calculated by dividing the national yearly product by the quantity of circulating money. The exchange rate, he argued, was an index of the health of the foreign trade of a country, although its fluctuations were influenced by speculative capital movements.

Public expenditure was another issue to which Verri turned his attention. He was in favour of public works, especially infrastructure, which he defined as *lusso di consumazione* [consumption luxury], while he rejected *lusso infecondo* [sterile luxury], reiterating in this case a typical physiocratic argument.

Direct taxes were incisively defined as '*a portion of property which each individual deposits in the public treasury, in order that he may enjoy in safety the property remaining to him*' (Groenewegen translation 1986: 83; Italian text, Verri 1964a: 222 – italics by Verri). In discussing the tax effects on equilibrium, Verri had a clear idea of the shifting nature and incidence of taxation. In particular, he realized that taxation of wage-goods would have the effect of raising monetary wages (by shifting backwards onto the producers), while taxation of non-wage goods would cause forward-shifting to consumers.

A very important observation put forward by Verri was that in order to assess the effects of a tax on market equilibrium, a certain period of time should be allowed to elapse to allow for a situation where taxpayers initially react by trying to evade the tax, then later opting to adjust their behaviour to the new situation.

Verri enumerated five 'canons of taxation' – which are similar to those considered in the fifth book of the *Wealth of Nations*. They are: (1) reducing the expense involved in tax collection to a minimum (see Groenewegen: translation: 89; Verri 1964a: 229); (2) ensuring '*that there is the least possible difference between the amount paid by the people and the total amount on the treasury books, while allowing as much freedom as possible to the nation*' (Groenewegen translation: 90; Verri 1964a: 230 – Verri's italics), which corresponds to Smith's fourth canon; (3) observing maximum clarity in fiscal laws, and impartiality in their application (see Groenewegen translation: 91; Verri 1964a: 231), substantially Smith's second canon; (4) avoiding increased transportation or exchange costs between seller and buyer by tax interference with domestic trade (see Groenewegen translation: 92; Verri 1964a: 231–2), and, finally; (5) 'a tax must never be made to follow hard on the heels of growth in industry' (Ibid.) in the sense that a tax must never discourage industrial improvements or more technical progress generally.

As far as direct taxes were concerned, Verri favoured the land tax based on the cadastre, but – quite differently from the Physiocrats – he rejected the idea of an *impôt unique*, inasmuch as the land tax is subject to amortization *via* land value depreciation and it would be unjust if this tax were left unaccompanied by a system of indirect taxation.

Before closing his book, Verri acutely observed that the Finance Minister is required to be impartial and energetic, while the Minister of Economy is called upon to act with caution and measure. It is in the nature of financial laws to be straightforward – because they principally impose or forbid modes of behaviour – while it is the nature of economic laws to be indirect, because they encourage or discourage certain types of behaviour. The market's efficiency must be the guiding light for the policy maker. The Minister of Economy should be

> active in destroying [the institutions which are not consistent with the market], and most cautious in building [new institutions because] most of the matters that concern him are inaccessible to the hands of man. The rest must be left to the principle that is the direct driving force of the universe ... which we call ... *nature*.
>
> (Groenewegen 1986: 116–17; Verri 1964a: 259–60)

Verri's 'consulte'

Concluding, mention should be made of the '*consulte*' [official reports] written by Verri on behalf of the Milanese government. These reports dealt with money circulation, the wheat trade, duties involving domestic trade, and the regime of state monopolies. In particular, Verri fought a memorable campaign against the *Ferma generale*, a very lucrative public concession of the trade in salt, tobacco and gunpowder, etc., which was entrusted to a powerful private enterprise. Verri's battle against the *fermiers* was eventually won in 1770.

Beccaria: 'the Italian Smith'

His interest in the economics of crime

As introverted and lazy as Verri was extroverted and dynamic, Marquis Cesare Bonesana di Beccaria (of Milan, 1738–94), author of the *Dei delitti e delle pene* (1764) that brought him international fame, was appointed to teach 'cameral sciences' (a synonym for public economics) at the Palatine schools of Milan, thereby arousing the envy of Pietro Verri, his former friend and companion in the *Accademia dei Pugni*.

Beccaria manifested his economic views very early. In his most famous book he argued that the death penalty is as useless as it is cruel:

> the evil of the punishment exceeds the good [for the criminal] that springs from the crime, and in this excess of evil over good must the infallibility of

the pain be calculated, as well as the loss of the good that crime produces. What goes beyond this has to be considered as superfluous and therefore tyrannical.

(Beccaria 1970 [1764]: 60)

The vantage point from which the question is examined is that of the criminal's mind, exactly like the *Caffè* article on smuggling. Following Helvétius's *De l'esprit* (1758), Beccaria concluded that the concepts of *good* and *evil* should be translated into those of *useful* and *harmful* (Francioni 1990: 77, in VV. AA. 1990a; see also Gianformaggio 1982).

In another passage Beccaria observed that every citizen sacrifices a small portion of his own liberty in order to induce 'the others' (that is, the State) to defend his own rights: 'The aggregate of these minimal portions forms the right to punish. All portions beyond are abuses' (Beccaria 1970 [1764]: 13). This definition is in symmetry with the nineteenth-century liberal theory of fiscal imposition, exclusively based on utilitarian principles (see Ferrara's approach in Chapter 5 below).

More a Physiocrat than a Smithian

In spite of Schumpeter's definition of Beccaria as the 'Italian Smith' – though it should be remembered that Schumpeter conversely defined Smith, without irony, as 'the Scottish Beccaria' (Schumpeter 1994: 180) – Beccaria appears to have drawn his doctrines from the Physiocrats, and was a very different thinker from Verri. The latter's fear of being plagiarized by his former friend therefore seems altogether unfounded.

In his *Elementi di economia pubblica*, written in 1769 and posthumously published by Baron Custodi in 1804, Beccaria presented a model of the circular flow of an economy, illustrating the ways in which the different social classes spend their incomes and transform them into demand for the goods and services which the same classes cooperate in producing. There is identity between total product, total income and total expenditure. Beccaria assumed that non-agricultural workers need their wages in advance – while agricultural workers may directly draw from what they produce – under the classical assumption that wages exactly cover subsistence.

After sketching his general model, he examined the main features of growth, which consists of the increase of *prodotto contrattabile* [marketable product]. This result is achieved by maximizing the *travaglio utile* [useful labour], which in turn influences the population level. The relationship between population and subsistence is taken in the sense that the capacity of the latter to grow is seen as a limiting factor affecting the increase of the former. However, Beccaria showed no special concern with regard to the possibility that the two trends may, in effect, be increasingly divergent. Hence he cannot properly be considered a forerunner of Malthus's two progressions, though possibly an *ante litteram* corrector of them.

Seven years before Smith, Beccaria (1958 [1769], vol. II: 387–8) gave a precise definition of the division (specialization) of labour:

> Through experience everyone draws the realisation that as a person applies his hand and his mind always to the same kinds of works and products, he more easily obtains the results than if he were to make all things by himself, alone and in an isolated context.

A certain Smithian flavour may also be perceived in another passage dealing with the origin of towns and the evolution of the town-country relationship. But while Smith considered this relationship from the perspective of the flow of agricultural commodities to the towns, and of capital investments to the country, Beccaria was more attracted to questions pertaining to the different degrees of concentration/dispersion of populations, which he insightfully explained in terms of the prevailing size and structure of landed property. When large estates exist as *latifundia*, the population is concentrated in only a few large towns and acts as a consumer, while in the case of a small- or medium-sized property regime, the population is scattered among villages or small towns and devotes itself to commerce and industry. He may have had in mind that the former case prevailed in the south of Italy, the latter in the north.

In line with the majority of eighteenth-century writers, Beccaria expressed concern about the risks associated with a declining population, and indicated several measures to counter the trend – public health policy, especially against contagious diseases; encouragement of marriage; discouragement of the absolute liberty of the testator; prohibition of the *fidei-commissa* that hindered free land ownership; and placing limits on the number of churchmen. In dealing with such subjects Beccaria manifested his propensity for quantitative and applied research. Many of these measures, had they been adopted, would have accelerated the crisis of the *Ancien Régime*.

Value and money

Only in the fourth and last part of *Elementi*, dealing with commerce, did Beccaria deal with value. Acutely, he observed that in the first stages of the economy emphasis was placed on use value, while in the more mature (i.e. commercial) stage, the notion of exchange value gained greater relevance. Beccaria based value on utility and scarcity in a relative sense, but his analysis of the equilibrium of exchange between two dealers and two goods goes much further. He observed that if demand is the same (here he is evidently referring to demand curves), it is supply that determines the exchange value between the two goods; but if reciprocal demands are different, the exchange value of the commodity for which demand is higher will be greater than that of a commodity which is less in demand. Here Beccaria foreshadowed the mid-nineteenth-century theory of international trade (see A. Graziani Sr 1889, Chapter 4).

An interesting point underlined by Beccaria is that when the number of both commodities and operators increases, a particular commodity assumes the role of money. As such, it presents two properties: (1) that of being a measure of value, and; (2) that of being a 'pawn' accepted in exchange for all other commodities. At first a commodity is accepted as money due to its intrinsic utility, but subsequently, once metallic money has been introduced, care must be taken to ensure that the value of the coin is the same as that of the metal. Variations in relative values, he pointed out, will lead to revaluations or devaluations of the coin, followed by new coinages.

Against old bullionism, Beccaria observed that it is the velocity of circulation, not the absolute amount of money, that expresses the good health of the economic state of the country (Beccaria 1958 [1769] vol. I: 598–9). Beccaria espoused the quantitative theory of money, and held that there is a proportional relationship between the quantity of money in circulation and the number of everyday exchanges, this proportion depending on the general economic conditions of society (Beccaria 1958 [1769], vol. I: 600–1). Beccaria also subscribed to Hume's theory of re-equilibrating trade balances through the movement of prices and metals. 'The nations that manifest a continuous trade and open mutual relations of commerce … cannot reduce themselves to a state of permanent excess or defect [of metallic money], but continually tend to equilibrium' (Beccaria 1958 [1769]: 607).

The last two topics considered in *Elementi* are the rate of interest and the exchange rate. The former is defined as a gain based on 'the utility of time', while the latter is determined by 'the utility of place'.

Beccaria's 'consulte'

Finally, Beccaria's liberal ideas are revealed in his *consulte* written on behalf of the Milanese government. Even though the objects of these reports may seem somewhat modest, the principles that inspired Beccaria were very clear-cut: protection of domestic production leads to retaliation and is therefore useless; workers must not be repressed too severely, because it cannot be precluded that the most skilled among them may decide to emigrate; furthermore, as far as seasonal unemployment is concerned, the wisest remedy is to encourage the temporal displacement of the unemployed workforce from the silk to the flax industry (see Vianello 1943).

The economy without progress: Giammaria Ortes

Physical science against economic 'fiction'

The singular personality of this Venetian monk (1713–90) attracts the reader's attention for two reasons: (1) his inclination for theorizing, probably enhanced by his scientific training under Guido Grandi, professor at Pisa University and one of the most renowned mathematicians of his time, and; (2) above all, his sceptical attitude towards progress and economic growth, which distinguishes him from all other eighteenth-century economists both in Italy and abroad.

Indifferent if not hostile to the ideas and in particular to the spirit of the Enlightenment, but open to the scientific revolution ushered in by Bacon, Galileo and Newton, Ortes reproached his fellow economists for their alleged lack of scientific methodology. Nowhere are they explicitly mentioned, although a careful reading of Ortes's texts reveals that he knew at least Petty, Mandeville, Locke and Smith (see Erba 2011), all of them condemned for their confusion between reality and imagination or, more precisely, between what is and what ought to be. Economics is especially insidious, Ortes claimed, and all its propositions must be carefully submitted to the tribunal of reason. Appearances are deceptive, and what seems to be real is often a mere deception. Ortes thus resolved to follow an entirely rational method of enquiry.

However, one may wonder whether this rigorous method was appropriately used by Ortes. One of his minor works, *Errori popolari intorno all'economia nazionale* (1772), aimed to disprove criticisms voiced by those Enlightenment writers who strongly opposed the extended landed properties of the Church that allowed ecclesiastical authorities to obtain high rents. Ortes objected that incomes were in no way dependent on property; rather, they were dependent on employment. Therefore the Church was not responsible for the poverty of the masses, because ecclesiastical rents were not unearned incomes; indeed, they were not incomes at all (see Ortes 1999 [1772]: 7–8).

This sophism was unveiled by Ortes himself, when he further suggested the Church should, as far as possible, renounce its feudal privileges and accept the market mechanism (pp. 94–109). Here, Ortes implicitly admitted that feudal rents were incomes as well, and that his previous definition of income as exclusively being the fruit of 'employment' was overly restrictive.

Ortes's propensity for making use of paradoxes characterized his otherwise subtle 'critique of political economy'. Ortes's criticism challenged the most entrenched certainties of economics to their very foundations. He challenged the viewpoint espoused by economists who taught that wants progressively increased. In fact, in Ortes's assessment this was a sheer deception produced by false assumptions; on the contrary, human wants are fixed, and only their external manifestations may appear different from time to time, and from place to place. Consequently, he argued, production does not grow under the impulse of new wants, but only as the consequence of population increase. The higher rate of growth of the national product as compared to growth of the population – the growth of per capita income – is also a deception that disguises a mere variation in distribution. In actual fact, Ortes asserted, the nations that seemed to be the wealthiest, such as Britain and France, were those blighted by the greatest number of poor. In contrast, the countries that appeared poorer, such as the Italian states, enjoyed a more balanced distribution of income and wealth and consequently were happier. Ortes thus perceived that any process of growth creates income disparities. For this reason Marx enthusiastically defined him as 'one of the great economic writers of the eighteenth century, [who] regards the antagonism of capitalist production as a universal natural law of social wealth' (Marx 1990 [1867]: 800).

Ortes was at his best as a mathematical economist when he engaged in calculating the population's vital food needs in order to estimate the total expenditure of the population in the Venetian republic. In this context he drew up an annotated list illustrating the minimal standard of living requirements, which called for the availability of a certain amount of *beni bisognevoli* (something akin to 'basic goods' in today's statistical research on poverty; Erba 2011: 66). The temptation to see Ortes as a pioneer of modern linear programming techniques is great.

However, Ortes's calculus expressed in material terms did not exhaust his discussion on the driving forces of society. As an additional factor, he acknowledged the economic importance of a fundamental psychological, and hence moral, factor – selfishness – which sparks a hoarding impulse for the mere sake of it. The result is that part of the national product is diverted from the economy. Saving is a net reduction of expenditure and therefore of income. In this fundamental aspect he was a veritable forerunner of Keynes.

Ortes's 'critique of political economy'

Ortes appeared to believe in the working of a *negative* invisible hand; or better, in the reverse of the Mandeville paradox. He claimed it was a mistake to maintain that 'any increase of goods for individuals corresponds to an increase for the community' (Ortes 1804 [1774]: 17); while saving may be an individual virtue, it is a public calamity. From this perspective, Ortes warned against the 'fallacy of composition'.

His critical, and to some extent destructive, view of the mainstream (both physiocratic and classical) economics of his time involved his definition of productive factors. In his account, capital is 'equivalent to all dead employments of resources' and is far from being an active principle of production. Ortes here appears to anticipate Marx's definition of capital as 'dead labour'. Money is likewise a typical abstraction and a *fictional element*. That is to say, although money is frequently identified with wealth, when considered by itself money has no actual value. This justifies Ortes's support for the quantitative theory of money. The transactional motive is the one and only justification to demand money.

Ortes believed that in every country there is a fixed proportion of 'employed' and 'unemployed', a concept that can be seen as a variation on the classical theme of productive and unproductive labour. Ortes prefigured Malthus in his concerns regarding overpopulation (overpopulation of the 'employed' population only; that is, the part which consumes agricultural goods). The main remedy for overpopulation is the celibacy of the priesthood, which is all the more essential inasmuch as it increases the number of idle 'unemployed' who provide further demand for non-agricultural goods, but does not increase supply. In this respect (his treatment of macroeconomic equilibrium) Ortes may also be considered a forerunner of Malthus.

He realized that all efforts to change the current state of income distribution through public policy were doomed to face insurmountable difficulties. There was, he believed, a philosophical-theological explanation for economic inequality, due to the working of the 'principle of sufficient reason' which Ortes borrowed from Leibniz and indirectly from Aristotle (see Erba 2011: 62). His reliance on this principle – a cornerstone of the theodicy tradition in Western thought – explains Ortes's defence of the status quo, beginning with the Church's *fidei commissa*, and more generally of the right of the aristocracy to be considered the natural ruling class.

Giambattista Vasco, the Piedmontese Beccaria

The Kingdom of Sardinia underwent a transition from the reformism of Victor Amadeus II to the conservatism of Charles Emmanuel III and Victor Amadeus III. After 1750 the growing intellectual reaction against the laziness and myopia of the government aroused an interest in research on the subject of economics.

Giambattista Vasco (of Mondovì, 1733–96) was the brother of the better-known democrat and revolutionary Francesco Dalmazzo, who died in prison in 1794. In order to escape the oppressive cultural climate of Turin, Giambattista moved to Milan, where he established contact with Verri and Beccaria. Upon his return to Turin he founded an interesting progressive journal, the *Biblioteca oltremontana*. In his final years he manifestly opposed to the French Revolution.[10]

Vasco's writings deal with economics and institutions, money, labour and social policy, and showed a solid doctrine, underpinned by noteworthy technical and mathematical training. His opinions were moulded by the work of his more senior friends Beccaria and Verri, and he may be considered a genuine follower of both of these figures.

In *La felicità pubblica considerata nei coltivatori di terre proprie* (1769) Vasco considered private ownership of land as bestowing a fundamental entitlement to participate in society. He did not advocate an altogether equal distribution of land, but suggested the adoption of a minimum and a maximum extension, in order to avoid, respectively, excessive fractioning and excessive extension. He therefore proposed that the term '*mansus*', which he drew from German medieval law, should be used to designate this minimum unit of landed property. The maximum amount for each landowner should be eight or nine *mansi*.

Vasco's *Della moneta. Saggio politico* (1772) expanded the theory of value of commodities (based on rarity and scarcity) to include money. There should be correspondence between the official and the current exchange rate fixed by the market, as both must respect the intrinsic value of money. He argued that two 'tariffs' (exchange rates) could be established: one representing the intrinsic value of money, the other indicating its value as determined on the basis of private contracting.

Along with metallic money, paper money could also be accepted when issued by private bankers and based on public confidence. This type of circulation required daily control by the State with the aim of guaranteeing its convertibility. Moreover, Vasco also envisaged the possibility of state-issued money, basically Treasury bonds necessary to finance public works, which could be withdrawn from circulation through amortization.

Among his various activities, Vasco was entrusted with drawing up a government report on the remedies for unemployment in the silk industry, especially *torcitura* [silk-throwing], due to a shortfall in the supply of raw material. Here Vasco suggested some forms of workfare, such as allocating the unemployed to carry out machinery repairs. But first and foremost he was in favour of the free export of raw silk as a consequence of the abolition of old mercantilist prohibitions.

Vasco showed a fairly good knowledge of the work of Adam Smith.[11] Additionally, in 1792, he published a pamphlet, *L'usura libera*, in which he appeared to converge with the positions held by Bentham in his *Defense of usury* (issued five years earlier). Finally, his dissertation *Delle università di arti e mestieri* (1793) is worth mentioning. As a witness of the apparent crisis of the corporative system that was accused of causing high prices, unemployment and low wages, Vasco discussed the economy of the crafts and professions, drawing inspiration mainly from Turgot and Smith. On the one hand, Vasco acknowledged that the measures introduced on the basis of corporatism could be of use in defending consumers against unauthorized employments; while on the other he rejected the practice of utilizing corporative institutions as tax collectors, objecting that this ran contrary to Adam Smith's canons concerning taxation, and in particular those relating to proportionality and certainty.

Neapolitan school: *laissez-faire*, law and economics, and political conservatism

So far our attention has focused on the most notable economists of the 'Golden Age' of Italian economics in the eighteenth century. Most of them contributed to laying the bases for various different schools that endured until the first decades of the next century.

Let us now offer a rapid sketch of their followers and disciples. Ideas and projects of economic reform, a fairly pronounced involvement with their governments, and scholarly activity that stood midway between scientific investigation proper and journalistic enquiry, unify this category of learned men, who can be described more as 'functionaries' than as producers of original ideas.

The ideal starting point is the Neapolitan school of economics, which was more strongly influenced by Genovesi than by Galiani. Two aristocrats, described in the following sections, can be cited among the main representative authors.

Law and economics in Naples: Gaetano Filangieri

Gaetano Filangieri (of Naples, 1752–88), the descendant of a princely family, was author of *La scienza della legislazione* (1780–91: the last volumes appeared posthumously), an extensive although unfinished treatise that compared the contemporary legal system with Roman law and probably drew inspiration from Montesquieu. The work, published in five volumes, was translated into French, German and Spanish and, for the first volume only, into English (see Maestro 1976; Ferrone 2012). Filangieri rose to fame rapidly, and appears to have been the only Italian intellectual who Goethe met during his 1787 journey through Italy (Goethe 1993 [1817]: 212).

Although Filangieri's main interests were not principally economic, he showed considerable knowledge of the international economic literature: Montesquieu, Hume, Wallace and Cantillon on population; Raynal on manufacturing; Schmid d'Avenstein (much read in Italy in the same years) on colonial expansion; and so forth (see Filangieri 2004 [1780], vol. II: vii). He also had knowledge of Adam Smith, although probably not so much from direct acquaintance with the original text as, rather, from the abstracts published in Italian journals (Ferrone 2012: 205).

Book 2 of *La scienza della legislazione*, devoted to *Leggi politiche ed economiche*, deals with economics as it stands in relation to institutions. A strict disciple of Genovesi, he had little faith in the automatic workings of the market, and still less in the invisible hand automatism. If, on the one hand, law must draw its inspiration from economics, it was equally true on the other hand that economics finds its key guidelines in law. A true representative of the late Enlightenment intellectuals, Filangieri can be classed more as a Liberalist than as a *stricto sensu* liberal.[12]

He was troubled by the low level of population in the Kingdom of Naples, a situation he blamed on the excessive concentration of landed property, especially in the hands of the Church. As a result of such anti-clerical attitudes, his book was published in 1791, posthumously. Nevertheless, it was immediately placed on the *Index librorum prohibitorum*. He also expressed concern about the excess population of the capital city as compared to the striking depopulation in the countryside. He therefore advocated measures which would encourage the establishment of industries away from Naples (see Maestro 1976: 20). In general he was in favour of a balance between agriculture, industry and commerce. These sectors should be allowed to develop in a framework of freedom; this belief, however, did not imply an absence of law, but rather the presence of sound regulatory norms.

Additionally, Filangieri discussed the advantages and disadvantages of the two alternative models for the national army, a subject that had attracted the attentions of many contemporary writers, including Adam Smith (see Winch 1978). While Smith was in favour of a standing army, Filangieri – himself a member of the armed forces by profession – advocated the alternative model; a militia, he argued, had the merit of making it possible to build up an army of citizen-peasants, rooted in traditional attachment to their land and therefore with a vested interest in defending it and the families that lived on it. At once both a 'democratic' and 'patriotic' concept, it inspired the notion of 'armed nation' that became widespread in the Italian *Risorgimento*.

On other issues Filangieri – who was also influenced by Verri's *Meditazioni* – was a staunch free trader, strongly critical of all trade policies based on the *beggar-my-neighbour* principle.

Palmieri's conservative economics

Like Genovesi, Marquis Giuseppe Palmieri (of Lecce, 1721–93) was concerned with the growth of wants that become manifested in societies during the process of growth. However, in contrast to his master, Genovesi, and also Filangieri, Palmieri in his book *Riflessioni sulla pubblica felicità relativamente al Regno di Napoli* (1787) proved to be a rigid conservative. He was openly hostile to the 'maximum of happiness divided up among the maximum number' principle shared by Verri and Beccaria. In particular, he was against the economic-utilitarian treatment of punishment presented in *Dei delitti e delle pene*, arguing it was better to condemn an innocent man than set a guilty man free, because 'absolving a guilty man is the same as condemning to death[!] one thousand innocents' (Palmieri 1991 [1787]: 92).

Palmieri followed Genovesi in maintaining that the most serious problem of the South was that of inducing people to work, but he was sceptical about the effectiveness of landed property reform. In his view, capital for agriculture could better be supplied by special credit institutions.

Virtue and the economy in Dragonetti

Recently, the attention of historians has also focused on Giacinto Dragonetti (of L'Aquila, 1738–1818), who could be considered a *trait d'union* between Genovesi's vision of 'civil economy' and Bentham–Beccaria's subjectivist approach. Dragonetti's *Della virtù e de' premi* (1766), a tract on the Utilitarian principles of law, was published in a number of Italian editions and underwent many translations – into English, French, Russian, German, Spanish, and even into Swedish and Polish. Bentham himself may have read it. Briefly, Dragonetti, a magistrate, endeavoured to complete Beccaria's treatment with reference to the incentives a legal system should provide in order to encourage virtuous conduct among citizens (see Bruni 2010; Zamagni 2010).

The hitherto rather undefined concept of 'public welfare' thus acquired one of its most skilful interpreters and defenders, whose thought was oriented towards an enlargement – not a dismissal! – of the individualist premises. Economic liberalism was therefore presented as embedded in a broader moral view.

Some minor voices

Tuscan school: the Bandini legacy

In general, economists from Tuscany have attracted greater interest among economic historians than among historians of economic thought. This is not surprising. Faced with the decay of commerce and manufacturing, due *inter alia* to the increasing marginality of the Florentine state with respect to the great streams of traffic throughout Europe, many Tuscan writers turned once more to the subject of agriculture, proposing a lightening of the tax burden on land, and a substantial plan of public works, beginning with land reclamation. In order to implement such an agenda, they claimed there was a greater need for reliable public servants than for original theorists.

Considerable credit must be given to the far-sighted wisdom of Grand Duke Peter Leopold of Habsburg-Lorraine, the 'shepherd prince' according to the Arcadian appellative coined for him by Mirabeau. During his reign (1765–90) corporative fetters were abolished, the inefficient *Annona* system (against which Bandini had fought his main battle) was reformed, and the internal tolls and other duties on domestic transport were cancelled. In parallel, an undeniable cultural openness was a prominent feature of the Grand-Duchy of Tuscany and the small republic of Lucca. Here it proved possible to publish the main works of Verri and Beccaria, and above all, two in-folio editions of *Encyclopédie* (Lucca 1750 and Leghorn/Livorno 1770, both in the original language).

Three Tuscan economists may be briefly recalled here. All three were members of the *Accademia dei Georgofili*, founded by Abbot Ubaldo Montelatici in 1753 in order to safeguard Bandini's legacy. Very soon the *Accademia dei Georgofili* came into conflict with the *Accademia della Crusca* on account of the latter's pedantic quest for language purity, while the main problem, in the economists' view, was to ensure 'the common happiness and good of mankind' (see Cochrane 1961: 213).

In roughly the same years, Gian Francesco Pagnini (of Volterra, 1713–89), a well-trained economic historian but a theorist as well, wrote in his *Saggio sopra il giusto pregio delle cose* (1751) appended to his translation of Locke's economic works, that in order to measure value it was necessary to consider both 'physical factors' and 'moral factors'. The former concerned the number of sellers and buyers and the quantity of commodities; while the latter dealt with consumers' tastes and the ability of the marketed goods to satisfy wants. Market equilibrium would be reached when the 'physical' and 'moral' quantities of the good demanded were equal to the physical and moral quantities of the good that was given in exchange (see Dal Pane 1953).

Parson Ferdinando Paoletti (of Bagno a Ripoli near Florence, 1717–1801) was the individual who was most faithful to Bandini's thought, which he attempted to harmonize with the Physiocrats. In particular, in *I veri mezzi di render felici le società* (1772), Paoletti distinguished the long-period equilibrium price of wheat, which should be appropriate ('decorous') in order to reward peasants for their toil, in analogy with the Physiocratic *bon prix*, from the short-period price, which was affected by the multiple difficulties springing from non-agricultural markets.[13]

Finally, Francesco Maria Gianni (of Florence, 1728–1821) in his *Pensieri sulla ricchezza nazionale* (1787) was possibly influenced by Ortes in considering the relationships between aggregate production, population and consumption as fixed, and in his attempts at calculating the population's average means of subsistence.

After Peter Leopold's departure from Florence to Vienna, where he was to be crowned Emperor Leopold II (1790), Senator Gianni – writing in a period that coincided with a change of policy in a more conservative direction brought about by Peter Leopold's successor – began to look more compassionately on the condition of the poor. In his *Discorso sui poveri* (1804) he observed that most of the poor were workers who were the victims of involuntary (technological) unemployment. But as a committed Liberalist, he rejected any form of public relief.[14]

Venice between agronomy and laissez-faire

The closing decades of Venetian rule, before Venice passed under Austrian dominion (Campoformio Treaty, 1797), witnessed a considerable flourishing of interest in economics, with lively contributions from *literati*, travellers and – above all – businessmen and agronomists.

Entrepreneur Antonio Zanon (of Udine, 1696–1770), in his *Lettere sull'agricoltura, il commercio e le arti* (1757–67), dealt with the excessive dispersion of the population in Friuli, a sub-region of the Venetian territory, where there were too many scattered villages and too few large towns. The remedy, he maintained, would be to boost wine and silk production (see, in general, Molesti 1987), thereby fostering positive integration between town and country, the ever-recurring problem since Machiavelli.

Francesco Mengotti (of Belluno, 1749–1830) was author of *Il colbertismo* (1791), a memoir presented at the Florentine *Accademia dei Georgofili* as part of a public competition. It tackled the subject of the role of manufacturing in economic development. Mengotti did not attack mercantilism in its more mature form, but rather bullionism; namely, the idea that an increase in metallic money could have real effects on production. In opposition to the latter approach, Mengotti championed the quantitative theory of money. He generally agreed with Adam Smith that Spain and Portugal, despite having colonial empires, did not benefit from this advantage due to their lack of manufactures at home.[15]

The Jacobin 'economists'

Italian 'Jacobins' – the intellectuals who shared the republican and democratic principles carried out by the French occupants of Italy during the triennium 1796–99 – constituted a surprisingly heterogeneous group. From the literary and cultural point of view, they appear to conclude the age of the Enlightenment rather than prefigure the ideas of the fast-approaching age of Romanticism. Elements of radical transformation merge with the drive towards modernization of the economy in the sense of market expansion and reduction of state interference.

Abbot Giuseppe Compagnoni (of Lugo near Bologna, 1754–1834) is best known for his proposal to adopt the three-colour flag for the Cispadana Republic, of which Milan was the capital. In his *Elementi di diritto costituzionale demo-cratico* (1797) Compagnoni embraced the position of a committed Rousseau fol-lower. In contrast to Beccaria, who argued in *Dei delitti e delle pene* that the social contract calls upon all individuals to surrender a small portion of their ori-ginal rights so as to safeguard their entire remaining range of rights, Compag-noni argued that all citizens should surrender the totality of their rights in order to reclaim them from the State. This approach, Compagnoni stressed, embodied the true sense of democratic sovereignty (see VV. AA. 1956a: 62–3).

With regard to other matters, Compagnoni conceived of the economic task of government principally as that of encouraging a regime of free enterprise, by granting protection to inventions, ensuring free domestic and foreign trade, and above all eliminating existing corporative constraints. All taxes should be certain, and their destination and allocation should be absolutely transparent. As far as property was concerned, Compagnoni distinguished property rights – admitted merely as 'ownership of immobile property' – from industrial rights – which should be encouraged, as 'ownership of mobile property' (VV. AA. 1956a: 51).

Another Jacobin, author of *Grammatica repubblicana* (1798) which was pub-lished anonymously under the classical pseudonym Nicio Etritreo (probably Claudio Della Valle, see p. 423), insisted on the importance of introducing chairs of agriculture and commerce in Italy – but he was by no means a Physiocrat. Rather, he appears to have drawn inspiration from Genovesi. In effect, he was concerned with the excessive inflow of gold and silver, stating that it caused a rise in prices that favoured the import of foreign goods and thereby impover-ished the nation. Money, he reasoned, should be proportional to the needs of commerce; it must not be hoarded but should be left free to circulate. Further-more, the wealthy class faced a twofold task; that of lending at low interest rates, or, alternatively, of purchasing luxury goods produced in the country. The unem-ployed should be channelled towards socially useful activities, and private charity should be substituted by public intervention. Finally, Nicio Eritreo invoked an 'agrarian law' (a literary echo of the Gracchan legislation of the Roman Republic) aimed at redistributing land to non-propertied families (p. 154).

An additional figure who should not be overlooked is Vincenzio Russo (of the province of Naples, 1770–99), one of the victims of the Bourbon reaction. His *Pensieri politici* (1798) is considered the most 'socialist' outcome of Italian Jacobin literature. For instance, he was the only Italian writer of the time to favour progressive taxation (pp. 301–2). However, one should refrain from over-enthusiastic judgements on his foresight. He had no confidence in manufacturing and commerce, believing that both these types of activity rendered the workers spiritually weak; moreover, industries in these spheres encouraged urban agglomerations which 'are lethal for democracy (p. 305). In contrast, Russo argued that agriculture forges men who are true patriots and soldiers, as well as active producers. Thanks to agriculture the population will also grow; Italy could rise from a population of about 16 million to as much as 48 million inhabitants

(p. 307). Note that Russo is unlikely not to have been acquainted with William Godwin's *Enquiry concerning political justice* (1793), which is similarly optimistic concerning property, population and democracy. A further aspect touched upon by Russo is that once the spirit of greed and selfishness has been removed from people's mind, the economy would be left entirely free (p. 349).

The Jacobin economists conclude the parable of Enlightenment studies on economics in Italy. A critical assessment of their failure to bring about substantial reform was pronounced by Vincenzo Cuoco (of Civitacampomarano, 1770–1823), who also wrote on economics and statistics during French rule (see Romani 1994: 31–7). In his famous history of the failed 1799 Neapolitan revolution, Cuoco – himself a Jacobin in his youth – ascribed the failure to the abstract mentality of the Neapolitan revolutionaries, who seemed to believe it was sufficient to argue rationally in order to achieve the accomplishment of their wishes (see Cuoco 1860 [1806]: 4). Here, Cuoco marked the ideal transition from Enlightenment to Romanticism in Italy.

Notes

1 Extract reproduced in the editor's note to Galiani (1958) [1770]: 9.
2 See Einaudi (1953) [1945]: 281. A slightly different text is presented in the English version of Einaudi's essay, in Spiegel (ed.) (1952): 73.
3 Galiani (1987) [1780]: 7. Preface not included in the English translation by P. Toscano (1977), henceforth quoted as 'English translation'.
4 For a comparison between Galiani and such authors as Davanzati, Broggia and – above all – Locke, which highlights Galiani's debt both to the earlier tradition and more recent works, see Rosselli (2001), in Faucci and Giocoli (eds) (2001).
5 For a thorough discussion of the various contemporary intepretations, see Giocoli (1997). Giocoli refers to Jacques (Jakob) Bernoulli's (or Bernouilli: 1654–1705) theory of expected values, and not to his nephew Daniel (1700–82), famous for his reflection concerning decisions relating to uncertainty conditions.
6 See the original French version, Galiani (1987) [1770]: 181; Italian translation, Galiani (1958) [1770]: 187–8.
7 At that time he wrote some comments on Hume's *Political discourses*, of which he owned a French translation that had come out in 1754. See P. Verri (2006): 63–83.
8 See Venturi (1977). A very sketchy presentation of Lloyd's ideas, revealing that he supported the quantitative theory of money, but at the same time undervalued the danger of paper money inflation, is revealed in Hutchison (1988): 344–5.
9 See the excellent biography of Verri by Capra (2002). A meticulous historian of himself and his family, Verri collected his public and private papers in one of the best-kept eighteenth-century private archives. See Panizza and Costa (eds) (1997): 2000.
10 Most of his writings have been collected in the Custodi collection of *Scrittori italiani classici di economia politica*, vols 34 and 35 (1804). A recent, more rigorous edition, is Vasco (1989).
11 Gioli (1993): 226–8, gives scant information. More exhaustive is Gioli (1972): 917–62.
12 The problem of whether Filangieri was a genuine 'modern' liberal, or not, first arose with Benjamin Constant's criticism of him for failing to establish his liberalism on the concept of a constitution, and in particular for misunderstanding the true spirit of English liberalism (see Constant (1822)). Since Constant rejected all proposals

of economic reform which were not included in a definite liberal-constitutional context, his appraisal of the Neapolitan author was *a priori* negative. For a rediscussion of this issue, see Pecora (2007): 20.

13 See his works in *Scrittori classici italiani di economia politica*, vol. XX (1804).
14 On Gianni, after the old book by Mori (1951), who generically insisted on the Tuscan economists' 'eclecticism', see the complete study by Diaz (1966).
15 Mengotti's main writings are also collected in Custodi's *Scrittori classici italiani di economia politica*, vol. XVI (1804).

4   Strengths and weaknesses of the early nineteenth century

A discontinuity?

With the opening of the nineteenth century, Italian economics showed indisputable signs of decline. Certainly, there were no lack of interesting writers who belonged to this period, but the type of reflection on the leading principles of political economy that had been undertaken in the previous 50 years, lost much of its original force.

This impoverishment is all the more regrettable because the early nineteenth century witnessed a remarkable progress of economics in other countries, with such scholars as Malthus, Ricardo, Say, Lauderdale and James Mill, to name just a few, successfully establishing a (comparatively) univocal scientific language based on accepted definitions of the main economic concepts and an acknowledged method of approaching economic phenomena ('normal science' according to T. S. Kuhn). Between 1800 and 1830 the key topics – population, value, income distribution, money, international trade – were rigorously clarified. Political economy began to attract people's interest and to occupy the pages of widely read periodicals – for instance the Whig *Edinburgh Review* (1802), the Tory *Quarterly Review* (1809), Bentham's *Westminster Review* (1824) (see Coats 1996). Furthermore, in 1821 the Political Economy Club was founded, stimulating discussions that influenced both parliamentary debate and government action (see Gordon 1976).

A number of explanations have been put forward in the attempt to highlight the increasing aloofness of Italian economics from the international mainstream. One reason can be traced, above all: the cultural setting. Romanticism, more so in Italy than abroad, did not encourage the study of economics. The great poet and scholar, Giacomo Leopardi, spoke out sarcastically against the Enlightenment ambition to sum up the laws of social development in a restricted number of propositions and render them popular through the media: 'Long life to statistics! Long life to all economic ... sciences, to all portable encyclopaedias, and to all such fine creations of our century.'[1]

Implicitly, his accusation was directed against the key concept of 'utility', which stood accused of suffocating the individual spirit of liberty and creativity. Economics, he believed, was the typical science of utility, and as such it aroused his hostile response.

With the benefit of hindsight, Leopardi can be said to have been too severe in his censure. Romanticism inspired many important voices, including Joseph De Maistre (see Camcastle 2005), Alban de Villeneuve-Bargemont, and, later on, Thomas Carlyle, who all endeavoured to present an alternative to mainstream economic thought by upholding traditional cultural and spiritual values and, in some cases, by advocating a return to the spirit of the Middle Ages as embodied by the Roman Church. The objection levelled by the Romantic 'economists' against the Enlightenment was that historical traditions held considerable importance for individual nations, and that respect should be paid to the heritage of bygone ages. This feature can be detected in the works of the great Geneva scholar, J.-C. L. Simonde de Sismondi (1773–1842), a close friend of so many Italian (especially Tuscan) *literati* that he himself could be considered a quasi-Italian writer. In fact, his ideal society – which largely coincided with the historical experience of the Italian cities of the Middle Ages (a topic he treated in one of his most praised works) – coincided with a pre-capitalist economy.[2]

Let us return to the post-1815 situation. In parallel with the worsening of the peninsula's political conditions due to restoration of old 'legitimate' dynasties, a silent theoretical counter-revolution began to make itself felt in the domain of social sciences, with serious negative effects on economics.

First, the relationship between economics and law was subverted. Verri, Beccaria, Filangieri and others had attempted to establish an 'economic analysis of law' centred on a cost-benefit approach to legislation and on the argument that legislation itself should be reformed to take into consideration its economic effects. After the 1815 Restoration, this tradition waned. The definitive rejection of the natural law tradition – together with the parallel rejection of economics as a science based on 'natural laws' – had a negative impact on a theoretical approach to economics. The result was that the study of law became little better than descriptive and a-theoretical work, and this aspect astounded many foreign scholars, such as Friedrich von Savigny the great German jurist and historian.

It can be objected, however, that during the first half of the nineteenth century a growing importance was attributed to statistics, as witnessed in European circles by a move towards a mathematical approach in this field. One need only recall the names of Gauss, Laplace, Poisson, Quételet and others (Schumpeter 1994: 448–9, 524–6). In Italy, on the other hand, 'statistics' was mainly understood in the sense of *Staatswissenschaft*, or 'science of the state'. This represented the outcome of an early eighteenth-century tradition inherited from the Austrian Empire, which identified statistics with the collecting of data for use by the government.

Concluding, after the pioneering age of Italian economics, an age of consolidators could have been expected. Unfortunately, no such development came about. Overall, analysis of the economic system, so brilliantly carried out by the Enlightenment economists, was interrupted in the first decades of the nineteenth century.

The Custodi project

In the previous chapters reference has frequently been made to the 50-volume collection of *Scrittori classici italiani di economia politica* by Baron Pietro Custodi (1771–1842), still a fundamental source for the knowledge of Italian economists of the past (see Rota 1989). Custodi, a former Jacobin who had switched allegiance and espoused the Napoleonic cause, dedicated his monumental enterprise to 'those Italians who still wish to benefit their common fatherland'.[3] Naturally, he was addressing the ruling class of the Napoleonic Kingdom of Italy.

However, some shortcomings of this enterprise cannot be brushed aside. Composed in no more than 18 months between 1803 to 1805 (an appendix with a general index was issued in 1816), it was devoid of a comprehensive introduction, apart from a short preface to volume one; the information on individual authors was scanty and incomplete, and it suffered from a generally poor philology. Moreover, it was debatable whether all the economists included could be labelled as 'classics'. Thus, alongside the most prominent authors, one also finds minor or even negligibly important writers. This is all the more surprising given that the collection omits important authors such as Botero and Muratori.

In order to reach a wider audience of readers, another Milanese writer active between Napoleon and the Restoration, Count Giuseppe Pecchio (1785–1835), summarized the contents of the whole collection in a slim book, *Storia dell'economia pubblica in Italia*. Pecchio was a political exile in England (in 1821 he had been condemned to death in Milan) and possessed first-hand knowledge of the political and social situation of the country that hosted him. Wishing to present Italian economic thought in a sympathetic light for an English audience, Pecchio stressed that economics in Italy was primarily the outcome of a reaction against despotism, and – amplifying Custodi's original intention – he defined economics as 'la scienza dell'amor patrio' [the science of love for one's fatherland] (see Pecchio 1849 [1829]: 270).

This statement was certainly too benevolent, since most eighteenth-century economists had been obedient to the absolute monarchies of the peninsula and the reforms they advocated were far from incompatible with the *Ancien régime*. Count Carli himself, who employed the term 'fatherland' in an article cited in Chapter 2, had given the term a mere cultural meaning. On the other hand Pecchio appended to his book, *Comparison between Italian and English economists*, a commonplace destined to last for a protracted period of time, from the *Risorgimento* to Fascism, which implicitly corrected his former statement on English economics. Pecchio described British economics as arid, selfish and coldly calculating, while he depicted Italian (as well as French) economics as philanthropic and sensitive to moral considerations. It is noteworthy that this reductive opinion of English *economics* was balanced by Pecchio's sympathetic assessment of English *society*, whose industrial workmanship he praised (Pecchio 1976 [1831]) in spite of the frequent economic crises he described in another book (Pecchio 1826).

Reflecting on the contrast between the two countries, Pecchio sought to derive some suggestions that could be of use for Italy. Given the indisputable backwardness of the overwhelming part of the peninsula, a strong injection of sound economic principles could only but improve the country's performance. Yet, somewhat unexpectedly, Pecchio concluded that Italy should rely mainly on beneficence and philanthropy in order to respect its intrinsic vocation.[4]

Melchiorre Gioja's ultra-empiricism

The last Enlightenment man?

The two most representative figures of early nineteenth-century Italian economics were Gioja and Romagnosi. According to consolidated interpretation their thought is to be considered closely connected if not perfectly complementary (see Porta 1993).

Here a rather different view is offered. In actual fact their approach to economics was altogether different, and their sensitivity towards economic phenomena reveals substantial contrast, albeit one never explicitly declared by either of the two scholars.

Gioja – despite his repeated attacks on several eighteenth-century economists – was more closely linked to the dominant tradition of the previous century than Romagnosi. A critic of the Custodi enterprise, which he deemed a cultural failure and a waste of money, Melchiorre Gioja (of Piacenza, 1767–1829; on Gioia see Barucci 1965; Romani 1994, Chapter 2) introduced himself as an adversary of conformism and a declared iconoclast. His biography is that of a man who changed his mind several times in life. A priest up to 1797, later on an ardent Jacobin, subsequently a moderate republican, then a public servant under French rule and finally a comparatively free-minded intellectual under the Restoration, he achieved considerable acclaim among his contemporaries, as well as provoking fierce dissent. For example, Charles Babbage, the mathematician, favourably mentioned Gioja in his *Economy of Machines and Manufactures*; Adolphe Blanqui rhetorically extolled him as 'l'Atlas de la science en Italie' (Blanqui 1882 [1837]: 476) and several *literati*, including Stendhal and Foscolo, showed interest in and respect for him. On the other hand, Alessandro Manzoni, novelist and connoisseur of economics (see Barucci 1977), considered him no more than a plagiarist (Manzoni 1885: 125); and Jean-Baptiste Say ironically wrote of him 'il se rendait utile à l'économie politique, en copiant les bons auteurs' (Say 1832, vol. IV: 353).[5]

Gioja's philosophy was that of the French *idéologues*, who insisted on seeking to identify the well-springs of human action, and regarded them as associated with sensations. Moreover, Gioja was attracted by moral calculus, in accordance with Jeremy Bentham's doctrine, to which he added a complicated case list of the actions man performs in order to reach satisfaction, avoid boredom and idleness and, above all, obtain the consensus of others (see Badaloni 1973: 911).

An initial glance at Gioja's main political ideas shows that even during his Jacobin years he claimed that the principle of equality could not endorse any programme of absolute equality of wealth among citizens. For only 'tyrannies consider peoples as a homogeneous mass in all their parts. In contrast, the republican regimes' morality is based on *the real disparity of rights and qualities*, which, if good, must be encouraged, if bad, repressed' (Gioja 1962 [1798]: 85; original italics).[6] In his framework, true justice was based not on the distributive but rather on the commutative criterion, which consisted in giving reward proportionate to merit; in turn, the central focus of *merito* was the principle of *convenienza sociale* (Gioja 1830 [1818–19]: 1). That is to say, all merit should be based on social acknowledgement of the individual qualities of cleverness, workmanship and education (although not of line of descent or blood-line). Gioja therefore rejected Verri's objective of 'the maximum of happiness divided by the maximum number', which he regarded as excessively egalitarian.

With the advent of the Industrial Revolution and its attendant economic crises, Gioja took a position that coincided neither with Jean-Baptiste Say's optimism nor with Jean-Charles Sismondi's pessimism. Rather, he argued that the forces of industrialization should be channelled through the converging actions of state power and private initiative. This policy was precisely the approach adopted by Napoleonic rule according to the lines traced by Minister Chaptal. Gioja defined the government's action as involving 'Education, Example, Encouragement, Prescriptions, Prohibitions' (quoted by Macchioro 1990: 279).

The framework of Nuovo prospetto

A tireless writer, Gioja published such eccentric books as *Teoria del divorzio* and *Galateo*, plus a series of monographs on the economic districts of the Napoleonic Kingdom of Italy. A collection of his 'minor works' was issued posthumously in 17 volumes (published by Ruggia of Lugano between 1832–37). The present survey will be limited to his main work on political economy.

'I do not announce a collection of works on economics, which is an enterprise that must be left to publishers' (a clear taunt directed against the Custodi project), but 'the collection of all ideas relating to this science, an intellectual enterprise that must be accomplished only by a man of letters' (Gioja 1838 [1815–17]: 1). With these condescending words Gioja presented his monumental *Nuovo prospetto delle scienze economiche*, a six-volume, 2,600 page treatise, featuring more than 200 statistical tables and a host of explanatory charts.

The work opens with a comparison between mathematics and political economy, arguing that the former is characterized by simplicity and exactitude, the latter by complexity and approximation; the former by the universality of its applications, the latter by the need to take all circumstances into account and, above all, by the presence of 'an indefinite variety of elements that must be calculated' (Gioja, op. cit.: xxi). Which method was the most suitable? In barely two pages Gioja explained that the true scientific method in economics was that of decomposing and recomposing the phenomena under scrutiny, thereby adopting a typically empiricist approach.

The first two books deal with the production of wealth. Quite correctly, Gioja defined production as the most effective way to reduce costs and allocate factors. Achieving such goals required (1) *power*, namely, man's ability to appropriate natural as well as artificial (industrial) forces; (2) *knowledge*, that is to say, the application of science to the economy, and; (3) strength of *will*, enhanced by recourse to reward or by resorting to imitative modes of behaviour developed by fashion.

The third book examines distribution. Gioja equated the community with a business enterprise, whose *caratisti* [shareholders], including both workers and employers, are owners of the productive factors. Functional distribution, in his framework, was determined according to their respective contribution to production (of course, Gioja did not refer to marginal productivities).

The fourth and fifth books deal with consumption, both productive and unproductive. Gioja observed that a crisis cannot come about as a result of a lack of demand, but only from a deficiency of supply. This was an approach that moved in parallel with Ricardo (the *Nuovo prospetto* and the *Principles of Political Economy and Taxation* were issued in the same year).

The sixth book is devoted to the State's *agenda* and *non-agenda*. Any state action, Gioja maintained, had its *strong* and *weak* points, and must take into consideration the interest of individuals who are recipients of these actions; moreover a balance between costs and benefits was always necessary before any public choice could be made.

Gioja's attitude towards other economists

Gioja was a voracious consumer of different theories. The last volume of *Nuovo prospetto* contains a 150-page long critical assessment of all other economists: a critique mainly of a semantic type, which aimed at showing that many definitions or statements present in the economic literature were loose or, more often, self-contradictory. According to Gioja, Say and Verri sometimes maintained that nature is generous, sometimes that it is not; Smith sometimes wrote that the division of labour increases the inventive spirit, sometimes that it does not; and so forth. In expounding his critical assessment, Gioja's aim was not merely to censure the apparent shortcomings of many celebrated economists, but more ambitiously to demonstrate that many theories of economics were not really theories – that is to say, they were composed of falsifiable statements in Popper's sense – but rather mere verbal utterances. Unfortunately, Gioja himself was far from being univocal on such topics as the function of money, the role of machinery or the definition of the entrepreneur. These shortcomings often weaken Gioja's *vis polemica*.

Gioja's 'industrialism', not unlike that of Saint-Simon, was above all a eulogy to the opportunity given to all self-made men (as he himself was) to achieve success: in short, the definition of an open society. But an apparent contradiction can be perceived in his sympathy for control from above, directly or indirectly influencing the individual spirit of competition. In this sense his suggestion of distributing cockades and other non-monetary distinctions among the ablest factory workers may call to mind certain contrivances belonging to twentieth-century real socialism. In Gioja's mind, however, such schemes were to be promoted to satisfy the plausible intention of creating a competitive mentality among workers, as well as encouraging the rise of a select aristocracy of labour.

Giandomenico Romagnosi's uncontrasted influence

An economist by necessity

It would be beyond the scope of this book to attempt to give a systematic account of the imposing work in the fields of philosophy and law of Giandomenico Romagnosi (of Salsomaggiore, near Parma, 1761–1835). Instead, attention will be directed here towards the comparatively small amount of his writings devoted to economic subjects. Almost all of his economic writings were composed in the last years of his life, when the aged scholar – who the Austrian government had deprived of the *venia legendi* [licence to lecture] for political reasons – decided to contribute to the *Annali universali di statistica* as a means of earning an income, despite not having studied economics and statistics previously.[7]

Romagnosi, like Gioja, straddled two eras. More acutely than Gioja, he felt the contrast between the dying Enlightenment and the rising Romantic spirit. In Kent R. Greenfield's pioneering work, *Economics and Liberalism in the Risorgimento* (1934), Romagnosi is linked to Vico rather than to the Enlightenment thinkers, but Greenfield concludes that Romagnosi's idea of progress was typically linear, not cyclical, and this feature differentiated his thought from pure Romanticism (Greenfield 1964 [1934]: 391).

Apart from those aspects concerning 'vision', it should be stressed that Romagnosi's major theoretical undertaking – which led him to study law, economics and statistics as part of a coherent philosophically oriented research programme on social sciences – addressed the challenge of conciliating the individual and society. This could not be achieved through the forces of the market alone, as the aim of economics is that of guaranteeing the 'social order of wealth' (Romagnosi 1932 [1827]: 8–9).

In this respect Romagnosi was probably influenced by Adam Smith's definition of economics as 'a branch of the science of the statesman and legislator'. However, in contrast to Smith, who did not identify the whole subject matter of economics with the science of the legislator, Romagnosi tended to consider economic prescriptions and juridical norms as substantially coinciding, and only formally distinct.

Incivilimento and the role of statistics

In *Dell'indole e dei fattori dell'incivilimento* (1829–32) Romagnosi presented his original concept of civilization, which can be considered as a later version of the Enlightenment idea of progress. He maintained that the natural order, based on the impulse any society feels to improve its own condition, needs the support of law and politics, and therefore of economic policy.

Difficulties in interpreting Romagnosi's framework may arise from the fact that he interpreted *incivilimento* [civilization] both in the sense of a *process* and also as a *result* of the process itself. Taken in the former sense, it could be likened to an 'art', and in the latter as an 'ideal state', namely, a situation of final rest attained by a society when all its potentialities have been developed – a concept not dissimilar to John Stuart Mill's stationary state. The concept of 'ideal state' met with objections from the young Francesco Ferrara, who observed that such a mechanical vision of progress was attributable to the short-comings of the concept of *incivilimento* itself, if construed as an abstract *a priori* model of society which, necessarily, could be no more than approximated by existing societies (see Ferrara (1955) [1836]: 78–88). Implicitly, Ferrara accused Romagnosi of endorsing a philosophy of history similar to that of Hegel, in which freedom to follow one path or another was excluded.

In our opinion, however, Romagnosi fruitfully devoted attention to selecting the institutions capable of triggering the process of improvement, developing his approach through his conviction that private law, rather than public law, was the most powerful engine of progress. Seen in this perspective Romagnosi closely fol-lowed Adam Smith, who wrote in Book III of *Wealth* that the transition from medi-eval to modern times was primarily due to the transformation of property rights.

On the other hand, Romagnosi did not follow Henri de Saint-Simon, who had written that the progress of humanity was necessarily compelled to pass through the successive steps of religious reform, educational reform and industrial reform. Moreover, as compared with Gioja, Romagnosi was by no means an 'industrialist' – he felt that the progress of industry (in the sense of workmanship) should always be accompanied by the establishment of *possidenza* [ownership] which guarantees the stability and peaceful evolution of social relations. As far as the division of labour was concerned, Romagnosi – who, unlike Gioja, was rather indifferent to matters of productivity – considered it a special manifestation of human sociability.

Linked to the concepts of *incivilimento* and *stato ideale* is Romagnosi's notion of statistics. Jean-Baptiste Say wrote that the task of statistics was to collect transitory data, while that of economics was to record permanent data (see Say 1827). Romagnosi raised several objections to these arguments, perhaps exaggerating in the opposite direction. In contrast to Say, he assigned to statis-tics not only the task of measuring both permanent and transitory phenomena, but also the goal of defining the Laws of Progress themselves. Put another way, according to Romagnosi's vision, statistics was the true philosophy of history, or at least the crucial instrument to penetrate into its recondite features. The duty of the statistical service organization was to take all these aspects into account (Romagnosi 1839 [1827]: 13), although from a practical viewpoint Romagnosi recommended that statistical offices should be privately administered. This was due to his fear that 'official' statistics could easily be manipulated by a despotic government. In this respect Ferrara was in agreement.

On value and development

Romagnosi's conception of economics was decidedly objectivist. He endorsed the idea that any good has a natural value, in the sense that this value is given by nature itself and cannot be changed by human will. Such a statement may have owed its origin to his espousal of the doctrine of natural law (see Mannori 1984, vol. I, Chapter 1). Nevertheless, this approach was tempered by his belief that there exists an 'estimation judgement' – that is to say, an evaluation of the saving of labour obtained from the appropriation of a good. Some decades later Francesco Ferrara integrated this reasoning into his 'cost of reproduction' theory of value (see Chapter 5 below).

In Romagnosi's view it was of little importance whether a good had a material conformation or not. The crucial issue centred on whether a thing could be owned or not. Goods that could be appropriated, like sunlight, were not economic goods; whereas property rights that could be bought and sold – like administrative concessions – were, and independently so of the material things to which they were subservient.

He was at his best when he addressed concrete phenomena. In *Del pauperismo britannico* (1829) he observed that pauperism was not the direct outcome of Malthus's Law, but of complex historical circumstances resulting from the persistence of obsolete institutions such as Queen Elizabeth's statutes, the problem of rules on enclosure, and the perverse administration of the Poor Tax (see Romagnosi 1829 in Sestan 1957).

The solutions Romagnosi proposed reflected the same approach as that adopted in the eighteenth-century Lombardy experience. He suggested an expansion of the market both for agricultural and industrial commodities, a reduction in taxes on land ownership, and abolition of restrictions on the emigration of workers. In effect, Romagnosi's ideal economic system, the only one which could succeed in combining efficiency with equity, was not dissimilar to the system that achieved success in Northern Italy, especially with regard to the regime of forestry and waters (both of which he considered as important sources of externalities). Here he drew strongly on Beccaria.

Romagnosi stated that, in general, a system is optimal when 'government has a minimum of tasks and the people a maximum of commercial activities' (quoted in Valenti 1891: 42). However, his system assigned important goals of 'tutorship' to economic policy – defending rights, and protecting the weakest ranks of people. Such a position prefigured that of John Stuart Mill, and can shed insight on the question of whether Romagnosi was a genuine economic Liberalist.

The truth is that Romagnosi subscribed to the invisible hand parable; indeed in his *Assunto primo della scienza del diritto naturale* (1820) he denied the existence of a *visible* hand. But he also underlined that free competition cannot stand alone without the protection of a framework of laws and rules that would safeguard the 'civil coexistence' which, to his mind, was the crucial factor behind progress and, at the same time, the main (or the one and only) goal to be pursued.

Followers of Gioja and/or Romagnosi

A comparative glance at the reception of Gioja and Romagnosi suggests it was the latter scholar who exerted greater influence during the *Risorgimento*. In *Annali universali di statistica* (1831), Giuseppe Sacchi wrote that while Gioja argued in terms of sheer balances among different individual self-interests, Romagnosi's arguments – underpinned by a more strongly moral thrust – took into consideration 'all social exigencies' of a nation (quoted by Barucci 1965: 180). The undisputable vagueness of Romagnosi's thought attracted many scholars looking for contacts between social and political sciences. Consequently, any economist or jurist from Milan or Palermo or the other major cultural centres felt entitled to appeal to Romagnosi's superior authority, confident of finding the answers they needed from within the broad vision portrayed by Romagnosi. Last but not least, Romagnosi, the freemason, encountered after 1870 the approbation of many Catholic thinkers belonging to the Historical school (see Chapter 5 below).

A police report written in the 1830s denounced that in Palermo there were two 'political circles' which drew their inspiration respectively from Gioja and Romagnosi (Spoto 1988: 120–1). A circle of followers of Romagnosi had taken shape in Catania as well, and featured among its members two economists, Vincenzo Cordaro Clarenza and Mario Rizzari, the latter also influenced by Saint-Simon through Michel Chevalier (see Grillo 1996: 22). It is perhaps on account of these political ramifications that many of Gioja's and Romagnosi's followers attempted to link their thought to previous local traditions. This was the case, for instance, of Archdeacon Luca De Samuele Cagnazzi (1764–1852), who held a professorship in Naples from 1806 to 1821, when he was removed for political reasons as a former supporter of Murat. In 1848 he became President of the ephemeral constitutional Neapolitan Parliament.

In contrast to many economists in the South who were predominantly lawyers, Cagnazzi came from studies in natural science and also wrote on such subjects as climatology and meteorology (see Salvemini 1980). In his *Elementi dell'arte statistica* (1808) Cagnazzi rejected the 'empirical' approach to economics, censuring it as a sequence of remedies lacking an appropriate analysis of the causes of the illness of the social body. Furthermore, Cagnazzi was one of the first in Italy to comment on Malthus's law of population growth, to which he introduced a fundamental correction. He argued that an increase in population did not depend on subsistence only, but also on 'moral and political welfare'; namely, the standard of living and the quality of life, which he believed to be higher in northern and central Europe than in Italy. In this regard he was following a strand of thought present in Romagnosi.

Cagnazzi was also a follower of Smith, mainly on the treatment of the stages of economic growth. He was also acquainted with Genovesi, although the latter was not directly quoted perhaps because he was still included in the *Index librorum prohibitorum*, together with Verri, Mill, Bentham, Saint-Simon, and a few years afterwards, Coquelin-Guillaumin's *Dictionnaire*.

Cagnazzi's main disciple, Matteo De Augustinis (1797–1845), was active in the early years of the reign of Ferdinand II, a period that raised short-lived hopes of freedom. In his *Condizione economica del regno di Napoli* (1833) De Augustinis advocated measures for the privatization of *demani* lands [state property] in Puglia. Additionally, in *Il progresso*, a journal modelled on the Florentine *Antologia*, De Augustinis published a long article, 'Discorso storico-critico sulla economia sociale' (1836), which shows greater traces of the influence of Romagnosi and even of Cattaneo – who was writing some of his most important essays in those very same years – than of the Southern economists' tradition. In the last years of his rather short life De Augustinis abandoned his earlier caution and took up a position in favour of absolute *laissez-faire*, even on the question of the literary copyright regime which De Augustinis – here foreshadowing Francesco Ferrara – defined as a 'useless oppression for all people and only a very slight benefit for authors' (*Della proprietà letteraria e de' suoi giusti confini* (1837), quoted by Parente 1973: 69). De Augustinis's principal economic work, *Istituzioni di economia sociale* (1837) is more dependent on Say, Senior and Rossi than on Italian economic literature.

It is worth noting that Say's authoritative *Cours complet* was translated and printed in Palermo in four volumes issued between 1834 and 1836 (see Spoto 1988: 123). This project owed its origin to the Palermo chair professor of political economy, Ignazio Sanfilippo (1784–1842), whose reliance on the French writer was so great that he entitled his own textbook *Catechismo*. However, his successor Giovanni Bruno (1818–91) is to be considered a follower of Romagnosi's thought.

The chair economist at the University of Catania was Salvatore Scuderi (1781–1840), a follower of Gioja and a critical commentator of Ricardo. In 1841 a competition was announced to nominate his successor. Significantly, the competition – which required a written dissertation – was centred on proposing the most suitable policy for industrialization in the South. The winner was Placido De Luca (1803–61), a moderate protectionist subscribing to the line taken by Scuderi (see Travagliante 1994). De Luca – who later was appointed to a professorship in Naples – had the historical merit of publishing the first (indeed, his one and only) Italian book expressly dedicated to *La scienza delle finanze* (1858).

Francesco Fuoco, or the (partial) reception of Ricardo in Italy

The Fuoco–De Welz case

Quite different from the work of Gioja and Romagnosi is that of Francesco Fuoco (of Naples, 1774–1841). This abbot was a 1799 revolutionary who turned to economics only after the unsuccessful 1820 revolt. While in exile in France he met in Paris a silk entrepreneur from Como – Giuseppe De Welz (1785–1839) – a follower of Saint-Simon who commissioned Fuoco to write

Saggio sui mezzi da moltiplicare prontamente le ricchezze della Sicilia (1822). This was a project presented to the King of Naples' minister, Luigi De' Medici, as a proposal for reform of the banking system in the kingdom. The book was then published in Paris under De Welz's name alone. This bizarre editorial agreement continued with *La magia del credito svelata* (1824), likewise inspired by Saint-Simon's ideas on credit as a 'wizard' with the ability to create wealth. In the book Gioja's echoes were also present in the reflections on the role of entrepreneur.

A couple of years later Fuoco published under his own name two volumes entitled *Saggi economici* (1825–27), whose content was completely independent of his earlier writings. Today the perennial debate on Fuoco–De Welz has been definitively settled, and Fuoco has been credited with exclusive authorship of the so-called 'Dewelzian' works as well as of the book published under his own name (see VV. AA. 1977; Barucci 2009: 175–89).

The Saggi economici

The scope of commentary in this book will be limited to the *Saggi economici*, with regard to which, and analogously with two preceding churchmen-economists, Galiani and Ortes, Fuoco informed the reader that he had composed his work in absolute isolation (see Fuoco 1969 [1825–27], vol. I: v).

Beyond the objective difficulty of the subjects dealt with in *Saggi economici*, this work is not an easy read, owing to the manner in which the subject matter is presented – almost as a running commentary on Smith, Ricardo, Say, Malthus, Lauderdale and others. In his method of economic analysis, Fuoco can be seen as an opponent of Romagnosi, for while the Northern lawyer invoked the methodological unity of the social sciences, the Southern abbot distinguished between pure economic theory, applied economics and the science of administration (corresponding to economic policy), asserting that their different aims required the use of separate methods. With regard to theory, Fuoco supported Nicolas-François Canard's argument in favour of the use of algebra, and rejected the opposite position shared by Say (vol. II: 61–120).

On account of his propensity towards theoretical reasoning, Fuoco's name has been traditionally associated with the Ricardian line of thought, although on several issues he was more dependent on Smith and Malthus. For instance, he dealt with natural price and the 'venal', or market, price. The natural price, which depended on the quantity of labour contained, was the centre of gravity for the market price, which depended on 'the quantity of labour that must be expended in order to obtain a good' (Fuoco 1825–27, vol. I: 12). This is a clear reminiscence of Smith's labour-commanded theory of value – in equilibrium, there must be a correspondence between the two prices. But in contrast to the classics, Fuoco assigned this dependency to a subjective evaluation made by each trader. Moreover, Fuoco apparently abandoned the classical doctrine of value when he argued that equilibrium is reached when there is a proportionality between labour (in the two meanings mentioned above) and the degree of utility of commodities (ibid., p. 176). Thus Fuoco's line of reasoning was developed here in a rather more subjectivist context.

On the other hand, Fuoco set out his arguments in the manner of a classical economist when he dealt with the notions of capital (as accumulated labour) and profit (as a surplus exceeding production expenses). Similarly to Ricardo he singled out agriculture as the sector where the general rate of profit was formed; but, unlike Ricardo – and following Malthus – he did not believe that an increase in the price of wheat determined an increase in wages and hence a fall in profits. Fuoco maintained, instead, that all prices would grow proportionally and the rate of profit would remain unaltered. Once again he dismissed the Ricardian inverse relation between profit and wages in favour of the Smithian–Malthusian 'adding-up' theory. However, Fuoco was still a Ricardian when he observed that the cheap price of wage-goods, while favourable for profit, was not favourable for rents. In general he believed that protecting rents meant 'sacrificing to the utility of a few men that of an entire people' (ibid., p. 123). In this context, the rent from land was presented as a monopolistic income.

Besides sharing Ricardo's concept of differential rent, formed through the decreasing returns of land, Fuoco grasped that in manufacturing the industries benefiting from more efficient machinery enjoyed a special rent, and he argued that this kind of rent was destined in the long run to disappear owing to the spread of innovation throughout the entire economy. Almost 70 years afterwards Marshall would label this as 'quasi-rent'.

Very thoughtful are the pages where Fuoco connected individual labour with 'social' labour via the division of labour and the operation of the market. The role of money was that of translating the various individual values into 'abstract labour' – an expression devised by Fuoco but which a few years later appeared independently in Marx. On the other hand, in accordance with harmony economists, Fuoco concluded that income distribution in equilibrium was proportional to the wants of the various social classes (cf. Fuoco 1825–27, vol. II: 40–51, quoted in Perri 1998: 139). In this context, Fuoco – abandoning Ricardo – repeated Romagnosi's appeal for 'just and well-proportioned distribution, from whence derives the good both for capitalists and workers' (Fuoco 1825–27, vol. II: 147–8, quoted by Malagola Anziani 1979: 99).

In conclusion, both Fuoco–De Welz and Fuoco-Fuoco appeared as hetero-geneous voices with respect to post-1815 Italian economics. For the first (and last) time, classicism and industrialism were closely associated in Italy. However, this singular author reaped a meagre harvest from the practical outcomes of his original thought: Fuoco–De Welz was not taken seriously as a reform projector, and Fuoco-Fuoco fell into obscurity as a theorist.

In general, no courageous economic experimentation in the Saint-Simonian spirit was attempted in Italy, nor was there any continuation of in-depth reflection on the political issues of a conflicting theory of distribution à la Ricardo. The vast majority of Italian economists preferred to write eulogies to the status quo. The *Risorgimento* movement paid a heavy tribute to this timidity in both programmes and ideas.

The role of scholarly journals

Lombardy and the North

Despite the unfortunate political conditions of the peninsula, after 1815 a considerable number of scholarly journals were launched. The most renowned journal was *Il conciliatore* of Milan, dubbed 'the blue sheet' on account of its colour. Although published for just one year (1818–19), this organ of the Lombardy liberal aristocracy hosted articles by Romagnosi, Gioja and Pecchio, among others. Several book reviews on Lauderdale, Chaptal and the Florentine Georgofili were written by the patriot Silvio Pellico (later imprisoned by the Austrians in the Spielberg fortress and famous for his captivity memoirs, *Le mie prigioni*).

Another Milanese journal was *Biblioteca italiana* (1816–41), sponsored by the Austrians, and comparatively open to economics. This journal hosted articles by Romagnosi and Gioja in which the latter, during his frequent disputes with Say, claimed a sort of primacy of Italian economics over French and English works in this field (see Maccabelli 1996: 160).

A third journal, destined for a much longer life, was *Annali universali di statistica* (1824–71), which contained many translations and detailed review articles of foreign publications (see La Salvia 1977). In 1826 two book reviews appeared in *Annali*, respectively on Ricardo's and on Malthus's *Principles*. Both reviews bore the signature 'V ... a', and their author was Alessandro Volta, the scientist. Against Ricardo, Volta objected that the increase in the price of wheat was not due to the difficulties of producing it, but rather to the increase in demand, which in turn increased the price of wheat and therefore encouraged farmers to cultivate the worst lands. In his objection to Malthus, Volta contended that he had failed to make it clear whether rent was a neat original product or the effect of a redistribution of income (in other words, whether rent is absolute or differential).

In comparison to Lombardy, the accomplishments of post-1815 economics in Piedmont were far more modest. At the University of Turin there was no chair of economics.[8] Consequently, no journal dealing with economics was set up and the (few) existing economists opted to publish their work in Lombardy, in journals such as *Annali di statistica* and *Politecnico*, or in Tuscany. Before 1848 it was generally considered that the best Piedmontese economist was Carlo Ilarione Petitti di Roreto (1790–1850), who shared the same leaning towards statistics displayed by Gioja and Romagnosi. On other matters Petitti was one of the first Italian economists to seriously consider the social consequences of industrialization; he was not against child labour per se, but he did advocate the spread of elementary and professional schools for the purpose of educating young workers (see Petitti di Roreto 1969 [1841]).

As far as public works were concerned, Petitti distinguished between investments that secured a return some years afterwards, and those that obtained a rapid return. Among the former, he addressed the question of railways, suggesting that the right to build railways should be restricted to state-owned companies, a solution he considered cheaper than financial support to private enterprises (see Petitti di Roreto 1969 [1845]).

Another economic expert in Turin was Carlo Ignazio Giulio (1803–59), professor of rational mechanics at the university there, and the author of several official reports – among them one in favour of the free market price of bread and another that addressed the concept of 'optimum population' as one where the proportion of the adult labour force was at a maximum. Giulio belonged to the Turin tradition of physicists and mathematicians, with solid interests in social and economic disciplines (see Einaudi 1953 [1935]).

Tuscany

Among the learned men active in Tuscany one finds an exceptional character who can be described mainly as a cultural organizer – Gian Pietro Vieusseux (1779–1863). In 1812 this man of Swiss origin founded a *gabinetto di lettura* [reading room] that produced the important journal, *Antologia* (1821–33). But the timing was unfortunate, and the journal was suppressed for political reasons. Vieusseux then concentrated on the *Giornale agrario toscano* (1827–65), associated with the *Accademia dei georgofili*, whose chairman Cosimo Ridolfi (1794–1865) hosted at his farm a private school devoted to the professional education of bailiffs. Ridolfi was acquainted with many French and Swiss agronomists and economists, including Sismondi, and enjoyed the protection of Grand Duke Leopold II of Tuscany, himself a trained natural scientist. In 1840 Ridolfi was appointed to the chair of agrarian economics in the first faculty of agriculture in Italy, which was established at the University of Pisa. In his lectures and essays he advocated stronger integration between agriculture, mining and manufacturing. He also explored the issue of *mezzadria* [sharecropping], which he considered as less efficient than high farming, especially when agricultural prices were falling (see Ridolfi 2008).

Ridolfi's advanced thinking on husbandry, as well as on general agrarian policy, were opposed by the Tuscan economic and political establishment, whose leading figure was Abbot Raffaello Lambruschini (1778–1873), a Catholic liberal whose interests focused above all on agriculture and pedagogy.

Naples

In the years after 1815, Naples, which was traditionally more inclined towards theorizing than was the case elsewhere, experienced a growing interest in economics, manifested among philosophers influenced by French *idéologues*, who in turn were economists – such as Say, Destutt de Tracy and Cousin. This situation continued until 1850, but thereafter the growing influence of Hegelianism in Naples had the effect of extinguishing any further philosophical interest in economics (see Oldrini 1973).

In this context some attention should be paid to the contribution of a 'minor' economist, Costantino Baer (182?–1896, exact dates unknown), to the interesting journal *Museo*, which was launched in 1844. Baer addressed the awkward topic of the distinction between wealth and value, a controversial issue that placed Ricardo in opposition to Say (see Ricardo's *Principles*, Chapter 20). Baer pointed out that a country might be endowed with abundant uncultivated land that can neither be ascribed actual value nor considered as an actual rich. Value and riches, he noted, had the same meaning but from a different perspective (the former to be understood as actual value in exchange, the latter as actual value in use), while special kinds of riches, for instance the intellectual energy of a people, could only be considered as having potential value once they were successfully exploited (Baer 1844a).

In another article Baer highlighted the imperfect scientific nature of the so-called economic truths, given the difficulty of transferring the *ceteris paribus* method from experimental sciences to economics (Baer 1844b). This observation reflected the influence of John Stuart Mill's *Unsettled Questions of Political Economy*, published that very same year. From 1856 to 1872 Baer – who had moved to Turin and held high-ranking civil service positions in the Kingdom of Italy – corresponded (in French) with Mill on economic matters. In his book *L'avere e l'imposta* (1872) Baer distanced himself from the well-known positions held by the British thinker on the so-called double taxation of saving. In his correspondence, Mill did not refrain from vindicating his own position on such an important topic as the concept of taxable income (see the correspondence in Urbinati 1990: 221–9). Baer was also a contributor to *Nuova antologia*, in which he wrote several articles on self-government in Britain. Finally, he translated J. Goschen's *Theory of foreign exchanges* in the fourth series of *Biblioteca dell'economista* (see Chapter 5).

Sicily

Following the French occupation of Naples, King Ferdinand I moved to Palermo in 1806 with his court, under the British Army's protection. The British presence in Sicily may have encouraged the debate on *laissez-faire* and free trade (see Grillo 1994). After 1815 a heated discussion on the comparative merits of Gioja and the classical school arose, and was fiercely debated in the *Giornale di scienze, lettere e arti per la Sicilia* of Palermo, launched in 1824. In this context, Gioja's message was restrictively interpreted in the sense of being merely protectionist. With regard to other subjects the journal translated articles by Dunoyer, McCulloch and Say.

The years 1830 to 1837 saw a flourishing of Sicilian journals open to questions of economics, but after the latter date a new wave of political repression reduced their number, such that on the eve of the 1848 revolution only two could be considered as having an independent voice (see Travagliante 1996). The first was the *Giornale di statistica*, the organ of the Palermo *Ufficio di statistica*, established in 1832, that was published between 1836 and 1864. Francesco Ferrara, at the time *commesso* [clerk] at the office in question, contributed several important articles dealing with economic methodology, economic history and the history of economic thought. The second journal, the *Giornale del commercio* (founded 1840; a new series started in 1844) was the organ of the local Chamber of Commerce, whose secretary was, once more, Francesco Ferrara. It hosted an anonymous, magisterial, work on *La città di Manchester*, depicting that great town under the Industrial Revolution. For many years this article was attributed to Ferrara himself (see Ferrara 1965), but in actual fact it was written by Léon Faucher, the French economist, and possibly translated by Ferrara.

Carlo Cattaneo's march into modernization

The category of complexity: 'native' and 'dative' elements

In discussing the work of Carlo Cattaneo (1801–69), the Milanese intellectual, attention will concentrate here on his contribution to the social sciences, although it should be mentioned that he also composed noteworthy writings on a wide range of subjects including geography, local history, comparative history and anthropology, linguistics and philosophy. He was also renowned for his action as a federalist patriot during the 1848 Milan *Cinque giornate*, which concluded with the expulsion of the Austrians from the city. Cattaneo chose voluntary exile in Switzerland after Unity.

In focusing on his work in the field of the social sciences, it should be recalled that he was a committed disciple of Romagnosi. Like the latter, Cattaneo held Vico in high esteem and was imbued with Vico's powerful conception of history. Nevertheless, in comparison to Romagnosi, Cattaneo cultivated further wide-ranging interests, as mentioned above, with an open-mindedness that was also a typical feature of his economics. In a nutshell, Cattaneo was attracted by the multi-faceted aspects of progress, and went beyond his master's concept of *incivilimento*.

It has been written that in dealing with economic problems, Cattaneo 'aims at giving a complex solution: all social facts are conceived as the conciliation of natural conditions and spiritual acts, of traditions and innovations, of individual motives and collective exigencies' (Bertolino 1956: xi–xii). The 'complexity' category dominated his conception both of economics and of society. Cattaneo reflected on humankind's intellectual abilities, abilities that he considered to be moulded by an uninterrupted interaction between mind and experience: 'Man makes history, and history makes man' (quoted by Levi 1928: 27).

In his vision, just as human beings were never insulated in their interaction either with nature or with society (but rather underwent continuous transformation), so they also perpetually constructed their own environment, eternally creating and modifying their ideas, always prompted by the urge to make new discoveries and achieve intellectual breakthroughs.

As a thinker, Cattaneo is generally considered as a Positivist, on account of his attention to empirical data and his declared anti-Idealism and anti-Spiritualism (see Bobbio 1970: 124–38). Some features of Cattaneo's thought –first and foremost his enduring interest in anthropology and the comparative history of economic systems – descend from the French Enlightenment. On the other hand, his attention to the different degrees of development of nations, with his consequent awareness of the particularity of the different paths towards progress, seems to reflect Adam Smith's thought, from which Cattaneo drew the concept of the division of labour. Last but not least, Cattaneo was always a staunch supporter of *laissez-faire* and free trade, and in 1843 he wrote a committed critique of Friedrich List's protectionism (Cattaneo 1972 [1843]).

Cattaneo's vision was centred upon the dialectics between the concepts of 'native' and 'dative', two terms that are present in the work of Romagnosi, Cattaneo's master (see Barucci 1961: 716). The history of civilization, Cattaneo believed, showed that original elements are continuously enriched by cultural factors derived from foreign parts which, in tandem with the 'native elements', contribute to the 'creating' of history – though the comparative weight of the two forces naturally differs from people to people. For instance, he maintained that the peoples of Africa owed much to Western colonization, and only a great country such as China, with a thousand-year-old 'native' tradition, had been able to isolate itself from the rest of the world for so many centuries. This unique situation had allowed China to develop its economy, thanks to an admirable system of irrigation and public works, and also to the thriftiness and propensity of its population for work. He predicted that in the future even China would open up to modern civilization, and introduce the idea of liberty alongside that of equality (see Cattaneo 1957 [1861]).

'Intelligence' as the main motive force of social history

There is nothing in Cattaneo that is akin to Hegel's 'cunning of reason', and still less, to a transcendent Providence governing the course of history. Yet, in spite of the fact that considerations on the economy occupied such an important place in Cattaneo's worldview, he did not regard economic matters as the *primum movens* of history. Cattaneo, the empiricist, was consequently very distant from any form of historical Materialism or determinism based on the prevailing force of the 'economic factor'.

In *Del pensiero come principio d'economia publica* (1861), Cattaneo reproached classical economists for neglecting the very first principle of any progress, which is always of a spiritual kind: intelligence or, more generally, 'thought'. He argued that in reducing the productive factors to the three canonical elements of land (nature), labour and capital, the classical economists were legitimating the false and distorting conclusion that certain kinds of works are unproductive. Moreover, their approach seemed to imply that accumulation and investments were not the product of reason and intelligence, but the result of mechanical and merely speculative actions. Here Cattaneo's line of reasoning calls to mind Antonio Genovesi and the eighteenth-century Italian economic tradition, in which education and intelligence were regarded as substitutes for the lack of accumulation in such a backward country as Italy. In comparison to Genovesi, however, who remained an underdevelopment economist, Cattaneo showed his pride in being a native of Lombardy, a region where nature's generosity had fruitfully collaborated over the centuries with human intelligence.

Yet despite his eulogy of intelligence, Cattaneo did not interpret this factor as a synonym of rational economic *choice*. Intelligence did not enjoy the same role in his vision as rational behaviour in the marginal approach. Rather, it was an original element of production embedded in society, which could be made to emerge through collective knowledge and education. Correspondingly, he was more inclined to extol institutions that most greatly encouraged the development of collective intelligence, rather than to analyse the best economic use of the 'intelligence factor' as an alternative to other factors (see Raffaelli 2012: 304–8).

Cattaneo believed that the progress of humankind was prompted by two main forces. These were not identifiable with the traditional pleasure-pain antithetical pair encountered in the eighteenth-century economists, to be found again later in F. Ferrara. Rather, in Cattaneo the philosophical intelligence-knowledge-will triad was inspired by Romagnosi's *posse, nosse, velle* principle, appropriately reformulated according to a different outlook. The progress of improvement, Cattaneo believed, followed the same steps as the progress of human civilization: instincts, experience, rational will: 'Will-power, like intelligence, is a principle of wealth.' In particular, 'the impulses that lead our will to purchase goods are called interests'. Intelligence, in his view, should enlighten labour so that the latter becomes creative as well (this effect was not extensible to factory workers, whom Cattaneo, like Smith and most classical economists, regarded as condemned to a brutal existence), while man's will (which Cattaneo best represented as embodied in the entrepreneur as an 'ideal type' in the Weberian sense) should be given absolute freedom to operate.

The role of institutions in the march to development

Cattaneo was aware that the forces of development must act as a counterbalance against institutional constraints, such as the persistence of ancient rights that hamper improvement. In his *Bonificazione del piano di Magadino* (1851) he analysed the conditions of an extended area in Canton Ticino, where the survival of ancient communal and corporative rights hindered rational reclamation, since many of these rights, especially the common right of pasturage, were incompatible with economic exploitation (see Cattaneo 1939 [1851, 1853]). This observation was a striking anticipation of the modern concept of the 'tragedy of the commons'.

On the other hand, the attempt to introduce into new areas institutions that had proved favourable to development in other areas was no easy task. The case of Ireland, where Viscount Palmerston's cabinet sought to implant some of the institutions that had proved highly successful in Lombardy, prompted Cattaneo – whose wife was English – to write a memoir, addressed to the Vice-Consul of

Britain in Milan, pointing out that Ireland's economy was very different from that of Lombardy. In Ireland, land ownership was unevenly distributed; the particular regime of inland waters rendered the irrigation system through the *servitù d'acquedotto* [water mains easement] impossible; the income deriving from landed property was not taxed through the cadastre; too many entails and other medieval burdens severely overloaded the farmers; potato monoculture condemned labourers to idleness for a large part of the year; and so forth (Cattaneo 1939 [1847]: 133–204). Once these differences were made clear, Cattaneo concluded, it would be possible to operate in the direction of ensuring property rights and modifying agrarian contracts towards a more modern and capitalist system.

In dealing with these subjects, Cattaneo most clearly showed his debt to Romagnosi. He strongly believed that a limit on absolute private property was necessary in order to ensure a rational system of irrigation as a source of positive externalities.

Transport and poor relief

Cattaneo was personally involved as an investor in the building of the railway line from Milan to Venice and wrote an important study on its possible effects. 'What is the railway layout that offers the largest private return and the highest public utility?' Cattaneo asked (Cattaneo 1956 [1836]: 112). Put in a slightly different form, the question was: for a given population, what is the amount of traffic that will maximize the enterprise's return and give the highest benefit to the existing population involved?

In this context, he reasoned as a neo-classical economist rather than as a development economist. Basically, he did not believe that the new line would succeed in modifying the urban settlement pattern along its tracks. He may have realized that the extraordinary population movement towards the West in the United States, boosted by construction of the railway, could not be reproduced in the North of Italy where, as a result of the medieval settlements, the distribution of inhabitants over the territory was to be considered as quite stable. Historical experience confirms the correctness of his analysis, with only the surplus population in Northern Italy choosing to migrate.

Finally, Cattaneo examined the question of the Poor Law reform in England, approaching the subject more from the viewpoint of a classical economist. He felt that the compulsory system based on the Poor Tax was flawed inasmuch as it implicitly became an incentive to laziness; furthermore, it placed an excessive tax burden on landowners, and the absurdity of the public works that beneficiaries were obliged to perform led to widespread discontent. Given that these factors increased public expenditure while failing to reduce indigence, Cattaneo advocated a regime of absolutely free and voluntary charity. Additionally, he suggested fostering internal as well as international emigration and increasing the number of savings banks and insurance companies (see Cattaneo 1956 [1836–37]: 392).

First stirrings of a more open-minded attitude towards reforms

After 1840 an undeniable change of attitude towards administrative as well as economic reforms began to make itself felt throughout Italy. Early attempts can be singled out that endeavoured to converge towards a broader political and economic design, and to distinguish between a democratic and a liberal-moderate initiative.

While the democrats (if one excludes some individual cases, such as Cattaneo) were comparatively indifferent to economic programmes and concentrated on patriotic and often merely demonstrative actions – for instance, *Pensiero e Azione*, Giuseppe Mazzini's motto, focused mainly on action – the moderate liberals showed a strong commitment on the level both of civil society and economic initiative. They aimed to build a free market among the Italian states through commercial treaties, as a premise for political and economic federation rather than for a direct unification. Further, they were favourable to a policy of public works based on railway construction. Interestingly, they also advocated a discipline of literary property rights and inventions, to be implemented partly through international treaties.[9]

Among the most significant enterprises of this period, it is worth mentioning the yearly *Congressi degli scienziati italiani*, of which the first meeting was held in Pisa in 1839, with subsequent meetings being hosted in various towns until 1862. Despite the exclusion of economics – for evident political reasons – from the list of 'sciences' whose presence was allowed, the mere fact of a project whereby scientists belonging to all states of the peninsula (and possibly foreign scholars as well) could meet and discuss acted as a powerful drive towards overcoming parochial attitudes of isolation and self-sufficiency.

Until 1860 there was uncertainty regarding the political model for the to-be-unified state. As is well known, victory went to the supporters of centralization on the French (Napoleonic) model, in the direction of uniformity and compression of local forces. This was indeed the easiest way to proceed rapidly towards national unification, but it represented a betrayal of the traditional moderate positions. In the long run it gave rise to unrest and difficulties in the transition to democracy, implicitly favouring the success of Fascism in 1922. Politically speaking, the two main *Risorgimento* economists, Cattaneo and Ferrara, both sincere federalists, were losers.

The democratic side of economics: Mazzini

In the case of Italy's most famous democratic patriot, Giuseppe Mazzini (1805–72), no discussion of his achievements can afford to disregard the profound influence of Henri de Saint-Simon on his social thought. Although Saint-Simon's message was not easy to decipher – was he a lucid reformer, a founder of a lay religion, or a mere visionary? – Mazzini not only took a number of key concepts from him, but some features of his expository style as well; the mystically inspired overtones, the dialectics between 'critical' and 'organic' ages, the frequent stress on 'organization' and on the 'association principle', the tripartite division of society between capitalists, entrepreneurs and workers where an alliance between the latter two classes was preached as the best way not only towards economic improvement, but also towards the moral improvement of society.

In 1860, after a 20-year preparation, Mazzini published his main theoretical work, *Dei doveri dell'uomo*, a synthesis of his entire social thought. The eleventh chapter, *Questione economica*, contains his main ideas on the subject, highlighting the contrast between the formal equality of all citizens before the law, ensured by the liberal doctrine, and their underlying economic inequality. Mazzini, who had read the classical economists, subscribed to the wage fund doctrine, according to which the rate of wages depends on the (fixed) amount of capital divided by the number of workers (see Mazzini 2009 [1860]: 936). Consequently, he implied, a durable increase of wages through strikes and other forms of protest was not feasible. Rather, the disparities of wealth depended on the uneven distribution of property. In this conception, he departed from the vision put forward by Marx. While by no means rejecting the principle of property per se; Mazzini presented it as 'the *sign* ... of the quantity of *labour* by which the individual has transformed, developed, increased the productive forces of nature' (ibid., p. 939). And as we will see in the next chapter, a Liberalist such as Francesco Ferrara argued in almost the same manner.

Mazzini furthermore distinguished between property as a *natural* right, and property as a *positive* right, and argued that the *actual* distribution of property needed to be corrected, without abolishing property rights as a whole. For in such a case

> you [here Mazzini addressed a hypothetical socialist interlocutor] would abolish a source of wealth, of emulation, of activity, and you would be little better than a savage who, in order to pick fruit from the branches of a tree, first sets about felling the tree itself.
>
> (Ibid., p. 940)

His observations reveal that he shared the same critical approach to collectivism as that evinced by his great political adversary, Cavour. Mazzini insisted that collectivism led not to freedom, but to a 'renewal of the ancient serfdom' (ibid.). He thus compared the principle of forced collectivism from above with the principle of free 'association' from below, among workers who organized themselves into cooperatives based on the principle of sharing the fruits of their enterprise, with the sole exclusion of the capital owned by the enterprise. Mazzini also considered the problem of how to raise the funds necessary for capital creation. In accordance with his basic principles, he rejected any perspective of expropriation, arguing that the main source of accumulation was to be found in the workers' voluntary savings.

Concluding, Mazzini's thought displayed the influence of the British democratic-reformist writers, and particularly of John Stuart Mill, not only in matters concerning the latter's sympathy towards the workers' condition, but also with regard to Mill's distinction between production – which could not be modified by politics – and distribution, which was the policy-maker's primary goal (see Rancan 2006; Faucci and Rancan 2009).

The moderate side

Scialoja: the Italian Say

Antonio Scialoja (of Naples, 1817–77), a disciple of De Augustinis, is well known to *Risorgimento* historians as Finance and subsequently Education Minister in several *Destra* cabinets. His main works on economics have recently been republished.

His early handbook bears the title *Principi di economia sociale esposti in ordine ideologico* (1840), where 'ideological' – here in the sense of abstract reasoning – was a tribute to French thought. Scialoja presented himself as a follower of Say, and centred the presentation of his arguments on the *loi des débouchés*, the so-called Say's (or Say-Mill's) Law of Markets, which denied the eventuality of a general glut (in Scialoja's terminology *ingombro* [obstruction]). One can but admire the straightforward way in which Scialoja argued that since all products were transformed into incomes, and incomes were distributed to productive agents, equilibrium between total supply and total demand would always be reached. Moreover, since the greater part of expressed wants was connected to vital needs, demand would, in his view, always adjust to supply through the influence of the population law. Therefore, there would be no risk of general overproduction. However, partial crises were always possible, whenever a sector was involved in a process of technical innovation that increased production by reducing prices, but without expanding purchases, leading to a fall in profits. Here, Scialoja assumed an inelastic demand curve. If, vice versa, demand were elastic, the increase in production would lead to a more than proportional increase of purchases, profits would increase, and the partial crisis would be overcome (Scialoja 2006a: 34–6).

Scialoja further argued that as a result of the spread of innovation, equilibrium would be established at higher efficiency levels. He believed that partial crises could also be offset by entrepreneurs through insurances, and by workers through individual provision for lack of work and mutual aid. Machinery could also cause technological unemployment in the short run only, but in the long run an expanding production structure would be able to absorb all surplus manpower.

Scialoja's distribution was based on his definition of the neat surplus in agriculture, the *estaglio* (from Latin *extalium*); namely, that which is paid to the landowner by the mere fact of his property rights, independently of the land's productivity. In a nutshell, this was the equivalent of the Smithian and Marxian absolute rent, and corresponded to the price for the use of a factor whose supply is fixed. On the other hand, Scialoja also acknowledged the existence of Ricardo's differential rent.

As far as population was concerned, Scialoja – again following Say – distinguished between means of *subsistence* and of *existence*, arguing that as shown by historical evidence, the former type tended to transform itself into the latter. Once the transformation process was accomplished, then the nation would have reached its maximum of population.

In 1846–47 and 1847–48 Scialoja held two courses whose details have been published only recently. In his framework, theoretical economics is involved with ends, practical economics with means (Scialoja 2006c: 41). Scialoja rejected Romagnosi's definition of economics as *scienza operativa* –based on the triad *nosse, velle, posse* – which risked confusing the two moments of pure and applied science. Faithful to this distinction, Scialoja observed that the seeming 'exceptions' to Say's Law of Markets concerned its application only, and not theory per se (ibid., p. 43). Economics, he maintained, was a value-free science (ibid., p. 45).

The two major authorities from whose teachings he drew inspiration were Genovesi and Smith, who in a sense exerted a complementary influence on Scialoja's thought (Ibid., p. 67). Scialoja appears to have awarded priority to some strands of the philosophical history of economics that stem from a few basic principles which then act as a spur to the analysis of facts. He firmly believed that examining 'facts' per se, without the help of theories, was misleading, as statistics provided only empirical generalizations, mainly based on the concept of the mathematical mean (ibid., p. 83).

Scialoja's *Trattato elementare*, written in 1848 shortly before his return to Naples, is essentially a didactic text. Here too the main source is Say, particularly Say's *Cathéchisme*. Also taken from Say is the distinction between direct producers (such as workers and entrepreneurs) and indirect producers (owners of natural agents of production and capitalists). Against Ricardo, Scialoja rejected the inverse relationship between wages and profits, maintaining that only a sudden increase in monetary wages, with unchanged productivity and prices, leads to a reduction in profit.

Scialoja also examined the question of property rights. An industrial patent, he argued, does not protect an inventor who cannot economically utilize his discovery; moreover, it retards the spread of technical-scientific progress. Rather than a copyright, he suggested that a system of prizes in favour of inventors, and the publication of their discovery, would be more appropriate (Scialoja 2006b: 70; in general see Grembi 2002: 267–94).

Scialoja's best contributions are probably the memoranda on economic subjects he gave at Cavour's request. In *Carestia e governo* (1854) he defended the liberalization of the price of bread introduced by Cavour, as well as Cavour's decision to maintain a light duty on flour for fiscal reasons. A short time later Cavour repealed even the light duty, and Piedmont could boast having introduced legislation that was akin to that of Robert Peel. In 1861, as a representative of Cavour in Naples, Scialoja republished his pamphlet together with a preface against *camorra* and the enemies of Piedmont. Another important paper concerns a comparative study on the finances of Piedmont and Naples, which was published in 1857 (see Scialoja 2013: 317–24; 135–235).

Minghetti's 'just' economy

Marco Minghetti (of Bologna, 1818–86) occupied a major position among the *Risorgimento* figures. After belonging to the entourage of Pope Pius IX during the latter's 'liberal' pontificate, Minghetti became Finance Minister and twice Prime Minister of the *Destra*. From his extant unpublished manuscript papers it can be inferred that he had a good knowledge of Bentham, Senior and Mill, whose texts he carefully summarized and annotated.

Even as a young man, Minghetti showed a deep interest in the relationships among social sciences according to the 'tree of human knowledge'. In his view these relationships were not of *sub*ordination, but of *co*ordination, and equilibrium should be established among the various domains of human thought – and of human action as well. As far as economics was concerned, this meant that if equilibrium were not achieved, production would threaten to suffocate distribution. Minghetti conceded that the degree of state intervention required in order to ensure equilibrium may differ according to the different stages of a nation's progress, but he felt that a certain degree of intervention was necessary because the economy, if left to its own devices, 'causes incertitude … that poisons the pleasures we are enjoying, renders each of us an enemy to everybody, and almost all of us detestable even to ourselves' (Minghetti 1896 [1841]: 58). Minghetti sent this article, rich in humanistic flavour, to the elderly Sismondi, who appreciated it.

As a careful observer of the surrounding economic reality, Minghetti underwent a change of attitude with regard to the actual trend of the economy. In 1832, at the age of 14, he visited England with his mother (who was of English origin), and was struck by the polarization of wealth and misery, the severe demographic pressure, and the difficulties in providing an outlet for the increasing amount of commodities. Observing the dramatic class conflict that was wracking Britain at that time, in 1843 he declared that the tranquility of the Italian countryside, where the poor were supported by a network of private and religious charitable institutions, was infinitely preferable. In particular, Minghetti applauded the pedagogic virtues of Italian sharecropping, seen as educating labourers to be happy with their own condition (Minghetti 1872 [1843]: 46).

In 1846, however, during another visit to England in the very midst of the Anti-Corn Law League campaign, Minghetti was remarkably impressed by the vigorous growth of the economy, which was accompanied by comparatively stable social peace. On that occasion he met several British statesmen and economists – among them Senior, McCulloch and Whately – and admired their willingness to ameliorate the conditions of the poor without disturbing the march of economic progress (Minghetti 1872 [1846]). Naturally, Minghetti was aware that the British model could not be mechanically imported into Italy, and some adjustments had to be introduced. Social happiness *and* economic welfare could only be achieved, Minghetti concluded, through cooperation between economics, law and morals. While emphasizing that economics was the science of means, he believed it should benefit from the resources provided by all other social disciplines, especially those concerning the ends pursued by human action.

In his ambitious book *Dell'economia pubblica e delle sue attinenze colla morale e col diritto* (Minghetti 1859; translated into French in 1863), he integrated Romagnosi's approach with that of Pellegrino Rossi, with whom Minghetti had become well acquainted when both of them formed part of the Pope's entourage in 1848.

Rossi's influence on Minghetti

Pellegrino Rossi (of Carrara, 1787–1848) taught constitutional law in Geneva and subsequently political economy at the Collège de France in Paris, where he succeeded Jean-Baptiste Say. Thanks to his widely read *Cours d'économie politique* (1840–41) Rossi was the Italian-born economist who reached the widest international audience in the mid-nineteenth century. In the present survey, it is important to remember him above all for the distinction he drew between pure and applied science, a distinction he based on his belief that the former is independent of morals, while the latter – *qua* inclusive of economic policy – should consider morals as well.

Another point concerns Rossi's critical view of the classical distinction between productive and unproductive labour. This was a discussion Rossi deemed old-fashioned because all actions producing enjoyments that satisfied a demand were *ipso facto* productive. Minghetti, on the other hand, objected that a clear-cut distinction between pure and applied economics was hardly defensible without the addition of some supplementary 'backward warranted conditions' (to use a modern expression) that are external to economic models but necessary to circumscribe the economic phenomenon itself. He referred to these conditions as 'proportions' (see Minghetti 2012 [1859]: 34), a term that was slightly (but significantly) different from Frédéric Bastiat's 'economic harmonies'. Minghetti rejected the argument that all social conflicts can be resolved by recourse to unbridled *laissez-faire*. Applied economics, he maintained, needed to interact with morals and law –in reasonable proportion – in order to solve issues that cannot be settled by unilateral recourse to any single sphere.

Consequently, his picture of a 'good' society was one that would provide for some mitigation of the market's excesses, if necessary by means of basic government interference. Minghetti manifested this view many years before the 1870s, when the debate between absolute and 'self-restrained' Liberalists began to dominate the political scene.

Minghetti was able to bridge the historical gap between modern economics and the traditional social attitude of the Roman Church. Thus, while during the first decades of the nineteenth century the Church had embraced the most reactionary positions in politics as well as in economics, from 1850 onwards the new Jesuit journal, *La civiltà cattolica*, sought to present an alternative view to current liberal economics that was not altogether hostile to the new ideas, in an attempt to reconcile the traditional religious and moral discourse with substantial reception of the 'laws of the market' (see Bianchini 1996).

In this context it is also worth mentioning Father Luigi Taparelli d'Azeglio (1793–1862), brother of the better-known liberal statesman Massimo. Father Taparelli perceptively distinguished between Bentham and Beccaria, the Utilitarians, both of whom he firmly rejected, and Say, the *Idéologue*, who he mildly tolerated. Implicitly this was a bridge between Catholicism and political economy,[10] and it marked a crucial step towards a new political alliance between Catholicism and liberalism that could not fail to influence the Catholic vision of economics.

Cavour's economics

Early writings

When just 18, Camillo Benso, Count of Cavour (1810–61), made some particularly perceptive observations (in French – his first language) concerning Smith, Ricardo and Say (Cavour 1971). He generally praised the formal rigour of classical economics, but also insinuated that many of the discussions concerning the first principles concealed verbal disputes or ad hoc reasoning. This was the case, he argued, with regard to the labour theory of value, which could be maintained only if it dealt with the difficulty in obtaining the foodstuffs necessary to 'command' (in Smith's sense) given quantities of labour. Since these quantities varied according to the conditions of society, it was not possible to treat the quantities of subsistence that could be purchased by the average wage rate as an invariable measure of value – unless one were to conclude, tautologically, that value depends on value. Likewise, he contended that it was useless to choose as the standard of value a commodity whose value undergoes no change, because no such commodity exists. In this sense Cavour would have rejected – had he been acquainted with it – the 'solution' to the invariable standard of value problem presented by Ricardo in his posthumous *Absolute value and exchange value*.

Thus, value could not be defined as an absolute property of commodities, as the argument would thereby be shifted to a metaphysical level. Accordingly, the young Cavour subscribed to Say's approach, in which value is a mere relation between utilities, and since utility implies the concepts of scarcity and want – both of which are ceaselessly changing – the utility-values are likewise changeable. This notwithstanding, Cavour admitted that Ricardo was right in arguing that the production conditions of a commodity contribute to defining its value. Considering value from the cost side was as legitimate as considering it from the demand side. Cavour appears to have been an *ante litteram* Marshallian.

In another unpublished manuscript, Cavour discussed Ricardo's claim (*On the principles of political economy and taxation*, Chapter 16) that a tax on wages had the effect of increasing production costs and therefore reducing profits. Cavour objected that the wage rate did not depend only on the production conditions of food, but also on the standard of living prevailing in a country, so that countries at the same level of development may present different wage rates. Moreover, the increase in the price of wheat would not necessarily have negative consequences on real wages, as it would be likely to attract new wheat growers, leading to a growth of the sector. This, in turn, would result in higher wages and profits, even in the presence of a tax on wages. In general, Cavour concluded, it is not possible to assign absolute validity to the Ricardian proposition.

Against socialism and collectivism

Unlike most of his contemporaries, Cavour avoided the rhetoric of *bene pubblico*, in the sense of public happiness, and concentrated on the economic interests that come into play, arguing that knowledge of economic laws may be precious for anybody who intends to follow a strategy of reconstructing economic and social equilibrium.

As a political leader, Cavour has traditionally been considered a moderate on the right, but his moderate attitude was somewhat unconventional. He declared his preference lay with 'a state that is unquiet, but strongly endowed with freedom, as compared to a state that is quiet, but living under a rule of compression and regression' (Cavour 1962a [1847]: 288). Cavour's vision foreshadows an idea also found, among others, in Ferrara and Einaudi, namely, that only a society inspired by liberal principles is an open society and therefore subject to constant growth. On the other hand, his criticism of socialism and 'communism' – a term circulating in Europe even before 1848 – appears to prefigure several twentieth-century objections to planning that were voiced mainly by the Austrian-libertarian school.

According to Cavour, an egalitarian distribution of income not only failed to guarantee general plenty, it could actually be harmful to the economy if it interfered with the capital accumulation mechanism. This was a mechanism in which saving was conceived as 'abstinence' from consumption in the present with a view to a greater gain in the future – a tenet Cavour had learned from Senior, the British economist he met in Britain. If the market-oriented accumulation process is successful, Cavour observed, a decision to substitute it with a state-oriented, coercive mechanism, resorting either to indirect means – by limiting the consumption of luxuries – or direct means – by increasing taxation and expanding public expenditure – would mean making a leap in the dark. Cavour pointed out that there was a necessary link between private accumulation and entrepreneurship: the latter cannot stand without the former. That is to say, there was no guarantee that a system based on a state accumulation mechanism would be able to respect and maintain the function of entrepreneurship:

> In order to achieve abundant production, capital and works alone are not sufficient, but the contribution of intelligence, as well as of a guiding,

enterprising, firm mind is also required. It is hardly conceivable that such a mind will continue to operate, if the hope of acquiring an inviolable property right over the products of its industry were to cease.

(Cavour 1962b [1848]: 324–5)

In this regard, the market-oriented literature circulating today could not be clearer.

Another vital sector in which socialism aimed to intervene was that of industrial relations. In particular, Cavour opposed the typical 1848 claim to the 'right to labour'. Discussing the numerous difficulties likely to be encountered in achieving such a goal, Cavour expressed his concern that the best organized groups of workers would be the most favoured, leading to the rise of a new medieval-style corporatism, even if it were presented as 'socialism'.

The eternal dilemma: efficiency versus equity

The equation socialism equals return to medieval society was shared by many Italian liberal economists including Ferrara, Pantaleoni, Pareto, and (in more veiled terms), Einaudi. Implicit in the argument was not only that the goal of efficiency must have priority over that of equity, but that equity was, per se, diametrically opposed to efficiency; reciprocally, efficiency would also provide the conditions for equity.

Ferrara and Pantaleoni represented the extreme position, which excluded the quest for equity from the realm of economics. Pareto, on the other hand, depicted a situation known as the Pareto optimum, where the goal of the maximum efficiency could be attained without changing the existing distribution. In actual fact, Pareto also admitted redistributive policies via his second theorem of welfare economics (see below, Chapter 6), but his notion of income distribution gave limited hope with regard to the feasibility of systematic redistribution. Independently of Pareto, Einaudi also attempted to define justice (a term he used synonymously with equity), starting from a definition of 'normal income'. Yet, as we will see in Chapter 7, Einaudi had difficulty in convincing his readers that taxing normal income was the *only* solution capable of guaranteeing equity as justice in taxation. Therefore the issue was left unsettled.

Cavour himself was far from indifferent to the condition of the poor. But again, he was alarmed that public relief could weaken awareness among the poor that they should seek to make provision for their own future, and this could undermine the whole economy's efficiency. Accordingly, he praised the transformation of the Old into the New Poor Law, which adopted the 'less eligibility' principle, so that the assisted poor should not be granted greater relief than that to the poorest worker. On the other hand, Cavour approved of the abolition of the compulsory settlement of the poor in their birth parishes, and looked favourably on the resulting possibility for the poor to move throughout the entire territory in search of work (Cavour 1962c [1835]). This essay was also translated into English.

Public works and public budget

Cavour was always a staunch free trader, but not an out-and-out advocate of *laissez-faire*. Addressing the development problems of a late-comer country such as the Kingdom of Sardinia, he included in his economic vision a positive function for state expenditure. Railways, in particular, called for a special public effort, since railway enterprises faced a prolonged waiting period before fixed costs could be recouped; a situation that might discourage private investment. Cavour distinguished between first-order railways – namely, those connecting the main towns – and second-order railways, which served local traffic only. The former should be built by the State, while the latter could be built and managed by private companies (see Cavour 1962d [1846]). Apart from these technical reasons, the first-order railways also fulfilled a political function; namely, that of facilitating links between the North of Italy and Europe by crossing the state borders. In this context it is worth noting that the Fréjus tunnel between Italy and France was opened in 1871, ten years after Cavour's death.

Cavour put forward similar ideas concerning the State budget. In contrast to many liberals who considered – and today still consider – budget equilibrium as a dogma, Cavour maintained, as Finance Minister, that 'in consequence of the improvement of society, we observe a growth of wants; in consequence of this, public expenditure increases' (Cavour 1855 [1852]: 450). And in order to clarify that such a trend was independent of any political regime, he asserted that 'this is an ineluctable necessity which must perforce be obeyed not only by constitutional governments, but by absolute governments as well'.

Such a perspective, which subordinated the reasons of finance to considerations of the economy, in opposition to the mainstream (pre-Keynesian) doctrine that subordinated economics to finance, was shared by several enlightened political figures who worked closely with Cavour. In 1857 Antonio Scialoja, at that time exiled in Turin, engaged in a heated debate with the then Bourbon functionary Agostino Magliani (or Magliano) – who would later be appointed as Finance Minister during the Sinistra rule in the 1880s. Since Magliani had extolled the 'lightness' of the Neapolitan budget as compared to the 'heaviness' of that of Piedmont, Scialoja invited his adversary to consider the different economic effects of public expenditure in Naples and Turin on the general economy of the two states. The acknowledged budget deficit in the Kingdom of Sardinia (heavy taxation, large public expenditure) contributed to fostering growth, while the restrictions enacted by the Neapolitan budget (low taxes, low public expenditure) were of no help at all (see Scialoja 2013 [1857]: 135–235; Einaudi 1953 [1939]: 215–27). In this respect Scialoja foreshadowed the strategy of economic policy – severe fiscal pressure in order to cover a massive public expenditure for the economic take-off – which was followed during the post-Unity decades.

Notes

1 Leopardi (1967) [1834]: 540. Note that Leopardi considered the nineteenth century as being not too different, from a philosophical point of view, from the eighteenth.

2 See the recent proceedings in three languages – French, Italian and English – of an international Sismondi conference, VV. AA. 2011d.

3 *Dedicatoria, Scrittori classici italiani di economia politica*, Milano: Destefanis, (1803), vol. I: 2.

4 For a conciliatory interpretation, according to which Pecchio was critical of Ricardo but not of British economics as a whole, see Isabella (2012).

5 In a later edition he mitigated his assessment, albeit in a quite malicious way: 'en puisant dans [drawing from] les bons auteurs' (Say 1840: 602).

6 Gioja (1962) [1798]: 85; italics by Gioja.

7 See the testimony of Giuseppe Sacchi, the editor of *Annali*, reported by Barucci (1961): 701–2.

8 The first chair was established in 1819. Suppressed two years later for political reasons, it was finally re-established in 1846: see Pallini (1988).

9 Almost a century ago Raffaele Ciasca, the economic historian, published a massive reference book on all economic publications issued around 1848, from lengthy tomes to slim pamphlets, all of which testified to the fervour of initiatives during that period: see Ciasca (1916).

10 See Taparelli d'Azeglio (1845): 626, 641. For a different interpretation of Taparelli, stressing the predominance of the concept of 'order' as fixed by the Church, see Corrado and Solari (2009), especially pp. 31–3.

5   Francesco Ferrara and the economic schools in Italy (1850–90)

A changing background

The timespan covered by this chapter embraces the concluding *Risorgimento* years and the first decades of the new state's life. It is divided into two parts. The first 20 years or so are dominated by the outstanding figure of Francesco Ferrara, patriot, polemist and statesman, as well as major economist. Ferrara's manner of thinking could not fail to be influenced by the tumultuous changes set in motion after 1830 in Europe, when liberalism obtained its most substantial conquests. The great number of topics he tackled – from federalism to value theory, from state-Church relations to the role of statistics, from fiscal reform after 1861 to the theory of money and credit – and above all the originality of many of his indications both at a theoretical and a practical level – made him a personality of special importance in the landscape of intellectuals who 'made' Italy.

By about 1875 Ferrara's star had begun to wane, and hegemony was achieved by a variegated host of economists and high civil servants; the so-called *vincolisti* – that is to say, those in favour of state intervention – who rapidly occupied almost all university posts, sat in Parliament, took cabinet office and frequently wrote in the daily and periodical press. Their thought was eclectic, revealing a juridical approach and a historicist background of a Positivist derivation. Many of them, especially those from Lombardy or the Venetian region, boasted of their ideal descent from the *sommo* [highly praised] *Romagnosi*.

Francesco Ferrara's vision

The civil function of economics and of economists

The long life of Francesco Ferrara (1810–1900) extended throughout the whole of the *Risorgimento* years and into the first decades of the new state's life. A Sicilian, he began by studying medicine, but was spurred to dedicate himself to economics by virtue of a very stimulating intellectual milieu that made up the entourage of his mentor, Prince Carlo di Castelnuovo, an English-style liberal and one of the promoters of the 1812 Sicilian Constitution. As a young clerk at the Statistical Office of Sicily, and an officer at the Chamber of Commerce of

Palermo, Ferrara founded two journals – the *Giornale di statistica* and the *Giornale di commercio* – which hosted important articles by himself and his brother-in-law Emerico Amari (1810–70), a scholar of law and philosopher who applied the comparative method to conduct an in-depth appraisal of the concept of 'progress' in law (see VV. AA. 2011c).

Despite the fact that both Ferrara and Amari were sincere patriots, they were aware that in matters of science an excess of nationalism could be dangerous, especially concerning cultural matters. In particular, against those who boasted of the prominence of Italian economic science, Ferrara objected that the advancement of science could not but lead to rejection of any Nationalist arrogance.[1]

The economist's mission, Ferrara believed, was above all that of enlightening the political class with regard to economic truth. To perform this duty, comprehensive freedom – of thought, of speech, of action – was a necessary prerequisite. He felt that neither Gioja nor Romagnosi, who had been working during the age of despotism, had been entirely free to manifest their views, still less Galiani, Verri and Beccaria, whose roles had been as mere consultants and/or public servants entirely dependent on absolutist rule. In a nutshell, Ferrara's viewpoint was that of an intellectual who was aware of his own rights, and he defended them with tenacity. An exile from Sicily after the 1849 reaction, he was appointed to chair of political economy in Turin where he became acquainted with Cavour, who attended Ferrara's lectures and summarized them in articles in his newspaper, *Il Risorgimento* (see Cavour 1962: 447–65).

In 1850 a rift developed between Ferrara and Cavour, soon after the latter entered into politics. Ferrara's objection was that Cavour appeared to have betrayed his early liberal economic and political ideals. After Ferrara's resignation from *Risorgimento*, his political battle continued through three journals he subsequently founded: *La Croce di Savoia* (1850–51), *Il Parlamento* (1853), and *L'Economista* (1855–56). In 1859, after a suspension from his chair for political reasons, he resolved to leave Turin and moved to the University of Pisa. In 1860, after Garibaldi's liberation of Sicily, he returned once again to Palermo in a vain attempt to support a federalist solution for the island. After Unity he became actively engaged in politics, as Finance Minister and Deputy in 1867, as Director of the Venice School of Commerce in 1868, and as Senator in 1880. But for the last ten years of his life he withdrew into absolute silence.

The government's natural (and unnatural) duties

Ferrara was not so naive as to neglect the weight of 'sinister interests' (as Bentham defined them) over political decisions. In particular, Ferrara feared the collusion of pressure groups and interest lobbies with the State, arguing that if monopolistic interests obtain favours in the form of legislative measures, then freedom – either political or economic – is severely compromised. His view was that a free market could fight monopolies by the strength of its own forces; state regulation, on the other hand, far from reducing all monopolistic situations, is driven to create them – and often does so deliberately.

In the 1850s Ferrara spoke out against many features of Piedmont legislation that protected vested economic interests. His opposition to Cavour was probably excessive, and to some extent unjustified, but it stands among the first examples in Italy of modern independent journalism seeking to denounce all situations provoked by the perverse interaction between political and economic interests. Ferrara mounted a press campaign against the appointment of the Banca di Torino, which Cavour was personally involved with, as the bank of issue of the Kingdom of Sardinia. After Unity, Ferrara opposed the more subtle practice of appointing special parliamentary commissions, officially set up with the aim of 'studying' solutions, but effectively acting as pressure groups in order to favour sectional interests. These commissions, Ferrara sarcastically commented, were expected to 'prepare a dish of *facts* which can be used as pretext' to obtain advantageous laws in Parliament (Ferrara 1976 [1875]: 282).

The 'dish of *facts*' alluded to the vagueness of designs, a vagueness that masked the intention of favouring particular economic forces at the expense of the entire community. According to Ferrara, and exactly as maintained by Einaudi almost a century afterwards, the 'knowing-for-acting' principle – which requires the policy-maker to give a very clear indication of the goals he aims to achieve as well as the best economic way of attaining them – must be the golden rule to ensure the transparency of public action. In the absence of such control a liberal economy risks failure.

In criticizing the ruling class of his time, Ferrara had in mind an ideal scheme of the functioning of the political system based on a federal state. He was an admirer of the American institutions, and in moments of distress he confessed to his friends that he wished he could migrate to the US. In his political articles Ferrara cited Tocqueville as a statesman involved in the 1848 revolution, not as the author of *Democracy in America*, which he probably had not read; yet in many respects Ferrara's conception of liberty is very similar.

Ferrara (1976 [1884]: 358) wrote:

> The office of governing is but one of the thousands of jobs, one of the many industries ... which, taken as a whole, give the idea of social activity. All of us, each one for his own part, produce, exchange and consume utilities embodied, to varying degrees, in matter.... Hence there exists a class of producers, appointed to supply that special utility that is named justice, order, protection, in a word government.... If governing is producing, the innate laws of production must inexorably be the predominant task of the ruling class.... The social utility that government produces cannot be directly evaluated by government itself, or by government alone; those who can indeed measure it, receive it with agreement or reject it and who thus assign a value to it, will be its buyers and consumers, our nation itself. Indeed, we ourselves, nation-governed, are the only ones entrusted with deciding whether this utility deserves the price the producer-government imposes upon us, or, shall we say, the sacrifices to which it condemns us, in

the form of taxation as a device to meet the cost of the utility.... This is the significance of the expression we use: economic freedom.

In Ferrara's framework, government – far from possessing an ethical justification – is merely the outcome of a process of division of labour; that is to say, the transposition into economic terms of the concept of the social contract in Locke's version. Chapter 7 will call attention to the persistent influence of this representation in Einaudi's theory of optimal taxation, and implicitly of optimal government.

Ferrara added that the above representation is merely an ideal abstraction. In most historical cases the exchange of utility between state and citizens tends to 'change its nature: law very early becomes an artifice created with the aim of absorbing the individual existence of man; law, created in order to defend freedom, becomes an instrument of serfdom' (Ferrara 1935 [1858]: 711).

A few decades after Ferrara's denunciation of the malfunctioning of the relationship between the citizen as a consumer and the State as a producer of public goods – a relationship which, he felt, could not be trusted – a fully-fledged critical assessment of the distortion of information between state and citizens was developed by Amilcare Puviani (1854–1907), who held a professorship at Perugia University. Working almost in isolation, in his *Teoria dell'illusione finanziaria* (1903) Puviani skilfully highlighted the techniques through which the ruling class succeeds in dissimulating the correspondence between public expenditure and public wants, and in convincing taxpayers that the sacrifices required to obtain the State's services are genuinely necessary (see Puviani 1973 [1903]). In order to muster evidence for his theory, Puviani mainly relied on antiquity and the *Ancien Régime* rather than on modern times; nevertheless, his book can be considered an ideal bridge between the sociology of Ferrara and that of Pareto.

The *Biblioteca dell'economista* enterprise: an idiosyncratic work?

The core of Ferrara's economics can be found in the 19 massive introductions to the 26 volumes of *Biblioteca dell'economista* that he edited (in two series) from 1850 to 1868. It was a remarkable editorial enterprise carried out by the Turin publisher Giuseppe Pomba, who had already attracted attention for his projects in the field of encyclopaedias and other collections addressed to a broad audience of readers.[2]

It is disputable whether Ferrara had in mind a precise editorial model. In France a 16-volume *Collection des principaux économistes* had been issued between 1840 and 1848 by publisher Guillaumin, which hosted the works of the main French and British authors. The most frequently cited volume of this collection remains Eugène Daire's edition of the *Économistes financiers français*, which probably represented a model for the opening volume, *Fisiocrati*, of Ferrara's collection (Ferrara 1955 [1850]: 105).

A bird's-eye comparison with the previous Custodi collection shows that the Pomba project was altogether different. While the former enterprise was intended to enhance both the peculiarities and the merits of the Italian tradition, the latter – that is to say, Ferrara – relegated the Italian authors to the third volume of the first series, 'Italian treatises of the Eighteenth century' and in 1852 he wrote such a critical presentation of these writers that it raised a number of protests (see Faucci 1995: 184–6).

In his preface, Ferrara severely rebuked the eighteenth-century Italian economists for being too state-oriented in a mercantilist sense. Therefore, although Genovesi, Beccaria, Verri and Filangieri did have their place in the collection, their merits were seriously underrated. Gioja, Romagnosi and Fuoco were not included. This was not all. In the two volumes on 'Money and its surrogates' (1856–57), Ferrara made reference to Galiani only to raise the suspicion that *Della moneta* may not have been his own work (due to his very young age) (Ferrara 1961 [1856–57]: 315), and, as far as its content was concerned, he criticized Galiani's support for *alzamento* (ibid., pp. 100–1).

Instead, Ferrara included several Italian authors, mainly from Tuscany and Lombardy, in the two volumes on 'Agriculture and related economic questions', issued in 1859–60. Overall, a reader of this work of Ferrara's could gain the general impression that the Italian contribution to the development of economics was almost exclusively confined to applied and practical questions.

The *Biblioteca*'s greatest attention was reserved for the British (and French) eighteenth- and nineteenth-century classics, from Adam Smith to John Stuart Mill, including some early critics of Ricardo on value (such as Bailey and Rae), accompanied by the most representative post-classicists like Carey, Rossi, Bastiat, Dunoyer, Chevalier and Cherbuliez. Moreover, works by Babbage and Ure on industrial production and productivity were included, as well as von Thünen's *Isolated State* (translated from French) on the natural wage in land economics. All the volumes of the first series, which included general treatises, were supplied with an introduction by Ferrara, who wrote very comprehensive essays – with one exception, Smith's *Wealth of Nations*, for reasons that can be easily imagined (*Tanto nomini nullum par elogium*). In this case Ferrara preferred to attach a rather colourless presentation written by Victor Cousin, the French *idéologue*.

Ferrara also composed substantial introductions to the volumes of the second series on agriculture, money, wages, crises and foreign trade. Only the last three volumes, issued after 1866, presented no introduction at all, owing to the political commitment which by then was absorbing Ferrara's attention.

On method and value

Ferrara's subjectivist approach

Ferrara's approach to the history of economics was strictly theoretical. He was comparatively uninterested in looking for precursors, and indifferent to reconstructing the historical and material background of theories. The authors were filtered through a strictly analytical examination. Far from being ecumenical, Ferrara by no means refrained from severely criticizing all authors who did not share his own theory of value. In fact, value represents the core of Ferrara's reflection. As is well known, classical economics had faced the problem of the exchange value of commodities according to an objectivist perspective. Value was regarded as an intrinsic quality of commodities, something akin to its weight or volume, which, it was assumed, could therefore be measured through an invariable standard, or rather through a special commodity whose value was invariable because its production conditions were likewise invariable. This problem had attracted both Smith and Ricardo; the former opted to select 'labour' since its value was expected to undergo no change whatsoever, although the Scottish economist did acknowledge that natural prices no longer corresponded to their value as expressed in labour. Ricardo, on the other hand, maintained that both labour and capital were the true sources of value, and that capital could be translated into past labour, though he realized that the passage of time had serious consequences in this calculus.

It is common knowledge after the Piero Sraffa edition of Ricardo that the British economist acknowledged in the last months of his life that there were serious analytical difficulties in defining the properties of an (ideal) commodity possessing an invariable value. However, at the time when Ferrara was studying Ricardo, the general opinion was that by Ricardo's own admission the labour theory of value was valid only for reproducible commodities – not those that were rare or unique – commodities whose value depended on the intensity of demand; namely, on consumers' tastes and incomes. This led to two different explanations, 'objectivist' for the former group of commodities, and 'subjectivist' for the latter.

In opposition to this conclusion, Ferrara objected that a single fundamental principle was absolutely necessary; value, he maintained, was mainly based on human judgement. Ferrara was not the first Italian economist to follow a subjectivist approach to value; before him Beccaria and Verri were subjectivists, and Galiani partly subjectivist and partly objectivist, exactly like Genovesi. Only Ortes could be considered a pure objectivist, but none of them reached Ferrara's conclusion – namely, that not only is there no opposition between exchange value and use value, but neither is there any opposition between production and consumption.

Ferrara's vision was one in which everyone toils [*travaglia*] both in producing and in consuming. In either case each of us undergoes pain in order to obtain a pleasure; even the very act of eating requires some pain in order to satisfy hunger. Nor does opposition exist between labour and utility; *travaglio*, in Ferrara's approach, represents any sacrifice of utility that is accepted for the sake of obtaining another (greater) utility, and labour employed for productive purposes is but a special case of transformation of given utilities into other utilities.

In this conceptual framework, Malthus's law of population represented a perfect case of humankind's improvement through suffering. For this reason the

Sicilian economist, a committed Malthusian, was classified by some interpreters as a 'theological finalist' (see Guidi 1990: 215–39).

But notwithstanding transcendence-inspired overtones, Ferrara firmly relied on Utilitarianism and frequently referred to the 'great Bentham'. He was particularly skilful in demonstrating that the two categories of cost and utility absorbed all remaining explanations of economic value. For example, according to the French tradition (at that time represented by Auguste Walras and later by his son Léon), *rareté* was merely a feature of particular utilities, a factual circumstance that could increase the *travaglio* necessary to obtain a given utility, but which should not altogether be considered as a determinant of value.

Ferrara argued that the fundamental economic act is human occupation of nature. The right to property was not to be seen as the historical product of a social relationship among human beings, but was instead a starting point per se. It is important to stress that Ferrara did not appeal to natural law for his conception of property, but rather to the sensualist psychology of the French *idéologue* Destutt de Tracy, whose *Traité de la volonté* Ferrara included in *Biblioteca dell'economista*. In Ferrara's words (1955 [1854]: 428–33):

> occupying is the destiny of humankind.... Occupying is a 'travaglio' that men must inevitably and progressively perform.... There is no need of institutions, codes and juridical systems in order to legitimate the isolated occupation of matter that is the fact and the condition itself of existence.... If all property rights are absent, any effort to occupy goods is impossible.

After clarifying that value is a mental judgement on the relationship between goods and human sensations, Ferrara specified that there exist three judgements concerning value: (1) that on *use* value, namely the ability of a good to extinguish a pain by the consumption of the good itself; (2) that on *cost* value, namely the ability of a good to inflict pain through the process involved in obtaining the good, and; (3) that on *merit* or *exchange* value, namely the comparison between (1) and (2). The price of a good is merely the monetary expression of the ratio between utility and cost. The merit value is therefore 'value *par excellence*' (Ferrara (1955) [1854]: 339). When merit value coincides, on the one hand with utility, and on the other hand with cost, then equilibrium is reached in the sense that either utility or cost can indifferently be chosen in order to determine the commodity's value.

This notwithstanding, what are the effects, Ferrara wondered, of a divergence between merit value and cost, and between merit value and utility? He pointed out that a good cannot have a merit value (namely, a price) *higher* than its cost, because this would mean that, as consumers, we would bring upon ourselves a pain higher than the *travaglio* necessary to produce it. This would be repugnant to human nature, which seeks to economize on effort. On the other hand, neither can a good have a merit value *lower* than its cost, because cost is governed by physical laws which man cannot break. Moreover, a good cannot have a merit value *greater* than its utility, because nobody would desire it. However, he observed that a good can have a merit value *lower* than its utility, in which case value is lower than utility, and the situation in which (total) utility is greater than (marginal) value would result in a gain for the consumer (see Ferrara 1986 [1856]: 47–52). In modern terms, this represents a consumer's surplus. Ferrara's lack of knowledge of the concept of margin precluded him from solving Smith's so-called 'paradox of value', but the road he traced, although a little tortuous, was headed in the right direction.

Reproduction cost as the foundation of exchange and distribution

Consider the example of Robinson Crusoe. As long as he is either the only producer or the only consumer, and knows both the cost and utility of a good, he is able, after meeting Friday, to perform a comparison between the cost of the good he is willing to give up and the utility of the good owned by Friday he wishes to obtain. This barter operates under the rule of two fundamental laws: that of decreasing utility and that of increasing costs, i.e. in a situation in which it can be assumed that Robinson knows the cost of his own good and the utility he can obtain from Friday's good but he has no knowledge of Friday's cost of his own good or of the utility he can obtain from Robinson's good. The same holds for Friday.

Each exchanger is willing to perform the exchange if the price of the good he wishes to obtain is less than the 'reproduction cost' of the good itself. But does the reproduction cost consist of? Ferrara claimed that because of the objectivist approach, as well as the materialist approach espoused by classical economists, the latter failed to realize that prior to any exchange there must be a mental calculus with regard to the cost that would be involved if one attempted to obtain the good in some alternative way – for instance, by producing it directly, or by resorting to a surrogate. Thus, the strategy for each exchanger will be that of exaggerating the *production* cost of his own good, with the aim of matching the other exchanger's view of its *reproduction* cost:

> Each exchanger feels that, after esteeming, in his mind, the other's product in quantities of labour ('travaglio'), it will be necessary to exchange it with his own product, yet not according to what it effectively cost, but according to what it is valued by the other exchanger.
>
> (Ferrara 1956 [1863]: 237)

The process – defined by Ferrara as 'tentatively groping', and anticipates Walras's *tâtonnement* – ends when the two goods are exchanged in accordance with the reciprocal reproduction costs.

With indisputable shrewdness, Ferrara showed that all exchange phenomena in the market are based on the reproduction cost. For instance, he reasoned that those who delay the purchase of a good because they foresee that its price will be lower tomorrow are acting as if they were intending to 'reproduce' the same good, rather than 'looking for it in the field of the multitude, looking for it in the field of the future' (Ferrara 1956 [1856]: 354).

Ferrara used the same criterion in the case of very rare goods, such as works of art. A painting by a supreme artist has a physical reproduction cost that is practically infinite, in accordance with its uniqueness. Yet it can be sold at some positive price because buyers will reason in terms of its reproduction cost through surrogates, i.e. by comparing it with other slightly less rare works by contemporaries. Thus a value theory based on production costs refers to the costs that have already been expended before the exchange, while a value theory based on reproduction costs refers to the costs that have been saved owing to the exchange itself (see Ferrara 1956 [1856]: 299).

Ferrara presented the competitive market as the place where innumerable evaluations are made concerning the reproduction of goods. These evaluations, in turn, descend from subjective evaluations concerning pleasure and pain. Owing to the fact that the data for these calculations are continuously modified, the system is in perpetual motion.

In addition to its function as a yardstick for market exchanges, the reproduction cost is of use for determining the distributive shares as well. Again, Ferrara accused the Ricardian theory of distribution of resorting to different principles for each kind of income – subsistence for wages, capital accumulation for profits, decreasing productivity of land for rents – when to him 'there is just one law instead of three' (Ferrara 1986 [1855–56]: 307).

As far as wages are concerned, in Ferrara's framework the capitalist makes a comparison between the production cost of the wage-goods that he pays and the reproduction cost of the labour he obtains; whereas from the worker's perspective the production cost refers to the labour he sells and the reproduction cost to the wage he gains. The work of the more highly skilled workers has an elevated reproduction cost – inasmuch as it is hard to find substitutes – and therefore skilled workers enjoy higher wages than unskilled ones. Furthermore, pointing out that the rents of the best land depended on the latter's reproduction costs, Ferrara maintained that the limited supply of fertile land explained the existence of a rent on such land. But rent was by no means 'unearned income', as the Ricardian Socialists were claiming; rather, he argued, there exists no such thing as a purely net surplus in the classical sense.

Ferrara was proud of his theory, although he acknowledged that its antecedents were already largely present in Henry Carey and Frédéric Bastiat, two authors he included in *Biblioteca dell'economista* (see Ferrara 1956 [1856]: 511–13). Indeed, Bastiat is presented almost as hero and martyr in his battles for economic freedom.[3] Ferrara was personally acquainted with Carey, who he met when the American economist visited Turin in 1857.

Unfortunately for Ferrara, his theory did not achieve the success he had hoped for. Alfred Marshall, who presumably had not read Ferrara, but was certainly familiar with Carey, observed in his *Principles of economics* that the cost of reproduction theory was forced to neglect the importance of technical improvements when evaluating the current price of old products, or the price of products that are in high demand during special circumstances (e.g. a famine). Two opposite cases are that of a picture by Raphael (infinite reproduction cost), and that of a commodity for which there is no demand at all (zero reproduction cost). In all these cases the only determinant of price was effective demand.[4]

The question of the materiality of goods

Ferrara rejected Smith's distinction between productive and unproductive labour, as well as Say's distinction between 'material' and 'immaterial' goods. The Sicilian economist observed that this distinction is merely a matter of definition; all goods could be described as '*immaterial*, since they all promise a utility that is always an abstraction', or as '*material*, insofar as the utility they promise can be obtained only through the contribution of a material element'. And the concept of 'material' can have a fairly extended meaning   for instance, the teacher's voice itself (Ferrara 1955 [1855]: 473) is a prompt that stimulates the students' sense of hearing merely in the act of striking their ears, and therefore acts 'materially'.

Nevertheless, although Ferrara considered the materiality–immateriality issue as devoid of sense, he maintained that in all goods the material element prevails over that which is immaterial. For instance, he suggested that even in the case of literary or scientific production, where all material factors seem absent, the crucial property right worthy of protection is that of the publisher, without whom the poem or the scientific theorem would never become known to the wider public. In discussing the economic foundations of copyright, Ferrara adopted a rather paradoxical, yet coherent, position. He contended that authors should have no right to demand payment for reprints of their work, as their right to be paid refers exclusively to the moment when they consign their work to the publisher. Thereafter, the publisher stands as the only legal owner of the work, over which the author has no further right; consequently, all trademarks and patents are viewed as monopolies which hinder competition and should be abolished. It can clearly be seen that Ferrara's position exactly foreshadows that of present-day ultra-liberal economists (who are probably unaware of their antecedent).

Ferrara clung so strongly to his theoretical position that he renounced all payment on the occasion of the reprint of his statistical writings (1890), and raised no objection to a new edition of his *Prefazioni* (1889–91) – even though it was incorrect and full of interpolations. At the root of this stance was his scepticism towards the possibility that an author's merits could be clearly distinguished from the merits of earlier authors. He felt that truly original or 'new' ideas which were genuinely entitled to protection were very rare and hard to detect, and political economy – Ferrara sarcastically concluded – was a field that was particularly unoriginal: *Nihil sub sole novi*.

Ferrara's drive for the unification of economic categories did not prevent him from acknowledging the distinction between capital goods and consumption goods. In his view the former had two distinctive characteristics: (1) they were the source of 'indirect' utilities, through the 'diversion' of produced goods from their natural destination; that is, final consumption; (2) they were the result of past labour. There was no such thing as entirely 'free' capital; rather, he claimed that what determines the difference between final and capital goods is a human decision to use the capital as a source of direct or indirect utility, namely, to consume it or to save it through accumulation. One may discern here a premonition of Böhm-Bawerk's capital as a mean of indirect production, and also of Fisher's destination capital.

Money and credit

On the subject of money, Ferrara contended that its main function was that of acting as an intermediary in exchanges. He saw money as 'a pawn' that 'divides the exchange into two parts, and the interval [between the two] assures us that the thing we relinquish will find its equivalent in the desired thing' (Ferrara 1961 [1856]: 111–12).

Its function as a general equivalent is made possible by the fact that, insofar as money is a commodity per se, it has a value determined by its reproduction cost 'within the limits of its utility'. As noted above, utility cannot be less than the reproduction cost.

The theory of value based on the reproduction cost allowed Ferrara to solve the issue of the value of money. For, if money is a commodity like all others, this means that metallic money, *qua* commodity money, can be produced by private citizens according to the reproduction cost. The only constraint will be that of indicating its weight and *titre*. He rejected all alternative 'cartalist' theories of money as a mere symbol or sign, considering such theories as *étatistes* and as the mere expression of the despotic will of the sovereign or the government.

Ferrara then dealt with credit, viewed as the necessary bridge between the supply of savings and the demand for investment; by virtue of credit, what stands useless in one hand becomes useful if transferred into another's hand (see Ferrara 1961 [1856]: 225). He pointed out that faster mobilization of resources, made possible by credit, could accelerate the growth of dynamic countries like the United States. In his appraisal, credit played a special role in either preventing or worsening crises. Examining two different remedies for crises of excess or insufficiency of supply in comparison to demand, he noted that one possibility consisted in reliance on the market itself, as the market would alter the relative prices and restore the system to equilibrium. The other alternative involved making use of credit. By means of credit, a dealer in a market unsupplied with certain commodities would be able to purchase them elsewhere and sell them so that the chain of purchases and sales remain intact. If, however, due to an error in forecasting, sales prove to be insufficient, then the debts that have been contracted will not be honoured, leading to a chain of failures. Any credit that does not result in new production for sale is a factor of further crises and instability. Moreover, Ferrara continued, credit becomes self-defeating when the State intervenes in promoting it through specialized institutes for industry, agriculture, land and so forth. In fact, such action does not avert, but merely postpones, the outbreak of crises. And if a crisis is unavoidable, merely delaying its onset is of no aid whatsoever.

Ferrara as an opinion-maker on policy matters

After 1861 Ferrara entered the third stage of his life, becoming a freelance writer for *Nuova Antologia*, a periodical that drew inspiration from the French *Revue des deux mondes* which hosted contributions by numerous *literati*, economists and political leaders. For some years Ferrara supported the *Destra* cabinets, and worked closely with Finance Minister Quintino Sella (1827–84), a University professor of natural sciences who had a good background in economics. Ferrara supported Sella's project of a tax on *macinato* [grist] on the assumption that the higher price due to the tax would produce a rise in monetary wages and therefore a beneficial drive towards technological improvement (see Ferrara 1976 [1865]: 129).

The tax was eventually introduced in 1868 by Sella's successor, Luigi Cambray-Digny, but the difficulties encountered in determining the amount of tax due, calculated by means of a mechanical counter placed in the mills, as well as the population's protests against what was called the 'tax on poverty', led to its abolition by the new *Sinistra* cabinet in 1881.

Another moment of the *Destra* policy was represented by the forced circulation of paper money, established in 1866 for the purpose of defending the Italian lira and Treasury bonds against international speculation. The National Bank, the first bank of issue (out of six) in Italy made a loan to the government in exchange for the right to increase its paper circulation. The subsequent war against Austria worsened the financial situation; paper inconvertibility became a measure that was able to tackle not only the bank crisis, but the public finance crisis as well. In his *Nuova antologia* articles Ferrara pointed out that the value of paper money was independent of its quantity, since it depended only on public confidence. This was a perspective Ferrara shared with the Banking school (Tooke, Fullarton); he was an opponent of the Monetary school (Torrens, Overstone) based on the quantitative theory of money. His position was that an excess of paper money would not lead to price troubles because once the banks had lost their reserves they would reduce their assets and thereby readjust their accounts.

Nevertheless, for political reasons Ferrara remained critical of the forced circulation measure. He regarded the privilege of inconvertibility assigned to the National Bank as an intolerable favour, in perfect continuity with the Cavour line of reasoning that Ferrara had persistently criticized during the 1850s. In fact the other five smaller banks of issue – two of which had their head office in Florence – did not enjoy a similar privilege. Ferrara believed it would be more expedient to utilize state-issued money, to be withdrawn from circulation once taxes were paid. The circulation of state (Treasury) money, he argued, would avoid the monopoly of forced emission graciously reserved for the National Bank. On other matters, and independently of crises, Ferrara was favourable to a fiduciary circulation of banking money, whose issue was to be left free within the limits of the banks' balance sheets.

Finally, during his term of office as Finance Minister, Ferrara was involved with the awkward issue of the purchase of the *Asse ecclesiastico*; namely,

Church estate that was expropriated in 1866. A private company was created in order to sell this asset, and an advance payment of 600 million lira was made to the State. But difficulties encountered in selecting appropriate foreign bankers to carry out the manoeuvre, and above all concerns about fairness, prompted Ferrara to resign after less than four months in office in July 1867. His ambitious project to settle Church-state relations through a process of purely economic bargaining without any prior definition of the constitutional position of the Church was therefore rejected.

Ferrara's adversaries

'A large number of ill-paid professorships' (Schumpeter)

Schumpeter (1994: 856) observed that after Unity 'there were a large number of ill-paid professorships'. In effect, the new state's needs led to a considerable increase in the number of teachers, despite a very limited budget. This increase was also due to the decision to award a central role to state rather than private education – an approach shared by the whole *Risorgimento* ruling class. There was a widespread conviction that the problem of creating a national identity in a country whose territory had for centuries been a patchwork of small separate entities involved education. The alternative of allowing private initiative to create institutions for higher learning would have implied awarding an almost exclusive power of educating the future ruling class to the directives of the Catholic Church, which had strongly opposed the process of unification (the 1870 occupation of Rome put an end to the Church's 1,000-year-old temporal power) and never accepted the 1871 *legge delle guarentigie* [Law of Guarantees] that established absolute separation between state and Church. The liberal state, in assuming the task of supplying higher education, was deemed more suitable to ensure absolute freedom of teaching and therefore enable the broadest possible dissemination of ideas. Unavoidably, most teachers of economics in the first decades of the new state's life had no special scientific training, but were recruited from journalism and politics, including several patriots who had experienced the Bourbon prisons.[5]

With regard to the teaching staff in the field of economics, from the mid-1870s onwards the picture began to change, with a thrust toward the achievement of a more professional scientific standard and the creation of new institutions where the ruling class received advanced training. Alongside the faculties of law, which had been the traditional route through which knowledge in economics and finance was acquired, the high schools of commerce were now introduced, which did not depend on the Ministry of Education but on the Ministry of Agriculture, Industry and Commerce (MAIC). This Ministry therefore more explicitly assumed the crucial function of acting as a forum and interest group for private business.[6]

Accordingly, the high schools were designed to train both high-ranking public servants and top executives in the private sector. The first high school was established in Venice in 1868, the other two in Genoa (1884) and Bari (1886) – all three towns being important centres of commerce and business.[7]

By 1924 the high schools of commerce had been renamed faculties of economic and commerce, and were placed under the authority of the Ministry of Public Education.

The faculties of political sciences were established later, during the 1930s, and owed much to the Fascist intent of creating a 'new' leading class. It is noteworthy that prior to Fascism there was only one high school of political sciences, founded in 1874 in Florence as a private institute by a group of moderate liberal intellectuals and named after Cesare Alfieri, a Piedmontese political writer. Among its professors of economics, mention should be made of Carlo Fontanelli (1841–90) and Arturo J. De Johannis (1846–1913). The civil service's needs also prompted the establishment of many chairs of public finance. The first chair was held at Modena University in 1880 and assigned to Giuseppe Ricca Salerno (1849–1912), who is to be remembered for his learned and still usefully consultable *Storia delle dottrine finanziarie in Italia* (1881; 1896).

The decades from 1870 to 1890 also witnessed the development of statistics, which was cultivated either as a quantitative discipline requiring mathematical training (this was the case of Messedaglia, more of below) or as a discipline bordering on administrative law and organization. At least two noteworthy scholars deserve to be recalled in this context. First, Luigi Bodio (1840–1920), a junior colleague of Ferrara's at Venice who was appointed as the Director of the Statistical Office at MAIC, and was later President of the *Institut international de statistique* and a Senator of the Kingdom. He reorganized the periodical publications of *Direzione generale di statistica*, and encouraged statistical research on emigration (for more on him see Soresina 2001).

Second, Carlo F. Ferraris (1850–1924), who held a university chair of administrative science at Padua, published many statistical reports on higher education and, as Minister of Public Works in 1905–06, carried out the nationalization of Italian railways (see Ferraris 2007).

Bodio completed his studies in Innsbruck and Paris, Ferraris in London and Berlin. They both had an excellent knowledge of German, but Bodio appears to have been a liberal in the strict sense, while Ferraris is closer to the concept of the 'chair socialist'.

In parallel, this period was characterized by the birth of associations of economists, the spread of professional journals, and regular public competitions for the appointment of university professors, through the establishment of uniform rules that have passed down to the present time almost unchanged.

The Italian 'Methodenstreit'

Around 1874 a battle about method in economics was waged in Italy. It was a minor anticipation of the better-known *Methodenstreit*, which arose between Carl Menger and Gustav Schmoller about ten years later. It is worth recalling that the impact of German economics had been marginal in Italy throughout the first half of the nineteenth century – Friedrich List was criticized by Cattaneo, but also by Ferrara who did not include his *National System* in *Biblioteca dell'economista*. In 1870, however, the victory of Prussia over the Second Empire directed attention towards the so-called Historical school of economics, led by Wilhelm Roscher and, later on, by Gustav Schmoller. At once Germany was seen to possess valid economists as well as able statesmen and redoubtable soldiers.

Furthermore, strong reverberations of the first conference of the Verein für Sozialpolitik, held in Eisenach in 1872 as an offshoot of a group of economists labelled 'chair socialists', were strongly felt in Italy. As is well known, these economists were by no means *stricto sensu* socialists; on the contrary, they aimed at approaching the issue of 'proletarian' socialism through social reforms enacted from above, especially concerning labour legislation and social insurance, a field in which imperial Germany rapidly reached a leading position in Europe. In Italy such social reforms had not even been envisaged, as bitterly remarked by Pasquale Villari, the historian, in his *Lettere meridionali* (1872). In particular, no limits were imposed on night labour and child labour.

Ferrara's article 'Il germanismo economico in Italia', issued by *Nuova antologia* in August 1874 (Ferrara 1972: 555–91) covered the following areas:

1   undervaluation of the features of German economics, which according to Ferrara, rested on Hegel's category of the 'Ethical State';
2   a similarly reductive assessment of the Italian 'Germanic' school, the main character of which was the lack of scientific unity and hence an apparent heterogeneity of theoretical positions;
3   rejection of the political implications of the theoretical tenets of the Italian 'German economists'.

Now, the theoretical argument raised in point (1) was inexact, since many economists in Germany were influenced by Positivism rather than by Idealism, which at that time undergoing a wide-ranging crisis; point (2) was based on Ferrara's personal idiosyncrasy with regard to his esteem – or lack thereof – for many of his colleagues, whose names were being connected with the rival sect, and, finally; point (3) is central in Ferrara's argument because he accused the *vincolismo* [restrictionism] preached by 'German'-Italian economists of being nothing more than the economic by-product of the sort of political *trasformismo* [opportunism] that prompted many right-wing deputies in Parliament to rally to the Left not on idealistic grounds but merely as the result of selfish calculations.

Undoubtedly, the political differences between *Destra* and *Sinistra* progressively disappeared after 1870, and this led to an impoverishment of political competition. Ferrara, himself a man on the centre-left, was worried about this tendency towards elimination of a clear-cut dialectic among different parties, convinced as he was that interaction and exchange of ideas was fundamental for a liberal system (naturally he considered Britain as the positive model, and post-Napoleonic France as the negative model). Distressed by these developments,

Ferrara bitterly confessed to his daughter in 1876, just a few months after the vote that gave the *Sinistra* the majority in Parliament (a result Ferrara himself had been instrumental in promoting): 'The Right was populace, the Left is a cloaca' (see Faucci 1995: 278).

The anti-Ferrarians

Soon after Ferrara's article on *Germanismo*, a circular was sent from Padua in September 1874 which started from a rather loose reference to the 'progress' of economics in the sense of realism and concluded with a critique of 'the fatalism of the Optimists', i.e. of the supporters of absolute *laissez-faire*. The scientific content of the 'Padua circular' was indeed very poor, but the political implica tions – the case for more state intervention – were very clear.

But who were Ferrara's adversaries, really? Four names signed the Padua letter. Three of them were found not to have been directly involved in the *Risorgimento*, and came from Lombardy and the Venetian region. They were imbued with the economic as well as the administrative culture of the Austrian (rather than the German) Empire. Fedele Lampertico (of Vicenza, 1833–1906) was a Catholic-liberal intellectual who sought to reconcile the Church with the Italian state. His most ambitious work was the five-volume *Economia dei popoli e degli stati* (1874–84: note the use of plural), where he insisted on characteristic trends of economic laws. Lampertico was among those who looked favourably on the possibility of applying the Darwinian approach to social sciences through the mediation of the Malthusian population theory (see Sensales 2011: 120).

Another signatory, Luigi Cossa (of Milan, 1831–96), professor at Pavia University, was a scholar of greater erudition than originality (Maffeo Pantaleoni defined him as 'tutto schema e scheda', i.e. exclusively devoted to composing lecture notes and erudite bibliographies). He left several introductory courses in economics that were translated into various different languages (French, English, German, Spanish and even Japanese).[8]

Cossa's main merit, however, was that of training an entire generation of scholars who moved to Germany or Britain to follow courses and then returned to Italy to embark on an academic career. Cossa also encouraged research into the history of economics by financing – even using personal funds – numerous grants and prizes. Several well-documented historical monographs written by his pupils – including Tommaso Fornari, Giulio Alessio, Augusto Graziani Sr, Andrea Balletti and, above all, Giuseppe Ricca-Salerno – can be usefully consulted even today.

The youngest signatory of the Padua circular letter was Luigi Luzzatti (of Venice, 1841–1927), who would become one of the main representative statesmen straddling the two centuries. A converted Jew (in particular he was a devotee of Saint Francis), Luzzatti was an 'apostle' of popular cooperative banks according to the Schulze-Delitzsch model. Money, banking and finance were his favoured topics, though he was comparatively less sensitive towards industrial and agricultural problems (see Pecorari 1983).

Luzzatti personally replied to Ferrara that there existed many intermediate positions between absolute *laissez-faire* and absolute state intervention, and that in Britain the new Liberal Party, headed by William Gladstone, was not averse in principle to a certain degree of interventionism.[9]

Quite a different case was that of Antonio Scialoja, a man from the South who had also been an active patriot. As we saw in the previous chapter, in his youth he followed Say's absolute liberalism, but after 1861 he was struck by Italy's negative economic performance and began to favour prudent interventionism.

The 'Germanists' organized themselves into an Associazione per il progresso degli studi economici and convened a meeting in Milan (1875) where several projects of social reform were illustrated. The association gradually spread throughout the national territory, setting up local sections, particularly in the South, so that the epithet of *lombardo-veneta* coined by Ferrara was no longer suitable. The supporters of *laissez-faire* were less well organized. Many of them were Sicilian or Tuscan landowners, whose association, the *Società Adamo Smith*, had its headquarters in Florence. The association elected as its President the former Interior Minister Ubaldino Peruzzi (1823–92), a businessman and engineer (who had graduated in Paris) with a good training in economics. Peruzzi and his wife Emilia had an important salon where a visitor might meet, among various *literati* and politicians, the young Vilfredo Pareto. The *Società Adamo Smith* also published a pugnacious periodical, *L'Economista*, to which Ferrara and Pareto frequently contributed.

A journal that was fundamental in creating a climate favourable to an appeasement between the two schools was the *Nuova Antologia*, founded in 1866 in Florence – at that time the capital of Italy (subsequently transferred to Rome in 1871). Its editor, Francesco Protonotari (1832–88), was himself a (scientifically rather poor) university professor of economics; but he had the vision to open up the journal to an array of economists interested in policy issues, such as money and banking, tax reform and budget control, agriculture, commercial treaties, and railway regulations. By virtue of this broad-based range of interests, the many different positions that were vying for position were extensively represented. The *Revue des deux mondes* model was subsequently copied, even in the style of its editing (see Barbieri 1988 [1934]).

Ecumenical as he was, Protonotari accomplished the miracle of building a relationship of cooperation between such contrasting characters as Ferrara and Luzzatti.

In contrast to developments in Germany, the 'struggle for method' added little to science in Italy. This may explain why the most eminent economist of the anti-Ferrara front, Angelo Messedaglia (of Verona, 1820–1901), took no direct part in this debate (see VV. AA. 2011a).

Messedaglia was interested in *applying* scientific and quantitative methods to economics rather than in engaging in idle discussions. In 1858 he corrected Malthus's population law, using the double difference method to show that the subsistence constraint transformed the geometric progression into an arithmetic one. He further observed that Malthus's method was flawed, as the latter had first logically simplified the concrete phenomenon, and then had subsequently applied the abstract principle to the effectively oversimplified concrete phenomenon, thereby committing a serious logical mistake (see De Viti de Marco 1980 [1901] in Finoia 1980: 281).

A veritable Positivist, Messedaglia praised the fact that statistics had transformed itself from a discipline that was the handmaid of the public administration, as it still was according to Gioja, into an autonomous science. Faced with the increasing call for more data, demanded by several disciplines including criminology and medicine, statistics was compelled to adopt a rigorous method based on abstraction, deduction and experimental testing. Messedaglia, exactly as Marshall did some years afterwards, considered biology as the model science for the economist. In contrast with many Italian scholars of his time, he maintained that economics was 'neither the science of happiness, nor of wealth', but the science which 'studies the laws according to which labour, in its twofold natural and civil relations, provides the external conditions of existence and of the process of refinement (*incivilimento*)'.[10] In so doing he was able to maintain Romagnosi's tradition, linking it to the more updated Positivist and 'scientific' views and freeing it from all ethical and meta-scientific implications.

The *Biblioteca dell'economista* once more

The third series: Boccardo's encyclopaedism

During the period when, as editor-in-chief, Ferrara composed the first and second series of *Biblioteca dell'economista*, he did not perceive – in keeping with a scholarly background steeped in the culture of Romanticism – the new trend in economics that was beginning to emerge in Europe in the wake of Positivism. This new climate, which was to dominate during the last quarter of the century, inspired the third and fourth series of *Biblioteca*. The third series (1874–93) was edited by Gerolamo Boccardo (of Genoa, 1829–1904), author of the syncretic *Trattato teorico-pratico di economia politica* (1853), and of *Dizionario della economia politica e del commercio* (1857) which in many ways reflected the achievements of Coquelin and Guillaumin's *Dictionnaire* (see Augello and Pavanelli 2005).

In the new series of *Biblioteca*, Boccardo broke away from Ferrara, and hosted the contributions of many German authors including Gustav Schönberg's mammoth *Manual of political economy* and the massive monographs by Wilhelm Roscher, Adolf Wagner and Albert Schäffle. But he also issued two important books representative of the British classical tradition: John Stuart Mill's *Unsettled Questions* (1844) and John Elliot Cairnes's *Character and Logical Method* (1857). Both had previously been excluded by Ferrara, probably on account of his distaste for methodological disputes.

Boccardo aimed to present himself as thoroughly up-to-date by hosting Jevons's *Theory of Political Economy*. Jevons himself, in his preface to the second edition (1879), very generously placed Boccardo among the European scholars who had successfully presented economics in a mathematical setting. Jevons deplored that fact that 'the followers of Mill and Ricardo' (namely, his British fellow economists) showed little interest in economic mathematics, whereas in 'the hands of [the] French, Italian, Danish or [the] Dutch' this approach was likely to become the leading strand of thought (Jevons 1970: 65).

Other mathematical texts hosted in Boccardo's series included Augustin Cournot's *Recherches* and Léon Walras's *Théorie mathématique de la richesse sociale*. But in presenting these authors Boccardo identified their merit as residing in their use of some unspecified 'quantitative method', without stressing the crucial point; namely, the introduction of a logically rigorous approach in economics. But despite a lack of full understanding of the importance of Léon Walras's scientific message, the anti-Ferrara school obsessively courted him by implying that a small Walrasian school was about to be founded in Italy ('tres faciunt collegium', Walras wittily wrote to his self-proclaimed disciple, Alberto Errera).[11]

Indeed, emphasis on the 'new school' was not totally innocent; rather, it formed part of a cultural strategy. Ferrara consistently declared his opposition to any application of mathematics to economics, as in his view economics was a 'science of man' based exclusively on introspection. Implicitly replying to Ferrara, Boccardo hosted in *Biblioteca* the leading French statistician Adolphe Quételet, who had studied the regularities of man's behaviour from the perspective of psychology. Statistics, Quételet believed, fulfilled the same function as experimental physics in pure science, while the function of mathematical analysis in economics could be likened to that of theoretical physics.

Another feature of *Biblioteca*'s third series was the inclusion of the so-called heretical economists, such as Owen, Lassalle, Proudhon, Tchernicewsky and Marx, whose first volume of *Capital* had been translated from French. Most disappointingly, however, instead of discussing the theoretical issues of the various authors, Boccardo limited himself to illustrating the main economic institutions for the relief of the poor, such as cooperatives, popular banks and so on. Here, he principally relied on Jevons's *The State in Relation to Labour* (1882) (see Boccardo 1882: iii–lxii).

Despite the shallowness of his interpretive performance, Boccardo succeeded in communicating two important messages to his readers; that society was undergoing rapid change and that the proletarian challenge should be addressed with intellectual weapons radically different from Ferrara's diktat, which stated straight out that 'il socialismo non si discute, si schiaccia' [socialism is not to be discussed, but crushed] (Ferrara 1976 [1875]: 319).

Cognetti's evolutionary economics

The editor of the subsequent fourth series of *Biblioteca* (1896–1905) was Salvatore Cognetti de Martiis (of Bari, 1844–1901), professor at Turin University. A committed Positivist, Cognetti assumed that history represents the economist's laboratory. A materialist as well, his explanation of the transition from classical political economy to the new views was based on his analysis of the changes in the economic structure of the West after 1870 – culminating with the 1873–96 Great Depression – which called for an altogether new approach.

Although he was an admirer of Darwin, Cognetti was not driven by the aim of proclaiming the predominance of 'the fittest' in the economy; rather, he limited himself to maintaining that just as all societies of living beings are progressively evolving, so human society is likewise subject to constant change (see Cognetti de Martiis 1881: 55).

In another work he claimed that 'the foundation of sociology and therefore of economics [which he considered as part of sociology] lies in biology' (Cognetti de Martiis 1886: 186), prefiguring the well-known statement made by Alfred Marshall. It is therefore hardly surprising that Cognetti included Marshall's *Principles of Economics* in *Biblioteca*.

Another noteworthy aspect of Cognetti's thought concerns his enquiry into possible early traces of 'socialism in ancient societies' (principally Greece and Rome), as potential precursors of a critical attitude towards the class structure of society of that time. A learned Latinist, he translated Plautus and wrote a book, *Socialismo antico* (1889) which presented the (indeed very loose) ideas of the ancient writers on economics as 'intrinsically rational' if set in their historical context.

Finally, Cognetti's name is to be remembered as the founder (1893) of the first seminar for political economy in Italy, called *Laboratorio* in accordance with Cognetti's science-oriented creed. The *Laboratorio* acted as a training ground for a number of economists who were destined to become the leaders of the discipline in the following decades – first and foremost among them, Luigi Einaudi. Its motto was Ovid's line 'Haec placet experientia veri', a maxim that well represented its activities, where junior members presented and discussed papers mainly dealing with matters of applied economics, such as labour economics, local rates and trade policy.

After Cognetti's untimely death, *Biblioteca* was continued by Pasquale Jannaccone (1873–1959), a former disciple of the *Laboratorio*, who edited the subsequent fifth series. This series published such important works as Sydney and Beatrice Webb's *Industrial Democracy* (1912) and J. B. Clark's *Distribution of Wealth* (1916). Jannaccone wrote no introductions at all. The translations of the main authors included in the five series (Smith, Ricardo, Malthus, Mill, Marshall) were reprinted, with a few formal alterations only, in the UTET economics series until the late 1940s.[12]

The 'utility principle' and Catholic doctrine: Giuseppe Toniolo

Considered as the founder of the still-active Catholic school of sociology, Giuseppe Toniolo (of Treviso, 1845–1918), professor of economics at Pisa University from 1879 to his death, endeavoured to link the Church's teaching (in which Pope Leo XIII definitively crowned Aquinas as the supreme source of authority) with historicist Positivism, according to Romagnosi's 'mild' version of *incivilimento*. It may appear strange that Toniolo elected to publish his treatise on economics only a few years before his death. In fact, the bulk of his previous publications mainly concentrated on the history of medieval economy and economics, borrowing extensively from German economic historians (see Spicciani 1990: 115–17). Economics, Toniolo admonished in the opening pages of his manual, was a science of means, not of ends, the latter being the exclusive domain of the Church (Toniolo 1915: 4).

In effect, Toniolo maintained that political economy had begun to take shape after the victory of Catholicism over Paganism, for whereas in classical antiquity 'positive social sciences played no role as they were confused with private and public law' (ibid., p. 7), the principle of free will introduced by Christianity, together with the distinction between the natural and supernatural order, allowed the autonomy – albeit still in a subordinate position – of social science from religion.

Within the natural order to which economics belongs, Toniolo argued, one should distinguish what is necessary from what is contingent. He held that the principle of utility, upon which economics is based, belongs to the domain of the necessary, while all historical circumstances belong to that which is contingent. The latter may be contrary to nature, as in the case of slavery, for which the economic – although not moral – justification was attributable to the backward state of productive forces in antiquity, but in his view such reflections underlined that by fostering greater conformity between the economy and nature the Catholic Church had a relevant function through its teaching that the Useful must be always co-ordered with the Honest (ibid., p. 48). Thus he believed that since economics was a science of means, not of ends, the doctrinal order should be offset by the true domain of economics; namely the factual order, which is determined by the material and historical conditions of each people. Furthermore, as a science of the 'factual order', Toniolo's economics rejected not only the unbounded *laissez-faire* preached by Liberalist economists, but also the nationalism of the German Historical school, which he defined as intrinsically 'relativist' (for the Church, an altogether negative term) and as a by-product of the materialistic spirit that had spread throughout Europe since the time of Lutheran Reformation.

To conclude, Toniolo appears to have been not so much engaged in converting economists to Catholicism, as in convincing the Catholic faithful of the importance of economics (which, *qua* science, was to be regarded to some extent autonomous, although not independent, of faith). Overall, Toniolo can be seen as a highly active figure, a vigorous advocate of reforms in the field of the legislative protection of workers, and a promoter of a new Catholic labour law (see Spicciani 1997). He should also be remembered as a co-founder of the *Rivista internazionale di scienze sociali* and an inspirer of many other cultural initiatives.[13]

He was particularly influential in introducing economics into the political programmes of the Catholic movements – although it is probably too drastic to conclude that the European Welfare State was an almost-exclusive merit of the Catholics,[14] rather than (also) of the reformist socialists or the liberals on the left, *à la* Beveridge.

As is well known, Toniolo was – together with the prominent Jesuit priest Matteo Liberatore – among the inspirers of Leon XIII's encyclical *Rerum novarum* (1891), which opened the Church to the modern world's problems after the adverse experience of Pius IX. This may explain why numerous Catholic economists came to the forefront in the wake of Toniolo's teachings; emerging relatively unscathed from the Fascist dictatorship (once again, it should be borne in mind that they shared the Fascist corporative 'solution' to the issues of industrial relations), they were among the protagonists of the reconstruction after the Second World War. In this respect, Giuseppe Toniolo, both as a Catholic activist and as an economist, has left a much more enduring trace than many other celebrated scholars.

Achille Loria's ultra-Positivism

The season of success

During almost 20 years, from 1880 to 1900, the name of Achille Loria (of Mantua, 1857–1943) shone in the pale sky of Italian economics. His case is all the more remarkable, insomuch as his striking success was followed by a similarly dramatic eclipse. However, while Loria has a particular historical and intellectual context of his own, numerous factors underlying his success can be identified. At that time Italy suffered from what could be described as an inferiority complex towards the more advanced culture of Europe; thus the time was ripe for a thinker who could attract an international audience by proposing a personal, intriguing, view of the economy.

Loria entered the fray at the age of 23 with a mammoth volume bearing a mysterious title: *La rendita fondiaria e la sua elisione naturale*. This work presented a model of an economic system based on landed property, where land rent (both absolute and differential) was the fundamental income. His main argument was that in all past societies rent was destined to be 'elided' – that is to say, eliminated through its transformation into some other kind of income that was consequently redistributed to subjects other than *rentiers* – whereas in the capitalist societies of his time, rent was no longer elided but increased by the concomitance of other phenomena, first and foremost the monopolization of the economy, and was thus inexorably becoming indistinguishable from profit.[15]

It is not clear whether in Loria's system the passage from rent to profit is viewed as the outcome of a new alliance between industrial capitalists and landowners – as in Marx – or rather, the result of a struggle between these two categories – as in Ricardo. Be that as it may, the economic history of the West showed, Loria claimed, an intrinsic tendency of landed property to increase in dimension at the expense of small-sized property. Consequently, Loria's political message focused on defending small land tenures and/or encouraging the birth of cooperatives in agriculture, a defence to be accomplished by recourse to legislative action. Loria was opposed to land nationalization and criticized Henry George's proposal, as presented in his *Progress and Poverty* (1879), to elide rent by directly expropriating land.

Although some crucial assumptions of Loria's were seriously controversial – his central thesis that agricultural prices were rising compared to those of industry was not statistically proven – his basic argument that the conditions of agrarian production explained the main course of the Western economy, and that 'hunger for land' was the fundamental driving force of modern capitalism, rapidly gained popularity. In the US a group of historians, the so-called 'frontier' school, led by Frederick Turner, was influenced by Loria, whose work had been translated and circulated widely (see Benson 1950).

One of his books that presented state institutions as closely dependent on landed property, *La teoria economica della costituzione politica* (1886), was translated into French with the title *Les bases économiques de la constitution sociale* (1893), giving rise to a heated discussion in France. In Italy, many scholars of law hailed Loria's applications of economics to the legal system as a genuine breakthrough. A criminal law professor and leader of the Socialist Party, Enrico Ferri (1857–1929), depicted the legal system as entirely dominated by the capitalist structure of society, merging Darwin, Spencer, Marx and, of course, Loria, who he praised highly as a leading social scientist (see E. Ferri 1894: 39).

As well as his commitment to evolutionism and determinism in economics, Loria also tackled the task of confuting Karl Marx's 'solution' to the so-called transformation problem; that is to say, the transition from a system of values to a system of prices under capitalism. In an obituary of Karl Marx that he published in 1883, and even more explicitly in his *Analisi della proprietà capitalista* (1889), Loria pointed out that the action of the labour theory of value was seriously undermined by the theory of a uniform rate of profit, as calculated on the entire accumulated capital (both 'variable' and 'constant'). He thus attempted to determine the price of commodities as proportional to the quantities of labour required, plus the profit rate, by recourse to the concept of 'basic goods' – those goods that contribute to determination of the profit rate, and thereby, to determination of the exchange value of goods (Perri 2012: 646). In this sense Loria prefigured the more rigorous treatment of Marx's theory undertaken by Ladislaus von Bortkiewicz some years later, and more generally the twentieth-century debate on Marx's economic analysis.[16]

Loria was not shy of taking an outspoken position with regard to the main currents of marginal economics. He rejected the Austrian school's approach on account of its complete concentration on consumption and disinterest in distribution (see Loria 1890: 492); but he had considerable respect for Marshall and Edgeworth and from 1894 onwards he acted as the Italian correspondent of the British Economic Association (later on, Royal Economic Society) from Italy (see Marchionatti 1999: 305–28).

The season of critical assessments

Criticism of Loria developed in two main directions. Benedetto Croce, who at that time was interested in economics as a key to understanding history, found Loria's materialist interpretation of history exceedingly loose if not *naïve*. Where did the driving forces of society come from? Was the first principle of development based on: (a) population pressure over resources; (b) the struggle for land exploitation; (c) selfishness of the capitalist class, or all three together? Moreover Croce insinuated the suspicion that Loria's 'originality' was based on his skilful counterfeiting of Marx's theory in order to appropriate it more comprehensively (see Croce 2001 [1896], 54).

Another set of criticisms were more circumstantial. Given that rent is the outcome of land monopolization, how were the labourers to find the capital necessary to buy land, as Loria desired? Noting that capitalists preferred to leave their estates uncultivated rather than allow the workers to occupy them, Loria contended that such a manner of operating was anti-economical and could in no way be presented as 'natural' (see Conigliani 1903 [1899]: 170–5).

Another commentator observed that fighting for higher wages was a more attainable goal than fighting for some mysterious 'right to land' (see Valenti 1901: 67–8).

In contrast, no serious discussion was raised on the issue of Loria's critique of the Marxian theory of value. After all, the majority of economists agreed with Maffeo Pantaleoni's opinion that dealing with Marx was simply a waste of time, and comparing Marx with Loria – namely, an untrained economist with another untrained economist – made no sense at all. The result was the untimely demise of Marxian economics among Italian scholars.

From Lorianism to industrial policy: Nitti's evolution

Loria had only one disciple who surpassed him in terms of fame and honours received: Francesco Saverio Nitti (of Melfi, 1868–1953).[17]

Nitti was a bright young freelance journalist who, unlike Loria, succeeded in translating his economic intuitions into political programmes. In effect, the poor reception of Loria's sympathy towards cooperation in agriculture, which led to no specific party programme, contrasted with the response to Nitti's ideas on emigration as a remedy to surplus population in the South, as presented in his early work *Popolazione e il sistema sociale* (1894). The book was well received and prompted state-guided assistance for emigrants.

Another successful work by Nitti was his *Socialismo cattolico* (1891), published immediately before the *Rerum novarum* encyclical and shortly thereafter translated – between 1893 and 1895 – into Spanish, French and English. Here the background of Loria's reflections comparing the economic transformation of society with the evolution of theories and programmes was particularly evident. The expression 'Catholic socialism' was probably chosen to attract the curiosity of readers, because the actual contents of the book made it clear that modern

Catholicism presented many crucial differences from socialism. Nevertheless, Nitti envisaged a form of collaborative interaction between the two movements, inasmuch as both approaches showed a concern for social reform and improvement of working class conditions.[18]

In the second part of his life, Nitti abandoned sociological and ideological studies and reverted to more operative policy issues. In *Nord e Sud* (1900), attempting to counter the argument that the South had been the greatest beneficiary of unification, Nitti objected that the bulk of public works was still concentrated in the North while the fiscal pressure was comparatively higher in the South; and he noted that this had led to a considerable transfer of resources from the South to the North and not vice versa as uninformed public opinion was inclined to believe. Nitti's book spurred intense debate, and – after his election to Parliament (1904) – it became the basis for approving a special law for the industrialization of Naples.

From 1904 onwards, Nitti increasingly devoted himself to politics. As Industry Minister of Giolitti (1911–14), he promoted the establishment of the *Istituto nazionale delle assicurazioni* (INA), which was designed to provide a general system of insurance for workers through the monopoly of life insurance. During the war, as the head of the Treasury, he was able to keep inflation down, but in the early post-war years he headed a very fragile government and was compelled to resign. He was also an opponent of the spirit of the Treaty of Versailles, and agreed with Keynes's *Economic Consequences of the Peace*. Later, as an anti-Fascist, he moved to Switzerland in 1924 and subsequently to Paris, returning to Italy after the Second World War.[19]

Even though his scientific production was somewhat limited in comparison to his political writings, it is important to underline that he was the founder of *Riforma sociale* (launched in 1894), a journal which in the first ten years of life acted as a genuinely international tribune, with many prestigious contributors. Its models were likewise decidedly international – possibly *The Economic Journal* and *Revue d'économie politique*. During its first year, *Riforma* hosted articles by Gustav Schmoller, Achille Loria, Beatrice Webb and other renowned sociologists and historian-economists, while articles on pure theory did not form part of its mission and were thus not accepted. At the turn of the century Nitti's political commitment absorbed more and more of his time, so that the editorial position was left to Luigi Einaudi.[20]

The early revision of Marx's economics: Croce and Graziadei

In discussing Marx, Benedetto Croce (of Pescasseroli, 1866–1952) followed an approach that was quite peculiar. In his early years, Croce argued that Marx had the merit of dwelling upon the meaning of the related concepts of value and surplus value. The latter, Croce observed, was not an empirical-inductive concept but a mental-abstract construct that Marx drew from an 'elliptical comparison' between the *actual* capitalist system and an *ideal* society where there is only one productive factor, namely, pure labour – which corresponded to Adam

Smith's society of hunters of deer and beavers (*Wealth of Nations*, vol. I, Chapter VI). Stated in these terms, Marx's work did not concern economics in a proper sense, but rather could be defined as form of 'comparative sociology'.[21]

While Croce made no objection to Marx's general *methodological* premise, he rejected Marx's main *analytical* conclusion that involved the prediction of the general crisis of capitalism. In Marx's perspective, the capitalist system was destined to fail because the value of 'constant' (machinery) capital will increase more than the value of 'variable' (wage) capital, with the consequence that the rate of profit will decline despite any possible increase in the rate of labour exploitation, corresponding to labour productivity. On the other hand, Croce reasoned, since Marx himself did admit that constant capital can diminish in value owing to technical progress, the alleged 'law of the decreasing rate of profit' was undemonstrated.[22]

In the subsequent years Croce accentuated his critical attitude towards Marxism. He felt that Marx's methodology based on historical Materialism was heavily deterministic, no different from old-fashioned Positivism. Moreover, he rejected Marx's economics inasmuch as they appeared to be flawed by a false concept of value. Croce continued to maintain that a theory of value was still a crucial concept for any scientific economics, but he then rapidly embraced the subjective value theories in the Austrian version, which he praised while failing to realize it was incompatible with the classicist-Marxian approach. After his dispute with Pareto, he recognized that the 'new' economics had abandoned all interest in the definition of value, and – to alleviate his disappointment – he resolved to abandon any further reflection on economics (see the next chapter).

Antonio Graziadei (of Imola, 1873–1953) represented the kind of economist whose approach Croce could not share. Graziadei's early work, *La produzione capitalistica* (1899), tended to distinguish two aspects in Marx's personality – the value theorist, who he rejected, and the empirical researcher on capitalist development, who he praised. Graziadei's negative assessment of Marx as a value theorist was due to the latter's failure to take into consideration that the primary objective of any theory of value was to determine the exchange ratios among commodities. How, Graziadei wondered, could Marx conclude his treatment of the transformation problem by affirming that total values are equal to total prices? Marx was most certainly aware that the capitalist system accumulates and develops through technical progress and rapid improvement in the quality of capital – an improvement that can be measured in physical terms. In Graziadei's view, the Physiocrats' accounting criterion stated in terms of *quantities* should to some extent be considered as more appropriate than the classical-Marxian criterion stated in terms of *values*. Thus, instead of surplus value, Graziadei suggested, one should speak of surplus labour; namely, the excess of unpaid over paid labour. He believed that existence of such extra-labour was ascribable to the presence of non-competitive elements in the capitalist system, in particular a monopsony of the labour force, or an extra-price that the monopolist firms can obtain from the sale of their commodities. These aspects of Graziadei's work were influenced by the thought of Marshall.[23]

Concluding, Graziadei believed that the workers' movement should take the form of a *political* struggle for free trade instead of the old-fashioned and lesser *economic* class struggle. Yet despite this 'revisionist' attitude, Graziadei assumed a position favourable to the October revolution and was among the founders of the Communist Party of Italy. However, he was very soon expelled under the charge of 'right-wing deviationism'. During the Fascist dictatorship he was stripped of his chairship, but he was not deprived of his personal liberty and continued to write critical essays on Marxism (see Gattei 2012: 632–7).

It would be beyond the scope of this historical survey to provide an in-depth examination of the relationship between academic economics and socialism – the latter not necessarily identified with Marxism. If the characterization of an academic publication as 'socialist' is held to include all critical treatments of poverty, income distribution, crises and cooperation in agriculture, seen from the vantage point of their effects on social structure, then the borders of Italian 'socialist' economics would indeed be exceedingly far-reaching.[24]

Notes

1 See Ferrara (1875): 295–319, an open letter addressed to Senator Fedele Lampertico, who Ferrara accused of cultural nationalism.
2 On Pomba see Firpo (1976). The Pomba publishing house was transformed into UTET in 1854. See Bottasso (1990).
3 See Ferrara's introduction to the *Biblioteca dell'economista* edition of *Harmonies économiques:* Ferrara (1956) [1851]). Ferrara was personally acquainted with Carey, who he met when the American economist visited Turin in 1857. See Faucci (1995): 196.
4 See Marshall (1986) [1890]: 333.
5 From a recent study, it emerges that out of roughly 80 teachers of economic disciplines, inclusive of *ordinari* [full professors] and *incaricati* [senior lecturers] active in Italian universities during the nineteenth century, about ten had no publications at all in economics. See Augello (2012). Unfortunately, this reference book does not distinguish between the years before and after 1861.
6 In this sense it was a fulfilment of Cavour's legacy. See Caracciolo (1968), Chapter 1.
7 See Augello-Guidi (1988), in Augello *et al.* (eds) (1988): 335–84.
8 See Cossa (2000) [1880]. The original Macmillan edition was prefaced by Jevons: this was probably due to an exchange of favours, since Cossa had translated Jevons's *Primer* as early as 1879.
9 For a historical appraisal of the Welfare State's early steps in England, see D. Gladstone (1999).
10 Quoted by Pellanda (2003): 243.
11 See Jaffé (1965); Barucci (1972); Potier (1998).
12 For all the series of *Biblioteca*, see the essays by various authors in Augello and Guidi (2007).
13 See Vistalli (1954), Chapter XXVIIII; Bazzichi (2012): 68.
14 Negri Zamagni (2012): 728.
15 See the summary given by Loria (1891–92): 108–11.
16 On Loria's attempts to build up a 'classicist' theory of profits that would overcome the difficulties of Marx's transformation of values into prices, see Faucci and Perri (1995): 116–69; Samuelson (1997): 179–87; Faucci and Perri (2003): 203–38.
17 The acquaintance between Loria and Nitti is documented by Fiorot (1983).

18 Both works are included in Nitti (1971) [1891].
19 See his correspondence with and from Keynes, reproduced in VV. AA. (1983). For all these topics see VV. AA. (2011b).
20 See VV. AA. (2000); Bianchi (2007), especially Chapter 1.
21 See Croce (2001) [1897]: 67–118; see, among many other interpreters, Bellanca (1997): 73.
22 See Croce (2001) [1899]: 156.
23 See Gallegati (1982): 226–9.
24 See the rich, although somewhat heterogeneous, collection by Michelini and Guidi (2001).

6 Pure economics in Italy (1890–1920)

Introduction

The anti-historicist reaction

In a review of the economic studies in Italy written for an American journal, a member of the Historical school, Ugo Rabbeno (1863–97), admitted that the Austrian school had, in previous years, aroused some interest in Italy, but 'the new school seems still too young to attempt to bury the historical school alive – for this school has never been more alive' (Rabbeno 1891: 460).

Even more trenchantly, in that same year Achille Loria depicted the demise of the 'optimistic school' of Francesco Ferrara as the best proof of the emergence in Italy of a historical-critical and materialistic approach to economics (Loria 1891: 59–80).

Despite these self-confident statements, within no more than a few years the Historical school faded away and was definitively supplanted by the Marginal Utility school – although the latter is not necessarily to be identified with the Austrian school that goes by the same name. The season of the Marginal school in Italy had enormous reverberations abroad. Schumpeter (1994 [1954]: 855) stated that, although 'the most benevolent observer could not have paid any compliments to Italian economics in the early 1870s; the most malevolent observer could not have denied that it was second to none by 1914'.

The victory of the Marginal school in Italy coincided with its victory throughout the entire Western world. Carl Menger and his disciples in Austria, Léon Walras in the French-speaking world – William Stanley Jevons and Alfred Marshall in Britain, and John Bates Clark and Irving Fisher in the United States – came to the forefront of the scene and converted the new generation of economists to the new approach, which held that the relationship between individual subjects and the goods that can satisfy their wants occupies a central position. In their perspective, the two basic concepts are choice and equilibrium. All agents are called upon to choose – among final goods, according to their tastes, income and prices if they are consumers, or among productive factors according to the techniques, income and prices, if they are entrepreneurs – in order to maximize utility or profit, respectively. More generally, the process of reasoning in terms of measurable infinitesimal – indeed, 'marginal' – variations rather than in terms of average values, enabled the new school to devise a solution for many economic problems by considering them as problems of maximization under constraint. If economic agents, presumed to be rational, operate in a world dominated by scarcity of means, and are faced with a plurality of alternative ends, and no agent is endowed with market power, then economic equilibrium will automatically be reached. An analytical demonstration of the existence and stability of general equilibrium was still several decades away – it would not become available until the 1930s – but at a more intuitive level this result was accepted very early. What was true for a single agent was true for the entire system. Adam Smith's 'invisible hand' metaphor was established as the economic principle *par excellence*.

The analytical progress represented by the new school in comparison with the Classical school – and *a fortiori* in comparison with the Historical school that rejected analysis altogether – was evident. Economic phenomena were conceived as a set of functional relations among variables, and no longer of causal relations among quantities. The very idea of 'cause' in economics was rejected as metaphysical (Pareto).

However, what was gained in accuracy and rigour by virtue of the Marginal school was probably lost as regards realism, i.e. in understanding economic phenomena in their actual manifestation. 'Pure' economics intended to deal with the formal properties of an abstract system, which was based on a fiction: that of *homo oeconomicus*. As a consequence, the bridge between economics and the other social sciences, above all history and law, was broken forever. In fact, when Léon Walras strove to tackle a problem that included both institutional and normative aspects – the case for land nationalization – he was severely criticized by his strictest disciple, Vilfredo Pareto, who labelled him a 'thaumaturge', which, in Pareto's negative scale of assessment, ranked even worse than a utopian (see Pareto 1973, vol. II: 720).

The decision to limit the scope of economics to the theory of wants and exchange had the consequence that some of the main features of Western economy – the alternating of development and crises – were expelled from the agenda of 'respectable' economic studies, and left to sociologists, economic historians and statisticians (or even to sunspot watchers). Generally speaking, applied economics was considered as a descriptive region not worth exploring by a scientifically oriented economist.

The Italian way to marginal theory

On the other hand, the premises portending the advent of the Marginal school in Italy were numerous. Italian eighteenth-century economists were in the main subjectivists (since they regarded value as a mental judgement), hedonists (with the assumption that all humans seek maximum pleasure), and utilitarians (believing that the supreme aim is 'the maximum of happiness for the maximum number'). Admittedly, by the early nineteenth century the bulk of this tradition had been partially dispersed, but it was fairly effortlessly refreshed and presented in a new and more formally refined dress; from ethical hedonism to economic Marginalism it was but a short step. Only the more mature reflection carried out by Pareto would subsequently show that the theorems of economic equilibrium needed no hedonist premises, thereby paving the way to a more advanced season of marginal economics.

However, if compared to what was happening in other countries, the Italian school presented two special features. The first was positive, consisting in a more realistic approach to economics. Generally speaking, Italian marginal economists were aware of the significance of institutions in the economy. It was not merely by chance that numerous major figures among marginal economists were attracted by public finance, which allowed reflection on the nature of the State and the effects of public decisions as well, thereby offering a vantage point for political scientists. The Italian tradition of *scienza delle finanze* occupied a special position in Italian economics and gained widespread international consensus.

The second feature was, on the other hand, rather negative (with the proviso that 'positive' and 'negative' are objectionable terms if used to define the characters of scientific research!). It reflected the strong ideological bias that inspired the works of many Italian economists, in whose hands Marginalism was principally a weapon against their scientific and political adversaries, instead of being principally a 'box of tools' in Joan Robinson's sense (Schumpeter 1994: 15). This is particularly the case of Maffeo Pantaleoni, but Umberto Ricci and even Luigi Einaudi also followed this path. In these authors, Marginalism was presented as a quintessential outcome of liberal-individualist thought, in a strongly anti-reformist and anti-socialist version. In conclusion, Ferrara's teaching was relaunched with force.

From the point of view of the history of economics, the advent of Marginalism coincided with the start of Italian industrialization. It will suffice here to mention here the establishment of the Terni steelworks, the foundation of the Fiat car plant, and the birth of the Milan–Turin–Genoa 'industrial triangle',[1] with the concomitant conflicts between workers and employers, the foundation of the *Confederazione generale del lavoro* (CGL) trade union and, above all, the mass emigration towards North and South America. All this led to a fundamental transition from an agricultural, static society to an industrial, dynamic context, which led to the hard-fought, yet undisputed victory in the First World War.

Finally, it should be pointed out that Italian Marginalism had considerable resonance in the English-speaking world, although this acclaim was achieved many years after its heyday. Thanks to such scholars as Lionel Robbins and John Hicks at the London School of Economics, Pareto's definition and mathematical treatment of optimal equilibrium became widely known in Britain and later on passed into American economics, where its renown was enhanced through the interpretation of eminent scholars such as Henry Schultz and Paul Samuelson.[2]

But it should be noted that the other face of marginal utility economics – namely, Marshall's approach – also found numerous followers in Italy mainly (although not exclusively) among economists who were more open to empirical research. For instance, among those more akin to Marshall than to Pareto, one finds Pasquale Jannaccone, Antonio Graziadei and Guglielmo Masci.[3]

The Giornale degli economisti and its role

In the article by Rabbeno mentioned at the opening of this chapter, the author omitted to mention the creation (1890) of the *Giornale degli economisti*, which played a decisive role in the growing influence of marginal theory. The journal was the continuation of a Padua journal, founded in 1875 by the historicist economists, closed in 1878 and resurrected in Bologna in 1886 with an undefined programme. Four years later three young exponents of the new theories – Maffeo Pantaleoni, Ugo Mazzola and Antonio De Viti de Marco – assumed the co-editorship together with the former editor, Alberto Zorli, who was de facto set aside.

At the beginning, the idea was that of launching a periodical that would be engaged in politics as well as in economics. Pantaleoni wrote to Walras that the journal's aim was, first and foremost, that of 'supporting a policy that can save Italy from the forced circulation of money and in economics to fight against protectionism and socialism in all its forms' (Jaffè 1965, vol. II: 392).

Curiously enough, the theoretical aspects were left in the background: 'Pure science is not excluded – as Pantaleoni in 1890 wrote to a disciple of Ferrara's, Domenico Berardi – It is simply not at the forefront of attention' (Bilotti 1988: 25–6).

The *Giornale*'s political line was principally defined by its *Cronache*, political-economic comments that were authored in succession by Vilfredo Pareto (1891–97), Antonio De Viti de Marco (1897–99), and Francesco Papafava (1899–1909), the latter not a professional economist but a freelance journalist well-trained in economics as well. For these reasons the *Cronache* are still an invaluable source for any general historian of liberal Italy.

Effectively, there was a need *both* for a more pronounced economic liberalism after the undefined policies followed in Italy in the 1880s, *and* for a more rigorous form of economic reasoning, after the inconclusive logomachies of the *Methodenstreit*. These two different levels were clearly distinguished by Pantaleoni himself, in a letter to Berardi in which he clarified his previous assumptions:

> I am very happy that, from the practical point of view, both of us are involved in the defence of freedom. We must [nevertheless] observe that any practical action departs from the field of pure science. I myself at times wrongly confused the two things.... Science studies only the relationships between things, the uniformities of facts, and is not a faith that prompts us to make proselytes. In all sciences the boundaries distinguishing them from art are blurred at the beginning; for this reason, economic science at its beginning was regarded as economic art; but now it is time for science and art each to stand alone and go their separate ways.
>
> (in Bilotti 1988: 147–8)

In 1910 the *Giornale* merged with *Rivista di Statistica*, edited by A. Beneduce and G. Mortara, adding the name of this latter journal to its own. Its scientific line remained unchanged.

Pantaleoni's personality and research programme

An unquiet spirit

In spite of the fact that the secondary literature on Pantaleoni is very extensive,[4] no comprehensive intellectual biography on this major figure is available. This is a serious omission, probably due to an approach that awards greater importance to analysing circumscribed 'technical' aspects, than to reconstructing the entire personality of past economists within their cultural and material context.

As a scientist, Pantaleoni (of Frascati near Rome, 1857–1924) corresponded as an equal with some of the greatest economists of his time. At 27, still a young lecturer at the small University of Camerino, he established contact with Léon Walras, engaging him in a debate by letter on the subject of the Austrian school and the use of mathematics in economics. When, in 1889, Pantaleoni published his book *Principii di economia pura*, Walras dwelt on the work at length in an extended commentary (Jaffé 1965, vol. II: 337–8).

In the 1880s Pantaleoni entered into correspondence with Alfred Marshall, who allowed him to utilize some diagrams taken from the papers the British economist had arranged to have printed privately in 1879, on *The Pure Theory of Foreign Trade* and *The Pure Theory of Domestic Values*. Marshall admired Pantaleoni; writing to John Neville Keynes in 1889, he stated that he considered Pantaleoni as having 'much truer mathematical instincts than Jevons, Walras, Launhardt & Co' (Whitaker 1996, vol. I: 283).

In 1890 Pantaleoni met Pareto and initiated a long-life dialogue with him. A year later he introduced Pareto to Walras, who in 1892 nominated Pareto as his successor in Lausanne. The Pantaleoni-Pareto correspondence (unfortunately, only the Pareto side has survived) is one of the most important in the history of economics.

A passionate researcher, Pantaleoni was a master and teacher of extreme severity and rigour, and he was instrumental in the renewal of Italian university teaching staff in economics. In a dramatic pen-picture, his successor in the Rome University chair, Umberto Ricci, described him as 'the archangel with flaming sword, who burst onto the scene to make short shrift of all false schools and proclaimed pure economics as sovereign' (Ricci 1939 [1925]: 44).

Pantaleoni also wrote extensively in the daily press and non-specialized journals. Until 1900 he preferred to contribute to left-wing newspapers, such as the democratic *Il Secolo* and the socialist *Avanti!* In the closing years of the nineteenth century, Pantaleoni stood up for the socialists and the other left-wing democrats who were imprisoned by the reactionary government of the time. At the turn of the century, however, when the new Centre-Left Giolitti cabinet began to favour the lower class in comparison with the other classes,

Pantaleoni's perspective changed and he gradually shifted towards conservative positions. Between 1917 and 1922 five collections of his articles that had appeared in an extreme right journal, *La vita italiana*, were published by G. Laterza. In 1922 he approved of Mussolini's rise to power and was rewarded with appointment as life-long Senator of the Kingdom of Italy.

As a social scientist, Pantaleoni was a 'purist' in a rather idiosyncratic manner. Although firmly maintaining his Marginal school creed, he sought to remedy the main limits of this approach, which was confined to statics. He therefore chose to investigate all the factors of dynamism, such as crises and instability, which had received no adequate treatment in the studies by the main spokesmen of general equilibrium: Walras and Pareto. In following this research programme, Pantaleoni was helped by his marked versatility. Working in an era of increasing specialization, Pantaleoni was one of the last 'masters of economics', interpreted in the sense of a global science. He wrote on public finance, statistics, economic history and methodology of the history of economics, as well as on credit, banking and the economics of cooperation. His openmindedness enabled him to penetrate the complexity of social problems and to grasp their essence.

While not necessarily resulting in a dispersion of his energy, Pantaleoni's openness and intellectual curiosity may have led him to something akin to an intellectual uneasiness in dealing at length with a given subject. Thus, in reading Pantaleoni's work, one senses that no sooner has the author competently settled the main point of an issue he is then seized by the desire to pass on rapidly to another topic. In this respect Pantaleoni is the exact opposite of Pareto, who was eminently a system-builder. However, this feature by no means implies that Pantaleoni's research project failed to be intrinsically coherent and unitary. As Gustavo Del Vecchio has written, his work must be considered as 'original, fragmentary in its form, organic in its content' (Del Vecchio 1925: 114).

Pantaleoni and Pareto: affinities and divergences

Pantaleoni and Pareto present many affinities, above all as far as *Weltanschauung* was concerned. Both thinkers were conservative liberals, alarmed by the fact that the dramatic surge of the uncultivated (working) 'masses' into political life could disrupt the social equilibrium that the bourgeois class had forged in the previous century. The young Pantaleoni had hoped that education of the masses could be achieved via a market-oriented socialist force (see Michelini 1998, Chapter III). But he was soon disenchanted, since the socialists preferred to advocate legislative protection for the workers at the expense of society as a whole. Pantaleoni considered socialism, *qua* movement in defence of the weakest classes, as intrinsically unable to grasp the positive values of natural selection through free competition and social improvement. On the contrary, he felt that the ideals of mutuality and solidarity espoused by socialists hindered the ideals of self-help and individual ascent, which he saw as the true driving forces of progress.

A major difference between Pantaleoni and Pareto pertains to their respective views on the future of bourgeois society. While Pantaleoni foresaw that the bourgeoisie as a whole, *qua* social class, would defeat the proletariat as a whole, Pareto was endeavouring to build up a more detailed study of the various components of bourgeoisie. Pareto's aim was to show that any class conflict stated in simplistic Marxian terms of radical polarization was no longer conceivable, and a more complex system of alliance between separate segments of the bourgeoisie and the proletariat was at work in Europe. Pareto's theory of élites was based on this preliminary factual consideration, and was considerably more realistic than Pantaleoni's monolithic vision of class struggle.

As far as pure theory is concerned, Pantaleoni did not subscribe to Pareto's general economic equilibrium. But it would be superficial to suggest that Pantaleoni was not as well trained in mathematics as would have been necessary in order to manage the general equilibrium equations. A more convincing explanation is that his scientific curiosity prompted him to investigate those very topics that are traditionally outside the general equilibrium approach – such as technical change and consumers' changing tastes. In this perspective, Pantaleoni felt somewhat closer to Alfred Marshall, who in his *Principles of Economics* (1890) presented a qualitative and quantitative analysis of the factors of economic progress. Indeed, both Pantaleoni and Marshall believed in social Darwinism and in hedonism-utilitarianism as driving forces of human improvement; whereas Pareto considered these as mere relics of old philosophic creeds.

It is certainly true that Pantaleoni and Pareto both considered the relationship between economics and sociology as crucial. But while Pareto held that economics and sociology have different objects of investigation – insofar as they are related, respectively, to 'logical' and 'non-logical' actions – Pantaleoni argued that sociology and economics converged into a single social science.

The Principii

As was briefly mentioned earlier, Marginalism in Italy was linked to the eighteenth-century tradition in economics. Pantaleoni underlined this legacy in his early work, *Principii di economia pura* (1889). From the very first pages of the book, Pantaleoni faced a fundamental issue; once hedonism has been acknowledged as a basis for human (economic) behaviour, is it possible to compare the pleasures and pains of different subjects?

Bentham's utilitarianism gave an affirmative answer to this question. The British thinker had classified pleasures and pains according to the following circumstances, which influence their value: (1) intensity; (2) duration; (3) probability/uncertainty; (4) proximity/distance in time; (5) fecundity, or probability that a sensation of the same kind will follow; (6) purity, or probability that a sensation of the opposite type will follow; (7) extension of the same sensation to other individuals. Pantaleoni accepted Bentham's table, enriching it with Gossen's law of the optimal distribution of pleasures. He therefore appeared both as a utilitarian and as a hedonist (see Pantaleoni 1931 [1889]: 19, 37–9).

Most attracted by Edgeworth's distinction between individual and universal hedonism, Pantaleoni observed that there is a fundamental difference between the two kinds of hedonism. The former allows for comparisons that are not difficult to make, insofar as they regard the same subject, while the latter allows for interpersonal – or even international – comparisons that have a broad margin of error (Pantaleoni: 40). Meditation on this latter kind of hedonism was to become a crucial part of Pantaleoni's life-long scientific research programme.

Subsequently, Pantaleoni introduced the concept of wants, directly dependent on the existence of an unpleasant feeling one wishes to eliminate, or on the existence of a pleasant feeling one wishes to maintain and enhance. To describe this field of enquiry, he devised the term 'hedonimetrics', which referred to the transformation of psychological wants into quantities of goods. Since, in his frame work, the essence of goods is to provide utility, he regarded the distinction between material and immaterial goods as irrelevant.

Value in exchange, which he defined as 'an abstract relation between two quantities of two goods', was represented graphically as the angular coefficient that measures the ratio between the two goods that are being compared (ibid., p. 168). Pantaleoni highlighted that the transition from the Ricardian theory of comparative costs, to the theory of exchange based on a difference between utilities, was altogether natural, since the comparison involves the same subject. On the other hand, the comparison cannot regard the utilities of two different subjects that are not comparable (ibid., p. 177).

The general conclusion is that there is no fundamental difference between classical cost theory and marginal utility theory. The latter is simply a more 'modern' version of the former (ibid., p. 234).

The second part of *Principii di economia pura* deals with the application of the 'new' value theory to special categories of goods; namely, productive factors and money.

Although the book was translated into English (1898), Pantaleoni already considered it as old-fashioned, especially after Marshall's *Principles* (1890) and Pareto's *Cours* (1896). Accordingly, after a reprint in Italian in 1894, he dismissed the idea of providing a revised edition.

Economics and sociology

Pantaleoni accepted the theory of general economic equilibrium as a first approximation to economic reality, dominated as it is by factors of change and conflict. Again, his vision of economic competition was very different from that implicit in the general equilibrium approach; rather, it tends to recall the Darwinian selection process.

In 1898, in an article published in English (Pantaleoni 1898: 183–205), Pantaleoni started by arguing that sociology is 'a theory of social struggles'. He felt that most of the relationships defined as 'economic' are not of a contractual nature as they do not assume a perfect equality of position between the exchangers. Instead they belong either to a 'predatory' type – e.g. big business versus small business – or to a 'parasitic' type – e.g. landlord versus farmer – or else to a 'mutual' type. The latter type of relationship, implying some sort of cooperation between two parties whose rights and duties are not clearly fixed, was to become increasingly widespread in democratic societies, but in Pantaleoni's view it was intrinsically unstable. He believed that the difference between such relationships and those commonly observed in the economic sphere resided in the fact that an interpersonal comparison cannot be made in economics, since there is no bridge between the utility evaluation made by A and that made by B (all individuals are their own best judge). On the other hand, outside the confines of economics all utility comparisons can be made directly by the parties involved (everybody can be a fairly good judge of others), and consequently a judgement concerning 'strength' and 'weakness' raises no difficulties because there exists a common standard. In economics, a similar result can be reached indirectly, namely, through reference to the consumer's surplus; all consumers who maximize their own surplus are 'strong'.

> A contract is possible, only if either parity of strength exists, or … disparity is not known to exist…. If there is a stronger unit, who knows his strength, he will not enter into a contractual process but make use of his strength.
> (Pantaleoni 1898: 205; see also the Italian version, Pantaleoni 1925b, vol. I: 358)

It is the lack of knowledge – the veil of ignorance, as John Rawls would put it – that allows contractual, and therefore purely economic, relationships.

In Pantaleoni's essay *Nota sui caratteri delle posizioni iniziali e sull'influenza che le posizioni iniziali esercitano sulle terminali* (1901) alterations are induced into competition not by different levels of knowledge, but by the influence of temporal and institutional elements. Unlike a horse race, where the initial and final positions are predetermined by fixed rules, in all economic competitions a continuous shift both of initial as well as final positions is observed. Indeed, a shifting of the former positions *produces* a shift of the latter. The conclusion of the essay is a negative appraisal – in terms of costs and general inefficiency – of the efforts made by socialism to equalize the starting positions.

In defining the nature of economic behaviour, Pantaleoni's position was far-removed from that of Pareto. As will be seen below, Pareto assigned to economics the study of logical (rational) modes of behaviour, in the sense of the congruity between ends and means; and to sociology the study of non-logical conducts, regarded as devoid of this congruity yet perfectly adequate to reach some goal (for example, obtaining victory at the polls). In his essay *L'atto economico* (1913) Pantaleoni dissented from Pareto's distinction, and presented many instances of actions that are certainly logical, but not economic in the proper sense. It would thus appear that Pantaleoni had a different concept of 'logical actions', identifying them with all repetitive and statistically testable actions. This implied that animals would be 'logical' (and therefore 'rational' as well), a conclusion that Pareto – and not only Pareto! – would not be willing to admit.

Economics versus politics

In his essay *Di alcuni fenomeni di dinamica economica* (1907–09), Pantaleoni acutely defined statics as a special case of economic dynamics.[5] In his framework, dynamic movements must be distinguished into: (1) those which allow the system to return to the former equilibrium position; (2) those which bring the system into a new equilibrium position; (3) those which open the way to further disequilibria. He maintained that free competitive equilibrium is static, while monopolistic equilibrium is 'pregnant with dynamism'; furthermore, statics itself, taken as the expression of perfect competition, is none other than the result of a balance among conflicting forces. This *bellum omnium contra omnes* produces equilibrium. In monopoly, equilibrium is the outcome of a violence perpetrated by one against all; for this reason, Pantaleoni argued, monopolist situations cannot endure over time.

Pantaleoni was mainly interested in analysing the (3) factors, which tend to divert the system away from equilibrium. Among these factors he underscored those which are derived from a rise in 'general', or overhead, costs, as compared to variable and 'specific' costs, noting that this rising trend depended on the increasing size of firms. The errors that may derive from an inaccurate market evaluation lead to disequilibria and their effects are irreversible.

Expanding on this theme, Pantaleoni highlighted the tendency of modern society to adopt institutions that result in the introduction of more and more rigid elements, and he pointed out that even these alterations could be assimilated to increasing overhead costs. In foreseeing the fatal trend towards increasing rigidity of the system, Pantaleoni's pessimism was absolute, and to some extent preceded Schumpeter's dark prophecies on the future of capitalism put forward in *Capitalism, Socialism and Democracy* (1942), and in *The March into Socialism* (1949).

In such a context, Pantaleoni continued, the economic sphere tended to be reduced in favour of the political sphere – and also of the 'sexual' sphere, through a redistribution of power in society from males to females, the latter being considered as prompted by sheer instinct, vague sentimentalism and therefore impenetrable to reason (and, of course, to economics). In the same span of time the Italian Nationalist Manifesto (1910) expressed an attitude of virulent anti-feminism, partially transmitted to Fascist ideology. Pantaleoni shared the entire Nationalist programme – protectionism aside – and on many occasions depicted the female gender as invincibly dominated by irrational impulses. Pareto, probably distressed by his bitter personal experience as an abandoned husband – his wife, a Russian aristocrat, ran away with a servant – likewise indulged in many anti-feminist platitudes.

Another powerful source of disequilibrium was the growth of the state sector that led to political prices fixed by the public authority beyond the confines of the market (Pantaleoni 1919 (1911): 1–53).

In opposition to these negative factors, Pantaleoni called attention to other countervailing and, in his view, quite positive forces he noted in his observation of the trends of the economy. He extolled the 'new countries' – such as the US, Argentina and Canada – which were far from being textbook cases of the law of decreasing returns. The argument he adduced as the main reason for the rapid progress of those countries was that

> in the new countries all technical innovations, all instruments in agriculture *as well as in political systems* [italics added] are always of the latest model, without any prior expenditure on the everlasting series of tests that were necessary in the old countries to reach the same results.
>
> (Pantaleoni 1925 [1907–09], vol. II: 124)

Once more foreshadowing Schumpeter, Pantaleoni was relatively unconcerned about the eventuality that industries with decreasing costs could develop into monopolies. He adopted a similar approach in the essay *Definizione dell'economia* (1913), which investigated the possible threats to free competition. His underlying fear was that the rule of optimal resource allocation and consequent income distribution according to the marginal productivity of factors was being undermined by the popular masses who, through the universal franchise (introduced in Italy in 1912, albeit for adult males only), had become politically powerful and, as he saw it, were pursuing the one and only aim of gaining 'parasitic' incomes at the expense of the whole community. In the same year he branded justice (in the sense of equity) in economics as 'an abstract concept, *technically*, namely, *logically* false' (Pantaleoni 1925 [1913], vol. I: 124). The scepticism he expressed in this concept can be seen as presaging Hayek's well-known attitude against the 'myth of social justice'.

Finance and statistics

In Italy pure economics allowed the theory of public finance to free itself from the excessive burden of law in favour of an approach based on economic reasoning.

Pantaleoni's essay *Contributo alla teoria del riparto delle spese pubbliche* (1883) represented a pioneering attempt to extend the application of the hedonistic calculus, particularly Gossen's law of the equality of weighted marginal utilities as a condition for the consumer's equilibrium, in order to provide a guideline for the allocation of money among the different items of expenditure in the state budget. Parliament, *qua* rational consumer, was called upon to allocate its receipts by taking into account: (1) the intrinsic utility of the expenditure; (2) the utility of the same expenditure as compared to other possible items. When he wrote this paper, Pantaleoni was still optimistic that 'the Parliament's average intelligence' could be taken as a reliable proxy of individual choice. In subsequent years he rapidly abandoned this hope.

Another essay, *Cenni sul concetto di massimi edonistici individuali e collettivi* (1891, written with A. Bertolini) dealt with the definition of private and public wants. Three classes of hedonic maxima needed a (minimum) sacrifice of other wants: (1) if a sacrifice involved individual wants (and did not affect other people), then this was a case of individual maxima; (2) if a sacrifice were imposed on the entire population, this could be construed as a case of collective maxima; (3) finally, if a sacrifice were imposed on one group of people against another, the calculation would be far more difficult, because there is no 'collective sensory organ' in nature (Pantaleoni (1925) [1891], vol. II: 15) capable of directly measuring and comparing losses and gains of pleasure. However, Pantaleoni remained confident that some solution would be reached, provided that the entire community's sacrifice was minimal.

The same issues were touched upon in an essay which, prima facie, was extraneous to these topics. In *Delle regioni d'Italia in ordine alla loro ricchezza e al loro sistema tributario* (1891) the starting point also was the concept of a collective hedonist maximum and the difficulties of linking it to other 'sectional' or relative and more circumscribed collective maxima, as could be seen with regard to the various Italian regions if compared to the entire nation's collective maximum.

Pantaleoni shared the Benthamite principle of the 'maximum of happiness for the maximum number' as the highest goal.[6] Consequently, regional maxima necessarily had to be sacrificed to the largest maximum represented by the national interest. In this context, what Pantaleoni had in mind was a pyramidal succession of optima, from the lowest to the highest, whereby sacrifices would be borne by 'local' hedonist maxima in order to reach the nation's *maximum maximorum*.

The theory of banks' bailouts

The 250-page long study on the fall of the *Credito mobiliare* has been considered a classic of quantitative and institutional economic history applied to the phenomenology of a banking institution of the Pereire type, which principally dealt in bonds issued by state and public utilities. Pantaleoni distinguished between bank losses that can no longer be recovered, and immobilizations that can still give a return albeit in the long term. This latter type of operation justified the bank being bailed out. 'The history of losses is the history of human decline, the history of immobilizations is the history of human progress', Pantaleoni emphatically claimed (Pantaleoni 1936 [1895]: 348).

But who was entitled, and according to what perspective, to salvage the bank? Pantaleoni observed that all bailouts were performed by appealing to the 'public interest'. But he also noted that an ostensible public interest, if confined to the interests of the shareholders or of another consortium of men involved, could hardly be considered as 'public'. Consequently, there would be no alternative to acknowledging the political class as representative of the 'public interest', in which case, however, the inevitable result is that the entire nation would be saddled with the burden of salvaging the costs. Therefore Pantaleoni's position was that only the private sector must bear the burden. Moreover, the Bank of Italy should not be made to bear the burden of any bank rescue operation through additional liquidity.

Another essay concerns the 'mixed banks' according to the German model; namely, the institutions that provided mid-term credit to industry. The article was written in 1915, on the eve of the war, and was included in a book written by a disciple of Pantaleoni's who denounced the German economic penetration into Italy, held to have come about mainly through Jewish bankers (in particular, Giuseppe Toeplitz's Banca Commerciale).[7]

Pantaleoni proposed that such banks should have a special juridical regulation, and should never be allowed to use their clients' deposits for loans to industry, but rather should resort exclusively to their own capital (Pantaleoni 1936 [1915]: 473).

Finally, it is worth recalling Pantaleoni's address to the International Conference on Saving (Milan, October 1924) – his last speech before his sudden death – in which he evoked the historical origins of the savings banks as 'the poor man's moneybox'. He argued that the greatest savings banks, like the Milanese *Cassa di risparmio delle province lombarde*, should act as business banks, by investing in company shares rather than in debentures and state bonds. Similarly to Schumpeter, Pantaleoni concluded that the greater part of new capital did not derive from past saving, but from innovations – a concept which in his view socialists were, and always would be, unable to understand (Pantaleoni 1936 [1924]: 520).

Pantaleoni and 'economic dogma'

Pantaleoni concerned himself with 'economic dogma' in the inaugural lecture for his economics course in Geneva in two successive years. This may explain his exceedingly assertive manner. The first of these lectures opened with the shocking statement that there are just two schools of economics; that of those who know economics, and that of those who don't (Pantaleoni 1925 [1897], vol. I: 158).

Despite its ultimate tone, Pantaleoni's statement was not unremittingly categorical. In the same inaugural address he also admitted a modicum of methodological pluralism: 'Ideas resemble keys; each of them opens only a small number of doors.... Today nobody is entitled to reject the use of any logical method' (ibid., p. 161). The choice of one particular scientific tool rather than another was to be justified by the type of scientific demand.

On other matters, Pantaleoni was convinced that economics advances through increasing additions 'at the margin', not through cataclysmic disruptions or revolutions. He drew a comparison with a *boule de neige* that swells as it rolls down to the valley. This simile was in agreement with his view of continuity between classical political economy and Marginalism that inspired his *Principii*.

The second essay on the same subject focused on a comparison between the task of the historian of economics, and that of the statistician. Statistical interpolation, Pantaleoni acutely observed, restricts the domain of controversy, but increases the risk of self-deception. In contrast, abstaining from interpolation does make it possible to 'respect' history, but risks missing its meaning. Both approaches are to be deemed as acceptable ways of charting the history of economics, but there is a third way that is indeed altogether wrong, in the sense that it explains nothing at all. Pantaleoni dubbed this third route 'mesological' because it aims to explain economic theories through a generic reference to the 'social environment'. He objected that the environment per se produced no direct demand for scientific products, but at most an indirect demand for the latter through a direct demand for practical policy measures. 'The result of inquiry', namely, scientific theory, 'is independent of the environment' (Pantaleoni 1925a [1898]: vol. I: 234).

On the other hand, Pantaleoni equated the work of a clever historian of economic thought to that of a geologist who succeeds in finding traces and sediments of dead doctrines in doctrines that are still current. To some extent, Pantaleoni possibly foreshadowed Michel Foucault's idea of research as 'archaeology of knowledge', which is very far from a dogmatic approach to truth.

We are in the habit – Pantaleoni observed, to some extent reopening the whole discussion – of considering as 'classics' only the orthodox economists; namely, economists who operate in the mainstream, and for whom the mainstream represents the truth. But if the object of economic science were to undergo a sudden change, and those who today are considered as heretics were to be considered as the new orthodoxy, the entire situation would be different, and this could occur if, instead of equilibrium, value were again at the centre of economics. Here, as in other parts of his work, Pantaleoni reached a conclusion that is somewhat 'weaker' and more problematic than his general statements.

The Pantaleoni school

Even though Pantaleoni considered economic schools as 'syndicates of imbeciles', his scientific example had several followers, not only among conservative economists, but also among liberal and even leftist thinkers as well. In this context it is interesting to single out an economist who could be genuinely considered as a 'Marginal-socialist' in the proper sense – Enrico Leone (1875–1940),[8] a peculiar character of Marginal-socialist thinking, and author of two books: *La revisione del marxismo* (1909) and *L'economia edonistica* (1910). Leone's main (or unique?) contribution to economics was the concept of *plus-marginalità*; namely, an alternative explanation of the origin of the Marxian surplus value by reference to the monopsony of the labour force. This allows capitalists to pay wages that are lower than the marginal productivity of labour and therefore to appropriate unpaid work (see Santarelli 1982).

Vilfredo Pareto

Pareto's engagement in his early years

Nine years senior to Pantaleoni, Marquis Vilfredo Pareto (Paris, 1848–1923), from a patriotic Genoese family in exile, approached economics in his forties, after participating in the battles waged by the Florentine liberals, who had their own journal, *L'economista*, their own political association, the *Società Adamo Smith*, and their own learned society, the *Accademia dei Georgofili*. An engineer, Pareto was a manager in an ironworks factory (see Busino 1977), and was a regular visitor at the Peruzzi salon (Ubaldino Peruzzi had been Interior Minister before becoming Lord Mayor of Florence), where he had the opportunity of meeting, *inter alios*, such renowned novelists as Edmondo De Amicis and philologists such as Domenico Comparetti.

Pareto's writings in the Florentine period mainly concerned politics, but they already display a well-defined model of thinking. Somewhat similarly to the work of Ferrara, in Pareto's thought the *leitmotiv* was represented by the theory-praxis nexus. Against the historicist and statist economists, who accused liberal thinkers of being too abstract, Pareto maintained that without theory there could be no adequate praxis, so that so-called 'practical men' who despised theory achieved poor results in their capacity as practical men as well.

The political debate in the 1880s mainly centred around the effects of tariff protection on the entire economy. Pareto observed that as a result of protection Italy failed to benefit from the international division of labour because no effort was made to exploit her comparative advantages (mainly concentrated in agriculture). Thus, the 1880s were years of stagnation. While the national income was decreasing and fiscal pressure was increasing, state expenditure – Pareto pointed out – produced a redistribution of wealth from the 'undefended classes' of entrepreneurs and workers in the market-oriented sectors (silk, wine and oil) to those that enjoyed privileges (corn and cotton) deriving from tariffs and other political advantages.

In the 1890s Pareto also manifested solidarity towards the socialist leaders who were imprisoned and treated as public enemies. He believed they should be recognized as having the merit of denouncing the *scandali bancari* [banking mismanagements], rising expenditure on the army, and colonial expansion. In a *Cronaca* written for *Giornale degli economisti* in 1895, Pareto maintained that socialism, although erroneous from the point of view of pure economics, 'approximated to the truth' from the point of view of sociology, for it expressed the proletariat's effort to become the leading class in Italy by replacing an exhausted bourgeoisie (see Pareto 1965b: 334).

Pareto was never a Marxist. But in contrast to Pantaleoni, who repeatedly declared his lack of esteem for Marx as a thinker, Pareto read Marx quite carefully and wrote a preface to a selection from *Capital* edited by Paul Lafargue (see Pareto 1894 [1893]). Moreover, while Pareto wholly rejected the labour theory of value, he adopted a respectful attitude towards Marx's materialist approach to history (Pareto 1966: 356). Politically speaking, in his forties Pareto was a liberal on the left. In the same years he participated in the movement for international disarmament led by Ernesto T. Moneta, later (1907) a Nobel Prize-winner for peace.

Pareto's change of mind

In the early years of the new century, Pareto's political attitude changed. Para-doxically, soon after the victory of the liberal-progressive forces he had sup-ported up to that time, Pareto began to manifest a more pessimistic outlook with regard to future trends. In his view, the new course of the parliamentary alliance between the more moderate wing of the Socialist Party (the reformists led by Filippo Turati) and the progressive Liberals led by Prime Minister Giovanni Giolitti was little more than a mediocre compromise which, on the one hand, sanctioned the 'death of socialism' as an original movement (this was also Bene-detto Croce's opinion) and, on the other, signalled the demise of the original bourgeois ideals of improvement through competition.

The manifesto of the 'new' Pareto view was probably the magmatic essay *Un'applicazione di teorie sociologiche* (1900), where he surveyed the factors he regarded as having jointly contributed to impairing the original spirit of the leading classes in the West over the centuries – from ancient Rome depressed by Christian mysticism, to modern France shaken by the Dreyfus case – in an appraisal that showed a decidedly conservative, if not reactionary, vision of the course of European history.

But the underlying focus of Pareto's attention was not so much the actual historical process of transformation as, rather, the transformations affecting the ruling classes in Europe. He construed the whole nineteenth-century *sub specie* of the internal struggle between the two main sections of the bourgeoisie in their attempt to acquire a hegemonic position in society:

> The most advanced countries are those in which the two components of the bourgeoisie are present in a particular proportion.... When one component becomes preponderant, the country suffers – politically, whenever specula-tors prevail; economically, in the case of the predominance of *rentiers*.
>
> (Pareto 1966 [1911]: 475)

At present, Pareto maintained, in Western Europe the trend was leaning towards speculators.

Pareto's insightful analysis allowed him to foresee the transformations of the economy arising from the increasing importance of financial activities in the economic system worldwide. On the other hand, he failed to grasp the formid-able improvement in techniques and productive capacities that were an outcome of the Second Industrial Revolution. It may be surprising that, trained engineer as he was, and with past experience as the manager of a firm, Pareto manifested no special interest in phenomena that other contemporary observers (Frederick W. Taylor wrote his *Scientific organization of labour* in 1911) had been able to describe and analyse.

Moreover, the years from 1900–14 were not only characterized by technical progress, but also by industrial reorganization through cartels, trusts, and the general practice of dumping. Although several Italian economists took great interest in these phenomena, Pareto devoted little attention to an analysis of the effects of economic change on the existing social classes, preferring to give free rein to bitter invective bewailing the decline of the traditional ruling classes (in his vocabulary, 'aristocracies'). These considerations inevitably seemed to point to a deep regret for the inevitable decline of the old aristocracies rather than a penetrating analysis of the actual economic factors that had led to the new situation.

Strongly distrustful of the decadent leading classes of his age, and a die-hard adversary of any collaboration between socialists and moderates, Pareto began to sympathize with some non-mainstream heterodox intellectuals. Before the war he praised Georges Sorel, whose *Réflexions sur la violence* (1908) influenced many left-wing socialists of the time – first and foremost young Benito Mussolini – on account of its eulogy of *will* over *necessity* (that is to say, revolutionary versus gradualist-reformist action). Rapidly, however, Pareto followed his friend Pantaleoni and turned to the Nationalists. At least one point was common to revolutionary socialists and reactionary Nationalists: the cult (or myth) of violence as the 'sole matrix of history'. Furthermore the Nationalists, in Pareto's view, had the merit of incarnating the *rentiers* (of agrarian origin) who opposed the *spéculateurs* (of financial origin). In the end, Pareto wholly shared the Nationalists' critical attitude towards the enervated bourgeoisie.

In contrast to Pantaleoni, however, Pareto abstained from taking active part in the war propaganda and was substantially a neutralist. This attitude *super partes* can be partially explained by the fact that he had been living in Switzerland since 1893, as a professor of economics at the University of Lausanne. After the First World War, Pareto was struck by the virulence of the class conflict. In this context, Pareto displayed, so to speak, a split personality. As a scientist, he undertook the task of collecting evidence of the passing of power from the bourgeoisie to the proletarian élite. As a die-hard conservative, he felt an instinctive rejection of all riots and other manifestations of popular unrest. Nevertheless, he remained fundamentally a moderate liberal. In his last article, '*Libertà*' (July 1923), published in the Fascist journal *Gerarchia*, he warned the Fascist government that excessive repression would unleash a counterproductive backlash, and respect should be shown for the traditional (individual) liberties, principally of the press, teaching and worship.

Pure economics and pure sociology

Vilfredo Pareto was both a great economist and a great sociologist. That one and the same thinker mastered to the same (high) level two disciplines which, although presenting some affinities, are undeniably different, is perhaps a unique case in the history of modern social sciences. The founders of modern sociology, Comte, Spencer and Durkheim, were no economists; the founders of modern economics, Jevons, Menger and Walras, were no sociologists. Pareto mastered both fields of research.

It would be trivial to explain this feature merely by invoking his powerful mind. If he felt motivated to cultivate economics and sociology in parallel, the reason should be sought in his unitary conception of the social sciences. Such an attitude was certainly favoured by the late nineteenth-century cultural climate, which was imbued with scientism and strove to trace all the regularities that could be found in human behaviour. In short, there was a widespread belief that social disciplines should be treated as 'logical-experimental' sciences, by virtue of which they would become accessible to definition, measurement and empirical testing.

In this effort to build up a solid general theory of society, Pareto was helped by his great curiosity for the most disparate social phenomena. He was a restless collector of 'facts' that could confirm his social theories. From ancient history to crime news, he reviewed an enormous amount of prima facie heterogeneous material in order to map out the lines of a 'pure' theory of social action. Compared to a vast undertaking of this kind, he found the task of economic science comparatively easier, since the scientific status of 'pure' economics was more advanced than that of 'pure' sociology.

Nevertheless, Pareto felt that both current economics and current sociology were flawed by the same faults – namely, a contamination with metaphysics (statements that were not empirically tested) and with ethics (confusion between 'to be' and 'ought to be'). Positivism itself, which in his early years he had considered as genuinely scientific, now appeared to him as far from irreprehensible.

Here a distinction should be drawn between Positivism as a method (in the sense of an experimental method) – to which Pareto always remained faithful – and Positivism as an ideology, which Pareto progressively repudiated. Indeed, the very idea of human progress seemed to Pareto altogether misleading. In his view the true scientific vantage point for the study of society was not that of progress, but rather that of the formation and circulation of élites, whose life-force was continually renewed by drawing upon the upper strata of the dominated classes. One may surmise that he regarded this particular perspective as allowing him to penetrate many collateral phenomena he did not aim to examine directly – e.g. the spread of a mass society through the media. For instance, during Pareto's lifetime the *Corriere della sera* newspaper reached more than a million readers.

Pareto undertook no detailed study of the organization of modern political parties and trade unions. However, the main work, *Il partito politico* (1916, by a disciple of his, Robert Michels (1876–1936), a German-born scholar whose first name was Italianized as Roberto after he obtained Italian citizenship), was conceived as an application of Pareto's theory of élites (see Faucci 1989).

It can be concluded that Pareto was mainly interested in political sociology, not in economic sociology as was the case of Weber and Veblen. Nevertheless, in Pareto's work sociology and economics are not altogether separate fields. What sort of melting pot gives rise to élites? A reply can be inferred from the 'law of incomes' (Pareto 1965a; Pareto 2009 [1896]: 132–43) that Pareto elucidated in the same years, which involved the question of income distribution. In his vision, the personal distribution of incomes, unlike the logistic curve of errors, depicts a curious curve that is far from being symmetrical; instead, it is more akin to a half-arrow or, better still, a half-whirligig, in which higher incomes are placed at the top (which is very thin), while the incomes representing the statistical mode (namely, those values that are statistically most frequent) remain on the middle-lower level. It is the section where the mode is located – and which corresponds neither to the mean nor to the median values – that represents the melting pot where the new aristocracies appear and prepare to succeed the old ones. In general, the elements at the bottom of the curve are expected to climb up from below and take the place of the elements that descend.[9]

From ophelimity to economic equilibrium

For Pareto, social equilibrium was the result of so many contrasting and clashing forces that any formal representation of the situation was impossible. On the other hand, the task of representing economic equilibrium was comparatively easier. Here, the point was to extend the properties of Walras's model, insofar as this was possible, to any feasible economic system, including the 'collectivist' model, thereby rendering the model absolutely general in the sense of meta-historical. If economics wished to become a true scientific discipline, it should present itself as rational mechanics (see Ingrao 1994).

It can readily be observed that Pareto's faith in the possibility of transforming economics into an absolutely rigorous discipline was the outcome of his 'scientism' – in Hayek's sense – namely, the belief that the status of the social sciences cannot differ from that of the natural sciences. Yet at the beginning of his studies on pure economics Pareto himself raised some doubts on the principles that could justify the scientific foundation of economics. In 1891, commenting on Pantaleoni's *Principii di economia pura*, he wrote to his friend: 'I fear the hedonistic principle is very far from the ideal of rational mechanics' (Pareto 1960, vol. I: 46).

Nevertheless, his first important contribution to pure economics, *Considerazioni sui principii fondamentali dell'economia pura* (1891) is centred on the notions of total and marginal utility, taken as the basis for any rational economic calculus. But at that early stage of his reflection Pareto did not address the issue of a definition of utility that was of use for economics. Rather, he identified utility with hedonism and pure economics with rational mechanics (see the English edition, Pareto 2007 [1892–93]; Italian text, Pareto 1952: 55–235).[10]

Pareto's subsequent reflection led him progressively further away from his early approach. In his two-volume *Cours d'économie politique* (1896–97), Pareto distinguished between generic utility and *economic* utility, defining the latter by means of the Greek term 'ophelimity' (which literally had the same meaning, but was used to avoid confusion), and limiting himself to the claim that ophelimity 'closely approximates an objective property of things' (Pareto 1949 [1896–97], vol. I: 12). After 1900, Pareto altogether rejected utility as the source of 'value', going so far as to state that the search for its causes is nonsense in a general equilibrium perspective.

> Value has no single cause: rather, it has infinite causes. Any theory that is willing to assign a cause to value is radically incorrect, whatever cause it indicates. We might indicate either production cost [Ricardo and Marx], or final utility degree [Jevons], or *rareté* [Walras], or something else.
>
> Pareto 1952 [1901]: 454

Pareto now believed that only the general equilibrium approach could be considered as definitely 'scientific'. Consequently, he did not judge Marshall's partial equilibrium approach as worthy of attention. Studying, as Marshall did, the equilibrium conditions of a particular market, even with the aid of mathematics, was of little interest. And in any case, what was actually achieved by the eighteenth and early nineteenth century 'classics' who didn't bother with mathematics? They posited the price of some commodity as unknown, subsequently they considered it as the result of 'a combination of known quantities, namely, the prices of the elements of production' (Pareto 1952 [1901]: 448), and believed they had thereby solved the problem. Similarly, the representatives of the Austrian school – which, according to many Italian economists, including Pantaleoni, represented the quintessence of 'new' economics – substituted a false causal relation (value-labour) by another false causal relation (value-utility). Only general equilibrium, based on the assumption of mutual dependence among all economic phenomena, escaped 'the chicken and the egg dilemma', as Pareto scornfully wrote (Pareto 1966 [1907]: 382).

Pareto also inveighed against another and still more evident error due to metaphysics, namely the twin concepts of 'essence-phenomenon'. The classical economists and Marx had interpreted the value of a commodity as its essence, and the price of a commodity as its phenomenon. But, Pareto insisted, a science that aims to be truly logical-experimental cannot accept that there exists a double level of knowledge: that of the 'thing in itself' and that of the sensory perceptions. It was the duty of any scientific knowledge to concentrate upon the study of phenomena and their regularities, not to rely on a metaphysical creed.

Tastes and obstacles

The most mature fruit of these reflections was the *Manuale/Manuel*, published in Italian in 1906 and in a French translation (not by Pareto himself) in 1909, with several additions, among which a mathematical appendix. The architecture of this book distinguishes it from all other textbooks of its time. The first chapter, an introduction to social science, provides a sociological basis for economics by inserting economic action among the so-called 'logical actions'. The latter do not depend on the desire to satisfy our own wants, but on 'tastes' – a deliberately neutral term used in order to avoid any possible hedonist implications.

As early as in his *Cours*, Pareto made use of the indifference curves (or 'lines'), drawing inspiration from Edgeworth's *Mathematical Physics* (1881). However, the Oxford economist had deduced them from economic utility, taken as known, whereas Pareto, in his *Manuale*, assumed the curves directly from agents' behaviour, from which he derived 'what is necessary for the theory of equilibrium, without the need to consider ophelimity' (Pareto 2006 [1906]: 123). The rejection of ophelimity – a term which Pareto was eventually willing to consider as a source of misunderstandings – is crucial. In his *Manuale* Pareto assigned an index to each indifference curve, so that the comparison between two curves gave the result of 'greater', 'lower', 'indifferent', but not that of 'twice as large', 'twice as low', and so forth. This constitutes the ordinal approach, as opposed to the cardinal approach followed by Edgeworth in conformity with the Benthamite tradition of directly measuring utilities, and accepted by young Pareto himself. The cardinal approach, on the other hand, implies a direct measurement of the different degrees of utility. But Pareto (ibid.: 189) raised an objection:

> A man may know that he achieves less pleasure from the third glass of wine than from the second; but he cannot know how much wine he must drink, in order to obtain from the third glass exactly the same pleasure that he derived from the second one.

In other words, ophelimity (exactly like utility) cannot be used as a measure of quantity, and vice versa.

Along with the indifference curves of tastes, Pareto also considered the indifference curves of obstacles. He identified two kinds of obstacles; those depending on the other party's tastes, and those due to the fact that the other party is a producer, whose indifference lines are his own possibilities of production (in more modern terms, the *isoquanta* of production). Joining the tangency points of the taste curves and of the obstacle curves resulted in obtainment of the 'complete transformation line' (ibid.:129) that defined the exchange equilibrium.

At this point Pareto introduced prices. The passage is justified as follows:

> So far we have ... avoided making use of prices.... It seemed appropriate to show how the theories of economics do not move directly from the consideration of a market where some prices exist, but rather start by considering equilibrium, which originates from the contrast of tastes and obstacles. Prices appear as auxiliary unknowns, most useful to solve economic problems, but they must eventually be eliminated, leaving tastes and obstacles alone on the field.
>
> (Pareto 2006 [1906, 1909]: 150)

Consequently, he defined 'the price of Y in X as the quantity of X that must be given in order to obtain a unit of Y'. Geometrically, the exchange ratio is the slope of the budget line (ibid.: 151). The tangency points between indifference curves and budget lines, when connected by a line, express the 'barter curve', in which any point is an equilibrium position.

Tastes and obstacles determine quantities and prices of the goods that are bought and sold if certain restrictive conditions are satisfied (the total expenditure of any consumer must be equal to the total income obtained by selling his own productive services (ibid.: 251). If all agents are in equilibrium, the 'maximum of ophelimity for a collectivity' is reached. This position implies that 'any displacement away from this position will necessarily cause an improvement in the condition of some components of society and a worsening in the condition of others' (ibid.: 253). This is Pareto's optimum, which to some extent appears to complete the Verri–Helvétius–Bentham proposition concerning the 'maximum of happiness for the maximum number', with the further fundamental recommendation: 'provided that nobody worsens his position'.

Pareto demonstrated that this situation can be reached only through perfect competition, arguing that it was indifferent whether ownership of the productive factors was private (as in a capitalist system), or public (as presumed to be the case in a hypothetical 'collectivist State' (see pp. 258–60). This important – albeit merely theoretical – issue was developed by Barone (see below). For Pareto, the necessary and sufficient condition was that all prices of goods and factors – starting with capital goods – should be determined by free competition.

This conception of economic optimum was apparently rigorous, but highly restrictive as well. How could it be maintained that *any* income redistribution from the rich to the poor violates the principle of the optimum, since there is no possibility of comparing the increase of happiness enjoyed by the poor with the reduction of happiness lamented by the rich? Pareto's implicit conclusion was that any economic policy aiming at increasing social welfare was the domain of politicians only, and that the economist had nothing to say on such matters (apart from denouncing these reforms as anti-economic).

Pareto himself indicated an alternative to this otherwise discouraging conclusion. He admitted that some redistribution of income could be made initially, before the start of the production process. This has been called the second theorem of welfare economics, which completes and integrates the so-called first theorem, according to which a competitive equilibrium is, per se, an optimum.[11]

Pareto's awareness that his concept of economic optimality excluded an important part of social reality prompted him to write his third great work: the *Trattato di sociologia generale* (1916).

At the very centre of the book stands the study of human behaviour, as it appears in a heterogeneous society, where a hierarchy of values, and implicitly of power, exists. Now, economic actions, *qua* rational actions – in Pareto's language, 'logical actions' – pursue the goal of the maximum of ophelimity. Social actions, on the other hand, are influenced by social stratification and particularly by the main division in society as conceived in Pareto's sociology, namely the distinction between the ruling and the ruled class. While the actions of the former are to some extent logical as regards their ends – driven as they are by the Machiavellian rule of maintaining power by all possible means – the actions of the latter are defined by Pareto as predominantly non-logical. *Vulgus vult decipi.* For instance, in primitive societies savages obey the witch doctor, dancing in order to trigger rain. If by chance rain falls, the savages' subordination to the witch doctor will be reinforced. People in the so-called evolved nations do not dance to invoke rain but, Pareto pointed out, they passively follow their political leaders' slogans. People act on the assumption they are pursuing their own expected utility – which is nonetheless a group utility: welfare, security, justice for many, not for all – without perceiving the deception to which they are subjected, either in the determination of their goals or in the choice of ways to attain them.

The two optima

As opposed to economics, Pareto believed that in sociology, which in his vision coincided with political science, a maximum of 'utility', either *for* a community or *of* a community, does indeed exist. The first of these two aspects was examined in a short article of a mathematical nature, in which his starting point was economic equilibrium. After defining the equations regarding an economic optimum, Pareto underlined that the main character of this kind of optimum is that the marginal ophelimities of the individual members of the community cannot be summed together, since they are heterogeneous. But if these ophelimities could be multiplied 'by certain positive quantities', they could be rendered homogeneous. Therefore their aggregation would be feasible. Thus, the connection between the two kinds of equilibrium can be found. In his view the main problem remained that of defining the coefficients that render those magnitudes homogeneous and comparable. Here, Pareto observed, the choice of the transformation coefficients is delegated to the world of politics. If the rulers espouse a left-wing approach, they will be inclined to assign high coefficients to the ophelimity of the poor, and low coefficients to that of the rich; if the rulers are on the right, the opposite will be the case. Once the transformation coefficients are fixed according to non-economic criteria, the community may genuinely reach a sociological maximum – a utility maximum, different from the ophelimity maximum, but not altogether extraneous to it. This result will correspond to a sociological optimum *for* a community (see Pareto 1966 [1913]: 661–5. English translation in Pasinetti 1992, vol. I: 39–43).

More frequent, however, are the sociological optima *of* a community. Pareto suggested that an increase in population could be seen as a target corresponding to the optimum *of* a community, for instance on issues that have political and military implications. Such a target requires no reference to any transformation coefficient – it is sufficient for people to be deceived as to their 'real' interests. In this case, Pareto moved towards Pantaleoni's conclusions on individual and collective maxima.[12]

History, Pareto concluded, teaches that the 'power élites', as Charles Wright Mills would call them half a century later, have always passed off the utility maxima *of* a community as utility maxima *for* a community – and even more as (economic) ophelimity maxima *for* a community. The clarion calls trumpeted by political élites in order to reaffirm their rule are defined by Pareto as *derivazioni*. These derivations have the same role as ideologies – 'false consciousness' in Marx's thought (see Bobbio 1971: 109–22).

An application of sociological theories to economics: Pareto's approach to public finance

Pantaleoni considered *scienza delle finanze* as fertile terrain to test the theories of pure economics, whereas Pareto consistently rejected any symmetry between the study of private (individual) economy and that of public (collective) economy. This is hardly surprising. Since 'the State' is embedded in the power élite, the science of finance, insofar as it aims to achieve a genuinely scientific character, seeks to penetrate the real and often unconfessed motives – Pareto called them *residui* – that lie behind formal and often-solemn ideological declarations, the *derivazioni*.

The true difference between economics and finance, as set out by Pareto, is as follows. The taxpayer – considered as a rational individual who acts in order to obtain the maximum of ophelimity – represents no more than a very restricted case, for taxpayers are quite unaware of the effects of taxes on the whole economic system. Their ignorance implies that a taxpayer's '*actions are not of the logical type*, which constitute the real centre of economics and can fairly easily be investigated, but *of the non-logical type*, with regard to which the theory is far more difficult'.[13]

On this issue, Pareto's statement was not fully original. As seen in the foregoing chapter, Francesco Ferrara had doubted whether an acceptable comparison between the pleasure of consuming a public service, and the pain of paying the corresponding tax, could be established. Amilcare Puviani, for his part, had pointed out that the State nudges citizens towards 'fiscal illusion'. Pareto went further. He wondered whether such concepts as 'collective' or 'social' wants had any scientific basis at all. His conclusion was that the impossibility of defining a maximum of ophelimity *of* the community made this quest absolutely sterile. The government cannot bring about the happiness of the wolf and that of the lamb at one and the same time. Consequently, establishing a collective hedonistic maximum in public finance is meaningless. This awareness marks Pareto's distance from Pantaleoni.

Pareto and Croce

It was shown in the foregoing chapter that Croce encountered economics via his early interest in the methodology of historical sciences and Marx's theory. After concluding that Marxism was per se unscientific, Croce felt he was sufficiently prepared to engage with Pareto on the latter's field: that of the scientific character of economics. The debate was hosted in *Giornale degli economisti* as an exchange of correspondence between the two scholars.[14]

Croce started by expressing his disagreement with Pareto's definition of pure economics as 'rational mechanics'. 'The economic fact is no mechanical fact', Croce commented, because it is 'a fact of evaluation' by man when the latter engages in economic action (see Croce 2001e [1900]: 223).

Engaging in economic action, Croce continued, means first and foremost *willing* something. As is well known, the volitional act of willing and the condition of 'knowing' are the fundamental pair of concepts that summarize Croce's philosophy. Since economic activity is practical and volitional, Croce felt that Pareto's terminology – where economic actions are defined as '*logical actions*' – confused the theoretical and practical levels. The correct distinction, Croce maintained, was not between logical and non-logical *actions*, but only between logical and non-logical *theories*. When people engage in economic behaviour they may commit errors of will, but not of knowledge. They may at most fall into the trap of committing *technical* errors (for instance, by giving a mistaken forecast of the course of bonds on the stock exchange), but in this case the kind of technical knowledge involved is, in Croce's framework, no more than a low-level form of knowledge which can be assimilated to information of practical nature.

It can be observed that Croce's critical approach was mainly of a semantic type because for Pareto 'logical' meant 'rational', in the sense of 'not merely instinctive'. But there was another and more substantial point in Croce's position that Pareto could not countenance. Croce considered the category of 'value' as fundamental both in *performing* economic actions and in *reflecting* on them; that is to say, in the whole territory of economic science. Pareto, on the other hand, regarded 'value' as a highly misleading word and a cause of great confusion in economic debate.

In his reply to Croce, Pareto rejected the goal of 'knowing the essence and origin of a thing'. Such an approach [which he named 'essentialist'] had, he believed, been

> thoroughly detrimental to ancient science … which had sought to start out from the origins and then to chart the path to the facts, whereas modern science strives, very cautiously, 'to set out from facts and … thence to proceed back to their origins'.
>
> (Pareto 1952 [1900]: 423)

In a nutshell, Pareto manifested his preference for an operational definition of science based on its empirical results, not on an a priori definition. But this outcome was unsatisfactory from the point of view of Croce, who in his second letter objected that the aims and scope of a science could not be established by – in Pareto's language, 'cutting a slice of reality' – without a preliminary indication of the type of mental tool with which the cut is to be made. Pareto's repartee stating that the 'cutting knife' is provided by mathematics was totally unsatisfactory in the eyes of Croce, according to whom mathematical calculus was not science in the proper sense, but a mere variety of formalist logic, by definition unable to make authentic discoveries (Croce 2001f [1900] in Croce 2001, vol. I: 234). Rather, in Croce's vision, science was identified with philosophy; all alternative roads to knowledge on reality were to be rejected as merely classificatory, descriptive, or worse.

Croce's position on the role of mathematics in economics was not far removed from that of Alfred Marshall. As is well known, Marshall was of the opinion that economics was basically a moral science dealing with man, while mathematics was no more than a useful language appropriate for clarifying certain relationships between man and things. Croce, embracing an even more radical view, considered mathematics as unsuitable for economics. A science of man, as economics undoubtedly was, could not be treated as a science of nature; accordingly, the dialectical logic that underlies human behaviour could in no way be assimilated to the formal logic on which mathematics is based.

It may seem somewhat astonishing that at the beginning of a century that was to make so many fundamental contributions to mathematics and scientific research in general, and to economics in particular, such an archaic position, leading to an identification of philosophy with metaphysics in the attempt to proclaim the superiority of philosophy over science, was reaffirmed by the man who would become the 'intellectual dictator' in Italy for the later decades. In his reply, Pareto chose to define himself as akin to the medieval nominalists, unconcerned with investigations into the intrinsic nature of things and interested only in classifying them as a function of the aims being pursued.

In subordinating 'classification' to the needs of scientific strategy, Pareto implicitly showed that he shared the Pragmatist project, whose pioneer in Italy was Giovanni Vailati (1863–1909), a philosopher-mathematician in contact with numerous economists including Einaudi and Pareto himself (see Bruni 1997: 577–91).

In this sense, Pareto clearly appears as more 'modern' than Croce. On the other hand, Croce was right in stressing that human will is central in the process of economic choice, although he viewed the process of choice as fundamentally a matter of sentiment rather than of rational knowledge (see Busino 1971: 1109–11).

Moreover, Croce was able to highlight a contradiction in Pareto's framework inasmuch as the operative conception of economics that Pareto favoured was in conflict with the latter's absolute confidence in 'facts' in the sense of objective data – a typical throwback to old-style Positivism.

Each of the two contestants emerged from the discussion with their own conviction stronger than ever. Indeed, it has been rightly noted that 'Croce's point of arrival as an economist is his point of departure as a philosopher' (Tagliacozzo 1945: 313). This is testified by the attention Croce devoted in the following years to developing his reflections on the philosophical 'principle' of Economics (with initial capital letter) as a distinct aspect of the life of the Spirit, more precisely as *volizione del Particolare*, corresponding to generic human activity and praxis. On the other hand, he identified economics (the economists' economics – note the initial lower-case letter) with applied mathematics. Thus the economist's task was reduced to the mere technical work of 'accounting, not of thinking' in the sense of philosophizing (Croce 1923 [1908]: 251).

The distance from Pareto's scientific method was crystallized definitively in Croce's review of *Trattato di sociologia generale*, where it was scornfully dubbed 'a case of scientific teratology'; namely, an immense collection of heterogeneous facts that could not easily be interpreted. In short, Croce dismissed Pareto as a failure both in his aspiration to cast himself as a philosopher of economics and in his desire to be recognized as a scientific sociologist (Croce 1932 [1924]: 169 and ff.).

The result was that Croce abandoned any further interest in economics, exactly as he had done a few years earlier regarding Marx's thought. In subsequent years Einaudi alone among economists would endeavour to establish a dialogue with the Italian philosopher (see Chapter 7 below).

Croce may have been over-hasty in seeking to eliminate economics from the cultural scene. Less than 30 years after the conclusion of the Croce–Pareto debate, Lionel Robbins's *Essay on the Nature and Significance of Economic Science* (1932; revised edition 1935) described volitional choices as the key elements of economic behaviour. Unhappily Robbins, a great admirer of Max Weber, whose concept of rational actions was not too far from Croce's, made no mention of Croce even though *Historical Materialism* had been translated into English as early as 1914 (see Borsari 1964).

Enrico Barone and the 'pure' approach to a collectivist economy

His fortunes (abroad)

Enrico Barone (of Naples, 1859–1924) should be considered the third great economist of the Lausanne school, after Walras and Pareto. Unfortunately, his personality is not yet well known, despite the fact that his multi-faceted career could have been expected to attract biographers. He was a teacher at the War School of Turin, a colonel of the Military General Staff, the author of books on strategy, ballistics, the military history of the First World War, and even the origins of the French Revolution. Moreover, he was a contributor to Nationalist journals, a film scriptwriter, an amateur painter, and, last but not least, a chair professor of economics at the Institute (Faculty) of Economics and Commerce in Rome (see in general Gentilucci 2006).

His merits have been well documented and acknowledged abroad. In his *Socialism, Capitalism, and Democracy* (1942), Schumpeter wrote of Barone's 1908 article 'Il ministro della produzione nello Stato collettivista', that it conclusively settled the theoretical problem of the working of a collectivist economy. In fact, the Austrian economist was sufficiently impressed to write an extended summary of Barone's article (Schumpeter 1994 [1942], Chapter 16).

Additionally, in his posthumous *History of Economic Analysis*, Schumpeter devotes considerable attention to Barone's treatment of the production function of the first degree in order to obtain complete exhaustion of the product (Schumpeter 1994 [1954]: 986–9). Finally, Schumpeter observed in his 1949 biographical profile of Pareto that Barone's article on collectivism had the merit of completing Pareto's argument by showing that

> faced with given prices of products and productive services, every individual distributes his receipts from the sale of his services between expenditures on

consumption goods and saving in a certain unique manner 'of which we are not going to investigate the motives'. This ... does away with any concept of either utility or indifference functions.

If one adds that Schumpeter edited Barone's *Principi di economia politica* in German as early as 1927 (see Schumpeter 1997 [1949]: 130) the picture concerning his high regard for the Italian economist is complete.

The list of important economists who looked favourably on Barone include Paul Samuelson, who in his *Foundations of Economic Analysis* wrote that Barone went beyond Pareto by using price index numbers instead of indifference curves in order to determine the conditions of exchange (Samuelson 1947: 217). Additionally, Richard Kuenne stated without hesitation that 'Barone's mathematical background was superior to that of Walras and Pareto'; that 'his desire to develop a scientific economics led him to draw upon British economics for inspiration to a greater extent than Walras or Pareto'; and finally that 'he cannot be viewed merely as an embellisher of the constructions of other economists or as a mediating agent between different architectural modes in economic theory' (Kuenne 1968: 16).

Kuenne's extended entry mentions Barone's contribution to the theory of international trade from the welfare perspective, and discusses Barone's criticism of the assumption of first-degree homogeneity in the neo-classical production function. Finally, it stresses the relevance of his shadow-price hypotheses, as well as the concept of 'iterative corrections' in the working of a collectivist economy, concluding that 'the minister's tasks' had a 'logical consistency' (ibid., p. 19).

In comparison with these positive appraisals of Barone by non-Italian economists, it should be noted that in Italy his merits were far from undisputed. The dictum *nemo propheta in patria* – literally valid for such personalities as Galiani, Rossi, Pareto and Sraffa, all of whom obtained greater success abroad than at home – applies to Barone as well, in spite of the fact that he always resided in Italy. Many of his Italian colleagues objected that Barone's originality – as compared to Pareto and/or Walras – was rather modest, and in one case went so far as to declare that he was little better than a slavish follower of Pareto if not a plagiarist acting with his master's consent. Other contemporary economists labelled him as a skilful eclectic, whose main effort was that of reformulating already-known theories in an elegant way rather than of building up an original system (see Jannaccone 1912: esp. 340 and ff.). Perplexities about the real weight of his contributions to economics emerge even in obituaries and in book reviews (see Del Vecchio 1977 [1925]: 122; Mortara 1937: 886).

The most striking instance of understatement was the treatment reserved in Italy to *Ministro della produzione*. In 1935 Friedrich von Hayek hosted this article in a volume on (or rather, against!) *Collectivist economic planning*. Soon after the war this collection was translated with a preface by the liberal economist Costantino Bresciani Turroni. It is surprising that the Italian edition did not include Barone's article, not even mentioning it in the reference list at the end of the book. Similarly, even though the book's preface referred to 'market socialism', it neither cited nor quoted Barone.

There is a political explanation for this otherwise unintelligible episode. The Italian edition of the book appeared in March 1946, less than three months before the referendum that led to the Republic and the general elections of the Constituent Assembly. At that time there was serious concern that the extreme left (socialists plus communists) could prevail. This may explain not only the very hasty design and layout of the publication, but above all the exclusion of the prestigious article by Barone, the only one in the collection which seemed to give some credit to the feasibility of 'collectivist planning'.[15]

Barone's main theoretical contributions

A true 'economic Euclid' – a well-known definition Einaudi coined for Pantaleoni but which seems more appropriate for Barone – this economist who was a member of the armed forces showed his great mastery using mathematical formulae to present not only his own thought, but that of other authors as well, frequently with the added advantage of making their thought clearer. In short, his main contributions regard the coordination between production theory, distribution theory and price theory; and the application of the general equilibrium approach to a centralized economy. In this context he made substantial contributions to microeconomics, taxation, international trade and welfare economics.

As far as general equilibrium is concerned, he contributed to rectifying Walras's capitalization formulas, and discussed the application of Euler's theorem to the marginal theory of production as developed by Philip Wicksteed (see D'Amico 1975: 183–211; Mornati 2012: 542).

Naturally, his major contribution to general equilibrium theory remains his *Ministro della produzione*, an unfinished study on the optimal properties of a 'socialist' system where public ownership of the means of production is accompanied by a market-based factor allocation. Barone demonstrated that this system could also reach a Pareto optimum. The fundamental reason was already implicitly admitted by Pareto himself thanks to the so-called second theorem of welfare economics, where any initial income distribution – including an equalitarian situation – is consistent with a final result of optimal equilibrium, provided that this takes place within a market of perfect competition. As well as the practical feasibility of this kind of 'market socialism', Barone's paper clarified the 'dual' character of Pareto's welfare theory. Not only – as Pareto had already demonstrated – was any competitive equilibrium a Pareto optimum, but also, given any initial distribution of income whatsoever, it will be always possible to reach a Pareto optimum through a competitive mechanism (see Petretto 1982: 147–67).

As far as public finance was concerned, Barone enunciated the theorem of the non-identity of the fiscal pressure exerted by an even amount of direct and indirect taxes. While Pantaleoni had argued that the loss of utility for the taxpayer depended only on the amount of the income subtracted, independently of the way in which it was subtracted (see Pantaleoni 1938 [1910]: 118 and ff.), Barone

– by utilizing indifference curves and budget lines – demonstrated that if the amounts of direct and indirect tax are equal, the sacrifice for a taxpayer affected by the indirect tax will be greater; and correspondingly, that if the sacrifice for a taxpayer is equal either with the direct or the indirect tax, the State will collect less revenue with an indirect than with a direct tax (Barone 1912: 316–53; Steve 1976: 267–77).

Another subject addressed by Barone concerned the loss of welfare – in terms of consumer's surplus – deriving from a monopoly. Part of this loss, a triangle, was recoverable only if the consumer pays a lump sum tax to the monopolist, subject to the condition that the latter reduces his price to the average cost supposed as constant, and produces the same quantity as in perfect competition (Barone 1936, vol. II: 17–18, Dooley 1998: 71).

Likewise, in the welfare perspective Barone reconsidered the Ricardo-Mill treatment of the gains from international trade in order to demonstrate that the growth of imports increases the consumer's surplus more than it reduces the producer's surplus; and vice versa in the case of an increase of exports (Barone 1915: 108 and ff.). A fiscal duty on imports is therefore admissible, provided that it is not prohibitive, and can compensate the 'wealth destruction' that results from the price increase and the quantity diminution (ibid., pp. 117–20). The second best criterion is here clearly envisaged.

De Viti de Marco's theory of public finance

A democratic economist

Marquis Antonio De Viti de Marco (of Lecce, 1858–1943) is perhaps the most enigmatic of Italian marginal economists. He left a much smaller bulk of writings than Pantaleoni and Pareto, in spite of a longer life than either of those two scholars. His political engagement led him to Parliament, but his speeches were both short and infrequent. In addition to the *Giornale degli economisti*, he also edited the political periodical *L'unità* – not to be confused with the communist newspaper founded by Gramsci – to which many Southern intellectuals contributed. He was one of the approximately 13 professors (the exact number was never precisely ascertained) who refused to swear obedience to the Fascist regime in 1931 and forfeited their university chairs. De Viti spent the rest of his life cultivating his estate near Lecce.

The tasks of public finance and the definition of public goods

As was seen in the appraisal of Pantaleoni presented earlier, many representatives of Italian Marginalism were attracted by the economic nature of the State. This largely depended on the fact that Italy as a state was still in the making and was thus a challenging subject of research per se. Theoretical discussion on the nature of the State also aroused interest as a testing ground for solutions to the most pressing economic issues of the time. More specifically, the Italian state, a second-comer in the industrialization process, was faced with the need to undertake crucial tasks that went far beyond tax-raising, in order to supply the most necessary public services.

In this context, De Viti adopted a surprisingly realistic way of thinking. He claimed in his early work *Carattere teorico dell'economia finanziaria* (1888) that *scienza delle finanze* should not aim to indicate which wants the State is called upon to satisfy once and for all; rather it should outline which type of economic conduct by the State can be regarded as most appropriate for satisfying the wants that are historically given. In this early work he limited himself to applying the marginal calculus to the State as an economic agent, while in his more mature *Principii di economia finanziaria* (1928 and 1934) De Viti introduced a fundamental distinction between individual wants, taken as the object of political economy, and collective wants, taken as the object of *scienza delle finanze* in the sense of public economics.

Defining public goods (and wants) is probably one of the most important results of the Italian public finance tradition. This branch of study has inspired the so-called 'purist' (or, as some scholars improperly define it, 'voluntarist') theory of finance, in contrast to the so-called 'sociological' or 'political' approach, which reveals the influence of the preceding Historical school and is more descriptive than theoretical (see Cosciani 1977, Chapters 2 and 3).

Together with De Viti, mention should be made of Ugo Mazzola (1863–99), whose untimely death prevented him from becoming an indisputable leader in his field. In his *Dati scientifici della finanza pubblica* (1890), Mazzola focused on the definition of public goods as those that are complementary to private goods (for instance, the public good of 'safety' is enjoyed together with the private good of 'personal property'). This was a typical liberal-individualist position. Mazzola then traced the path from public goods to public wants: 'collective [synonym of public] wants are not autonomous but reflected'. The demand for public goods – goods that satisfy public wants – was consequently a derived demand, whose value depended on the marginal utility of the private goods with which they were combined (see Kayaalp 1988: 15–25).

Analogously, De Viti maintained that the process of evaluating wants should be performed according to the marginal utility principle. However, in comparison with individual wants, De Viti believed that collective wants have the prerogative of producing 'contrasts of interests' among the various subjects, and such contrasts require mediation by the State. A quantitative measure of this contrast, and, by extension, of the public goods required by a community, can be expressed through

> the algebraic sum of positive and negative quantities, namely, of the positive needs some individuals feel for a certain service, which imply their desire that it should be produced, and the negative needs others feel with regard to the service in question, i.e. their desire that it should not be produced.
>
> (De Viti de Marco 1961 [1934]: 37)

It is apparent that De Viti, following Pantaleoni's *Teoria del riparto delle spese pubbliche*, believed that Parliament was the most appropriate institution to ponder the pros and cons. However, a noteworthy difference can be perceived between De Viti and Pantaleoni. According to Pantaleoni the distinction between individual and collective wants was based on determination of the subject that provides the means for wants satisfaction. De Viti objected to Pantaleoni that the State's intervention was an effect, not a cause. The fundamental distinction between the two types of wants consisted, De Viti observed, in the nature of the wants and in the way they manifest themselves. He pointed out that over time many individual wants become collective wants because their satisfaction (or non-satisfaction) produces conflicts among individuals and the State intervenes in order to supply the services that are necessary. If one were to follow Pantaleoni's approach – De Viti remarked with his characteristic wit – all that would be required for any good whatsoever to be designated as 'public' would be to entrust the State with the production of the given good. Following this line of reasoning, in 1890 De Viti manifested opposition to nationalization of the telephone industry; phone calling, he argued, is not a 'pure public good' because those who do not pay the subscription rate can be excluded (absence of non-exclusion). The only justification for nationalization of enterprises producing 'public' services that are not *stricto sensu* public goods was therefore political. De Viti maintained that most allegedly public goods are, so to speak, political goods. Unfortunately, he bitterly concluded, the ultimate decision to satisfy the want for these goods is not truly devolved to representative government, but is the sparring ground of pressure groups and economic lobbies.

The economic theory of the State

By virtue of this reflection, De Viti was able to define the two main ideal types of the State entrusted with providing the goods for which a collective (or public) want is felt:

1   the monopolist, or absolute, State, where a social class or caste, which pays no taxes, engages in production of collective goods for its own exclusive advantage and offloads the relative costs upon the subjected classes that derive no advantage therefrom;
2   the 'popular', or 'cooperative', State, where all citizens enjoy benefits through consuming the public goods whose production they have freely endorsed by voting. In analogy with private cooperatives, in a democratic state there is an identity of interests between rulers, as producers, and the ruled, as consumers of public services: 'all citizens who are the taxpayers are also those who enjoy the public services' (De Viti 1961: 41). However, the classical liberal position that limits the electoral franchise to owners of property is taken as the logical basis of the entire argument. De Viti's cooperative State is by no means a Welfare State.

The consequence is that in De Viti's cooperative State, tax is not a neat loss for the producer who is affected, but a necessary cost in order to obtain an advantage. This is a development of Ferrara's concept of the tax as the 'tiny price' we willingly(!) pay in order to obtain the utility of the public service. But such an approach skirted the problem of the 'calculus of consent', because De Viti assumed unanimity of decisions in the cooperative State on the very disputable basis that the buyers and sellers of goods belong to the same group. Admittedly, as has been objected (see Fasiani 1980 [1932]: 126), De Viti needed a more realistic political theory in order to solve the conflict of interest he himself had set at the basis of the State's economic action, which, however, he removed in his taxation theory.

De Viti justified the State's taxing power by reference to his theory of 'the State as a factor of production'. The State participates in the entire process leading to the formation of neat total income, defined as 'the mass of the first degree goods [namely, of final goods in the language of Austrian economics] produced and consumed yearly' (De Viti 1961: 218). Note that this income includes saving, which then has to be taxed (for an opposite position, see Einaudi, Chapter 7 below).

The transition from indirect to direct taxation is explained by assuming that citizens exert continuous control over the price of public services in order to ensure that prices remain affordable. While control over indirect taxes is 'posthumous' (subsequent) and comes about by consuming the service itself (e.g. an imported good), control over direct taxes is antecedent to the supply of the public service (e.g. justice), and is exercised through the Parliament's vote by assigning a special budget to the public office that is entrusted with the service. In particular, the subscription price, whereby the enterprise requires the customer to pay a fixed sum (e.g. for attending an opera season, or for parking in protected roads or squares) in exchange for unlimited use of the service, introduces the mechanism of tax: 'The subscription price is the cradle of tax' (ibid., p. 103).

In effect, while in the case of indirect taxes the demand for the service given by the State is individual and specific, in the case of direct taxes the demand for the service is general and non-specific. The presumptive index for the demand of public services is the taxpayer's income, under the hypothesis that 'the consumption of general public services is proportional to every citizen's income' (ibid., p. 117). However, this does not imply that proportionality alone is acceptable. Taxation must take numerous non-economic factors into account, such as 'conflicting interests' among the various classes of taxpayers, and *stricto sensu* economic factors such as the different effects of a progressive and a proportional tax system on the rate of capital accumulation. De Viti, implicitly following John Stuart Mill, showed a preference for a moderate progression via exemption of a minimum income.

Another topic discussed by De Viti concerned the validity of 'Ricardo's equivalence theorem' between a special tax and a loan whose interest is to be paid by an annual permanent tax. Pantaleoni had basically confirmed Ricardo's line, adding some further elements such as the possibility that the debtor may have no capital at all to transmit to the future generation (see Pantaleoni 1891, English abridged translation, 1992, vol. I: 45–9)

De Viti came to a similar conclusion, but via a different route. Faithful to his idea of a substantial symmetry between private and public economy, he started from an individual who, faced with an unusual expenditure, has to choose between alienating a part of his assets and contracting a debt. In public economics the decision to cover a special outlay through a capital levy will likewise compel some taxpayers to alienate their assets, while others will take on debt. If the State prefers to raise money through the national debt rather than by means of a capital levy, then a single public relationship (between the State and the subscribers) will substitute for a multiplicity of private relationships between individual debtors and creditors. Thus, on the one hand the State will be indebted towards the subscribers of the Treasury bonds, while on the other it will be the creditor – through a standard tax for servicing the debt – of the same taxpayers who, in the previous example, would have paid the tax (see De Viti 1961 [1934]: 395). The only difference between the two alternatives is that the capital levy is paid only by higher income taxpayers, whereas the tax for servicing the debt is paid by all citizens.

A radical objection to De Viti's (and Ricardo's) approach was raised by Benvenuto Griziotti (1884–1956), the founder of a theory of public finance which attempted to bridge the Paretian theory of politics with an institutional approach derived from the Historical school. In particular, Griziotti objected that De Viti's approach neglected the possible conflict of interests between different generations of taxpayers. Overall, decision-making in such a context was, in Griziotti's view, mainly political and pertained to an assessment of whether the expenditure was intrinsically worthwhile (see Griziotti 1992 [1917] in Pasinetti 1992: 81–97).

Money, credit and banking

Although De Viti's main field of interest was public finance, he also paid attention to money and credit. In the book dating from his early years, *Moneta e prezzi* (1885), he clarified the foundations and scope of the quantitative theory of money – the causal relationship between the amount of circulating money and the general price level – by showing the connection of this theory to the classical theory of distribution of precious metals.[16]

However, he emphasized that when passing from a purely metallic economy to an economy based on an unconvertible 'fiduciary' (in practice, paper) money, the proportionality between an increase in the quantity of metal and an increase in prices is no longer valid. Credit reduces the need for metallic money, which has the main role of compensating credits and debts.

In *La funzione della banca* (1898, 1934), De Viti developed a theory of a bank as an institution having the task of compensating two kinds of credit relationships – exchange credits based on bills of exchange (when the customer-creditor brings his bills to the bank for discounting) and bank credits in the proper sense (when a bank grants credit to the customer-debtor). The balance is covered by the metallic reserve of the bank. If the balance is zero there is evidence that the bank 'barters' two kinds of credits. In De Viti's view the banking company is an organ of *payments*, not of *investments*, the latter being the task of special credit institutions (*istituti di credito speciali*, such as security banks, agricultural credit banks and so on). De Viti argued, contrary to 'modernist' theories, as he himself called them, that the bank as an institution did not 'create' credit and that the modernists writers erred in maintaining that credits create deposits: rather, the opposite was true (De Viti de Marco 1990 [1898, 1934]: 63–71). However, De Viti added, the bank does in actual fact 'grant' credit: it is not a mere wardrobe that stores the customers' deposits, as the orthodox economists of his time believed. De Viti maintained that 'the credit the bank concedes springs from the credit it receives' (ibid., p. 72); in other words, it is not the deposits but rather the bank portfolio (bills of exchange owed by the bank) that determines its credit capacity.

De Viti's reflection on the bank's function led him to conclude that although metal money must remain convertible in order to guarantee the dealers and ensure stability of its value, the working of the monetary market through the bank can be ensured by paper money as well, or even by 'pure credit' (with compensation between credits and debts). This conclusion distinguishes De Viti from the orthodoxy of his day (see Graziani 1995; Realfonzo 1995 in Pedone 1995).

On the other hand, it should be borne in mind that in 1934 De Viti revealed a lack of awareness of the updated literature on money and banking; signally, the only recent book he cited was Hayek's *Monetary Theory and the Trade Cycle* (1932).

The question of the South

Between 1890 and 1910 there was a revival of initiatives for free trade and against protection. They originated from the needs of the most competitive Italian industries, such as the silk producers which were being suffocated by the alliance between landowners (mainly grain producers) and heavy industry (iron and steel). De Viti was at the head of the Southern opposition to protection, and strove to gain the support of the more reform-oriented section of the Socialist Party, led by Filippo Turati (1857–1932) who was also in contact with Pantaleoni, Pareto and other Liberalist economists. During the campaign before the general polls of 1904, De Viti launched a manifesto for an alliance between liberals and socialists, but without success. In subsequent years De Viti – unlike Pantaleoni and Pareto – remained on the left, together with his friend Gaetano Salvemini, the historian (1873–1957), who himself was likewise a committed free-trader.

De Viti's Southern programme was based on tax reductions rather than on further public works. His case against public works was both economically and politically motivated, based on his belief that public works were of use only when there was already an existing fertile terrain for development. If no such circumstance was present, public works would merely turn out to be unproductive expenditures serving only to enrich the (Northern) firms that were awarded the contracts through the procurement procedures. Moreover, financing public works through new taxes, instead of encouraging the development of the Southern regions via tax relief, made it difficult to attract new investments from the North.

But in De Viti's vision, the future of the South would be better served by the development of agriculture for export (oil, wine, citrus fruits), according to a specialization dictated by comparative advantages. Moreoever, he was sceptical not only towards industrialization in the South, but towards industrialization in the North as well, since in his view this industrialization was mostly artificial and largely depended on tariff protection.

As was briefly mentioned earlier, the policy lines De Viti and other Liberalist economists suggested were not put into action by Prime Minister Giolitti during his almost-uninterrupted period of government (1903–14). This notwithstanding, Giolitti's approach was not a mere continuation of the preceding era. He favoured the process of industrialization and, at the same time, he endeavoured to improve relations between capital and labour. Assisted by the general director (and subsequently governor) of the Bank of Italy, Bonaldo Stringher (1854–1930), and by Treasury Minister Luigi Luzzatti (see above, Chapter 5), Giolitti successfully defended the parity of the lira and carried out the conversion of Italian bonds from 4 per cent to 3.5 per cent, with positive relief effects on the Italian budget. This opened up the possibility of a fiscal reform along liberal 'Peelite' lines, a reform which, unfortunately, was never carried out.[17]

Giolitti's economic action has been considered in an increasingly favourable light by contemporary historians, inasmuch as he succeeded in promoting both an expansive policy based on public works and a more competitive private sector. However, the majority of the Liberalist economists of the time, including De Viti and Einaudi – not to mention Giolitti's outspoken political enemies Pantaleoni and Pareto – were harshly critical of this policy. De Viti accused Giolitti of being himself a *trasformista* who had no qualms about sacrificing all genuine reform programmes with the goal of defending at all costs his own political leadership, seen as flawed by an oscillating majority and lacking a solid and consistent programme. This led to the post-war crisis from which Fascism emerged as the winner in 1922.[18]

In 1928, reflecting on the previous decades of Italian history, De Viti pronounced an implicit recantation of his own political experience. He underscored that 'our [De Viti group's] critique against all degenerations of individual liberties and of the representative system' caused by Giolitti's rule 'did genuinely have the aim of defending and consolidating the democratic state. Therefore, our group was defeated' (of course, by Fascism) (De Viti de Marco 1994 [1930]: xlvii).

But here, some doubts may be raised on the overall effects of the liberal message. Why did the 'group' not become a party? The same question was asked by Einaudi in a spirited review of De Viti's book (Einaudi 1931). The liberal-Liberalist intellectuals admitted, too late, that they had been unable to enlighten public opinion on the point that their criticism of the *actual* working of democracy was not to be taken as a criticism of democracy per se. Through this somewhat inconclusive statement of intent, they added their authoritative voices to those who intended to subvert democracy.

Notes

1 See the by now classic anthology edited by Cafagna (1962).
2 For a very cursory sketch, see Weintraub (199): 252–9.
3 Masci (1889–1941) edited Marshall's *Industry and Trade* in Italian (1934: see Gallegati and Faucci (2010): 150–61).
4 Among the most recent contributions, see Augello and Michelini (1997): 119–206; Michelini (1998); Bellanca and Giocoli (1998); Bini (2007).
5 It has been rightly observed (by Montesano, forthcoming) that Pantaleoni never declared what he really meant by equilibrium – namely, whether he referred to a 'temporary' equilibrium in relation to given market conditions, or to a 'stationary' equilibrium that never changes over time. Since one can infer that Pantaleoni had in mind the former type of equilibrium, and Pareto the latter, this issue marked one of the most important theoretical differences between the two scholars.
6 It should be noted that Pareto likewise regarded the Benthamite principle as the essence of democracy. See his letter to Pantaleoni, 14 December 1892, in Pareto (1960), vol. I: 122.
7 See Pantaleoni (1936): 471–85, originally in Preziosi (1915). Giovanni Preziosi (1881–1945), an affectionate disciple of Pantaleoni's, later became a vehement apologist of racism and a supporter of Nazi Germany. He committed suicide during the *Liberazione* days.
8 Leone (of Naples, 1875–1940) has been studied more frequently as a leader of the so-called revolutionary syndicalism, a left-wing stream of thought opposed to the second international reformist line and much-influenced by Georges Sorel's subjectivism. See Zagari (1975).
9 Pareto (2006) [1906–1909], Chapter VII, esp. 271–80; see Persky (1992), esp. 184–5; Kirman (1998): 28–32. Ingrao and Israel (1990), Chapter 5, consider the connection made by Pareto between his law of distribution and his theory of élites as a mere rhetorical device.
10 It is worth noting that here Pareto dismissed the previous contribution given by Giovanni Antonelli (1858–1944), himself an engineer, who as early as 1886 wrote an unfinished memoir, rediscovered by Herman Wold in his work on pure demand theory published in 1943. In Wold's analysis of the relationship between production and consumption, Antonelli was acknowledged as having been at the forefront of the discovery of the 'dual problem' in linear programming. Antonelli's essay was reprinted by G. Demaria in 1951 (see his introduction to Antonelli (1951 [1886]: 223–31), and to Pareto ((1952): xviii), and translated into English in 1971. It is surprising that in a letter to Pantaleoni Pareto coldly commented that Antonelli's work was 'up in the clouds' (14 December 1891, in Pareto (1960), vol. I: 121). This was probably due partly to the fact that Antonelli assumed ordinal instead of cardinal utility, in contrast to the majority of economists of his day, and partly also to the fact that Antonelli employed matrix algebra; but above all, to the fact that he treated utility after treating demand, and not before, as Pareto was inclined to do at that time. On Antonelli see also Guerraggio and Mercurelli Salari (1985): 35–48.
11 These aspects were further developed by Enrico Barone. On the importance of Pareto and Barone for 'modern' welfare theory, see Samuelson (1947), Italian translation 1973, Chapter VIII.

12 In spite of this convergence, Pareto did not quote his friend on this issue and, in general, he was very self-restrained – only one citation in *Manuale*.

13 Pareto's letter to his disciple G. Sensini, quoted by Fasiani (1949), in VV. AA., (1949, 290); Pareto's italics.

14 The Croce–Pareto debate is available in English in *International Economic Papers* (1953), vol. 3.

15 See VV. AA. (1946). The publishing house's catalogue, *Cinquant'anni di un editore* (1983), states that the editorial supervision of the book was entrusted to Ernesto Rossi, a disciple of Einaudi's and an ardent Liberalist (on him see Chapter 8, below). In the abundant correspondence between Einaudi and Rossi, which contains extensive information concerning foreign books on economics – see Einaudi and Rossi (1988) – there is no reference to Hayek's book.

16 In the second chapter it was noted that De Viti blamed Antonio Serra for failing to focus on the connection between the two aspects.

17 See the critical articles published in *Corriere della sera* by Einaudi (1959–66), vol. II, esp. 382–405.

18 Modern historiography is much less severe towards Giolitti both as a statesman and a policy-maker. Giolitti combined 'more state' with 'more market', as summarized by Ciocca (2008) in Barucci *et al.* (2008): 83–110.

7   The post-Pareto generation
(1920–45)

Reasons behind a long silence

The Fascist constraint

From the economist's standpoint, it is only in the last few decades that the troubled quarter of century under scrutiny here has become an object of scientific research. There are reasons both of a theoretical and practical nature that have contributed to building a wall, if not of indifference, then surely of distance, around this epoch and its characters. The growing Anglo-Americanization of Italian culture subsequent to the Second World War has discouraged a rereading of a group of economists who – insofar as they were mainly anti-Keynesians or at least non-Keynesians – now appeared decidedly old-fashioned. Moreover, from the political point of view, the fact that the period under consideration includes the Fascist dictatorship has contributed to an understandable embarrassment. As the effect of a sort of self-censure, a 'blank spot' of oblivion has covered this crucial piece of intellectual history. Only recently, owing to the natural succession of generations, has a more open-minded scientific climate (and a new curiosity as well) come to the fore.

It should be mentioned, at the start, that Italian intellectuals learned very early the art of coexisting with Fascism. This attitude involved above all the *literati* – including law scholars, philologists, historians and philosophers – whose research fields had few defences against the dictatorship's penetration. Economists were no exception. Some of them nourished strong political sympathy towards the Fascist movement, attributing to Fascism the merit of defeating 'Bolshevism' in the 1920–22 unrest – a biennium of internecine struggle that assumed the features of a civil war – and of defending the patriotic values that had led Italy into war and brought victory in 1915–18.

Apart from these generic reasons, the liberal economists had a special motive for being favourable to Fascism. The huge burden of war economic legislation had imposed severe controls over the private sector. Foreign exchange regulations, compulsory manpower hiring in agriculture as a measure against unemployment, housing rent control (*affitti massimi*) to protect tenants, progressive income taxation and a special levy on capital, expropriation of war profits, and uncultivated land allotment to veterans, were all measures that were taken by democratic (Centre-Left) post-war cabinets (1919–22) that raised many protests. Mussolini – an extreme-left socialist until 1914, an ultra-patriot during the 1915–18 war, a left-wing democrat between 1918 and 1920, and finally an extreme-right demagogue after the latter date – was clever enough to interpret the middle class sentiments by assuming both an anti-socialist position in politics, and an ultra-*laissez-faire* position in economics ('let's put a stop to the State as railwayman, postman, insurance agent', he said in his Udine speech of 20 September 1922, one month before the March on Rome). Consequently, he gained the consent of the impoverished and disoriented middle class and obtained the praise of many economists, beginning with Pantaleoni and Einaudi.

As a result, Mussolini won the general election of 1924, thanks to a new electoral law that assigned two-thirds of the seats in Parliament to the list that obtained the highest number of votes. However, the assassination of the socialist leader, Giacomo Matteotti, in June 1924 and, even more so, the so-called 'January 3' (1925) speech, in which Mussolini openly declared his intention to establish a dictatorial regime, persuaded many liberals to differentiate their position from Fascism. In May 1925 Benedetto Croce wrote a manifesto of the anti-Fascist intellectuals, as a reply to another manifesto in favour of Fascism written by Giovanni Gentile. In contrast to the Gentile Manifesto, the Croce Manifesto was endorsed by many economists, including Einaudi. Subsequently, in 1926 several laws were approved, the so-called *leggi fascistissime* (Ultra-Fascist laws), that cancelled the constitutional guarantees and effectively suspended the 1848 Statuto Albertino.

Some victims

Two young economists paid a severe price for their opposition. Carlo Rosselli (1899–1937), a former lecturer at Genoa University and contributor to Einaudi's *Riforma sociale*, and later the founder of the *Giustizia e libertà* movement, was killed in France by Fascist *Cagoulards*. Antonio Pesenti (1910–73), a lecturer at Sassari University who participated in the 1935 Brussels international anti-Fascist meeting, was captured when he came back to Italy and condemned to 24 years of imprisonment.[1]

But the majority of university teachers limited themselves to paying lip-service to the regime. The 1931 requirement that all professors were to swear loyalty to Fascism was considered little more than a formality – rather than a humiliation, as it really was – and was passively accomplished. In 1938 the so-called 'laws for defence of the race' expelled all professors of Jewish origin from schools and universities. In particular, such economists as Gino Arias (himself a committed Fascist and an apologist of corporatism), Riccardo Bachi, Riccardo Dalla Volta, Gustavo Del Vecchio, Marco Fanno, Bruno Foà, Giorgio Fuà, Renzo Fubini, Franco Modigliani, Giorgio Mortara, Mario Pugliese and Giorgio Tagliacozzo[2] – some of whom were already well known while others were at the beginning of their career – lost their university jobs or had to abandon the hope of a promising future. A few were able to move to Britain, the Americas or Palestine. None among the 'Arian' professors made an official protest against this discrimination, and many of them obtained objective advantages from the anti-Semitic legislation, taking up chairs and other academic or editorial posts that were left free.[3]

An isolated case was that of Attilio Cabiati (1872–1950), a Genoa professor of economics who was obliged to resign from his chair due to an indirect criticism of the racial laws contained in a personal letter he addressed to the Education Minister.[4]

From October 1943 to April 1945, under the rule of Mussolini's so-called *Repubblica Sociale* in the regions of Italy occupied by Nazi Germany, the Italian Jews were officially considered as enemies, hunted down, and sent to German concentration camps. Among those who were unable to return home, at least two outstanding economists should be remembered: Renzo Fubini (1904–44), professor at Trieste and a disciple of Einaudi, and Riccardo Dalla Volta (1862–1944), former rector of the Florence University Institute of Economics and Commerce.[5]

In spite of all these political constraints, this period is of considerable interest from the point of view of the history of economic ideas.

Academic institutions, schools and editorial initiatives

Dramatis personae

In 1918, Umberto Ricci (1879–1946), a disciple of Pantaleoni, made a rapid sketch of the state of Italian economics at that time. After remarking that Italian economic thought was imperfectly known abroad, as demonstrated by the very restricted space reserved to Italy in the most widespread manuals of the discipline (such as those written by Gide and Rist, Ingram and others), Ricci bitterly deplored that the teaching of economics in Italy was not supported by adequate facilities, such as specialized libraries and other research tools, and its future therefore seemed far from promising.[6]

This notwithstanding, the following 25 years witnessed an indisputable increase in the number of chairs of economics, public finance, statistics, economic geography and the history of commerce – rising from about 60 to roughly 90.[7]

A bird's-eye view of the chairs of economics in the peninsula, from North to South, reveals the decline of Turin as a centre of gravity in this field as compared, in particular, to Milan.[8] Economics was taught in four different places in Milan: the Polytechnic (founded in 1865), the Bocconi University (1902), the 'Sacred Heart' Catholic University (1921) and the State University (1924). Public finance had its most important research centre in Pavia. In these institutions the teaching positions in economics were mainly occupied by non-Fascists. On the other hand, the posts in Florence, Pisa, Perugia and Bari (the latter founded in 1925 and named after Mussolini himself) were filled by corporatist (obviously Fascist) economists.

The staff at Rome University were the most variegated. The untimely death of Pantaleoni and Barone, and De Viti's retirement, were compensated by the new entries of Umberto Ricci,[9] Luigi Amoroso (the mathematical economist), and Corrado Gini (the statistician).[10] Finally, two non-Fascists held posts in Naples: Alberto Breglia and Epicarmo Corbino (both of whom were in touch with Einaudi);[11] together with two Fascists: Celestino Arena and Lello Gangemi.[12]

Minor figures can be found in the remaining Southern universities, with the possible exception of Attilio da Empoli (1904–48), a self-taught scholar who obtained success in the USA with an early book on equilibrium published in Chicago in 1931. The book concentrated on the theory of the firm and on cost curves (he coined the phrase 'ultra-marginal cost' that can be considered as fore shadowing J. Bain's limit-price). He subsequently taught in Messina, Bari and Naples. A Fascist, he sat in the *Camera dei fasci e delle corporazioni*.[13]

New and old journals

In 1924 the Bocconi University of Milan set up the journal *Annali di economia*, in which Einaudi, Bresciani and the young Piero Sraffa published some of their most important works. In 1938 the *Annali* merged with the *Giornale degli economisti e Rivista di statistica*, changing its name to *Giornale degli economisti e Annali di economia* and still in existence. The editorship passed from Gustavo Del Vecchio – a victim of the 1938 'racial laws' – to Giovanni Demaria (1899–1998), a disciple of Del Vecchio's who also was appointed to the post of rector of the Bocconi University (previously held by Del Vecchio himself). In 1942 the Fascist regime obliged *Giornale* to interrupt its publication, as it had hosted an article by Demaria that advocated – against autarky, an official Fascist dogma – resumption of a free international market after the war.

In the field of public finance the leading journal was *Rivista di diritto finanziario e scienza delle finanze*, started in 1937 under the editorship of Griziotti, a former reformist socialist who had by then *rallié* to Fascism.[14] Other journals extended their range of activity, as was the case of *Rivista delle società commerciali*, the organ of the Association among the joint-stock companies [*Assonime*]. Set up in 1911 under the political flag of Nationalism, in 1921 the journal became the still-existing *Rivista di politica economica*.[15]

It hardly needs stating that all the new economics journals heartily supported the official policy of Fascism, the so-called *corporativismo*. Among such journals it is worth mentioning *Economia* (1924–43), which hosted a pioneering study on Thorstein Veblen – at that time altogether unknown in Italy – and the more ambitious *Rivista italiana di scienze economiche* (1929–43), edited by the former Finance Minister of Mussolini, Alberto De' Stefani, himself a specialist on public finance.[16]

The regime carefully controlled these journals and did not hesitate to impose silence even on those that were suspected of belonging to the Fascist *fronda* [internal opposition]. This was the case of *Nuovi studi di politica, economia e diritto*, established in 1927, which, *inter alia*, hosted the translation of an important article by the law scholar Hans Kelsen, and published an essay on Max Weber. Despite the fact that this journal was edited by two leading Fascist intellectuals – philosopher Ugo Spirito and law scholar Arnaldo Volpicelli – it was suppressed in 1935. Another journal, *Archivio di studi corporativi*, the organ of the Pisa Advanced School of Corporative Sciences under the aegis of Corporations Minister Giuseppe Bottai, was more fortunate and endured from 1930 to the fall of the regime. In contrast, as we will see later, the journal edited by Luigi Einaudi, *La riforma sociale*, which had maintained a rigorous non-Fascist position, was closed as early as 1935.

Other editorial initiatives

Despite the heavy political control, two important editorial projects in economics were characterized by noteworthy independence. The first was the Italian series (1927–33) of the international project of the First World War economic and social history undertaken by the Carnegie Endowment for International Peace, jointly edited by Yale University Press and Laterza. Among the authors who contributed to the series, Bachi, Einaudi, De' Stefani and Mortara should be mentioned.

The second was a new series of *Biblioteca dell'economista*, entitled *Nuova collana di economisti stranieri e italiani* (note 'foreign' before 'Italian', a clear sign of non-conformism!). Its 12 volumes, issued between 1932 and 1937, offer a remarkable fresco of the state of economic theory at that time. Although the two editors-in-chief were the aforementioned Bottai and the supporter of corporative economy, Celestino Arena, its plan was relatively unaffected by the political climate of the time. Its scientific merit should be attributed to Gustavo Del Vecchio, professor at Bologna and at the Bocconi University, who acted as consulting editor. The collection included translations of Hicks (*The Theory of Wages*), Frisch (*Methods of Measuring Marginal Utility*), Rosenstein-Rodan (*Marginal Utility*), Sraffa (*The laws of return under competitive conditions*), Sraffa, Robertson and Shove (*Symposium on the Representative Firm*), Schumpeter (*Theory of Economic Development*), J. M. Clark (*Overhead Costs*), Mitchell (*Economic Cycles*), together with several works of the economists of the previous generation including Menger, Marshall, Edgeworth, Böhm-Bawerk and Fisher. The original project of *Nuova collana* included a second series dedicated to economic policy, inclusive of Keynes's *General Theory*, but the project was interrupted, mainly due to the racial laws of which Del Vecchio was a victim.[17]

Many Italian economists were also active on the international level, as witnessed by their involvement in the foundation and initial steps of the Econometric Society,[18] and by their presence as authors in top-ranking journals such as the *Review of economic studies*, *Revue économique*, *Econometrica*, *Economica*, *Zeitschrift für Nationalökonomie*, and others. Moreover, several Italian authors contributed entries to E. A. Seligman's *Encyclopaedia of the Social Sciences*.

Finally, a collection of books on current economic problems was published by Giulio Einaudi, son of Luigi, under his father's supervision. The series, titled *Problemi contemporanei* and launched in 1934, hosted *inter alios* books by Lionel Robbins and Arthur C. Pigou. Another important publisher, Zanichelli of Bologna, republished the main economic writings of Ferrara, Pantaleoni and Barone.

Doctrinaire attitudes and scientific neo-phobia

On the other hand, in assessing this production one cannot omit the observation that with the exception of a few cases, the undisputable economic learning shown by Italian economists – most of whom were competent in three foreign languages – was not accompanied by a corresponding open-mindedness to the new ideas that were debated abroad. In an international perspective, the interwar years have been adroitly defined as 'the years of high theory' (Shackle 1984 [1967]). This was an extraordinarily fruitful period in which the Keynesian revolution was only the tip of an iceberg; it saw the publication of innovative studies on the trade cycle, money, market forms, econometric methods, general equilibrium theory and macro-dynamics, in parallel with the early experiences of controlled economy in the West and of central planning in the East. Yet the response of the academic establishment in Italy to this ferment of activity was rather tepid. The legacy of Pantaleoni, Pareto and Barone, to some extent with the addition of Ferrara, was considered by many of its exponents as the appropriate (or the one and only?) route to follow.

An extreme instance of high learning accompanied by aversion to novelty is represented by the correspondence between two economists of the older generation: Achille Loria and Augusto Graziani Sr, who had their roots in late classical and in pre-Marginal (historical) economics. In 1933–43 the two scholars exchanged impressions with regard to the ongoing publications abroad. Besides Keynes, the list of authors on whom they commented embraced Chamberlin, Robinson, Haberler, Lindahl, Harrod, Douglas, Hicks, Mikesell and Kahn, concluding with Samuelson's 1940 article on 'pump-priming'. The two elderly scholars, at that time expelled from the academic world because of their Jewish roots, confirmed their faithfulness not to Pareto, but to the earlier Ricardo–Mill–Marshall tradition.[19]

The studies on dynamics, a terrain that attracted several scholars of the generation born around 1900, were obviously developed in the Paretian direction, with important additions in the sense of the application to economics of the latest discoveries in physics. In effect, this research, which required considerable training in mathematics, encouraged the reception of many aspects of the most recent discoveries in the field of physics, especially rational mechanics. Yet the scientific, epistemological and 'philosophic' implications of the analytical routes that were followed were unfamiliar to the majority of Italian economists of the time, so that the representatives of this updated line of research suffered from comparative isolation.

The reception of Schumpeter and Keynes

Schumpeter and Keynes, who came from different but equally important schools, provoked varied reactions in Italy. Schumpeter was personally in touch with first class Italian economists such as Barone and Del Vecchio, and edited in Germany a selection of the most representative texts of both of them. Schumpeter's sympathy towards the Italian school of economics can be explained as follows. On one hand, he descended from the Austrian school that exerted a notable influence on Italian Marginalism, especially at its origins. On the other, his predilection for the banker-entrepreneur as the main factor of economic change was partly due to the historical experience of the 'mixed bank' model, lending money both at short and long term – an experience that derived from Germany and provided capital for the industrial take-off in Italy (1896–1914). For these reasons Schumpeter's *Theory of Economic Development* was read and translated.[20] There was less agreement with regard to Schumpeter's theory of money and credit based on the bank's deposit creation – a heterodox theory in comparison with the traditional conception of the bank as a 'cloakroom', whose main interpreter was Edwin Cannan. This may explain why, among the early supporters of Schumpeter's banking theory, one finds a professional banker: Luigi Lugli.[21]

While Schumpeter's theories encountered few serious difficulties in their reception, the same cannot be said of Keynes, whose success in Italy was marked by a number of reversals. Keynes's main works prior to *The General Theory* were rapidly translated[22] and received favourable comments. In particular, *The Economic Consequences of the Peace* (1919; translated in 1920) was much praised, partly also because it was critical of the Versailles Treaty, which had provoked considerable discontent in Italy. In contrast, Keynes's *Tract on Monetary Reform* (1923), translated in 1925 by Piero Sraffa, met with attention but also dissent. As is well known, in this work Keynes rejected the arguments of those who wished to re-establish the gold standard at pre-war parities, objecting that such a 'return to gold' would have serious deflationary effects upon production and employment. Rather, he advocated a 'devaluation' policy, in the sense of stabilization accompanied by price and wage controls.

Another crucial point of the book was the trade-off between price stability and exchange stability. Keynes supported the former aspect, while the majority of Italian economists, headed by Einaudi, favoured the latter. The proposals put forward by Keynes[23] – and by Fisher – to stabilize prices not by re-establishing the pre-war gold standard automatism, but by using flexible monetary policies, were not shared by the majority of Italian economists. They observed that such policies would be unable to 'clear up' the crisis completely. Rather, this result could be best attained through a readjustment of the market disequilibria and the consequent expulsion of inefficient operators. In the interval, they considered a period of monetary deflation as necessary.[24]

The most severe criticism was directed against Keynes's idea of a demand expansion via the multiplier. Keynes's major critic in Italy was Costantino Bresciani-Turroni (1882–1963), who deployed his strong training as a statistician

– he had been one of the early critics of the so-called Pareto law of income distribution – and showed great familiarity with economic theory.[25]

Bresciani devoted a long and detailed article and a chapter of his post-war manual to criticism of the multiplier mechanism, with arguments concentrating above all on the alleged automatic character of it.[26] He raised two points. First, the multiplier did not take into account all the variables, both of a social and economic order, connected with an increase in investment. Second, he maintained that Keynes and Kahn overlooked the dynamic aspects of the multiplier deriving from the propagations of 'secondary expenditures' in the economy. These aspects mainly involved entrepreneurs' profit expectations. The role of the entrepreneur's 'animal spirits' was, he felt, neglected by Keynes (in spite of the *General Theory*'s famous allusion), while it was carefully underlined by Bresciani himself, who was very well acquainted with German economics and wrote many articles in German and Swiss journals.[27]

Bresciani argued that a recovery at constant prices, such as that implied by the multiplier process, should be considered as unrealistic – even if the existence of idle resources is supposed – as innumerable factors could contribute to rising prices. He reinforced his ideas on the shortcomings of the multiplier process – and more generally of any expansionist policy – in his research on Germany's economic vicissitudes after the war. Germany's initial recovery in the early 1920s, he contended, did not depend on an increase in 'voluntary saving' – namely, on a spontaneous accumulation process – but on high profits deriving from a delay in wage realignment to prices. This delay gave rise to a 'forced saving' in the Wicksell–Hayek sense. For those who followed the latter's explanation, 'forced saving' had the effect of exposing the economy to fluctuations according to a limitless price-wage spiral.[28]

In his massive study on German inflation, Bresciani observed that at first the increase in prices favoured the birth of 'profits from inflation', with consequent expansion of the economy. But once wages had aligned themselves to the new price level, then the growth of profits suffered a sudden stop, and unbridled inflation began to surge. However, he added, one could object that Nazi Germany had followed Keynes's therapy against the crisis by setting in motion an expansionist policy based on warfare and public works, and, implicitly, on the multiplier mechanism.[29] Indeed, Keynes himself seemed to justify this interpretation in his quite embarrassing preface to the German translation of the *General Theory* (1937), where he wrote that only a totalitarian state would be able to put into practice the policies he indicated.[30]

In a further study on the effects of public expenditure in Germany between 1933 and 1935 Bresciani – remaining faithful to his theory – retorted that the income increases observed at that time were those of the farmers, who had a smaller propensity to consume. This circumstance led to a greater accumulation via saving; namely, to a recovery on very different bases than those predicted by Keynes. Hitler was no Keynesian at all.[31]

In conclusion, many of Bresciani's observations could more appropriately be interpreted in terms of a critique of a popular version of Keynesianism, regarded as 'easy money' with inflationary effects, rather than of what Keynes really meant. But Bresciani's message was clear – *all* active economic policies are mostly useless or misleading, and the market must be given free rein to do its job.

Marco Fanno and the Wicksell–Hayek lineage

While Keynes encountered insuperable difficulties, Friedrich von Hayek's ideas were circulated, discussed and widely shared in Italy. In connection with Hayek, another author who was much-read and debated was the Swedish economist Knut Wicksell, who after 1898 had turned away from the quantitative theory – which he deemed tautological – in order to build up a theory of 'pure credit', where money is not a commodity available in given quantity but a product of the banking system and therefore is a magnitude endogenous to the system itself. In his framework, monetary equilibrium was seen as the equality between the bank rate of interest or discount, and the 'natural' rate of interest that expresses the productivity of capital (from another point of view, the natural rate of interest is that which balances saving and investment). If the money rate of interest is lower than the natural rate, there will be an increase in the demand for loans and a growth in the price level, and the economy will expand. Vice versa, if the money rate is higher than the natural rate, the economy will contract.

On this point it is worth mentioning the numerous contributions by Marco Fanno, undoubtedly one of the most insightful economists of the post-Pareto generation. He started as an expert on international economics, and gave a revised version of Ricardo's theory of international trade by introducing the question of emigration flows, accompanied by an analysis of the 'abnormal capital movements' that disturb the international monetary equilibrium and require a regime of controls. He linked these views to an interpretation of the crisis as provoked by the interference of monetary with real forces.

In his early book *Le banche e il mercato monetario* (1912), Fanno, following Wicksell, studied the market for credit, extending his analysis to the international monetary market. He observed that short-term speculative money and capital transfers depend on the divergence between monetary and natural interest rates. Equilibrium could by no means be reached by leaving the market forces completely free to operate. Rather, manoeuvering the discount rate by the central bank was of indisputable importance in the attainment of international monetary equilibrium. In fact, a high discount rate could, by reducing the price of the national bonds, recall short-term capital from abroad that would help to reconstruct the reserves and restore the trade balance without requiring gold movements (as shown in Hume's theory of automatic equilibrium). Fanno therefore admitted the possibility of some discretionary power for monetary policy. Moreover, he maintained that banks do not limit themselves to transferring credit, as held by the orthodox approach (see De Viti de Marco's positions, Chapter 6 above), but they can 'create credit'.

These reflections led Fanno to intervene with his own ideas in the debate on the causes of the Great Depression. As is well known, the two main dominant and contrasting positions were the theories of Keynes and Hayek. Keynes argued that crises were due to an excess of saving that could not be transformed into investment due to lack of demand. Hayek, on the contrary, claimed they were occasioned by an excess of investment stemming from a mistaken monetary and banking policy, with the main error consisting in the fact that the money rate of interest had been left below the natural rate (expansionist monetary policy), and this had caused an abnormal growth of prices and profits, an unhealthy boom of the economy, and an unnatural displacement of investments from the consumption goods to the capital goods sector. The consequent extension of the production period (a typical Austrian concept) had led to a distortion in productive activity, and therefore to a crisis.

Differences can also be observed in the therapies suggested by Keynes and Hayek. According to Keynes, the main goal should be internal price stability, to be reached through a flexible monetary policy and, above all, through a public expenditure policy in order to sustain internal demand. According to Hayek, on the other hand, the appropriate policy would be that of dismantling all measures of control over the economy until internal prices had declined and the market had spontaneously reached its natural equilibrium.

In Italy, as was mentioned earlier, Keynes was followed neither in his diagnosis nor in his therapy. The most prominent Italian academic economists, following their *laissez-faire* matrix, opted in favour of Hayek. In contrast, corporative economists – far from subscribing to *laissez-faire* – went beyond Keynes in advocating public policies of compulsory control of prices and wages.

An attempt at indicating a third theoretical path, composed of (many) elements of Hayek and (a few) elements of Keynes, was undertaken precisely by Fanno. He started from the Wicksellian tradition, by comparing a natural rate of interest – which Fanno called 'prospective or expected rate' – with a bank money rate corresponding to the discount rate. Equilibrium would be reached when the two rates coincided. In his framework, a disequilibrium can arise exogenously (on account of wars, technological innovations, etc.) or endogenously (by choices that modify the length of production processes, according to the Austrian theory). Such 'impulses' would have the effect of modifying the equilibrium between savings and investments, which depends on equality between the natural and monetary rate of interest. Fanno analysed the effects of disequilibrium on income and production. In this context, some 'Keynesian' traces can be observed, inasmuch as Fanno grasped the working of the cyclical mechanism of interaction between the acceleration of investment – due to a variation in income – and the multiplier of income, due to a variation in investment.[32]

As far as contact points between Fanno and Hayek are concerned, it should be stressed that Fanno's book on *Le banche e il sistema monetario* (1912; partially translated as *The Money Market*, New York, 1995) awakened the interest of young Hayek, who quoted it in his *Monetary Theory and the Trade Cycle* (1929),[33] and published an abstract of the book in 1933 in a collection entitled *Beiträge zur Geldtheorie*.[34] However, unlike Hayek – who invoked Wicksell in order to condemn all expansive monetary policy as the cause of harmful over-investment – Fanno observed that the banking system can help to reduce the economic cycle by adjusting the monetary rate to the level of the natural rate. It is not demonstrated, Fanno maintained, that the best monetary policy is that of neutrality. On the other hand, again in contrast to Hayek who was a supporter of free banking, Fanno was favourable to assigning extensive powers to the central bank.

Nevertheless, Fanno – in this case mirroring Bresciani – remained faithful to the Hayekian distinction between voluntary and forced saving. The former was physiological, inasmuch as it was the result of the spontaneous market mechanism, and represented the primary source of investment. The latter was pathological, inasmuch as it was attributable to a consumption shrinkage owing to the failure of monetary incomes to adjust to the price increases that resulted from an expansive monetary policy. 'Forced saving' – Fanno maintained – was a by-product of this expansion; for this reason, forced saving would end when the bank system raised the interest (or discount) rate, thereby prompting a deflationary policy. Once this had occurred, voluntary saving would be able to take the place of forced saving, leading the economy towards recovery.

However, Fanno considered deflation as an evil as well, maintaining that there is a 'critical point of deflation' (Fanno 1954 [1933]: 253–64), beyond which investments fall to such a low level that the whole system is seriously disturbed and the downward fluctuation is transformed into a depression. In such a situation, 'Keynesian' policies based on public spending may be approved. Yet Fanno's 'Keynesianism' was very limited. More than an organic programme based on public expenditure, Fanno advocated rigid controls in the exchange ratios and a severe discipline in industrial plant building. In the former case he advocated offsetting all 'abnormal capital movements' that were due to exogenous factors, while in the latter case he suggested control over all excessive plant capacity, thereby converging with the Fascist restrictive industrial strategy.[35]

Piero Sraffa's (mis)fortune in Italy

The young Piero Sraffa (1898–1983) successfully graduated under Luigi Einaudi's supervision. Sraffa's dissertation, soon printed in a slim volume entitled *L'inflazione monetaria durante e dopo la guerra*,[36] did not follow the traditional assessment of the question of inflation. Most observers, including Einaudi himself, ascribed inflation to excessive state expenditure and maintained that workers, via trade unions, were the main beneficiaries of inflation. Instead, Sraffa argued that profits benefited from inflation far more greatly than was the case for wages.

Furthermore, foreshadowing Keynes, Sraffa indicated the goal of domestic price stability as having priority over the goal of exchange stability (see Pavanelli 1993: 66–7). The same heterodox approach is shown in another paper[37] which aimed to explain to a foreign audience the complex Italian system of relations between banking and industry, with reference to the 1921 bankruptcy of the Banca di sconto. In contrast to Pantaleoni's essay on *Credito mobiliare*,

Sraffa did not seek to present a complete theory of bank bailouts, but limited himself to highlighting the concentration of economic and financial power in Italy, the new role of the central bank in coping with the insufficient bank credit supply for the industrial system, and – last but not least – the role of inflation in alleviating the banks' debt burden.

Subsequently, in his *Annali di economia* article 'Sulle relazioni fra costo e quantità prodotta',[38] Sraffa addressed a crucial issue in mainstream economics; namely, the symmetry between the theory of consumption and that of production/distribution. According to Marshall's *Principles of Economics* (Book V, Chapter III), while demand is dependent on the law of decreasing marginal utility, supply depends on the law of decreasing marginal productivity (that is to say, increasing marginal costs). Whereas classical economics, from Smith to Marx, argued that any variation in the quantity of manufacturing goods would not influence the marginal cost, which would be equal to the average cost, neo-classical economics, whose leader was Marshall, contended that costs are initially decreasing (because returns are growing) and subsequently increasing (because returns are diminishing) – as the well-known U-shaped curve demonstrates. But Sraffa objected that increasing and decreasing returns depend on elements that are completely heterogeneous (respectively, Smith's division of labour and Ricardo's sterility of land), whereas Marginalism had arbitrarily unified these elements. Moreover, increasing returns meant that all factors increase in the same proportion, while decreasing returns meant that one factor is fixed and the others have varied. Finally – and this is indeed the most important deduction – the non-proportionality of costs to the quantity produced implies either the escape from perfect competition (in fact, if returns are steadily growing there are no limits to the firm's expansion), or rebuttal of Marshall's typical *ceteris paribus* assumption on which partial equilibrium is entirely based. That is to say, all variations in a commodity's cost would affect the prices of the other commodities as well. Implicitly, this meant a re-evaluation of general equilibrium.

In a further twist of the story, Maurice Dobb, the Cambridge Marxist economist, was impressed by Sraffa's essay and suggested to Edgeworth and Keynes – the two editors of the *Economic Journal* – that they should publish it in abridged form.[39]

While in the English-speaking world the essay was well received and contributed to prompting research on non-competitive markets, in Italy the author's iconoclastic and trenchant tone was not appreciated, and the academic community was not generally sympathetic towards the work. Some of the reviewers did not even grasp the paper's real message. For instance, Vincenzo Porri, a senior colleague of Sraffa's in Turin, wrote that the 1925 article could encourage further 'empirical'(!) research. Gustavo Del Vecchio, for his part, although quite unhappy with Marginalism especially on account of its static approach, observed that 'returning to Ricardo' as implicitly advocated by Sraffa could not be a valid alternative to mainstream economics. Del Vecchio minimized the impact of Sraffa's attack on the symmetry between marginal utility and productivity and considered such symmetry as mainly of 'pedagogical' use.[40]

In this context one cannot refrain from observing that in his subsequent 1926 article Sraffa defined 'the fundamental symmetry between the forces of demand and those of supply' precisely as

> a pedagogic instrument, somewhat akin to the study of the classics, and, unlike the study of the exact sciences and law, its purposes are exclusively those of training the mind, for which reason it is unlikely to excite the passion of men, even academic men – a theory ... with respect to which it is hardly worthwhile departing from a tradition that has been finally accepted.[41]

Sraffa's use of 'pedagogy' as a synonym for intellectual conformism – besides being a playful jibe at Del Vecchio's remarks – is a typical Keynesian motif.

Finally, Sraffa's message was contested from the point of view of its originality. Turin professor Pasquale Jannaccone, editor of the fifth and last series of *Biblioteca dell'economista* and a renowned specialist on industrial economics, claimed his own priority in discussing the hypotheses of industries at constant, increasing and decreasing costs in an article he had published as early as 1914.[42] In effect, Jannaccone's article – centred on the phenomenon of dumping – can be considered as foreshadowing Clapham's discussion on 'empty economic boxes',[43] but somewhat less as a critical stance towards the marginal theory of costs and returns per se.

In March 1926, three months after his *Annali di economia* article, but nine months before his *Economic Journal* article, the 28-year-old Sraffa – at that time a lecturer at Perugia University – was appointed to the Cagliari University chair of political economy. But as early as July 1927 he moved to Cambridge and remained in Britain for the rest of his life.[44] His position in Cambridge gave him the opportunity to avoid taking the oath of allegiance to Fascism introduced in 1931, and he resigned that very same year from the Cagliari chair (Naldi 2008: 20, 27). Sraffa maintained his acquaintance with Einaudi, with whom he engaged in frequent correspondence, mainly on matters of rare editions and booksellers. Einaudi encouraged him to undertake the edition of Ricardo's work and called it 'a monument' when it was finally published.[45]

Quite different is the story of Sraffa's friendship with Antonio Gramsci, the founder of the Italian Communist Party who was imprisoned in 1926. The terms of his imprisonment allowed Gramsci to communicate only with family, so his sister-in-law Tania acted as intermediary with Sraffa. Sraffa gave Gramsci valuable assistance by providing him with books and journals, but did little to satisfy Gramsci's questions on economics, such as Machiavelli's economics and Ricardo's conception of a 'determined market'.

Gramsci's writings on economics were mainly contained in his *Prison Notebooks* and concerned the features of 'new' capitalism based on the combination of business organization and technology – the so-called Fordism. They do not appear to have been influenced by Sraffa.[46]

Del Vecchio, the Italian Schumpeter

While Fanno's reference authors were principally Wicksell, Hayek and Keynes, those of Gustavo Del Vecchio were Ferrara, Walras, Böhm-Bawerk and Pantaleoni. Of these, Ferrara and Walras influenced Del Vecchio's research on money, credit and equilibrium; Böhm-Bawerk, his work on capital and interest; and Pantaleoni his work meditations on dynamics. Although Del Vecchio never wrote a work explicitly devoted to method, his acute critical and historical sensitivity, more suitable for composing a work on interpretation than for creation, prompted him to engage in a continual quest for the origin and meaning of the different theories, as well as the trade-off between logical coherence and realism.

Unfortunately, Del Vecchio's stance presents a number of difficulties of interpretation. Balanced critic as he was, Del Vecchio made such a strong effort to weigh the comparative merits and demerits of the theories he treated with absolute impartiality, that a reader encounters serious difficulties in grasping the author's personal standpoint. Moreover, despite his ecumenical attitude, on various occasions Del Vecchio experienced a number of misgivings with regard to mainstream economics, praising pure economics for its formal perfection while at the same time berating it for its sterility. In contrast, although praising the Marshallian approach for its realism, he criticized the alleged narrowness of its vision of the economic phenomenon. Overall, Del Vecchio defined Keynes's thought as 'brilliant, but fragile' (Del Vecchio 1956: 11). Keynes's 'fragility', as Del Vecchio saw it, consisted in the lack of a coherently complete economic theory of money, as distinct from analysis of the various functions of money. Del Vecchio concluded that classical and Keynesian theories could be considered as fundamentally convergent. Such an attitude to some extent prefigured the subsequent neo-classical synthesis.

Finally, another stream of thought Del Vecchio considered as extremely important was Austrian theory, from which he drew many of his reflections on interest, capital and time. This multiplicity of strands of theory in Del Vecchio's thought has prompted one subtle commentator to define to him as a 'cultural mediator', rather than a mere eclectic (Zanni 1983: 26–7).

As mentioned earlier, Del Vecchio spent most of the interwar years meditating upon the current state of economic theory and its trends. He rejected the view of the development of economics as a succession of paradigms, schools, or, even worse, great individual personalities. More perceptively, Del Vecchio viewed this development as the outcome of a ramification departing from a single original tree – classical economics, especially Ricardian – and forming currents that were not mutually incompatible or conflicting, but had been *chosen* by economists in order to follow one particular path rather than another.

The most instructive case is that of the theory of value. In his interpretation, the fundamental categories at work were marginal utility, marginal cost and price. In Ricardo, it was the marginal cost (of wheat) that determined its price; in Jevons, it was marginal utility. At first sight the two theories are mutually exclusive. But in Ricardo, price determines marginal cost in the sense that if the price of wheat increases (as a consequence of a rising demand for it), then wheat cultivation will be extended and its marginal cost will increase owing to decreasing marginal returns, until it becomes equal to price. On the other hand, Ricardo could not deny that price determines marginal utility as well, for the reason that marginal utility will increase as price increases and demand consequently falls. Stated in these terms, Del Vecchio concluded, there is no conflict of theories between Ricardo and Jevons, but only a difference in the way of presenting the relations between the same variables. Thus, one may equally well choose to start from *c* (cost), *p* (price), or *u* (utility) in order to determine equilibrium (see Del Vecchio 1930: 75).

These concepts were to some extent generalized in 1932. Del Vecchio maintained that 'the Walras–Pareto system had closed rather than opened an era of economic theory' (Del Vecchio 1932: 407), but he argued that choice among the various doctrines was dictated first and foremost by what appeared most opportune and offered ease of approach. For instance, one could prefer to conceive of an economic system as a system of relations among material goods, in the manner of Ricardo, Thünen and Cournot; or of relations among psychical elements based on effort and satisfaction according to the approach favoured by Ferrara, Gossen, Jevons and Menger; or even in terms of 'the study of an abstract capital as distinct from capital goods' (an implicit reference to Marx *qua* opposed to Austrian economics: see Del Vecchio 1937: viii). The transition from one approach to the other was, to his mind, comparatively easy, owing to the fact that they deal with relative quantities and therefore abstract relationships. Hence, the idea of real progress in *theories* (as opposed to progress in *analysis*) was implicitly discarded.

Del Vecchio was of course aware that not all 'choices' among different theories were painless; each theory was to be submitted to a preliminary critical scrutiny. General equilibrium had to pass the test of the logical scrutiny of coherence; partial equilibrium, (also) that of realism. Here Del Vecchio finally acknowledged the importance of Sraffa's 1925 article, which demonstrated that Marshall's theory of the firm has its main limit in the concept of decreasing average costs (ibid., p. xiv).

As was the case for many economists of his time, dynamics was at the centre of Del Vecchio's scientific attention. Dynamics was rightly considered as different from the method of subsequent approximations in the Pareto tradition (Caffè 1983: 15), and was, instead, based on an integral reconstruction of economic phenomena through a connection between the historical method and the theoretical method. Economics, he argued, must originate from history and return to it 'without being dissolved in it', he wrote in 1952, adopting a philosophical mode of expression (Del Vecchio 1983 [1952]: 65).

But these words were not intended as a concession to old-fashioned 'historicism', in the sense of a mere reference to external and material conditions. Del Vecchio believed that the debate must remain within the field of economics, and that it should correct theoretical errors through a more exact theory, in accordance with the methodological lesson of Schumpeter who in 1930 edited a collection of Del Vecchio's monetary writings in German entitled *Grundlinien der Geldtheorie.*[47]

According to Del Vecchio (and Schumpeter as well), only a historical approach – that is, neither absolutist nor dogmatic – is able to reconstruct the genesis of theories. At the same time, only through work focusing on the 'hard core' of theory can the reason underlying its evolution be fully understood.

The Pareto school and dynamics

The 'years of high theory' in Italy were mainly characterized by numerous attempts to dynamize the Pareto-Walras model of general equilibrium. Quite distinct from Del Vecchio's indications on the need for a theory *within* history, a small but well trained group of economists examined the progress of mathematical economics, pioneered mainly in the United States by two professional mathematicians: G. Evans and C. G. Roos. It is interesting to note that Evans wrote his PhD thesis on the work of Vito Volterra (1860–1940), one of the most outstanding mathematicians of his time and the same man who had reviewed Pareto's 1906 *Manuale* and stimulated an important article by Pareto himself.[48]

The Italian mathematical economists active in the 1930s were principally Arrigo Bordin (1898–1963), Giovanni Demaria (1899–1998), Eraldo Fossati (1902–62), Valentino Dominedò (1905–85), Giuseppe Palomba (1908–86), Giulio La Volpe (1909–96), and, above all, Luigi Amoroso (1886–1965) – who had been a research assistant for the distinguished mathematician Guido Castelnuovo before undertaking a career as an economist. It should be stressed that their work not only concerned the formal properties of economic equilibrium – to some extent prefiguring the contributions by Abraham Wald on the existence and stability of equilibrium – but also included, in Amoroso's case, such elements as expectations, habits and other psychological elements in a cycle model and extended the inertia principle from mechanics to economics. The utilization of d'Alembert's principle was also in line with Pareto's legacy.[49]

It is beyond the scope of this book to examine the reasons that thwarted the development of this intriguing moment of cooperation between economists and mathematicians into a leading theme in the evolution of Italian economics. But it is likely that the political atmosphere of Fascism did little to encourage this line of research, prompting many economists to turn to the easier (and politically much more rewarding!) topic of *corporativismo*. Apart from this, the need for a more realistic approach to economics led the younger generation of economists – namely, the generation of the early decades of the twentieth century – away from an excess of formalism. This generation was to some extent prepared for the post-war 'discovery' of Keynes.

The concept of a close interdependence among phenomena was preferred to the nexus of a causal relationship that most economists considered as deterministic. This issue is especially apparent in Demaria (see below).[50] It is to be stressed that most of these attempts to establish a rigorous basis for theoretical economics moved in the direction of transporting the concepts of modern physics into economics; in Amoroso and Palomba the law of entropy; in Demaria the indeterminacy principle; and so forth. Naturally, if the basic implicit assumption was that the status of economics was closely allied with that of the natural sciences, such applications were almost obvious, and to some extent became little more than mere formal exercises. It is striking, however, that no parallel reflexion was undertaken to investigate the psychology of the so-called *homo oeconomicus*. Rather, Bentham's old categories continued to be considered as entirely valid. Keynes's intuitions on the nature of habits and propensities were altogether ignored by Italian theorists, who continued to work on the same anthropology as the previous century.

Giovanni Demaria's anti-determinism

Much more radically than Del Vecchio, his disciple Giovanni Demaria was in search of a unifying principle that could give economics the status of a 'hard' science. He too started from Pareto, but complained that Pareto's system was static as his equilibrium equations did not take time into account. On the other hand, Demaria observed, it would be wrong to re-introduce the ancient concept of cause in economics, and to identify the causal nexus with dynamic change. Against naive determinism, he chose to introduce into economics the indeterminacy principle which Werner Heisenberg had successfully introduced into physics in the very same decades.[51]

In fact, Demaria pointed out, just as it is impossible to measure both the position and speed of a particle – *mutatis mutandis* both the dimension and rate of variation of an economic quantity – it is impossible to make a rigorous forecast of the future state of an economic system. At best, all one can hope to achieve is to infer it statistically or probabilistically from an observed past event.

Demaria was also familiar with the American scene – as a young man he spent three years in the US and Germany (see Demaria 1981) – and declared his preference, among his fellow economists, for Frank H. Knight, the Chicago economist who introduced a fundamental distinction between risk (based on known probabilities) and uncertainty (based on subjective expectations). In 1932 Demaria was entrusted with editing the volume of *Nuova collana di economisti* dedicated to economic dynamics. The only Italian contribution to dynamics he hosted in the book was a short article by Amoroso, but the latter, rather than embarking on a discussion of the meaning of dynamics in economics, chose to explain the properties of differential equations, in order to offset some problems of dynamics, as consisting in 'fasces' of demand and supply curves instead of individual curves.[52]

Undoubtedly, Demaria went further in his methodological and philosophical position against 'causalism'. 'There is an error in interpreting economic phenomena as if they were invariably fixed in a time-place dimension devoid of activity and uniformly flowing' (Demaria 1934: 44). He did not refrain from introducing into economics a number of terms derived from other sciences. 'Entelechian' – an Aristotlean term describing the working of a vital force that leads the system to a state of quiet – was Demaria's favourite expression to define all facts that manifest themselves as unpredictable ruptures of the current trend. Here Demaria's conception was close to that of Schumpeter's demiurgic entrepreneur, whose action is often outside the traditional cause-effect sequence and is more frequently inscribed in the power-act sequence. It has been observed, however, that the treatment of 'entelechians' in Demaria more closely approximates Henri Bergson's intuitionism than Aristotle's rationalism.[53]

In subsequent decades Demaria worked on the so-called General Absolute System or Complete System, in which the traditional material of economics is treated endogenously (economic variables are endogenous by definition), but behind it there stands an exogenous non-economic sphere that exerts considerable influence. The outcome of the working of endogenous and exogenous forces is defined as 'complexity' and lies at the origin of fluctuations (see Bellanca 1996).

This ambitious intellectual programme led Demaria towards an increasing distrust of most of contemporary economics, especially the macroeconomic models which he considered as flawed by mechanism and determinism. He likewise rejected econometric research. In opposition to these studies, Demaria and his school developed a substantial body of historical research mainly into price fluctuations between the fifteenth and seventeenth centuries, with the aim of focusing on the 'entelechian forces' as primary factors, as well as their 'propagators' to the entire European economy. These studies concerned 'kinematics' rather than 'dynamics', since they recorded the fact of movement without providing any causal explanation, as the latter – given Demaria's scientific premises – would necessarily be flawed.

However, these attempts to provide empirical evidence for his theories on the realm of economic history encountered little success among professional economic historians, probably owing to the objective difficulties Demaria and his research group found in providing reliable data (see Demaria *et al.* 1968–87).

A man who embodied an era: Luigi Einaudi

A tireless journalist

During a period of over 60 years Luigi Einaudi (1874–1961) was astonishingly active as a journalist contributing to the Turinese *Stampa* (1896–1902) and the Milanese *Corriere della sera* (1903–25, and again after the fall of Fascism), which earned him great popularity and helped him build a subsequent career as a statesman. His positions were many and varied: editor of *Riforma sociale* (1908–35); lifelong Senator of the Kingdom (1919–43); Governor of the Bank of Italy (1945–47); deputy at the Constituent Assembly; member of the 'Committee of the 75' which drew up the Republican Constitution (1946–47); Vice-President of the Council and Budget Minister in the fourth De Gasperi cabinet (1947–48); finally President of the Italian Republic (1948–55). As such Einaudi enjoyed an influence over Italian public opinion greater than that exerted by any other economist, either before or afterwards. His militancy in the comparatively small Liberal Party was no obstacle to his success. On the contrary, somewhat paradoxically this circumstance enhanced his role as a man *au dessus de la mêlée* and therefore endowed him with the highest moral and intellectual authority.

As a journalist he commented upon all the main economic facts between the end of the nineteenth century and the sunset of the liberal state. He gathered together a broad selection of these articles in his eight-volume *Cronache*.[54] For many years he was *The Economist*'s Italian correspondent, writing short and incisive articles that have recently been published as a collection.[55]

An economic future for Italy

During the years around the turn of the century, Italy experienced some crucial moments in its economic and social history – mass emigration (more than ten million up to 1913) towards the two Americas; the start of industrialization and the making of an industrial working class in the North; the First World War economic effort; the post-war social and political unrest. All this was filtered through Einaudi's accurate day-to-day comments. In his careful scrutiny of facts, linking the analysis of the economic situation with that of the political and economic set-up, on many occasions Einaudi severely criticized the government's action, considering it as insufficiently market-oriented, or in other cases inordinately complaisant towards big business (Cassata and Marchionatti 2010).

Although a genuine liberal and an advocate of *laissez-faire*, Einaudi did not fully share the diagnosis of the other liberal economists. De Viti de Marco and the other free-traders considered Italy as condemned to specializing in the export of wine, olive oil and citrus fruits. Instead, Einaudi acutely perceived the birth of new entrepreneurial forces which would be instrumental in the development of modern and competitive light industry. In 1900 Einaudi examined the case of a Lombard textile entrepreneur – Enrico Dell'Acqua – who had gained a substantial fortune in Argentina and Uruguay through both the export of textiles from Italy and the establishment of new activities overseas with the aid of domestic (alas, protective) tariffs. The phrase 'merchant prince' – as Einaudi called Dell'Acqua – was borrowed from Walter Bagehot's *Lombard Street*, which Einaudi himself had translated in *Biblioteca dell'economista*. Einaudi's depiction highlighted an ideal continuity with the Renaissance noblemen active in trade and banking. Alexander Gerschenkron, the Harvard economic historian, has defined *Un principe mercante* as a 'fascinating' and excellent model for the study of entrepreneurship.[56]

Market and socialism

Einaudi was both a political liberal and an economic Liberalist, in exactly the same manner as Pareto and Pantaleoni. But in contrast to both of the latter, who were conservative liberals, Einaudi enriched his reflection – at least at its start – through a benevolent attitude towards the evolution of the socialist movement. As an observer of rapidly growing Piedmont, he did not believe the workers' 'leagues' (an earlier term for trade unions) represented a subversive menace; on the contrary he felt they were the outcome of the economic and political maturity of the working class. As early as 1897 he wrote:

> The workers' leagues are perhaps the first core of the institutions which in the future will morally, materially and intellectually elevate the conditions of the working classes. Today they are still simple tools of strikes.… But the Italian leagues are experiencing the same pattern of development as the British leagues…. Let the strikes and the working agitations of these years be the starting point for a transformation in which discussion will help to solve the controversies between capital and labour according to the English model![57]

Moreover, the unions were prompting employers to become organized and to substitute new updated industrial relations for old-fashioned paternalism. Einaudi was also in agreement with the concept that the unions should be assigned the task of raising funds for unemployment, disability and old age relief.

Consequently, Einaudi manifested his admiration for Fabian socialism and particularly for Beatrice and Sydney Webb, authors of *Industrial Democracy* (which he reviewed in 1898 and lauded as a 'masterly essay on economic sociology' that had achieved considerable progress over either Marxism or traditional *laissez-faire* literature). The Webbs' book was hosted in 1912 in the *Biblioteca dell'economista* collection (see Faucci 1986: 28).

During this period Einaudi contributed papers to the socialist journal *Critica sociale* – edited by Filippo Turati – whose aim was to create a task force of left-wing intellectuals for a truly reform-oriented programme. But Einaudi's early 'socialism' was by no means a state socialism of German inspiration. He believed the workers and employers should be left free to sign their agreements without any intervention by the State, not even as neutral arbiter. The behind-the-scenes opposition to corporatism shown by many liberal economists during Fascism had its intellectual roots in the 1890s.

In subsequent decades, however, Einaudi became increasingly dissatisfied with socialism. On the question of the political action of the Socialist Party, Einaudi followed Pantaleoni in remonstrating against the bureaucratic attitude and, still worse, the parasitism of many local organisms which had been set up in order to enlarge the electoral potential of the party. In particular, many cooperatives subsisted on the support of the socialist municipalities. In formulating these objections Einaudi was supported by his Turin colleague, and assistant to the editor of *Riforma sociale*, Giuseppe Prato (1872–1927).

Einaudi was mistrustful of the debate on planning and market socialism in the 1930s, a debate which on the international level involved such scholars as Lange, Dobb, Lerner and others. In his *Rivista di storia economica* Einaudi hosted a careful review essay on 'collectivist' literature written by his friend Attilio

Cabiati;[58] but Einaudi's own view was that 'all this belongs to the Kingdom of Dreams, namely, of pure schemes that economists are building with the aim of unreeling a guiding thread to help them find their way in the labyrinth of real life' (Einaudi 1940: 183).

Einaudi admitted that the perfect competition hypothesis was far-removed from reality, which tended to be increasingly dominated by 'monopolies, monopolistic structures, legal constraints, and so on' (ibid., p. 186). In the same years he rejected the Italian corporative experiment, which in the eyes of its apologists was expected to indicate a 'third way' between capitalism and communism. His feeling was that a genuine third way would not be found in Fascist corporatism, but only in a renewed form of economic liberalism; whereas socialism would be of little help in reconstructing the economy on a safer basis.

From the critique of 'justice in taxation' to the eulogy of ancient Athens

Einaudi's response to economic problems was very different from that of Pareto. This was not (only) due to the fact that Einaudi frankly admitted his lack of command over mathematics; rather, his mind spontaneously rejected excessively magnificent and complete constructions. In his early works he followed the path traced by his master Salvatore Cognetti de Martiis, and embarked on applied topics. His early studies in public finance were on local rates, a subject which at that time attracted the attention of many scholars because several towns, mainly in Northern Italy, had socialist administrations that were engaged in reforming taxation. The young Einaudi advocated taxation of the unearned increases of incomes in urban areas, not only for the sake of fiscal justice, but for economic reasons as well in the sense that such a tax would force landowners to build houses and thus transform themselves from *rentiers* into entrepreneurs. These ideas involved consideration of the elasticity of demand for dwellings, which led Einaudi to reject the commonly shared argument that since the demand was inelastic the tax would be shifted from owners to tenants.[59]

Some years later Einaudi addressed the same problem of efficiency versus justice in taxation from a more theoretical vantage point. In 1912 he produced an ambitious study of consumed income taxation, for which the theoretical framework was provided by John Stuart Mill and Irving Fisher. In Mill's framework (1848) taxing that part of income which is destined to saving would result in double taxation if the new income produced by invested savings were to be taxed as well. Fisher, on the other hand (1906), maintained that only income destined for final consumption is true income, while all income not actually consumed should be regarded as 'capital' and therefore not subject to income tax.

Both Mill and Fisher were worried about the negative effects of progressive taxation since it risked discouraging capital accumulation. Einaudi claimed that only proportional taxation led to 'equality', which he defined as that principle according to which '*if we tax one lira at 10 cents, each other lira of whatsoever income equal, higher or lower ... must be taxed at the same 10 cent tax*'.[60]

This statement, which he considered as axiomatic, implicitly assumed that marginal utility of income is constant, and this supported the case in favour of proportional against progressive taxation.

Surmounting all difficulties in coordinating Mill's classical (objectivist) theory of double taxation with Fisher's marginal (subjectivist) definition of psychological income, in the second part of his paper Einaudi attempted to demonstrate that all existing fiscal systems de facto exempt earned savings from taxation and mainly (or exclusively) affect the part of income that is destined to final consumption only. In so doing they respect the 'postulate of equality' by means of exemptions, deductions and other forms of qualitative discrimination. In this 'demonstration', or rather exemplification, Einaudi's profound knowledge of current fiscal systems was of great help.

The main implication of Einaudi's 'theorem' was that income taxation should not be based on the *source* of revenue but on its final *destination*, either for consumption or for saving. Einaudi naturally acknowledged that it was difficult to ascertain how taxpayers actually allocate their incomes. But in most cases, he observed, one can assume that a part of earned income will be allocated to consumption and therefore will be taxed, while another part will be allocated to *risparmio presunto* [presumed saving]. For instance, households allocate part of their income to the necessities of life in order to keep their capital's purchasing power unchanged. This destination is not to be considered as true consumption but rather as presumed saving, since it intends to improve people's ability to work and therefore must be exempted. Income from labour deserves a similar fiscal treatment. The part destined for paying for the necessities of life must be exempted.

Einaudi's essay gave rise to a lively debate[61] but the objections were more numerous than the endorsements. Internationally, Arthur Cecil Pigou – himself a supporter of the theory of the double taxation of saving – rightly observed that Einaudi should have more clearly defined the 'postulate of equality' that was the cornerstone of his doctrine. In Italy, Umberto Ricci and Benvenuto Griziotti replied to Einaudi that the returns on saved-invested income should be considered as newly produced income and therefore there were no grounds for a tax exemption.

In another paper, published in 1919, Einaudi refined his fiscal 'theorem' in two directions. First, he drew a distinction between the various kinds of tax according to their effects on the overall system. Three 'ideal types' were singled out: (1) the 'ransom tax' that is dissipated by a tyrannical government without any benefit for taxpayers (the simplest example is a tribute for the maintenance of a standing army); (2) the 'hail-tax' that leaves the economy uniformly poorer with no advantage for anybody, so that its effects are a pure loss; (3) the 'general', or 'uniform', or 'neutral tax' that 'leaves the *judgement of every taxpayer* concerning every unity of income invariant'.[62] In contrast to his 1912 article, here Einaudi formulated the postulate of equality in purely subjective terms.

Second, he examined not only the ways in which the State utilized the receipts of taxation, but also, more generally, the economic effects of public expenditure.

This aspect, with the partial exception of Pantaleoni's 1883 paper, was virtually neglected at the time. In treating the quite technical subject of amortization (the reduction in the capital value of a good whose income is taxed), he argued that the economic effects of public expenditure financed by the tax should be taken into consideration. Einaudi observed that if public expenditure had the goal of improving the economic environment, this outcome could not fail to increase all capital values. Therefore no amortization would take place.[63]

In subsequent years Einaudi realized that his statements on the basic postulates of a sound fiscal system could be addressed more satisfactorily in a general equilibrium rather than partial equilibrium context. The 'postulate of equality' – which in actual fact Einaudi never clearly stated – was set aside. Efficiency became the main (the one and only?) fiscal criterion.[64]

Last but not least, Einaudi's awareness of the relevance of historical research led him to find traces of the concept of 'normal' or 'ordinary' income in the most successful fiscal reforms carried out in the past. Both the 1750 Lombardy cadastre and the 1886 Kingdom of Italy cadastre were excellent instances of taxation that aimed to reward the best infra-marginal farmers and discourage the worst ultra-marginal farms (see Einaudi 1974 [1924]). Furthermore, he successfully identified many eighteenth-century theorists, especially the Physiocrats, as standing among the predecessors of his conception of 'optimal tax' (see Einaudi 1933).

In his last important work on public finance Einaudi not only harshly criticized all supporters of 'until-the-last-cent' taxation on actual income – by arguing in favour of taxation on normal income – he also added that a perfect fiscal system should encourage spontaneous and voluntary contributions as well. This had been the case, he recalled, in ancient Athens under Pericles, with the 'liturgies' paid by the rich in order to cover the expenses for public entertainments and other duties (see Einaudi 1959 [1938]: 267–8).

The Great Crisis: Einaudi versus Keynes

Along with many other Italian economists, Einaudi also enthusiastically praised Keynes's *Economic Consequences of the Peace* for its pacifist message as well as its critical attitude towards the Treaty of Versailles.[65]

In the 1930s, however, Einaudi engaged in a long-distance polemic with the English economist concerning both the vision of economic process, and Keynes's analysis. Keynes's provocative essay *Economic Possibilities for Our Grandchildren*, collected in his *Essays in Persuasion* (1931), triggered Einaudi's protests. As is well known, Keynes argued that 'the scarcity problem' would be definitively solved in the near future, and humankind would favourably reappraise goals with respect to means, and the good with respect to the useful. In the same essay Keynes presented capitalism as a mere conjuncture phenomenon, attributable to an exogenous fact – the influx of precious metals from Latin America in the sixteenth and seventeenth centuries – and presumably destined to end through the effects of another exogenous fact in the future. In a review article Einaudi voiced his disapproval of this 'history written by a latecomer Marx' (Einaudi 1932). The accumulation required for the capitalist take-off had been built up over several centuries of slow, painstaking saving, not through the casual piracy enterprises carried out by Francis Drake – as Keynes appeared to maintain.

Once again everything turned on the role of saving. Keynes, Einaudi observed, on the one hand viewed saving as useless, while on the other he spoke disparagingly of saving that was left idle instead of being employed. This point was then clarified by Keynes in his subsequent essay *The Means to Prosperity* (1933), where the author distinguished between crises that are due to insufficient resources – which should be remedied by 'abstinence, hard work and invention' – and crises attributable to the existence of idle resources. According to Keynes only the latter required public expenditure financed by loans, as well as public works capable of activating the multiplier process and thus creating new income.

In his review Einaudi ignored this possibility and insisted on the difficulty of raising the necessary money for the public loan, or the public expenditure that would have the result of ensuring full employment of idle resources. His response was that it should come from taxpayers' pockets, and only from them, since 'without a hare we cannot make a hare pie' (Einaudi 2006 [1933]: 127). Einaudi based his argument on the assumption that the formation of new incomes comes about through the banking system, but that the process goes from saving to investment and not from investment to saving. Moreover, the bank's reserves create a limit on credit expansion. Einaudi concluded by reaffirming the orthodox view; namely, that all saving deposited in the banking system is but a form of investment which savers regard as more secure than other forms of utilization. Only when the habits of investing-saving and those of mass consumption changed would the crisis be overcome.

Finally, three years after the *General Theory*'s publication, Einaudi wrote a passionate critical review of Keynes's book in which he maintained that liquidity preference could be a mere effect, and not *the* cause of crises. Hoarding, he asserted, was a typical phenomenon of historical periods of uncertainty, such as the Terror under the French Revolution. In normal times money performs its physiological tasks, and its demand is predominantly attributable to transaction motives.

After the Second World War Einaudi undertook an overview of all Keynesian strategies based on 'massive investments' undertaken by the State for the development of the South. Such investments, Einaudi objected, were inevitably destined to create inflation or to produce crowding-out effects against private investments (Einaudi 1956: 301–18).

Fascist economics, liberalism and the 'third way': Einaudi, Croce and Roepke

At the time of the evolution of Fascism towards an outright dictatorship, Einaudi took on the self-appointed role of defender of economic orthodoxy against the assaults of the regime's supporters. Many Fascist writers, including several economists, presented corporatism as a genuine alternative both to liberalism and communism. Einaudi therefore embraced the task of defending the independence of economics against the onslaught of (totalitarian) politics.

Einaudi's strategy was twofold. At the beginning he supported a 'Pantaleonian' view of economic dogma, rejecting any version of economics as a historical science and minimizing the influence of the social and material background in determining the pace of theoretical progress. He thus initially believed that the history of economics should be limited to the search for priorities in discovering this or that absolute truth (see Faucci 1986: 271). Einaudi went on to indicate the category of *price* as the pivot of economics, and the price of pure competition as the ideal standard to which any real economic system should be directed. By contrast, all alternative prices, such as monopoly prices or variously managed (including corporative) prices, could also become object of analysis; but they should be deemed as sub-optimal cases. Consequently, they should not be taken as policy goals (in Einaudi there is no room at all for a second-best approach).

Between 1927 and 1942, in an exchange of ideas with Benedetto Croce, Einaudi discussed the question of the relationship between political liberalism, economic liberalism and the 'third way'. After his discussion with Pareto, Croce had concluded that no true dialogue with economists was feasible, flawed as it was by their inability to engage in philosophical theorizing. In particular, he disdainfully remarked that they proclaimed themselves to be 'liberal', while they were, at most, simple Liberalists or followers of *laissez-faire*, understood as a mere empirical or practical norm of conduct. In so doing they were unable to contemplate any philosophical view of economics, and – Croce commented – this was good because there must be always a clear-cut line between empirical and speculative disciplines (see Croce 1945 [1927]: 316–20).

In the comment Einaudi wrote in response to Croce, he defended the liberal point of view of the economists. While acknowledging that *laissez-faire* was an empirical concept, Einaudi maintained that inasmuch as it contributed to the material improvement of society, *laissez-faire* could chart the road both to material and moral improvement for the whole of mankind, and could therefore contribute to an increase in general happiness (see Faucci 1986: 294). Thus, although the two scholars were in complete agreement on the description of an 'optimal society' – namely, a society enjoying Liberty – they continued to diverge as far as the essence of liberty was concerned, divided as to whether it embodied a lofty but also somewhat loose concept of Liberty of Spirit (as Croce argued), or a more commonsense concept historically restricted to the Western world and mainly based on free market competition (as Einaudi maintained).

In 1942 – a crucial date for the outcome of the war – Einaudi returned to the question of the ideal economic system, and implicitly admitted that identifying this ideal system with historical (Western) capitalism was faulty. In a long review article of the German economist Wilhelm Roepke's *The Social Crisis of Our Time*, Einaudi distinguished between historical capitalism – which had produced class struggle, industrial pollution and monopolies – and a pure 'economics of competition' that was full of moral elements including active cooperation, the sense of equality pervading the community, and, above all, a human (i.e. small) average dimension of firms. In 1943, fleeing occupied Turin, Einaudi took refuge in Switzerland, a country which appeared to him to best approximate his ideals of a 'good society'.

Indefinable corporatism

Let us return to *corporativismo* [corporatism], the official economic and juridical doctrine proclaimed by Mussolini. In 1926 Fascism forbade both strikes and lock-outs, and established that only the Fascist trade unions could sign collective agreements. Subsequently, Fascism promulgated the *Carta del Lavoro* [Labour Charter, 1927] in which the principles of the new corporative state were solemnly fixed, beginning with the regimentation of all workers and entrepreneurs in state organs, improperly called corporations – which invoked an allusion to the glorious medieval tradition.

Of course, no freely elected representation of workers was allowed. All worker representatives were appointed from above. In 1934 the Council of Corporations was created, and in 1939 the Chamber of Deputies was renamed *Camera dei fasci e delle corporazioni*.

Considerations of space preclude a detailed assessment of the real impact of corporatism on the Italian economy; suffice to observe that the three main economic decisions taken by the regime – the revaluation of the lira (1927), the birth of the *Istituto per la ricostruzione industriale* (1933) which contributed to rescuing the main Italian industries from failure, and the new Bank Act which assigned to the Bank of Italy special powers over the banking system (1936) – were made without a relevant contribution by the corporative organs.[66]

As far as corporative ideas are concerned, it is worth noting that many corporative ideologists wished to reconnect corporatism to an anti-classical tradition of economic thought which some of them regarded as 'voluntaristic', in contrast with the 'naturalistic' tradition represented by pure economics.[67] Indeed this line of thought, which intended to refer back to such past economists as Romagnosi and Toniolo, was undoubtedly present, mainly by virtue of Catholic social doctrine. But doubt can be raised as to whether it was genuinely of topical interest in the 1930s.

Moreover, Fascism also wished to present itself as a movement *à la page*, which had benefited from the contemporary debate on the 'end of capitalism' (Fried 1933). A remedy to the crisis of capitalism could, in the eyes of Fascist thinkers, be found by subordinating economics to politics. After all, this was Machiavelli's teaching – and Machiavelli was one of Mussolini's favourite authors.

The prospect of a 'third way' between unbridled liberalism and absolute collectivism attracted the interest of some Fascist economists in connection with the Roosevelt experiment, which they presented as a sort of American corporatism.[68] Additionally, as far as the European countries were concerned, they sought to present it in connection with France's *économie regulée*.[69]

It is indisputable that in the early 1930s these issues stimulated some of the most interesting political-economical contributions of the time. Nonetheless, the debate was very soon suffocated because the regime feared that unprejudiced discussion on the (negative) characteristics of market capitalism could spiral out of control. In 1932, at the second Meeting of Corporative Studies held in Ferrara, philosopher Ugo Spirito (1896–1979, a disciple of Giovanni Gentile), maintained that the main goal of corporatism was that of overcoming the liberal concept of private property in favour of the 'corporation as proprietor' principle.

This magniloquence concealed the modest aim of allowing some participation of the State in the executive boards of the greatest corporations, and entitlement of the workers to profit sharing. But the majority of the participants firmly opposed this proposal. As a consequence Spirito decided to abandon his economic studies and to return to philosophy.[70]

Apart from this current of thought, a more academic approach was that of 'translating' corporatism into the more familiar language of individual and collective maxima, according to Pantaleoni's standpoint as expressed in his *Massimi individuali e collettivi*. Finally, another perspective was that of defining corporatism as an economy in which one specific variable – namely wages – was removed from the interplay of economic forces and determined by a technical organ through some equitable criteria (Bini 1982: 253–83).

This position was not too far removed from that shared by the (few) liberal economists who approached corporatism from the vantage point of traditional economics. In their view, price in a corporative system was a non-competition price, to be approached in particular by reference to bilateral monopoly with its consequent indeterminacy problems.[71]

On other matters, most academic economists opted to label as 'corporative' their own conception of economic policy in order to avoid any political complications with the Fascist regime. This appears clearly in some manuals. For instance, Marco Fanno defined as corporative a policy that balanced the credit supply with the different duration of the productive cycles, and the supply of goods with consumers' tastes. Equilibrium was thus established between the pace of investment and that of saving – a topic which, as noted earlier, was Fanno's main research subject throughout his life (Fanno 1938). In contrast, Giuseppe Ugo Papi defined as corporatist a system that could stabilize the fluctuations in industrial costs, which Papi considered to be among the main causes of the Great Crisis (Papi 1943; on Papi's role in post-war years see Chapter 8 below).

The last five years of the Fascist regime were poor in terms of intellectual novelty. From 1938 attention was reserved to autarky and preparations for war. It was felt that the 'new order' which was to be imposed upon the whole of Europe, following the inevitable and overwhelming victory of the Axis, should first concern itself with exploitation of the 'great economic spaces' that would become available to the victors.

Many studies produced by technocratic *Istituto nazionale di finanza corporativa* (founded 1939) on war financing were partially inspired by Keynes's *How to pay for the war* (1940). Interest focused on the problems of necessary control over excess liquidity created by the growth of public expenditure (see Pavanelli 1989).

In 1942, a year that marked the decline of the Axis's fortunes, a debate on the perspectives of post-war reconstruction was held in Pisa. The general report was presented by Demaria, who proudly claimed the vindication of the truth of 'our own theorems' (that is, those of pure economics), and rejected not only autarky but economic planning as well.[72]

The debate resembled a conference, and a report was delivered by Cesare Dami (1915–1973), a young left-wing corporatist who became a member of the Communist Party after the war and whose works can be categorized as belonging to the 'market socialism' wave (for this reason he found himself struggling against the supporters of central Soviet-type planning). In Demaria's report, however, economic freedom and absence of planning risked becoming closely associated. These clear-cut positions would later be confirmed in the post-war reconstruction debate.

Notes

1 Carlo Rosselli's most important economic writings are collected in C. Rosselli (1973). On Pesenti see VV. AA. (2011).
2 Riccardo Bachi (1875–1951), an esteemed applied economist, fled to Palestine. Gustavo Del Vecchio (1883–1972) took refuge in Switzerland. Marco Fanno (1878–1965), a Jew who converted to Catholicism, escaped to a monastery near Padua. Bruno Foà (1905–99), a Neapolitan monetary economist, full professor at the age of 28, went to the US. Giorgio Fuà (1919–2000), a student of the Collegio Mussolini of Corporative Sciences of Pisa, was expelled from the Collegio as a Jew. He continued his studies in Geneva. See his wife's entertaining memories in E. Fuà (2004). Franco Modigliani (1918–2003), a Fascist in his youth as witnessed by his early articles on economic policy, went to the US (see his 1999 autobiography). Mario Pugliese (1903–40), a young full professor of public finance, expatriated to Argentina, while Giorgio Mortara (1885–1967), a statistician and economist went to Brazil. Finally, Giorgio Tagliacozzo (1909–96), author of a 1937 anthology which was praised by Schumpeter (1994: 136 and ff.), also went to the US.
3 Giovanni Gentile, the 'philosopher of Fascism', who was President of Bocconi University, expressed solidarity (privately) towards some Jewish colleagues. See the revealing correspondence published by Zanni in Bini (1996). There was the danger that *Giornale degli economisti* could close. See the important correspondence edited by Zanni (1977): 70–97.
4 See Marchionatti (2011): 49–51.
5 On Fubini, see Forte (2009a). On Dalla Volta see the anthology of his writings (mainly dealing with international economic relations) by Augello and Guidi (2009).
6 Ricci [1918] in Finoia (1980): 5–16.
7 A comparison between the 'state of the troops' in 1922 and in 1943, limited to *professori ordinari* [full professors], is attempted by Faucci in Becattini (1990): 221–5. No exact information is available on the global number of *liberi docenti, professori incaricati* [temporary teachers] and *assistenti*, but a projection of the data available for the *Laboratorio di economia politica* of Turin over the entire Italian university system (see Università degli studi di Torino, 1993) could suggest that the mass of university staff in economics totalled not less than 300. This was partly due to the establishment of the faculties of political sciences, where economics was also taught.

8 This by no means implies that the 'Turin school' had ceased to be regarded as having a respectable scientific level. See VV. AA. (2009).

9 There is insufficient space to present an extended discussion of the work of Ricci (1879–1946), who was perhaps the only authentic disciple of Pantaleoni, an expert in agrarian statistics and, as a 'pure' economist, a specialist on demand theory and saving theory (but see also his witty comments on economic policy: Ricci (1919)). In 1928 Ricci was forced to resign from his chair owing to an article he had written that was interpreted as a criticism of corporatism. He therefore moved to the Fuad University of Cairo, where he met another Italian voluntary exile, Costantino Bresciani Turroni. In 1942 Ricci finally moved to Istanbul University and died suddenly during his return journey to Italy. On his life and work see Bini and Fusco (2004).

10 Gini (1885–1965) is universally known for his concentration index, still of use in dealing with non-competitive markets, but he was an authoritative theorist of demography as well, with heavy 'totalitarian' (imperialist) implications. See Cassata (2006).

11 Breglia (1900–1955), a Catholic of left-wing allegiance, wrote mainly on the history of economic thought and on macroeconomics (his posthumous work can be found in Breglia (1965)). Corbino (1890–1984), a committed liberal and Liberalist, was an expert in maritime economics and a clever historian of Italian economy (see Corbino 1982 [1931–38]).

12 Arena (1890–1967) was an expert on labour economics and co-edited the *Nuova collana di economisti* (see below). On Gangemi (1894–1973) see in particular his useful survey, Gangemi (1924).

13 See Backhaus (2001); Di Matteo and Longobardi (2012).

14 On Griziotti, the founder of a public finance school centred on the close collaboration between economists and law scholars, see Osculati (2007).

15 See VV. AA. (2004a).

16 De' Stefani (1879–1969) authored above all manuals and surveys on economic legislation, but a number of his articles published in *Corriere della sera* were published as a collection (see among others *La resa del liberalismo economico* (1932)). In the dramatic Gran Consiglio meeting of 25 July 1943, he voted against Mussolini and therefore contributed to the regime's final crash. After the war he acted as an economic advisor to the Chiang-Kai-Shek regime in Taiwan. On De' Stefani see Marcoaldi (1986).

17 See Zanni (1985): 253–75.

18 See Brandolini and Gobbi (1990): 39–78.

19 See *Carteggio Loria-Graziani* (1990): 288.

20 See a complete international bibliography on Schumpeter in Augello (1990). For his influence in Italy see Santarelli (1984): 507–29; Graziani (1989): 41–83.

21 See Realfonzo (1990): 181–95.

22 For a complete account of the Keynes editions in Italy see VV. AA. (1984).

23 See Asso (1981–82): 211–25; 69–80.

24 See Pavanelli (1993): 68–80.

25 On Bresciani-Turroni (the hyphen between the two surnames means that Turroni was subsequently added for inheritance reasons) see Bini (1992); Rotondi (2006): 23–57.

26 See Bresciani Turroni (1939): 639–714; Bresciani Turroni (1951), vol. 2, Chapter VIII.

27 See a bibliography and a selection of these articles, drawn from *Weltwirtschaftliches Archiv*, in Bini (1986). The articles principally concern the application of statistical methods to price series.

28 On forced saving see the review article by Vito (1934): 3–46. It is a pity that this article is not included in the collection of articles from *Rivista internazionale di scienze sociali* translated into English in the special issue of the journal (2011, No. 3–4) and edited by S. Nerozzi and D. Parisi.

29 Bresciani Turroni (1931) (English translation 1937).
30 See Skidelski (1992), Chapter 16 (Italian translation 1996: 703–4).
31 Bresciani Turroni (1938): 76–88. More recent literature has observed that in Bresciani's critique of the multiplier mechanism the distinction between short and long period was not sufficiently taken into account (see Graziani 1981: 164).
32 See Fanno (1931): 329–71 (English translation 1993). See Delli Gatti and Gallegati (1991): 123–45; see also Magliulo (1998), especially 101–12, where Fanno is convincingly presented as a forerunner of the neo-classical synthesis. Finally, Meacci (2012): 593, examines Fanno's theory of prices (especially with regard to joint production) as an important development of Marshall's ideas.
33 See Arena in Meacci (1998): 124.
34 Some letters from Fanno to Hayek are in the appendix to this book, unpublished during the author's life, Fanno (1992) [1933].
35 See Fanno (1935), on which see Caffè (1966), vol. 1.
36 Sraffa (1920); see the introduction to a reprint of this work by M. De Cecco in *Economia politica*, 1994, 2.
37 Sraffa (1922): 178–97.
38 Sraffa [1925] in Pasinetti (1998): 322–82.
39 See Pasinetti (1985): 324 (English translation, 'Piero Sraffa: an Italian economist at Cambridge' in Pasinetti (1998): 375).
40 See Del Vecchio (1932) [1926]: 439–41.
41 Sraffa (1953) [1926]: 180–1.
42 See Jannaccone (1936): 21–24. This claim was authoritatively endorsed by Einaudi in his contribution to the *Festschrift* for Benedetto Croce: Einaudi [1950] in Finoia (1980): 107.
43 Clapham [1922] reprinted in Boulding and Stigler (1953): 119–30.
44 See Naldi in Kurz *et al.* (2008): 13.
45 See Einaudi (1953): 155–61.
46 See Gramsci (1994): xiii–xv. Some considerations are in Faucci (2010): 91–115.
47 See Del Vecchio (1997) [1930].
48 The analytical aspects involving the integrability of the related ophelimity functions are treated by Montesano (2006): 77–100; Scapparone (2007): 101–12. See also Pomini in Di Matteo and Donzelli (2012): 22–3.
49 On the difficulties Pareto encountered in transforming his system as part of the transition from statics to dynamics see Donzelli (1997) (*History of Economic Ideas* special issue dedicated to the centenary of Pareto's *Cours*). On Amoroso see Palomba (1966): 387–421. See now Tusset (2012): 43–63.
50 For a panorama of the international studies on dynamics, inclusive of the Italian contribution, see the proceedings of the 2009 Sienna Conference, Di Matteo and Donzelli (2012). See also Tusset (2004), especially Part II; Pomini (2009): 57–83; Pomini and Tusset (2009): 311–42.
51 See Demaria [1932] 'Di un principio di indeterminazione in economia dinamica', English translation in Pasinetti (1998): 149–82.
52 Amoroso (1932): 422.
53 See Raffaelli (1990): 172–3; Zanni (1996): 39–47.
54 Einaudi (1959–64). A supplement to this collection is M. A. Romani (2012), 2 vols.
55 See Marchionatti (2000), 2 vols.
56 See Gerschenkron (1965) [1962]: 83.
57 Einaudi (2012) [1924]: 68.
58 Cabiati (1940): 73–110.
59 L. Einaudi (1902). In his personal copy of Einaudi's article, Edgeworth annotated this aspect favourably.
60 L. Einaudi, (1958) [1912]: 13; italics by Einaudi. See the abridged English translation in *Italian economic papers*, III: 32.

61 See the review of different positions in Faucci (1986): 124–36.
62 See Einaudi (1958) [1919]: 181; italics mine.
63 There is no room to deal with Einaudi's general attitude towards public expenditure.
    Forte (2009a: 116 and ff.) praises Einaudi as the representative of an orthodox indi-
    vidualist liberal position, in opposition to a paternalist (*étatiste*) position mainly
    represented by Beveridge. Forte appears to have changed his mind since an earlier
    book in which he assimilated Einaudi to Keynes (Forte (1982)).
64 See Einaudi (2006) [1928–29]: 189–216.
65 See Einaudi (1961) [1920]: 643–50.
66 See Faucci (1975); for an institutional account see Gagliardi (2010).
67 See Fanfani (1942), where 'voluntarism' is more or less a synonym of normativism.
68 See Fossati (1937): ix.
69 See VV. AA. (1933). It must be said that in France the corporatist experiment was
    followed with particular interest; see Mornati (1997): 93–115.
70 See the collection of his economic essays in Spirito (1970).
71 Masci (1934), reprinted in Mancini *et al.* (1982), vol. II: 575.
72 See Demaria's text, reprinted in Demaria (1951): 473–502.

8   Post-war and recent decades

Political contrasts and economic issues during the reconstruction

The post-war years (1945–53) mark a far-reaching solution of continuity in the history of unified Italy. The main policy issues became a matter of public discussion, involving political parties, trade unions and entrepreneurial forces. In this situation, which corresponded to an accomplished democracy, it was increasingly felt that economists could play a significant role by disseminating their thought on a wide range of issues.[1]

Systematic research on the economists' participation in the political choices during the two crucial years, 1945–47, has so far not been attempted. Here, only the main guidelines for an assessment of the economists' role will be provided.

The basic essential problem was that of reconciling the necessary resumption of industrial production with the likewise necessary clean-up among the figures whose reputation was compromised through their involvement with the past regime. This point coincided with the need of new democratic industrial relations, to be centred on a more incisive presence of the workers' representatives within firms.

More generally, this also concerned the problem of the purge of Fascists from public life (especially from the public administration). The two moderate parties – the Liberals and the Christian Democrats – were in favour of 'normalization', namely, a substantial confirmation of the old personnel with the exception of the most striking cases of direct involvement with the Nazi-Fascist rule of 1943–45. The three parties on the left, and especially the *Partito d'Azione* (PdA) were, on the contrary, favourable to a severe process of regeneration of Italian society through a full-fledged purge of the most compromised personalities. However, the overall results were unsatisfactory. Count Carlo Sforza, an anti-Fascist exile, was appointed *Alto Commissario* [High Commissioner] for the sanctions against Fascism, but the public servants who eventually lost their posts were 1,300 out of 140,000 examined, with 13,000 put on trial. Moreover, in June 1946, soon after the proclamation of the Republic, Justice Minister Togliatti granted an amnesty for (minor?) crimes committed during the 1943–45 civil war. The normalization process thus effectively concluded with a collective pardon.

As far as professorial staff within the university system were concerned, only temporary suspensions from teaching were pronounced. All apologists of corporatism and autarky rapidly reoccupied their chairs, and in many cases were subjected to no penalization at all.[2]

These contradictions exploded in the first post-Liberation national cabinet, chaired by Ferruccio Parri, one of the leaders of the *Resistenza* movement in 1943–45 and the head of Partito d'Azione. Parri – also an economic expert, formerly in the Edison electric company *ufficio studi* – proved unable to conciliate such incompatible positions as those of liberals and of communists within the cabinet, and after six months he was compelled to resign. Subsequently, Alcide De Gasperi, the Christian Democrat leader, came to power and this contributed to a partial simplification of the political situation. The Partito d'Azione rapidly dissolved, and the three mass parties, the DC, the PCI and the PSIUP (the latter renamed as PSI after the January 1947 secession of its social democratic wing), eventually occupied the scene.

Knowing for reconstructing: the Economic Commission for the Constituent Assembly

An important outcome of the period was the creation of a Ministry for the Constituent Assembly, entrusted with collecting materials for preparation of the future Constitution (see VV. AA. 1995).

In October 1945 the Minister for the Constituent Assembly, the socialist leader Pietro Nenni, appointed a *Commissione economica per la Costituente*, headed by Professor Giovanni Demaria. Both the official reports and the hearings of the Commission are a precious source of information on the state of the Italian economy soon after the war, as well as on the ideas and programmes of reconstruction that independent personalities, entrepreneurs, civil servants and professional economists had in mind.[3]

Two features of the *Commissione*'s reports and hearings must be recalled. On the one hand, most economists who were interrogated – among whom there were several apologists of *étatisme* during the past regime – advocated a return (?) to free trade and *laissez-faire* without any further specifications. On the other hand, many entrepreneurs were pessimistic with regard to the prospects of the Italian economy. At that time it was impossible to foresee the 'Italian economic miracle' of the 1950s. Most economic experts limited themselves to signal that Italian industry, seriously damaged but not entirely destroyed, could draw temporary advantage from Germany's inability to compete at an international level. Correspondingly, it was unimaginable that Germany too would achieve a remarkable economic performance by virtue of the 'market social economy' model, ideated by Wilhelm Roepke, the ordo-liberal economist, and carried out by Finance Minister Ludwig Erhard.

Another committee, established on January 1946 and chaired by Pesenti, was that on labour. In the third volume of its proceedings, *Memorie su argomenti economici*, the young economist Paolo Sylos Labini advocated a 'Keynesian' programme of public works to alleviate unemployment. Once more, it is interesting to observe that in Sylos Labini's estimation it would take Italy at least 12 years to reach the 1938 GDP level (see Sylos Labini 1946: 271–306). It was actually reached as early as 1950.

However, this considerable effort to assess the state of the Italian economy in order to propose the necessary reforms was to some extent thwarted by the tumultuous succession of political events.

Economists at the Constituent Assembly

At the June 1946 political elections to the Constituent Assembly and the associated institutional referendum for the Republic, three-quarters of the votes went to the DC, the PSIUP, and the PCI taken together (DC 35 per cent, PSIUP 20 per cent, PCI 19 per cent). A degreee of success was also achieved by *L'Uomo Qualunque*, a right-wing group that advocated extensive tax cuts, absolute *laissez-faire* and the advent of the so-called *governo dei tecnici* who should have replaced all professional politicians in the government (a similar movement was present also in France). No neo-Fascist party had been admitted to the elections.

Among the Constituent Assembly members there were several economists (Barucci 1980: 31 and ff.), three of whom, all belonging to the DC, were particularly active.

Ezio Vanoni (1903–56), professor of public finance and financial law, came from the Pavia school of Benvenuto Griziotti, a school that was favourable to economic interventionism and to fiscal reform based on progressive taxation. Vanoni was appointed as Finance and Budget Minister in several post-war cabinets, and presented the first national economic plan (on Vanoni see Magliulo 1991).

Amintore Fanfani (1908–99), professor of economic history and of the history of economic doctrines at the Milan 'Sacred Heart' Catholic University, had in his early years published a study criticizing Max Weber's *Protestant ethics*.[4]

Fanfani was open to American institutional economics, insofar as it did not conflict with Catholic corporatism, which he had absorbed from the *Quadragesimo anno* encyclical. Some ambiguities in his thought are represented by his early sympathies – never disclaimed, to our knowledge – towards Salazar's *Estado Nuovo* (see the recollections of Demaria 1995: 227).

Fanfani initiated his political career as Labour Minister in 1947, concluding with his appointment as Budget Minister in 1989. He was six times Premier between 1954 and 1987, and twice Senate President. He was also appointed lifelong Senator.

His party and Constituent Assembly colleague Giorgio La Pira (1904–77), professor of Roman law at Florence University and mayor of the town in the 1950s and 1960s, manifested more than simple curiosity toward economics and probably foreshadowed a reading of Keynes as a crypto-Catholic economist that would be widespread in Italian politics in the following years. This resolved in a heated controversy with Reverend Luigi Sturzo (1871–1959), the founder of Partito Popolare in 1919 and representative of an extreme *laissez-faire* position.[5]

The third DC economist worth mentioning is Paolo Emilio Taviani (1912–2001), a *libero docente* of the history of economic doctrines and who studied at the Collegio Mussolini of Corporative Sciences of Pisa. In 1945 he directed the insurrection of Genoa against the Nazi-Fascists. From the 1950s onwards he held ministerial posts on many occasions. As an economist he touched on such topics as the historical origins of demand theory, the economics of cooperation, and equity in distribution. Moreover, he supported the critique to collectivism from a philosophic standpoint inspired by Maritain and Mounier (see Bartolozzi Batignani 1985).

All of these economists co-authored the so-called *Codice di Camaldoli*, from the name of the Tuscan monastery that hosted a meeting of Catholic intellectuals in the very last days of the Fascist regime (18–24 July 1943). This Code, once more following the lines of the Pope's social encyclicals, aimed to establish the guidelines for Italy's post-war economic and political reconstruction, by encouraging cooperation between capital and labour and advocating respect for the 'social function of property'. The leading concept in determining the scope of the State's action was the principle of 'subsidiarity'. The State should aim 'to encourage individuals, families and other groups to better solve their own problems with their own forces', but it should not be a substitute for them, in contrast to socialist and collectivist experiences (Magliulo 1991: 54).

The PSIUP economists were led by Rodolfo Morandi (1902–55), who had written a pioneering *Storia della grande industria in Italia* (1931) before being imprisoned by Fascism. As Industry Minister in 1946–47 he was a supporter of *Consigli di gestione*, an attempt to introduce supervision and control over the firms' management via the workers' representatives (see Morandi 1975 [1960]). Owing to the masters' prejudicial hostility, this experiment had very limited applications and ceased within a few years.

In addition to Pesenti, the PCI leaders who had received the strongest training in economics were Emilio Sereni (1907–77), a *libero docente* and author of a classical study on the structure of Italian land property (*Il capitalismo nelle campagne*, 1947); Pietro Grifone (1908–83), an *Assonime* [Joint-stock Companies Association] functionary during Fascism, whose book *Il capitale finanziario in Italia* (1945) drew on Rudolf Hilferding's category of 'finance capital' to interpret the structure of the Italian economy; and Bruzio Manzocchi (1917–61), author of *Lineamenti di politica economica in Italia* (1960). Most of them had experienced the Fascist prisons.

Altogether different was the approach to economics followed by the Social Democrats of the PSDI, who had seceded from the PSIUP in 1947. Their most representative economist was Roberto Tremelloni (1900–87), a *libero docente* at Geneva University and author of a *Storia dell'industria italiana contemporanea* (1947) prefaced by Einaudi. Giovanni Demaria also belonged to this group as consultant economist to Giuseppe Saragat, the PSDI leader. Both Tremelloni and Demaria were reformers in the Western meaning of the term – namely, they supported state intervention only in cases of the most evident 'market failures', principally monopolies.

Finally, the most prominent of the moderate (centre-right) economists at the *Costituente*, after Luigi Einaudi, was Epicarmo Corbino (1890–1984), an expert on maritime economics and a historian of post-Unity Italian economy.[6]

Other economists outside the parties

Several economists had a relevant function as freelance journalists, influencing public opinion especially on the right.

One figure deserving of mention is Libero Lenti (1906–93), who taught economics and statistics in Pavia and whad been a courageous commentator on economic policy during Fascism. His journal, *La Borsa*, was suppressed for political reasons (see Lenti 1983). Among the founders of the *Partito d'Azione* in the North in 1943, after the war he rapidly shifted towards conservative positions as witnessed by his *Corriere della sera* articles.

By the same measure we also find many who had transmigrated from their previous Fascist vision to a generically 'liberal' approach, including as Luigi Amoroso, who – after declaring in 1934 that free market competition had destroyed all medieval and Christian values which corporatism intended to re-establish – wrote in 1947 that the alternative between market economy and 'bureaucratic' (namely, planned) economy corresponded in political terms to the alternative between moral freedom and dictatorship (quoted by Barucci, Introduction to Saraceno 1969: 36–7).

The academic leader of this group of conservative economists was possibly Giuseppe Ugo Papi (1893–1989), an expert on international economics and, in the interwar period, a staunch supporter of a microeconomic approach to the Great Crisis (see Papi 1933). In the 1950s Papi occupied a leading role among the economic advisors to the government – he was strictly connected with Budget Minister Pella – and was for many years a (much contested) Rector of Rome University.

An awkward political collaboration

Despite their political divergences the three major parties succeeded in cooperating during the crucial years of 1946–47. The merit for this kind of armistice is to be assigned to the realism both of Togliatti and De Gasperi.

Palmiro Togliatti (1893–1964), the PCI leader, followed Einaudi's university courses in Turin before the First World War and defended his *tesi di laurea* with Loria. A close friend of Gramsci's, he fled to Russia in 1926. Togliatti, obedient to Stalin's directives, realized that the 1945 Yalta Conference had definitely assigned Italy to the American sphere of influence, and that the economic (and political) programmes of the Left could not disregard this basic state of affairs. Therefore, socialism as collectivism in its pure form couldn't in any way be advocated, while significant scope could be awarded to the so-called *riforme di struttura* in order to create a 'democratic' economic system limiting the power of 'monopolistic' companies and strengthening that of small firms and cooperatives. Structural reforms, Togliatti argued, should preferably be concentrated in the sphere of agriculture – partly also in order to attract the consensus of the traditionally conservative peasantry – where both communists and socialists were in favour of allotting land to cooperatives rather than to the individual *coltivatori diretti* [small farmers] traditionally protected by DC; moreover, PCI took the view that nationalization of industrial complexes could be contemplated only as an *extrema ratio*.[7]

A native of Trentino, Alcide De Gasperi (1881–1954) completed his political training under the auspices of the Austrian–Hungarian Empire. Up until 1915 he was a member of the Vienna Parliament. Although he never wrote on economics, De Gasperi's inner convictions can be inferred from his political conduct. An unbridled free market economy would not be the most suitable choice in order to reconstruct a backward, severely damaged economy, and some forms of intervention in order to improve the living standard of the poorest classes would be necessary. On the other hand, realist statesman as he was, he fully acknowledged that in addition to the three major official parties there was a 'fourth party'; namely the business lobby which should not be crippled with excessively advanced economic reforms. Governing without – or, even worse, against – the 'fourth party' was therefore impossible. This awareness prompted De Gasperi to expel PCI and PSI from the cabinet and to form (May 1947) a new coalition among DC and the minor centrist parties.

As chief of eight consecutive cabinets from 1945 to 1953 – an absolute record in the whole history of the Italian Republic – De Gasperi was careful to assign the ministries of Treasury and of Budget to moderate politicians, while reserving the ministries of Finance and of Labour to personalities on the left, initially from PCI or PSIUP, subsequently from the left-wing ranks of DC. This division of roles lay at the origin of a growing inability to make clear-cut decisions, especially after 1950. The consequence was the unfavourable result of the 1953 general elections – when DC lost the absolute majority of seats – which led to De Gasperi's retirement from politics.

The economic content of the Italian Constitution

The breakdown of the alliance between DC and the Left in 1947 didn't forestall the approval of the text of the Constitution, which was passed by the Assembly with an overwhelming majority on 22 December 1947, and came into force on 1 January 1948.

The Constitution aimed to establish a mixed, progressive economy, in line with the democratic foundation of the State. The Republic is 'founded on labour' (Article 1), as Fanfani proposed. Article 3 qualified this broad principle by maintaining that

> it is the Republic's task to remove the obstacles of an economic and social order which, by de facto limiting the citizens' freedom and equality, hinder the full development of human personality as well as the effective

participation of all workers to the political, economic and social organization of the country [Note, this elaborate formula was proposed by socialist deputy Lelio Basso].

The use of the term 'workers' instead of 'citizens' underlined the intention of recommending consistent income redistribution in favour of wages. Article 4, developing the same concepts, mentioned the 'right to work' as constitutionally protected.

Objections to the declarations contained in the Constitution were, however, voiced by elderly statesman and economist Francesco Saverio Nitti, who argued that such solemn promises could not be maintained – given the dramatic economic conditions of the country – and would merely become a source of dangerous illusion (see Barucci 1980: 44). Nitti and other pre-Fascist deputies expressed disapproval of the presence of the so-called programmatic norms in the text of the Constitution, which had no sanctions and were practically ineffective. Einaudi deemed those norms *di mero augurio* [merely augural].

Einaudi was active in the so-called *Commissione dei 75*, entrusted with drafting a project for plenary discussion and headed by the jurist-economist Meuccio Ruini (1877–1970). Quite surprisingly for an economist, in a *Corriere della sera* article Einaudi contended that reserving a special section to *Rapporti economici* (Title Three of the Constitution's project) was of no use at all. Einaudi's thought still reflected the influence of the 1848 *Statuto* of the Kingdom of Sardinia (after 1861 of the Kingdom of Italy). The *Statuto* was a typical *costituzione breve* [literally, short constitution] which remained silent with regard to social and economic matters and limited itself to establishing the rules for the state's supreme organs and guaranteeing the main individual liberties.

Nevertheless, in the plenary assembly Einaudi proposed a specific article against economic monopoly, which he depicted as 'the supreme injury to modern economy' (Einaudi 1982, vol. 2: 509). Unfortunately the article was not included. Only in recent times has this lacuna been reconsidered, adopting a more critical attitude to the absence of constitutional norms focusing on the (free) market as the centre of economic activity.[8]

Einaudi and the other liberals were more successful in inspiring paragraph IV of Article 81, which states that once the state budget has been approved, any further rule implying new or greater expenditures must indicate the means to cover them (the so-called *copertura*). In itself, however, this was no more than a partial application of the absolute principle of the balanced budget that was Einaudi's ultimate (and most cherished) objective.

Einaudi's ideas triumphed many years afterwards, with the 20 April 2012 constitutional law that introduced the 'balanced *structural* budget' principle (namely, the principle of maintaining the balance between expenditure and receipts independently of cyclical fluctuations, excluding special cases) into the constitutional text. This modification of Article 81 – which passed with almost no real debate either in the political arena or in the press – de facto cancelled any possibility of a markedly 'Keynesian' anti-cyclical policy.

Four articles in particular contributed to defining the Republic's 'economic constitution'. Article 41, which opens with the statement that 'private economic initiative is free', but limited by respect for the principles of 'social utility' and 'safety, liberty and dignity', clarified that the law should determine 'the programmes and checks' to be set in place in order to orient private and public economic activity towards 'social aims'. Use of the term 'programmes' instead of 'plans' (following the proposal presented by Taviani), and the plural instead of the singular, meant that the Italian Constitution did not envisage the feasibility of a general economic plan (see Sullo 1960).

In effect, the so-called 'Montagnana amendment' (9 May 1947), which was named after its first signatory and jointly presented by many PCI and PSI deputies, established that 'in the aim of allowing every citizen to exercise the right to work, the State will intervene to coordinate and address production according to a plan that ensures the maximum return for the entire community'. In a speech announcing his opposition, Einaudi objected to this formulation of the amendment on two grounds. The first, of a theoretical nature, was that a concept such as the maximum of social utility for a society is impossible to ascertain, owing to the 'no-bridge' assumption among different individual preferences.[9]

The second observation, empirically based, was that daily experience shows that 'all of us make plans'. Hence, referring generically to 'a plan' was pleonastic (see Einaudi 1982, vol. II: 496, 498). The Montagnana amendment was rejected.

Article 42 stated that private property was acknowledged, provided that it respected the 'social function' that was to be regarded as inherent in any property – a principle already contained in the Fascist 1942 civil code, still in force today. Article 43, which addressed the question of enterprises that had achieved a monopolistic position, admitted their expropriation not only in favour of the State, but also in favour of public institutions and 'communities of workers or of users' (a rule which, to our knowledge, has never been applied). Article 46 established that all workers have the right to 'collaborate', within certain limits, 'in the firms' administration' (a pale reminiscence of the aborted *Consigli di gestione* experience).

In short, the Constitution's 'economics' defined a model of society based on active synergy between the market and the State. In this sense the Constitution appears to be inspired by a philosophy nourished with progressive liberalism according to the American tradition, plus social Catholicism.

The burden of authority: monetary policy 1945–49

Italian monetary policy encountered serious difficulties during the 1945–47 triennium. An exemplary case was the question of the failed *cambio della moneta*.

After the war several Western European states – among them France, Belgium, Finland and the Netherlands – successfully performed a currency change, mainly in order to force all currency held by individual households out into the open (the intent was to introduce a special tax on all 'speculative' gains that could be attributed to the black market).[10]

In Italy this project met with considerable opposition, on the face of it for technical reasons but really because monetary changeover was perceived as a threat to the middle class (Einaudi, at that time Governor of the Bank of Italy, also had strong misgivings). The project was finally abandoned in July 1947.[11]

Another and still more serious problem was the struggle against inflation. Soon after the war, the liberal vision shared by Treasury Minister Corbino and Governor Einaudi offered encouragement for credit expansion and the opening of new banks. Throughout 1946 the reserve-deposit ratio diminished and business was delighted – especially the exporters, who were benefiting from a favourable exchange rate against the main international currencies (see De Cecco 1968: 126).

But from June 1946 inflation became apparent, rising at an alarming pace. In March 1947 Einaudi delivered his final report as Governor of the Bank of Italy, dramatically stressing the dangers of increasing inflation which 'in the long run ... [would reduce] the propensity to save', thereby negatively affecting both consumption and income (quoted in Faucci 1986: 354).[12]

Einaudi compared the monetary situation of Italy with the 1923 phenomenon of German hyper-inflation, when the cost of a new paper issue was greater than its real value – a situation he called the *punto critico* of inflation. Einaudi's theoretical argument was not altogether clear, but the political message was unambiguous; he was pointing the finger at an overly permissive public expenditure policy – especially the subsidized price of bread – as the main cause of inflation. This was a question he had already raised in many articles immediately after the First World War (see Faucci 1986: 160–1, 175, 353).[13]

On the other hand, the responsibilities of the private sector – mainly the bank credit expansion encouraged by Minister Corbino and tolerated by Governor Einaudi during the first part of 1946 – were neglected altogether. Liberalist economists and politicians firmly believed that inflation could be attributed solely to the state. As was noted in the foregoing chapter, Piero Sraffa in his *tesi di laurea* had vigorously challenged this argument, without, however, managing to convince his master.

In May 1947 Einaudi became Budget Minister in the fourth De Gasperi cabinet, from which the Left was excluded. The new ministry (see Faucci 1986: 369) was expressly created with the purpose of overseeing the entire range of public expenditure, which was to be supervised specifically by Einaudi himself. Einaudi was formally allowed to maintain his post as Governor, but his closest collaborator, Bank of Italy General Director Donato Menichella, acted as his *pro tempore* substitute. No temporary officer stood in for Einaudi at the Bank during his participation in the Constituent Assembly; but in any case, no 'conflict of interest' argument was raised. During three crucial years, the discreet and shy 73-year-old Piedmont economist concentrated in his own hands an impressive amount of decision-making power.

The 'Einaudi line' consisted of two combined measures; an increase in the reserve-deposit ratio in order to reduce the banking multiplier, and a reduction of the lending-bank assets ratio which had a powerful reductive effect upon credit supply.[14] This *stretta monetaria* [credit freeze] led to a severe recession that immediately resulted in rising unemployment and triggered a series of protests and riots. Fortunately these negative effects were partially offset by the launch of the ERP (Marshall) Plan, which allowed Italy and the other Western nations to benefit from the USA's free commodity grants and long-term loans through ECA (the ERP agency for Europe).

Questions were raised concerning the destination of the so-called *fondo lire*; namely, the sum reimbursed by the ECA agency to Italian firms in exchange for their purchases of US commodities. Since the *fondo lire* was to be administered by the Italian Treasury, it held the option of employing the fund for budgetary needs or for carrying out productive investment projects. ECA administrator for Italy, Paul Hoffman, in his 1949 report (*Country Study: Italy*) denounced the Italian government for not utilizing the money to bring about economic expansion, instead using it to build up the Treasury's monetary reserves. But this was exactly what pre-Keynesian (or rather, anti-Keynesian) 'sound' finance prescribed; monetary stability and a balanced budget were to be preferred to any other goal, including economic growth.

Hoffman's vision may have been unilateral. The course of history has shown that the take-off of the Italian economy began not long after 1949, (partly) thanks to the sound work of the Treasury and general budget conditions, but undoubtedly thanks also to the general improvement of the economic situation in the West, and, not least, by the favourable circumstances created by the Korean War.

Early projects of planning

In all cases, both the theoretical implications and the practical applications of the Marshall Plan sparked the formulation of a host of macroeconomic 'plans'. Pasquale Saraceno (1903–91), professor of management at the Catholic University of Milan and subsequently at Venice University, came from an important experience as IRI *direttore centrale* before the war. A DC member, as early as 1948 he presented *Elementi per un piano economico 1949–52*, in which the main goal was stated as that of absorbing unemployment and coordinating sector and territory (regional) plans.[15] Yet this plan lacked a precise theoretical model and reliable quantification.

It may seem odd that compared to the emerging DC economists, the economists of the Left appeared to be less timely in presenting an economic plan. But behind this apparent delay there lay a political calculation. The PCI leaders considered that devising a 'plan' would not be not electorally rewarding – insomuch as it would determine the main goals of public action and implicitly regulate, and conceivably limit, decisions made by the trade unions: in particular those regarding strikes.

It was only after the 1948 electoral defeat of the Left that Giuseppe Di Vittorio (1892–1957), the communist secretary of the CGIL trade union, launched the so-called *Piano del lavoro*. Several economists, including some who had not embraced the communist cause, attended the 1950 Rome Conference at which the plan was officially presented. The keynote speaker was Professor Alberto Breglia, a disciple of Einaudi's who had announced his vote for the PCI in 1946 (whether he adopted the same line in 1948 is unknown). In his address, Breglia, an expert on monetary economics, presented the circular flow of the economy where production and consumption interact. Given initial financing, the consequent increase in production and income would trigger a self-sustaining process. As Breglia put it, 'the plan finances the plan' by means of the increasing income it created, according to a theoretical framework that was more classical (and Physiocratic) than Keynesian (see Breglia 1973 [1950]: 143–8).[16]

For its implementation, the *Piano del lavoro* required the establishment of three public agencies to manage the following sectors: electricity (which implied the sector's nationalization), housing for low-income families, and agriculture in the South of Italy (see VV. AA. 1978). As far as the plan's financing was concerned, the workers themselves would also be called upon to contribute a modest amount from their wages.

Despite its timidity, the *Piano del lavoro* was deemed 'demagogic' and rejected by De Gasperi's government, which immediately replied with three noteworthy initiatives: the *Piano-Casa* for low-income housing (devised by Labour Minister Fanfani); the establishment of the *Cassa per il Mezzogiorno* (in which Saraceno was directly involved) in order to support economic projects in the South; and the so-called Segni reform (drafted by Agriculture Minister Antonio Segni) which aimed to create a strong network of small landowners in the South through a redistribution of land from expropriated large estates.

The main goal of the *Cassa del Mezzogiorno* (established 1950, formally abolished 1986) was to enhance economic initiatives located in the South (but some backward areas in the centre of Italy were also included); while the land reform was conceived as a partial response to the centuries-old 'hunger for land' that afflicted poor peasants. Although some positive effects were achieved, the land reform did not forestall the subsequent massive exodus of workers from the South to the North. In a historical perspective this exodus was no doubt a prerequisite for the subsequent 'economic miracle', but it represented a failure with regard to its original aim of increasing incomes and welfare in the South. Finally, the *Cassa del Mezzogiorno* functioned more as a device for financing Northern industry than as an engine for supporting industrial initiatives originating in the South. Saraceno himself, in his later writings, bitterly laid bare his disenchantment with the outcome of the government policies to which he had dedicated all his energies (Saraceno 1992: 401).

Another public initiative stemming from Saraceno's ideas was the creation of the so-called *poli di sviluppo* [development poles] concentrated in selected areas of the South. Such poles were to consist of heavy industry settlements, especially oil refineries and iron and steel plants. In consequence, a number of gigantic 'cathedrals in the wilderness', as their opponents called them, were built. Gioja Tauro, Taranto, Gela and Naples were the main sites hosting enterprises that provided employment and income for thousands of Southern workers, apparently triggering a multiplier in the Keynesian sense. All the plants in question belonged to the state. Inevitably, though, once the forces of the international division of labour made it more advantageous to produce steel outside the borders of Europe, most of these plants were shown to be economically obsolete. Industrial reconversion is still a major issue of Italian public policy.

The Vanoni Plan and beyond

Saraceno also contributed to the so-called *Piano Vanoni* (1955), officially 'Schema di sviluppo dell'occupazione e del reddito in Italia nel decennio 1955–64' [Scheme of the development of employment and income in Italy in the decade 1955–64], a product of the research team active in SVIMEZ (Association for the Development of the Mezzogiorno), founded by Minister Morandi in 1946. In comparison with earlier attempts, the Vanoni Plan explicitly drew inspiration from Keynes – or better, from Harrod – through a connection between the growth rate (in all its three specifications of effective, warranted, and natural), the Keynesian propensity to save, and the capital-output ratio of the economy. It should be noted that Vanoni's goal was not the attainment of a certain rate of growth of national income per se, but rather the attainment of full employment provided the growth rate could be maintained at the same level. The Plan's objective was to create four million new jobs within ten years. The rate of growth of the national income was set hypothetically at 5 per cent a year – through a considerable transfer of income from consumption to saving-investment, and consequently through a massive effort to accumulate. The Vanoni Plan was not endowed with detailed instrumentation; rather, it appeared as an extrapolation of the trends of the Italian economy where the actual rate of accumulation had been increasing since 1950. Moreover, no indication was given concerning the quality and direction of public intervention. Precisely for these reasons, the Plan – which Minister Vanoni illustrated in scientific meetings[17] – was generally considered more as a discussion basis for future action than as an immediately operative tool. In the most limitative assessment it was labelled as an intellectual exercise, and the 'politically not demanding'[18] nature of the Plan was ascribed precisely to this feature.

The 'common-sense' character (the expression is by Einaudi 1974c [1956]: 116) of Vanoni's scheme was praised by the liberal economist, who was personally acquainted with Vanoni and wrote a long assessment of his work on the occasion of Vanoni's sudden death. According to Einaudi the plan had the merit of very clearly outlining the sacrifices that would be involved in terms of foregoing consumption in order to attain the Plan's goal of an increase in employment in parallel with continuous accumulation. Einaudi concluded that the Vanoni Plan was not a book of dreams, but rather a severe lesson in realism.

Practically ignored was the 1961 appointment of a new committee entrusted with an 'organic[!] scheme for the development of economy and income'. Both Budget Minister Giuseppe Pella and the committee's chairman, Giuseppe Ugo Papi, were die-hard Liberalists.

Opening to foreign competition: Italy and Europe

By 1950 post-war reconstruction could be considered accomplished, since per capita GDP had finally reached 1938 levels. It was achieved in two successive stages. First, it was the outcome of Einaudi's policy of compression of consumption and of encouragement for savings, accompanied by severe control over public expenditure and a rigid monetary policy based on the quantitative theory of money; and second, Marshall Plan aid was utilized to improve investment and production. It is interesting to note that a further ingredient of a coherent classical policy – namely, trade liberalization – was achieved with greater difficulty owing to resistance in business circles to the opening up of domestic markets to foreign competition.

Nevertheless, from 1949 onwards – by virtue of pressure from OECE/OCDE (see Cavalcanti 1984, Chapter IV) – a movement towards increasing exchange liberalization arose. In 1951 Foreign Trade Minister Ugo La Malfa (1903–79), formerly an economic officer at the Banca Commerciale in the 1930s and a member of the *Partito d'Azione* during the Resistenza (see VV. AA. 1984; Soddu 2008), successfully accomplished the liberalization of foreign trade. His success can partly be explained by noting that Italy was, at the time, a net creditor towards the rest of Europe; accordingly, opening the frontiers to foreign trade was altogether opportune.

An economically unified Europe was the result not only of the actions of politicians and civil servants, but also of illustrious personalities. The European ideal had inspired many *Risorgimento* patriots, first and foremost Mazzini and Cattaneo, and helped guide the anti-Fascist movement. In 1942 Altiero Spinelli and Ernesto Rossi wrote the *Manifesto di Ventotene*, so named from the small island to which both had been banished under the internal exile – *confino* – system. This Manifesto sketched a post-war federalist Europe. In their view this process was to be created by starting from the grassroots – through strong participation of the masses – and should be based on substantial economic reform that championed not only absolute freedom of trade but also a serious fight against monopolies. Moreover, the 'new' Europe of their dreams should have no kinship with its pre-1914 predecessor.

Unfortunately, the road that was trodden was the much less appealing model of 'functional federalism'; namely the strategy of proceeding towards an economic union limited to specified sectors (as was the case with the European Coal and Steel Community). This more limited approach was justified by reason of prudence, but was viewed by public opinion as unsatisfactory if not sorely disappointing.

In his essays on European unity and in his informal suggestions to the government while he was President, Luigi Einaudi appeared to suggest a third way. On the one hand, conservative economist as he was he recommended a return to the gold standard as the soundest monetary system for Europe. On the other hand, enlightened thinker as he also was, he declared his preference for a quite different road map towards European unification – a path that would not proceed from economics to politics but from politics to economics. Indeed Einaudi often maintained that all political actions should move from values to interests and not vice versa (see Einaudi 1950; Einaudi 1956a).

The present dissatisfaction (or distaste) for European institutions – dominated by the economic constraints that Europe has imposed on itself – prompts us to reread the European writings of our illustrious scholar.

The absence of an anti-trust policy

The industrial organization inherited from Fascism was not substantially altered after 1945, and this inertia had a number of critical consequences. In particular, the great opportunity for developing a working competition between the state-owned and the private sector was missed.

In 1953 the *Amici del 'Mondo'*, an association that drew its origin from the Left-liberal weekly magazine of the same name, organized a conference on the oligopo-listic structure of Italian industry and proposed legislation based on the USA anti-trust experience. The speakers included Tullio Ascarelli, a renowned scholar of law, and Ernesto Rossi, who never refrained from denouncing the collusion between public and private monopolistic industry.[19]

The efforts to introduce something akin to the US rules were strongly opposed by the business press linked to *Confindustria*. Il *Mondo*'s initiative had no legis-lative sequel.

Some years afterwards, in 1961, under the pressure of the 1957 Treaty of Rome that founded the European Economic Community, a parliamentary com-mittee for study of the limits on competition was finally appointed. Its promoter and first chairman, the PSDI deputy and former Finance Minister Roberto Tremelloni, was a pioneer of the conception – now widely shared but at that time quite new for Italian politics – of the necessary linkage between free competi-tion, innovation and growth. Quite paradoxically, Tremelloni, a social democrat, attempted to teach the virtues of a free competition market to those who should have been most aware of these virtues.

The political vicissitudes of those years, connected with the initial steps of the centre-left experience, severely affected the parliamentary committee's activity. The majority of the members who made up the *Commissione sui limiti alla con-correnza* had little intention of producing any anti-trust law at all. A journalist depicted it as the *commissione anti-niente*, the anti-nothing commission. There-fore, despite extensive presentations and reports by many renowned economic experts, including Sylos Labini, Steve, Lombardini and Rossi-Doria,[20] the result was practically nil and the committee ceased in 1965 (see Granata 2007).

A law against monopolistic positions in the market, centred upon the concept of 'abuse of dominant position', was not introduced in Italy until as late as 1990, exactly a century after the USA Sherman Act and more in observance of Euro-pean Union recommendations than as a result of a strong drive from domestic politics. The merit was to be principally assigned to Professor Giuliano Amato (born 1938), a socialist jurist-economist who in the same years, as minister and Premier, did much to allow Italy's participation in the European Union.

IRI: from triumph to liquidation

IRI, the *Istituto di ricostruzione industriale* [Institute for Industry Reconstruction], established in 1933, was a public organism at the head of numerous financial holdings which, in turn, owned the majority of the assets of many firms originally involved in the 1930s crisis (see G. Toniolo 1978; VV. AA. 1981). For this reason, after 1945 nobody could seriously contemplate the idea that these firms could be restored to private ownership, not least because the capital necessary for such a vast business undertaking was totally lacking. The proper alternative was not between the status quo and privatization, but between the status quo and a more dynamic public management.

There were two distinct problems. The first was that IRI received substantial financial support from the state budget – the so-called *fondo di dotazione* [endowment fund] – which created a situation of objective privilege in comparison with the private sector. The second, and trickier problem was the apparent blurring of political and economic interests, demonstrated by the fact that from the 1950s onwards it was the DC that designated the President of IRI, reserving the post of Vice-President for the 'minor' allied parties. The practice of *lottizzazione* (a spoils system involving the allotment of political and economic posts to members of the majority parties) implied the other and still more detrimental practice of *sottogoverno* (a common term in Italian politics alluding to the benefits that the ruling parties obtain from uncontrolled flows of public expenditure), led to a spoils system that had no alternative, owing to the *conventio ad excludendum* regarding either extreme Left or extreme Right forces.[21]

Despite this original sin, IRI had the merit of reinforcing the position of Italy as an industrial power, through the presence of IRI-controlled companies in such crucial sectors as motorway construction and management (Società Autostrade), the shipbuilding industry (Fincantieri), the automotive industry (Alfa Romeo), the mechanical and military industry (Finmeccanica), the iron and steel industry (Finsider), airlines (Alitalia), as well as in the banking sector (inclusive of credit giants such as Banca Nazionale del Lavoro and Credito italiano). For some decades, the 'IRI model' was looked upon approvingly by the other European industrial powers as a case of cooperation between private and public economic initiative.

A serious shortcoming was the absence of a clear-cut and univocal industrial policy. The IRI-owned firms acted individually, without any meaningful coordination. Moreover, the *Ministero delle partecipazioni statali* [Ministry of State participations], the instrument created in 1956 to control the complex of the state's shares in the economy, was consistently occupied by politicians who were declaredly *personae gratae* to IRI. On the other hand, IRI remained a member of Confindustria, the association of private enterprises, until the 1959 *sganciamento* [exit] and IRI's consequent entry into the new association of state-owned enterprises, Intersind – an entry that was severely, but in this case unjustifiably, criticized by Einaudi (1974b [1959]: 62–90).

The IRI formula was destined to collapse when the 'financial crisis of the state' came to an end. The decision was made in 2000, and its liquidation followed in 2002. Exactly as in the case of the introduction of the balanced budget principle into the Italian Constitution, no public debate on the destiny of IRI took place. Even the IRI Foundation has been recently dismissed, and there are serious problems concerning the preservation of its monumental historical archives. On the other hand, some of the firms previously belonging to IRI, such as Finmeccanica, were transferred to the Economy Ministry. A definitive privatization of the sector is at present unfeasible, owing to the well-known economic difficulties of the country.

The ENI and ENEL cases

The electricity industry sector suffered from a monopoly; or rather, a collusive oligopoly of a small group of Northern firms led by the Edison company that followed a policy of high supply prices of energy, thereby discouraging the development of industrialization in the South. A competitor of the private companies in the field of production as well as the distribution of energy was ENI, a public company founded 1953 for the purpose of prospecting for methane gas in the Po Valley. ENI succeeded in expanding its range of activities to include the purchase of oil at favourable prices in the Middle East, inevitably clashing with the so-called Seven Sisters (BP, Shell, Gulf and others) of the international oil cartel.

The head of ENI, Enrico Mattei (1906–62), was a left-DC militant and had been a partisan during the *Resistenza*. Mattei, as a state entrepreneur, probably represents a truly unique character in the whole of the Italian experience. Realizing that a favourable reaction by the press was crucial, he also founded a newspaper, *Il giorno*, which launched a new aggressive style of journalism in contrast with the more conventional approach of newspapers like *Corriere della sera* and *La stampa* (the Fiat-owned journal).[22]

Mattei's highly distinctive attitude towards the 'fourth power' is best revealed by *Stampa e oro nero*, a publication in many volumes that highlighted the (generally abject) level of the press campaign against the ENI company, with objections being voiced not only by the Right, as one can easily imagine, but by the extreme Left as well. Mattei died in a mysterious plane crash in 1962.

The nationalization of the electricity industry was finally carried out in the same year, 1962, with the establishment of ENEL, and was destined to represent the one and only case of nationalization in Italian post-war experience. After a heated discussion among the parties it was decided that the indemnities for nationalization would be paid to the original companies, not to the individual shareholders as the Left would have preferred. This was officially due to the need to 'save' the entrepreneurial abilities of the electricity companies which had been expropriated. The result was that a huge amount of money was channelled into the creation of a new industrial firm, Montedison, which came about as a result of the merger between the old Edison and the Montecatini company, the latter being another monopolistic enterprise active in the chemical sector. The business of this colossus came to a sorry end (its last head, R. Gardini, after overseeing the accumulation of an enormous debt which all but brought the Italian chemical industry to its knees, eventually committed suicide in 1993). Here, exactly as in many other recent Italian cases, economic history was intertwined with mystery (and horror) stories.

Monetary policy once again

In the 1950s the absence of a clear-cut industrial policy in Italy was compensated for by a sort of surrogate in the form of safe (orthodox) money management. Here a crucial role was played by Donato Menichella, Governor Einaudi's successor as the head of the Bank of Italy. Menichella (1894–1980), a typical *servitore dello stato* [high-ranking civil servant] in the best Italian tradition, had been IRI's General Director in the 1930s and for this reason was submitted to the purge process in 1944–45, but was soon acquitted. Working in close collaboration with Governor Einaudi after 1946, Menichella acted de facto as a super-Minister for Economic Affairs during the 1950s. Monetary stability was tenaciously defended and this led to prestigious international acknowledgment – the so-called Oscar prize for the stabilizing the lira, assigned by *The Financial Times* on the occasion of Menichella's retirement in 1960.[23]

His successor was Guido Carli (1914–93). The son of a corporative economist, in his early years Carli worked as Executive Director at the International Monetary Fund (1947–48) and as President of the European Payment Union in 1950–52. In Italy he was in charge of the *Ufficio Italiano Cambi* (1945–52) before being appointed General Director (1959) and subsequently Governor of the Bank of Italy (1960–75). Later on he was President of Confindustria (1976–80), Treasury Minister (1991–92) and a DC Senator. Unfortunately, a general assessment on one of the leading personalities in post-war Italian economics and politics is still lacking.[24]

Carli had two basic tenets, both crucial for a consistent economic policy but perhaps not easily reconcilable. The first was monetary stability, which was necessary in order to attract foreign investment, thereby assuring international respect for the country. In pursuing this aim he continued the line of his two predecessors. The second was more strategic. He intended to transform the existing banking system, which was still governed by the 1936 banking law that fixed rigid models of credit institutions and placed obstacles against the banks' participation in industry, into a more flexible organization, competitive according to the international banking standards but in a sense returning to the experience of German pre-1914 'mixed banks' which favoured the early industrial revolution in Italy but were involved in the Great Crisis.

Carli believed the role of the Bank of Italy should be that of *banca delle banche* and no longer that of the *banca del Tesoro*. This was eventually brought about by the so-called 1980 'divorce' between the Bank of Italy and the Italian Treasury (originally, the Bank was obliged to buy Treasury bonds which found no buyers in the open market), put into effect by Treasury Minister Beniamino Andreatta (1928–2007), professor at the University of Bologna and the teacher and mentor of many leading DC economists and politicians now merged in PD, from Romano Prodi (born 1939) to Enrico Letta (born 1964). After this 'divorce' the autonomy of the Bank of Italy from politics – a central point in Carli's project – was assured.

A further aspect characterized Carli's actions. During the 1960s he was engaged in an open struggle against the Left (PSI and the left-wing of the DC) as far as the role of economic planning was concerned. In particular, he was vehemently opposed to any attempt to 'regulate' from above the direction of investment (see Carli 1993, Chapter 4). Carli was strongly in favour of merely 'indicative' planning, without any coercion involving the private sector. Eventually Carli's battle was brilliantly won.

The National Economic Plan, finally(?)

In 1962 the Centre-Left Fanfani cabinet carried out the nationalization of the electricity industry, and reformed the educational system through the establishment of the *scuola media unica* (compulsory schooling up to the age of 14). A season of reforms seemed to have started. In May, Budget Minister Ugo La Malfa presented a *Nota aggiuntiva* [additional note] to the 'General report on the country's economic situation'. This fundamental document, drafted by Saraceno, sketched the issues to be tackled by the Economic Plan. Besides the historical North-South gap, there was the increasing gap between private and public consumption, especially in health and education, defined as *impieghi sociali del reddito* [social destination of income].

The Technical-Scientific Planning Committee included some of the best Italian economists. It encompassed a variety of ideological positions and therefore different policy visions, all at a very high standard. On the one hand, Di Fenizio personified the liberal wing, favourable to a plan based on indirect constraints and incentives, as the only type of plan compatible with a free market and, indeed, with a Western economy. For opposite reasons, Di Fenizio rejected a mere indicative plan as a loose verbal exercise, and a 'normative' or compulsory plan as dictatorial. Di Fenizio's sophisticated analysis of the interplay of economics and sociology seemed to have drawn on Pareto's conception of élites (see Di Fenizio 1965).

It is striking, however, that Di Fenizio did not consider the solution of the so-called 'Southern question' as the main target of the Plan. On this point he diverged from the ideas shared by Saraceno as well as by Rossi-Doria, who distinguished two kinds of Southern agriculture; developed (the 'pulp') versus backward (the 'bone'). This dualist reality needed to be addressed by two differently structured strategies, respectively market-oriented and state-oriented. Accordingly, Rossi-Doria was highly critical of the *Cassa del Mezzogiorno*, whose action lacked flexibility and was totally subservient to bureaucracy and the parties (on Rossi-Doria see VV. AA. 1999).

On the other hand, two other members of the Technical-Scientific Committee, Giorgio Fuà (1919–2000) and Paolo Sylos Labini (1920–2005) chose to focus attention on a plurality of aspects concerning the Italian economy. The Plan, they maintained, should establish a multi-faceted reform project involving not only the economy, but the institutions as well. Their slim book (Fuà and Sylos Labini 1963) was the outcome of joint work among many specialists in different sectors, including S. Cassese and S. Rodotà (law scholars), G. Orlando (an agrarian economist) and S. Lombardini and G. Ruffolo (economists). Its starting point was a basic intuition; that the so-called 'economic miracle' of the 1950s and early 1960s could not be maintained unless the necessary measures of rationalization of the economy were introduced within a very short space of time. This interpretation was clearly irreconcilable with the absolute Liberalist view, which held that the economic miracle was to be explained by the unshackling of Promethean market energies and warned 'planners' against encroaching on the private mechanism of accumulation and distribution.

Fuà and Sylos Labini argued that there were at least four causes of economic inefficiency: (1) an uneven population distribution in Italy; (2) a low level of public consumption in the health and education sectors; (3) the presence of a backward commercial sector, composed of family-run and/or individual firms, which were too small to compete, and; (4) above all, mismanagement of the public administration. Taken together these aspects had the effect of a deadweight on the entire economy. It is striking that the issues raised and the proposals illustrated in the book never became the object of debate among the political forces, and were treated as mere intellectual exercises.

A third book on planning was written by another member of the Technical-Scientific Committee, Siro Lombardini (1924–2013), and it centred above all on the relationship between the general plan and the various local and/or specific plans.[25]

In 1968 a further step towards the realization of short-term planning was accomplished, thanks to a collective research led by L. Izzo, A. Pedone, L. Spaventa and F. Volpi. The final document (Izzo *et al.* 1970, 1975) focused on the goals and constraints of public action by distinguishing between endogenous and exogenous factors, and between final and intermediate targets, with special attention to the role of automatic stabilizers.

In subsequent years, however, the interest in planning began to decrease. Among economic experts, Giorgio Ruffolo (born 1926), former Secretary to the National Programming Board and author of a useful report on planning experience in Italy (Ruffolo 1973), continued in numerous publications his passionate defence of the idea of democratic planning, where politics inevitably prevailed over economic analysis.

Review of the troops

New periodical publications

If we shift from the sphere of policy to that of economics in the proper sense, after 1945 one finds an increasing number of economics periodicals. In particular, the banks issued first class journals, the most influential of which was probably *Banca nazionale del lavoro Quarterly review*, which started 1947 in English with such authors as V. Lutz, G. Ackley, B. Balassa, F. Machlup, J. R. Hicks, D. Patinkin, L. Spaventa, G. Fuà and F. Modigliani. The same bank also started *Moneta e credito* in 1948.[26]

Another journal in English was *Review of the economic conditions in Italy*, published by *Banco di Roma* (whose President after the war was Bresciani Turroni). *Banco di Napoli* (headed for some years by Corbino) also issued a journal, *Rassegna economica*. The Associazione bancaria italiana (ABI) continued to publish the monthly journal *Bancaria*, not to be confused with *Rivista bancaria*, the latter being the organ of the Associazione di cultura bancaria. The last important bank to publish a scientific journal was *Monte dei Paschi di Siena*, which started *Note economiche* in 1968, accompanying it with an English edition, *Economic Notes*. Meanwhile, Confindustria, the Confederation of Italian Industries, expanded its *Rivista di politica economica*, which hosted the annual proceedings of the *Convegni di economia e politica industriale* (started in 1947).

Among the most important university journals, the Catholic University *Rivista internazionale di scienze sociali* (RISS) continued to be active on both economic theory and policy, without neglecting the traditional topics of ethics and economics (F. Vito, S. Lombardini, G. Mazzocchi, L. L. Pasinetti, A. Quadrio Curzio). The University of Naples hosted *Studi economici*, established in 1941 and published by the faculty of economics and commerce. The journal *Ricerche economiche* was published by the University of Venice, while the University of Pavia continued to publish the *Rivista di diritto finanziario e scienza delle finanze*. A journal dating from over half a century earlier, *L'industria*, founded in 1886 as a mouthpiece of Milanese entrepreneurship, was completely transformed by its new editor F. Di Fenizio into a first class journal that devoted special attention to methodology, hosting articles by Hayek, Machlup, Popper and others.

Mention should also be made of the legendary *Giornale degli economisti e Annali di economia*, which bore the hallmark of Demaria's editorship for over 35 years. Demaria left *Giornale* in 1976 but his work was continued by a team of Bocconi economists. A journal that can be considered as sensitive to Demaria's ideas was *Rivista internazionale di scienze economiche e commerciali* (RISEC), founded by the Padua professor, Tullio Bagiotti (1921–83), and recently transformed into an English language periodical. The journal *Economia internazionale* (founded in 1948) was published by the Chamber of Commerce of Genoa, but it was independent of the University of Genoa.

A quite different case is that of Pesenti's *Critica economica*, launched in 1946 and explicitly modelled on the first series of *Riforma sociale* that was edited by Nitti, which was more reform-oriented than the subsequent series edited by Einaudi. Pesenti's intent was that of supplying an economic tribune for the Left, a project on which he was able to work together with a number of young scholars including Federico Caffè, Sergio Steve, Giorgio Fuà and Paolo Sylos Labini, all of whom were destined to rank among the leading Italian economists in the decades to follow. After 1948, as the political struggle in Italy became increasingly radicalized, many independent contributors to the journal withdrew, and *Critica economica* began to show an outspoken pro-PCI position. As a consequence the journal lost contributors and readers and eventually ceased in 1956. In 1970 the PCI launched a new journal, *Politica ed economia*, the organ of CESPE (Centre for Studies on Economic Policy), which attracted non-communist contributors as well, especially in the 1970s and 1980s. This was an outcome of the party's new strategy.

Moreover, it is important to mention several periodicals that contributed to disseminating economic information among a broader audience, such as *Mondo economico* (1945) of Milan, and above all two business daily newspapers, *Il sole* (founded in 1865) and *Ventiquattro ore* (founded in 1946). Both newspapers, and especially the former, espoused a conservative line, basically opposing all attempts at introducing something similar to workable competition into the Italian economy. They merged in 1965. The new *Il sole-24 ore*, owned by Confindustria, became a quality publication that succeeded in competing with the main specialized newspapers known on a worldwide level (see Bairati and Carrubba 1990).

Finally, several political journals, although not principally concerned with economic topics, hosted the writings of many economists. Let us first mention *Cronache sociali* (from 1947), a journal of the left-wing Christian Democrats and prompted by the law scholar Giuseppe Dossetti, which had among its contributors Federico Caffè and Siro Lombardini (see Glisenti and Elia 1961).

Another esteemed journal was *Nord e Sud*, of Naples (set up in 1954), under the editorship of Francesco Compagna (1921–82), an economic geographer who integrated the long-standing tradition of studies on the *questione meridionale* with a more updated economic and sociological approach. Among the main authors one may cite Augusto Graziani (1933–2014) – grandson of the early twentieth-century economist of the same name – who commented on the Bank of Italy strategy during the 1960s.

A few words about the publishing houses open to economics. Apart from the 'professional' presses that were close to the university world, such as Giappichelli of Turin, Giuffrè of Milan and Cedam of Padua, the 1960s and 1970s were also characterized by a steady or increasing focus on economics shown by 'generalist' publishers such as Giulio Einaudi and Laterza. Two new entrants to the economics domain were Il Mulino of Bologna, a publisher established in 1954, three years after the founding of the journal of the same name and which drew inspiration from a cultural convergence of Catholic and secularist democrats; and Feltrinelli of Milan, set up in 1955 and originally connected with the Istituto (later on, Fondazione) Giangiacomo Feltrinelli for research on the history and economics of the workers' movement.

Finally, an important collective initiative that should be mentioned was that of the Boringhieri press – a 16-volume *Dizionario di economia politica* (1982–90) edited by G. Lunghini (born 1938) and assisted by M. D'Antonio (born 1939). In sharp contrast to the traditional models of this kind, the *Dizionario* presented a restricted number of crucial entries – from Capital to Value – illustrating both the history and present state of the studies.

New centres of research in economics

The 1950s saw an increase in collective research in economics, by virtue of the substantial number of fellowships that also encompassed grants to Italian scholars for periods of research in the USA and the UK, principally financed by the Bank of Italy. Besides the Stringher Fellowship, established in 1931, a Mortara Fellowship – in memory of the renowned economist and statistician expelled from the university as a Jew – was established in 1967. Other fellowships were supplied by the USA Fulbright and Rockefeller Foundations. Significantly, the list of those to whom these fellowships were awarded includes the names of most professors of economics active after the war (see da Empoli 2004).

In parallel to this increase of opportunities for study abroad, there was a conspicuous growth of centres for advanced (*post-lauream*) research in Italy. The first institution – altogether independent from the university system – that undertook to provide advanced training for young economists was Svimez of Rome, whose researchers contributed to the 1955 Vanoni scheme. From 1957 onwards regular courses both in theoretical and applied economics were launched, with the participation of many renowned foreign scholars, including P. Rosenstein Rodan, F. and V. Lutz, H. Chenery and others, together with many young Italian teachers (see VV. AA. 1968).

More specific was teaching given by the Centre for Economic-Agrarian Research of Portici (Naples), established in 1959 through an agreement between the University of Naples, the Ministry of Agriculture, the Cassa del Mezzogiorno and the Ford Foundation, and due to the impetus of Rossi-Doria (Costabile 2004; Bernardi 2012).

Among the universities, two 'small' seats should be mentioned as active research centres that proved attractive for young scholars. Ancona presented an entirely new (founded in 1959) faculty of economics and commerce, initially a separate branch of the university of Urbino, which developed research mainly on applied economics under the leadership of Giorgio Fuà. After the years spent at the United Nations with Gunnar Myrdal and at ENI's *ufficio studi* with Enrico Mattei, Ancona-born Fuà headed a collective project in the late 1960s on *Lo sviluppo economico in Italia*, which saw the involvement of economists, law scholars, economic historians and statisticians in a common study. In subsequent years a more homogeneous group of economists was formed and the research undertaken in Ancona assumed a mono-disciplinary character, focusing on employment, productive capacity and international competitiveness in Italian industry (see Alessandrini and Crivellini 2004). Among the faculty's professors there were several economists who would later hold important positions in subsequent decades, including Napoleoni, Rey and Vaciago.

In the very same years the faculty of economics and banking of Sienna University – which benefited from the patronage of the *Monte dei Paschi* Bank – was characterized by a close connection with the major Anglo-American universities. Distinguished foreign economists, *inter alios*, Richard Goodwin (to which the faculty has been dedicated) and Frank Hahn, held professorial positions. As in the case of Ancona, Sienna recruited many teachers who became leading economists in the following years, including Romani, Izzo and De Cecco.

Among the other universities, Bologna became specialized in monetary theory and policy and benefited from the presence of the Italian branch of the Johns Hopkins University. Other competitive centres of propagation of economics in the North – apart from the historically established seats of Turin, Milan (where economics was taught in four universities), Pavia and Venice – were Bergamo and Trento. Both of the latter universities hosted several foreign scholars as teachers, including, respectively, Hyman Minsky and Axel Leijonhufvud.

In this context the case of Florence is distinct from the above-mentioned institutions. The faculty of economics and commerce there has a long-standing specialization in the fields of both the history of economics and in regional applied economics, with the school created by Alberto Bertolino (1899–1979). In particular, Bertolino's first disciple, Giacomo Becattini (born 1927) rose to prominence with a book on the history of industrial economics during the 1920s and 1930s (Becattini 1962). As part of his research Becattini dwelt on Marshallian topics, inquiring into their relevance for an understanding of contemporary economic phenomena, first and foremost the industrial districts. This flow of research, both theoretical and empirical (in particular the Tuscan industrial districts were scrutinized), obtained considerable success (see Pyke *et al.* 1991; Becattini 1998) and prompted renewed international interest in Marshall. Bertolino's second disciple, Piero Barucci (born 1933), who likewise started out as an applied economist, specialized later in the history of economics and founded a flourishing school.

Last but not least it is important to underline the role of the Consiglio nazionale delle ricerche [CNR, the National Research Council] in financing the most ambitious collective research on economics that was ever carried out in Italy – the 'Group for the study of distribution, technical progress and growth' which was active from 1964 to 1984 and contributed not only to disseminating Sraffa's critique of neo-classical economics, but also to promoting new lines of research on applied economics.[27]

The much-disputed success of Keynes's General Theory

As we have seen in the previous chapters, the policy proposals put forward by Keynes in the 1930s were not fully accepted by the Italian academic establishment (see Bacchi Andreoli 1949).

This attitude continued for many years after 1945. Ernesto Rossi – who was an admirer of the Beveridge Welfare State plan, and could by no means be considered an *a priori* enemy of the State's intervention – derided the host of public agencies that were called upon to comply with the Keynesian policy precepts. Even an economist of the younger generation, Paolo Sylos Labini, who had attended Schumpeter's lectures at Harvard, manifested scepticism both as regards Keynesian policy and Keynes's theory, and spoke out against the confusion among the different interpretations of Keynes's thought that were circulating in academic circles (see Sylos Labini 1966 [1950]). On the other hand, Keynes's 1936 *magnum opus* was not widely read in Italy and its translation did not appear until as late as 1948.

Generally speaking, many of the objections raised by Italian economists were not altogether trifling. They involved the whole methodology of aggregates – deemed simplistic – above all with regard to the relation between consumption and income. Moreover, critical observations were made on the issue of Keynes' indifference towards the quality of public expenditure, and insinuated that Keynes proposed a sheer programme of 'digging holes in the ground' (Keynes 1964 [1936]: 129). Here there was a striking misunderstanding of Keynes's true thought.

Apart from these polemical overtones, many critics observed that Keynes's prescriptions had been conceived for a mature economy characterized by idle resources and by an excess of saving over investment – which required action in support of aggregate demand – and were not suitable for an economy that had problems of structural unemployment, a large backward sector of the economy and, above all, serious difficulties of accumulation owing to insufficient private saving. Non-Keynesian economists could not deny that private demand was too low; but – they argued – the right thing to do was to encourage accumulation, which would subsequently create new income and therefore further demand.

On the other hand, many economists on the Left tended to lean more towards a 'Ricardian' view. They insisted that the main objective should be to reduce rents and develop a modern economy based on profits and wages. Stated in political terms, a strategic alliance between workers and 'non-parasitic capitalists' was definitely necessary, but would also be hampered by a number of adverse circumstances. Following Gramsci's adaptation of Marx's theories to Italy, they argued that in Italy capitalism suffered from an 'historical backwardness', due to the fact that the *Risorgimento* had not been a fully-fledged social revolution (as the French Revolution was), but the outcome of a compromise between old landowners and rising capitalists, so that profits presented themselves as inextricably tied up with rents. Once more the conclusion was that Keynes's thought – with such ambiguous economic characters as volatile investors and tenacious savers – was a misrepresentation of the real economic drama, and hardly a doctrine of any use for structural reform of the economy.

The communists' mistrust of Keynesianism also had roots in the 'real socialism' doctrine. In the Soviet Union Keynes was deemed the temporary saviour of Western capitalism – the economist who had taught decadent capitalists the best way to counter the fall in the profit rate. In this perspective the main tool of Keynes's policy was 'managed currency', which, through 'reasonable' inflation, contributed to maintaining high profit rates at the expense of real wages (see Pesenti 1946).

In fact, a widespread opinion – shared by such varied thinkers as Pesenti and Bresciani Turroni (and obviously by Einaudi) – was that behind Keynes's ideas there was a message in favour of inflation. Although it would be excessive to summarize the difficulties of Keynes's reception in Italy as a problem of cultural incompatibility, it would be not altogether false to conclude that the orthodox and the leftist economists found a convergence of ideas in their opposition to Keynes, even if for contrasting reasons.[28]

Be that as it may, Keynesianism was not the same as the economics of Keynes. What was lacking for many years in Italy was a careful textual study of the *General Theory*. In this context a pioneer was F. Di Fenizio (1906–74), who, in his journal *L'industria*, translated some important texts by and on Keynes, first and foremost the French preface to the *General Theory*, and several well-known articles on Keynes collected in a book of *Studi keynesiani* (see Garofalo 1984: 216).

In his *Economia politica* (first edition 1949) Di Fenizio fought against the most spread commonplace views on Keynes – that the multiplier was but a paradox; that Keynes's thought was incompatible with the 'classics'; and above all that Keynes was always favourable to sustaining effective demand, even in the face of the danger of inflation.

Two other economists shared with Di Fenizio the merit of offering a new, and more correct, interpretation of Keynes's thought. Vittorio Marrama (1914–83) was among the first young scholars to move to the US after 1945 and to come back with the results of his studies (*Teoria e politica della piena occupazione*, 1948). Federico Caffè (on whom, see below) studied at the London School of Economics and carried out his early research on the 'Keynesian' economic policy of the Labour government (*Annotazioni sulla politica economica britannica in un 'anno d'ansia'*, 1948).[29]

The Sraffa debate

This is not the appropriate place to review the debate raised by the publication – simultaneously in English (Cambridge University Press) and in Italian (Einaudi) – of *Production of Commodities by Means of Commodities*, certainly the book written by an Italian-born economist that was destined to be the most widely read and discussed in the world. Moreover, it is not our task to investigate the presence of one of a plurality of Sraffian 'schools' (see Roncaglia 1990: 233–74) which undoubtedly would complicate the picture. Here, just a short outline will be given.

In his life-long residence of Trinity College, Cambridge, the Turin economist, after concentrating on the theory of money under Keynes's suggestion, spent about 20 years collecting the works and correspondence of David Ricardo, and in so doing creating a great work of erudition and interpretation that Einaudi rightly defined as a 'monument' (Einaudi 1953 [1951]: 155–61). This task allowed Sraffa to reconsider the legacy of classical economics, from Quesnay to Marx, and to expound the main features of classicism in a modern guise, presenting it as a theory that was able not only to resist the attacks of mainstream economics, but even to suggest new lines of research.

In the book Sraffa aimed to define 'such properties of the economic system as do not depend on changes in the scale of production or in the proportions of "factors"' (Sraffa 1960: v). The logic was Ricardian, although the Ricardian simplification of assuming an output of the same quality as input (the wheat model) was not maintained. For Sraffa, commodities were heterogeneous, but a 'standard commodity' could always be conceived as a commodity that reflects the same proportions of goods as are observable in the production of the entire system. He made use of the term 'standard commodity', an aggregate of commodities that expresses in its composition the same proportion as that observed for the individual commodities which form part of the overall product. This standard commodity is produced by a 'standard system', within which the general rate of profit of the whole economy is calculated (and which corresponds to the ratio between the net product and the means of production).

In the second part of the book Sraffa addressed cases which may appear as special: the joint production of more than one commodity by the same industry, implying the use of different production techniques; the measurement of fixed capital; the commodities 'employed in production, but not themselves produced' (Sraffa 1960: 74) – such as land; and choice of productive methods in consequence of variation in the profit rate.

As is well known, after the publication Sraffa deliberately maintained his silence. Italian and international debate on the middle-aged, discrete, Sraffa highlighted a plurality of messages that this slim book inevitably communicated to an audience accustomed to reasoning in terms of mainstream neo-classical economics or, at most, in terms of Keynes's economics.

The first message was analytical. Reproducibility of commodities – instead of utility and scarcity – was declared to be the quintessence of economics. Sraffa presented an economic system where demand had no autonomous role (against Marginalism) and where relative prices were obtained directly from the quantities of commodities, without recourse to values (against Marx's imperfect solution to the 'transformation problem').

The second message was both ideological and political. It concerned the inverse relationship between wages and profits. Sraffa maintained that whether the wage rate was fixed, and hence the profit rate was calculated as a mere residual income or vice versa, was a matter of indifference (see Sraffa 1960, Chapter 5, sections 43 and 44). This argument prompted some writers to conclude that wages could be not only *abstractly*, but *genuinely* considered as the 'independent variable' of the economy, in the sense that it could indeed be possible to reduce profit to a minimum without excessive disruption in the functioning of the system (!). This extreme conclusion circulated in some sections of the political Left, but especially in the CGIL Trade Union during the so-called 'hot autumn' of 1969 – a season of strikes that eventually led to a considerable redistribution of incomes from profits to wages but was destined to create a deep rift within the progressive movement in Italy and indirectly contributed to its later crisis.

Turning to pure theory, Sraffa's lesson is part of the more general Cambridge message that was imported into Italy by a host of young scholars who had studied in Britain. This message had the undisputed merit of renewing the traditional portrait of the Italian theorist, which until 1960 was still based on Pareto and on the 1930 exercises on dynamics.

In 1960 Pierangelo Garegnani (1930–2011) published his Cambridge PhD thesis – which benefited from Sraffa's advice – on *Il capitale nelle teorie della distribuzione*. Garegnani addressed the crucial point of the marginal theory of distribution: namely, the assumption that capital was *valued* before being measured, and – above all – that the productivity of 'capital' determined the rate of wages through the increasing productivity of labour. The neo-classical production function, pioneered by K. Wicksell and E. von Böhm-Bawerk, and based on the inverse relation between the rate of interest and the amount of capital, was cast aside by Garegnani. In contrast, the classical theory of distribution was relaunched. This theory defined the rate of wage as independent of the productivity of capital; wages were determined by the actual situation of class relationships, as in Smith himself, or by historical factors, as in Quesnay (Garegnani 1981: 110).

Garegnani, for his part, set himself the task of rereading Keynes according to Marxian-Sraffian lines. The result was that a crucial distinction was made between the ambiguous Keynes of the neo-classical synthesis – reduced to a scholar who studied a special case of a capitalist economy dominated by the liquidity trap and sticky wages – and the original Keynes of the principle of effective demand (see Garegnani 1979).

In parallel with the Sraffa debate there was a lively debate between the 'two Cambridges' (British and American) on the limits of the neo-classical production function, a debate that took its cue from a seminal article by Joan Robinson and was animated by many young Italian economists such as Garegnani himself, Luigi L. Pasinetti (born 1930) and Luigi Spaventa (1934–2013) with their disciples, Italian and foreign. An important outcome of this debate was the concept of 'reswitching of techniques', which intended to demonstrate that the assumption of the canonical production function was undermined by the possibility of a return of a previously discarded technique, and therefore that it is not necessarily true that when the rate of interest or of profit (*qua* capital price) decreases, the consequence will necessarily be an increase in the quantity of capital per head, and vice versa. Technical progress, rather than the change in the rate of profit, may be the cause of such reswitching. This *prima facie* minor point assumes, according to Pasinetti, a fundamental importance in confuting the 'Marginal approach to distribution according to the marginal productivity theory' (see Pasinetti 1977: 173; see also Pasinetti 1966, quoted by Harcourt 1973 [1972]: 153).[30]

In recent years the interest in Sraffa has been refreshed by the new opportunity for access to his unpublished papers kept in the Trinity College archives. On the basis of new first-hand information, our knowledge of the scientific milieu of Cambridge before and after the war has been enriched (see Marcuzzo and Rosselli 2006). In particular, Sraffa's intellectual exchange of views with Wittgenstein, and the dialogue with Cambridge mathematicians including A. S. Besikovitch, have been examined or re-examined.[31]

Three independent voices

Before concluding this 'review of the troops', let us dedicate some attention to three thinkers who represent a *trait d'union* between the older and the present generation. These scholars can ideally be seen as concluding the long-lived story (or cycle?) of the Italian tradition of economic thought. Their sensitivity to the link between theory and policy, accompanied by a vivid sense of the role of the economist as a militant in the higher and proper sense, deserve all our admiration, together with the regret that their heritage has not, so far, been turned to the greatest advantage.

Federico Caffè's 'solitude'

Federico Caffè (of Pescara, 1914–87) was professor of economic policy in Messina, Bologna and Rome, and a consultant economist at the Bank of Italy. A great academic, and the teacher of a generation of economists, he fought for an economics without dogma according to an image of the economist who sets himself the task of determining not only the instruments and the intermediate goals but also the final goals of economic policy as well. In this approach he followed Jan Tinbergen's lesson, but also that of Luigi Einaudi, towards whom Caffè manifested great respect as well as – in many cases – spirited dissent.

It is fair to state, straight out, that in our opinion Caffè's economic thought was not 'original' in the absolute meaning of the term. Fundamentally he was an open-minded interpreter of selected great economists. These were authors who, as will be seen below, could appear to constitute a rather heterogeneous group but actually shared the features of clarity of mind and earnestness in declaring their own convictions.

Caffè maintained that the growth of economics is the result of a continuous construction of a building whose steps have to be superposed in harmonic succession over time. At first sight this utterance may appear as pure *Whiggism*. But Caffè clarified that this construction is first and foremost a building site, with economists as humble blue collar hard-hat workers. He humorously maintained that this outfit must not be mistaken for 'Harlequin's patchwork suit' made up of a multitude of different and heterogeneous pieces. Economic theory should be treated as a flexible instrument, provided that each economist who chooses what he needs from the toolbox of economics (as Joan Robinson would say) has a clear objective in mind.

Caffè soon clarified that the choice among the various tools is never a mere 'technical' task. Responsible economists must first establish a given order of priorities, according to a scale of values they are always willing to declare. The domain of economic policy rejects any attempts at 'neutrality'. Here, Caffè literally followed Myrdal's methodological insights (see Caffè 1966a: 28).

For these reasons Caffè was critical of Schumpeter's definition of 'economic *analysis*' as merely speculative and altogether different from applied economics and economic policy. Caffè objects: 'The whole of economic research is undertaken as a function of – and as a guide to – action' (Caffè 1966a: 12).

It follows from this statement that the traditional distinction between positive and normative economics is of little use if it is taken to be predetermined. Thus, Caffè argued that even in the positive phase, the normative framework – particularly as regards adopting the hypotheses that support models – may be present at least in an implicit form. Naturally, this distinction does not avoid surreptitious interferences of value judgements in positive analysis, resulting in evident negative outcomes as far as policy decisions are concerned.

Caffè suggested a tripartite division of economic theory, economic policy and applied economics, assigning economic policy the function of an 'intermediate step' between abstract reflection and practical economic action (Caffè 1966a: 21). Economists, he contended, should indicate not only the tools and intermediate goals of policy, but the final goals as well. Note that eclecticism may regard means, but by no means goals. All economists have a model of the ideal society of which they each form a representation in their mind. An ideal society, Caffè maintained, is a democratic society, democracy being identified in Caffè's vision with a continuous growth of the 'public spirit' (Caffè 1966a: 68). Here one may glimpse the best heritage of the Italian Enlightenment – the 'greatest happiness for the greatest number' principle which, according to Caffè, represents the core of an open society. The theory of economic policy is the field where both Genovesi's 'civic economy' and Romagnosi's 'civilization' find their natural place.

Caffè had two main sources of inspiration. The first was inter-war Cambridge. Clearly, throughout his life Caffè was a committed Keynesian; but his Keynesianism was of a special nature, namely, tending more towards emphasis on the elements of continuity within the Cambridge tradition than break-up of this tradition. Alongside Keynes there stood Robertson (whose monetary writings Caffè edited in Italian) and other junior economists of his milieu, starting with the 'indestructible Joan Robinson' as Caffè described her in an obituary. In this picture, Sraffa represented a slightly cumbersome presence, owing to the overwhelming echo – almost a retrospective shadow – created by his later work. Caffè was deliberately sceptical about efforts to translate Keynes into Sraffian terms – as several young Italian economists attempted to do in the 1970s (see Caffè 1977). Above all Caffè was never in agreement with the attempt to draw from Sraffa any operational indication for economic policy.

As a theorist Caffè substantially shared Arthur Pigou's welfare theory insofar as it allowed the possibility of comparing interpersonal utilities (see Caffè 1956). In particular, Caffè insisted on the existence of negative externalities (market failures), which Pareto did not take into consideration but which contradict the premises of Pareto's optimum. In Caffè's view the presence of a 'social cost' that individual firms tend to shift onto the collectivity was a fundamental element justifying public intervention. Caffè was therefore dissatisfied with Ronald Coase's solution, since the individual affected by the damage is often weaker than the individual who causes it (see Palmerio 1995).

On the other hand Caffè always opposed the Austrian school on account of its negative attitude towards any 'responsible economic action', which he regarded as the necessary guideline for the policy-maker. In particular he was quite unconvinced by Hayek, whose courses at the London School of Economics he followed in 1947.

The second source of inspiration was the Italian school of economics of the late nineteenth and early twentieth century. Caffè had the merit of nurturing interest in this tradition during the years of absolute predominance of the Keynesian paradigm in Italy. Rather than devoting substantial attention to Pareto and Pantaleoni, Caffè vindicated the merits of some comparatively minor Italian economists, among whom he favourably mentioned Luzzatti, the popular banks' apostle, and Bachi and Masci, who showed independence of mind from the neoclassical mainstream without falling into the excesses of corporative economics (see Caffè 1978).

Caffè edited several volumes of Francesco Ferrara's collected writings. On the one hand he praised Ferrara's deep knowledge of Italian society, with all its limits, which, Caffè bitterly observed, had remained unchanged throughout the centuries (Caffè 1975: 31). But although Ferrara's diagnosis of the evils of Italian society was very acute, the therapy Ferrara suggested – or rather, the absence of any therapy – had, in Caffè's opinion, reinforced the conviction among many Italian economists that public action is useless and that *laissez-faire* is the only way out.

Another great Italian economist whose writings Caffè carefully edited on several occasions is Luigi Einaudi. However, while praising Einaudi's historical-critical approach concerning the evolution of modern capitalism (see Caffè 1974), he objected to Einaudi's (mis)interpretation of Keynes's saving-investment principle and of the multiplier mechanism (see the Caffè-Einaudi correspondence in the appendix to Faucci 2002: 404–8). In short, Caffè preferred to highlight Einaudi's intellectual honesty than to extol his specific policy prescriptions.

The main problem of the 1970s was inflation. Caffè, probably spurred by reflection on the New Deal experience, suggested introducing control over public utility tariffs and the fixing of 'administered prices' for goods (see Caffè 1975c). In this sense he can be classified as a late institutional economist (see Cangiani and Frigato 2012).

Despite his background as a moderate reformist, Caffè wrote many articles for *Il Manifesto*, the 'communist newspaper', which willingly accepted the elderly economist's contributions. Numerous strands of analysis can provide insight into the reasons underlying this *prima facie* contradiction. First, *Il Manifesto* was a genuinely free voice, independent of parties and pressure groups. Second, Caffè was increasingly unhappy with the economic (and political) situation in the Western world, where the original Keynesian ideas of an international monetary order had been completely abandoned, giving way to the power of financial lobbies (the so-called *incappucciati* ['hooded ones'], a phrase which in Caffè's language clearly alluded to Freemasonry). The so-called Washington Consensus numbered Caffè among its early critics (see Caffè 2013).

In 1985 Caffè endorsed the CGIL Trade Union referendum against the law that reduced the *punti di contingenza* [cost of living allowance], openly criticizing Franco Modigliani, who was a supporter of the reduction proposed by the Craxi government.[32]

As is well known the referendum failed to obtain a majority vote, and this defeat, which was also a defeat for the CGIL, brought to an end a long season that had opened with the 1969 'hot autumn'. CGIL commemorated Caffè with two monumental books (Amari and Rocchi 2007; Amari and Rocchi 2009).

The 'passion of reason': Claudio Napoleoni, the economist-philosopher

Claudio Napoleoni (of L'Aquila, 1924–88), professor of economics in Ancona, Naples and Turin, was, like Caffè, a 'critical'economist, but his cultural background was markedly different from that of Caffè. While the latter drew on Marshall, Keynes, the New Welfare theorists and the Italian tradition, Napoleoni's favourite authors were Marx, Walras, Robbins and Sraffa. He dedicated no special attention to Italian thinkers (a partial exception was Croce) and showed little enthusiasm for Keynes (this can be attributed above all to Napoleoni's Marxian leanings).

A formidable teacher and communicator (see Bellofiore and Beltrame 2004), Napoleoni wrote textbooks on Walras (*L'equilibrio economico generale*, 1965); on the classical economists (*Smith Ricardo Marx*, 1970); and a much-read book on twentieth-century economic thought (*Il pensiero economico del Novecento*, 1963, 1990, translated also into English). Moreover, he undertook an important collective task, as editor of *Dizionario di economia politica* (1956), whose entries included contributions by scholars such as Dobb, Balogh, Demaria and Caffè. Napoleoni wrote the majority of entries himself, all of them of analytical content. Finally, he devoted himself to philosophical reflection on the destiny of research in the field of economics (*Discorso sull'economia politica*, 1985). Most of his articles were hosted in *La rivista trimestrale*, a journal which Napoleoni founded together with F. Rodano in 1962.

A Catholic, but standing completely apart from the DC, Napoleoni was for some years a Member of Parliament for the 'Independent Left' (which was sympathetic to the PCI) and actively participated in the political debate from the vantage point of an engaged economist-intellectual.

The plurality of interests showed by Napoleoni in his inexhaustible reflection has raised numerous comments, including the charge of being contradictory and incoherent. With his lucidly logical mind, Napoleoni could hardly be accused of this fault, but it is indisputable that during the course of his life he changed his mind on crucial theoretical points.[33]

In a well-timed review of *Production of Commodities*, Napoleoni praised Sraffa's analytical device of measuring the surplus by avoiding values, but also lamented that Sraffa was 'mute' on the historical origin of the surplus and therefore on the nature of capitalism itself. Rather than embracing the Sraffian approach, Napoleoni proposed Marx's historical-critical method. An example of this method was to be found, Napoleoni believed, in the so-called *Unpublished chapter 6* of *Capital*, which charted the distinction between a pre-capitalist and a fully capitalist society insofar as the subordination of labour to capital was concerned (*Lezioni sul sesto capitolo inedito di Marx*, 1972).

This is not all. In subsequent years Napoleoni increasingly reflected that Marx was unable to reconcile philosophical dialectics with the logic of economic science (here, Napoleoni implicitly agreed with Croce's notion of economics: see Chapter 6 above). 'Economic analysis, as based on measurable and empirically observable magnitudes, is not connected with social theory, and Marx's discourse appears divided into two non-communicating parts' (Napoleoni 1992 [1983]: 152).

After having thus disposed of Marx's scientific programme, Napoleoni had a further surprise. His concluding *Discorso sull'economia politica* offers a reappraisal of neo-classical economics, viewing the latter mainly through its representation in the famous epistemological assessment offered by Lionel Robbins's *Essay on the nature and importance of economic science* (1932, 1935). According to the last version of Napoleoni's thought the views of Robbins and Marx are not really antithetical, but rather complementary. Each of them depicted an aspect of the economic phenomenon, respectively the 'natural' and the 'historical' element. Napoleoni concluded that capitalist accumulation is *either* a result of abstaining from consumption (Robbins), *or* a result of surplus extortion (Marx). The definitions depend on the researcher's standpoint. Napoleoni's *Discorso* raised a host of objections to which Napoleoni – always open to discussion – patiently replied (Napoleoni 1992 [1986]).

Napoleoni applied his theoretical abilities to investigating the state of the Italian economy and suggesting the appropriate economic policy. In this context his perspective reflected the communist tradition, based on Gramsci's notion of the 'hereditary taints' of Italian capitalism. Translating this concept into economic language, Napoleoni stressed that the weight of Ricardian rents due to the absence of competition encroached on the accumulation of capital and therefore hindered the increase of wages above subsistence. But the affinity with Ricardo is only partial. Napoleoni advocated a reform in consumption (greater public consumption in education, health, leisure, etc., through an expansion of public expenditure instead of excessively high private, affluent, frivolous consumption) and his position was espoused by Enrico Berlinguer, the PCI secretary in the 1970s at the time of the *compromesso storico* between the PCI and the DC. At first sight it may seem strange that a Marxist should indicate a 'reform in consumption' instead of a reform in production as the main goal of a socialist strategy. In fact the link between human consumption, human wants and the essence of man was to occupy the final years of Napoleoni's thought, which were characterized by return to a severe and almost ascetic Christian vision of society.

The versatile economist: Paolo Sylos Labini

Paolo Sylos Labini (of Rome, 1920–2005), who taught economics in Catania, Bologna and Rome, had many affinities with Caffè and Napoleoni, in that he was interested in the history of the discipline and strongly believed that meditating on past economists was not a mere leisure pursuit but a fundamental step in the present day economist's training. His studies included a period in the USA, during which he attended Schumpeter's lectures in Harvard in 1948, subsequently completing his training in Cambridge, England, in 1949. He always considered himself an unwavering disciple of the Austro-American economist. Moreover, he was well acquainted with Joan Robinson and Nicholas Kaldor (and, of course, Piero Sraffa).

Sylos Labini's motto was 'R-R' ('realism and rigour', Roncaglia 2012: 718). His approach was 'realistic' in the sense that he liked to start from an overview of observed phenomena in order to single out the tools most appropriate to investigate their intrinsic connections. Another feature of his research was that of always awarding priority to structure over conjuncture, and the long view over the short.

In Sylos Labini's earlier writings, Smith, Ricardo and Marx marched hand-in-hand. The continuous broadening of the markets, as well as capital accumulation, were seen as the ingredients of economic advancement. A third ingredient, Sylos Labini observed, was supplied by the progress of technology, where development manifested itself as a succession of cycles. Here Schumpeter was his favourite author (see Sylos Labini 1970 [1954]).

Sylos Labini's main line of research concentrated on market forms. In his most important book, originally published in 1956, technological progress played a major role, but this time in connection with study of the circumstances of large enterprises, a context in which he benefited from inspiration prompted by Sraffa's 1925 and 1926 articles. He consequently rejected the traditional (Marshallian) presentation of static U-cost curves as a necessary prerequisite for the firm's equilibrium. If in a non-competitive market marginal costs are no longer the determinants of prices, this means that all potential competitors can be excluded by a strategy based on inventions and on the broad range of devices a monopolist can reserve for himself. An 'exclusion price' based on the mark-up would be able to ensure high profits without lowering prices. Sylos Labini was particularly successful in showing that the outcome of his own research on oligopolies converged with the most important achievements of the microeconomic revolution in the 1920s and early 1930s (Sraffa, Robinson, Chamberlin), as well as with Keynes's macroeconomics (the concept of effectual demand) and Schumpeter's dynamics of oligopolistic capitalism in *Business Cycles* and in *Capitalism, Socialism and Democracy*.

As is well known, Franco Modigliani's authoritative article *New Developments on the Oligopoly Front* (1958) contributed to the dissemination of Sylos Labini's work among an international audience. The fact that Sylos Labini was not a follower of the 'neo-classical synthesis' between Keynes and marginal economics was no obstacle. From Modigliani's article onwards, the main contemporary literature on oligopoly included the 'Sylos–Bain–Modigliani' approach, even though the three authors did not start out from fully unanimous theoretical assumptions.

Moreover, Sylos Labini was an admirer of Sraffa, and he once confessed to the present author that he had very much enjoyed explaining the Sraffian model to his grandson with the aid of some marbles. He developed Sraffian concepts in a stimulating article, *La spirale e l'arco* (1985), which convincingly argued in favour of the 'classical' vision of a system continuously reproducing its own conditions, as opposed to the marginal conception of economic phenomena as going from production to final consumption.[34]

A consistent number of Sylos Labini's works treated problems of economic development, offering a wealth of statistical information accompanied by a lucid strategic vision. One of the main issues was the relationship between economic structure and institutional and political constraints. While in his early years Sylos Labini was comparatively open to the planned economies of the East – partly also due to the fact that at the time in question both the Soviet Union and Mao's China were showing very high rates of growth – from the 1970s onwards he dismissed any benevolence towards Soviet-type planning, declaring that some crucial indicators of population welfare in the Soviet Union were worsening (e.g. the declining average lifespan: see Sylos Labini 1986: xii). Consequently, Sylos Labini manifested an increasing dissatisfaction with the prescriptions of Marx and Lenin for underdeveloped countries, turning instead to the Smith-Tocqueville approach based on the fruitful interaction between the market and property rights (Sylos Labini 2000).

Further, Sylos Labini engaged in study of the composition and dynamics of social classes in Italy, revealing admirable sociological skills. He drew attention to the crucial question of the comparative backwardness of Italian society, where a considerable part of the 'middle class' – which in other Western countries constituted the backbone of society – appeared parasitic and unproductive; while the lowest layers of society – especially in the South – inexorably coexisted with the Mafia and 'bad economy' (see Sylos Labini 1986). Sylos Labini's work was widely discussed in sociological circles, but there was a tendency to interpolate into his scheme a host of sub-species of social classes, thereby missing the central point of his research.

Let us conclude with a mention of his abundant political/polemical production. Although he never held political posts, Sylos Labini had been a committed activist in the secularist democratic (non-communist) front ever since the 1950s. A nephew of Giustino Fortunato, he was a disciple and personal friend of such democratic thinkers as Gaetano Salvemini and Ernesto Rossi. His civic commitment complemented his study of social class in Italy, in a relation of fertile interaction.

After Berlusconi's 1994 'entry into the fray of politics' Sylos Labini became increasingly vocal in speaking out against the dangerous influence a tycoon closely involved with the media and founder of a personal political movement could have on a democratic system (see Sylos Labini 2001, 2006). The centuries-old weakness of Italian society – an intrinsic lack of cohesion that had led to the recurrent call for 'a man sent by Providence' who would be expected to solve all problems from above at the wave of a wand – appeared to the ageing and disillusioned professor as fully confirmed.

Notes

1 The secondary literature on post-war Italy is very heterogeneous. The most readable book is still Lanaro (1992), written soon before the beginning of the Berlusconi era.

2 Quite paradoxically, among the processes of *epurazione* there was one that concerned Pasquale Jannaccone, the Turin economist, who never wrote in favour of Fascism but had been a member of the Fascist *Accademia d'Italia*. Eventually, Jannaccone was dismissed (see Faucci (1986): 347). In 1950 President Einaudi appointed him as a life-long Senator.

3 See the excerpts of the most significant hearings in Villari (1972), Part VII. The original documents are in Ministero per la Costituente (1946–47), 12 volumes.

4 Fanfani's book, written in 1933 and re-edited in 1944, was translated into English in 1935 with the title *Catholicism, Protestantism and Capitalism*, and reprinted twice in the last 30 years: by Notre Dame University Press, Indiana, (1984), in which a critical attitude towards Fanfani's work can be perceived; and by HIS Press, Norfolk, VA (2003) that was entirely favourable (see Fanfani (2005) [1944]: xxxv–xxxvi and 189–91). A lively debate on the book among American scholars is in the appendix to the Italian reprint (see pp. 187–269). On Fanfani see in general Roggi (2010); Michelagnoli (2010).

5 See Sturzo (1995). During Fascism Sturzo was in voluntary exile in America. Pagliai (2009) presents an appendix of correspondence between La Pira and Sturzo.

6 See Corbino (1982) [1931–38]). See also his collection of articles on newpapers (Corbino (1964), vol. I), and Corbino's life (Corbino (1972)). For his action as Treasury Minister during 1946 see below.

7 For the evolution of PCI's policy programmes see the documents collected in Barca *et al.* (1975).

8 See, among others, Padoa Schioppa (1997): 8–9. Tommaso Padoa Schioppa (1940–2010), formerly the Bank of Italy's General Vice-Director, was Economy Minister in the second Prodi cabinet, 2006–08.

9 Here Einaudi missed Pareto's distinction between the maximum of economic ophelimity and the maximum of sociological utility, implicit in the Montagnana amendment. For a different interpretation see Costabile and Scazzieri (2012): 750.

10 Among the professional economists, Demaria favoured money change most strongly; he considered it a valid alternative to the continuous issue of public loans and an antidote to inflation. See his articles in *La nuova stampa* (Turin) collected in Demaria (1951): 69–75.

11 See a historical reconstruction in Piscitelli (1975): 191–228. The reasons against *cambio* are defended by Ricossa and Tuccimei (1992): 30–8.

12 For Einaudi's general reports to the Bank of Italy, and further documentation, see Barucci (2006).

13 Giorgio Fuà commented that the two-year period indicated by Governor Einaudi as the span of time necessary to produce the complete annihilation of the value of lira was based on an unconvincing comparison between flow (expenditure) and stock (money) magnitudes. Fuà observed that Einaudi presented the 'punto critico' as the inexorable effect of a process based on arbitrary assumptions. See Fuà (1947): 89–101.

14 For a panorama of critiques to the *linea Einaudi* see De Cecco (1968). The best illustration in its defence is offered by Baffi (1965) [1954]: 177–93. Baffi (1911–89) was subsequently General Director of the Bank of Italy under Governor Guido Carli, and Governor himself from 1975 to 1979. He was obliged to resign under the accusation – which was demonstrated as specious – of not having provided the necessary controls over the banking system at the time of the Sindona case (involving a 'banker' who colluded with the Mafia and was protected by influential political men).

15 See Saraceno (1969) [1948]: 271–489. Barucci's introduction shows very clearly Saraceno's shift of interest from management to planning, a consequence of his involvement in politics.

16 It has been observed that the *Piano* concept of unemployment was not Keynesian (i.e. cyclical, as in Hoffman's *Country study*), but structural, based on disequilibrium between the labour aggregate demand and supply. See Bottiglieri (1984): 56.

17 The present author has consulted the typescript of the proceedings of a meeting between Vanoni and other professors of economics (held in Rome on 8 January 1955) to discuss the draft of the *Schema di sviluppo dell'occupazione e del reddito in Italia nel decennio 1955–64*. This document, probably never published, is kept in the Historical Archives of the European Community in Fiesole, Florence.

18 This minimalist definition came from Vanoni himself. See Lombardini (1967): 43. Siro Lombardini (1924–2013) has been a major character in Italian economics, as the founder of a flourishing school whose members were: L. L. Pasinetti, T. Cozzi and A. Vercelli. A specialist on monopoly theory, he was also minister of 'Partecipazioni statali'. See his interview in Di Matteo and Vercelli (2005).

19 See Rossi (1953); VV. AA. (1955). *Il Mondo* also published an article by Alfred E. Kahn, the American specialist on monopoly pricing and tariffs.

20 Manlio Rossi-Doria (1905–88), an anti-Fascist who spent many years in prison, was an agriculture economist at Naples University who was particularly active in denouncing the 'dominant position' of *Federconsorzi*, a semi-public agency that fixed the prices of many agrarian goods to be stored. See Rossi-Doria (1963). On Rossi-Doria see VV. AA. (1999).

21 For the origins of this phenomenon see Salvati (1982), especially Chapter 3 which documents the rapid success of DC from 1945 onwards in occupying IRI, initially thanks to its privileged relationship with the Allies.

22 Several economists frequently collaborated with *Il giorno*. One of them was Francesco Forte (born 1929), who succeeded Einaudi to the Turin chair of public finance. Subsequently Forte became ENI Vice-President and, later on, Finance Minister.

23 Concerning Menichella's discreet style, see Einaudi (1960). Particularly important are the recollections by Carli and Saraceno on Menichella in VV. AA. (1986).

24 Many of his ideas are clearly sketched in his autobiography (Carli 1993). On his intention to transform the Bank of Italy into a firm governed by a 'techno-structure' see Gigliobianco (2006), Chapter 6.

25 See Lombardini (1967). This volume was part of a collection of studies on various aspects of planning, whose publisher was Giulio Einaudi and whose editor was Antonio Giolitti (1915–2010), formerly a communist leader, later on socialist Budget Minister in several Centre-Left cabinets during the 1960s and 1970s.

26 See Roncaglia (2007). See also the volume collecting autobiographical essays issued in the same journal, VV. AA. (1988).

27 See Becattini, Sylos Labini, Garegnani, Graziani (1984). These reports are also invaluable in measuring the distance between Italian economics today and that of less than 30 years ago, as far as the intellectual background was concerned. The picture should be completed by referring to the strong connections that many Italian scholars established with Cambridge and Oxford (UK). From recent research carried out by Baranzini (forthcoming) it emerges that between 1950 and 1995 more than 40

volumes by Italian economists were published by Oxford University Press and about 1,000 articles authored by Italian economists appeared in the most prestigious international journals.

28 See the very instructive papers collected in VV. AA. (1984), including the many protagonists in the Keynes debate in Italy in the 1950s.

29 On Di Fenizio see Lunghini and Targetti Lenti (2004); on Marrama see Gandolfo (1987); on Caffè see below.

30 A selection of papers on these topics, including the translation of Garegnani's important article *Heterogeneous capital, the production function and the theory of distribution* (1970), are to be found in Sylos Labini (1973). Some papers by Italian economists on the issue of reswitching are collected in Harcourt and Laing (1971).

31 Several lines of modern historical research on Sraffa are already traced by Bellofiore (1986). After Roncaglia's contributions on Sraffa (Roncaglia 2000 and 2012c), Naldi is now expected to produce a comprehensive scientific biography. Naldi has presented the very first results of his research in Kurz, Pasinetti and Salvadori (eds) (2008): 7–29. Other noteworthy biographical and critical contributions are collected in Salvadori (1998). See also Pivetti (2000); Cozzi and Marchionatti (2001); VV. AA. (2004b).

32 It would be unthinkable not to mention Franco Modigliani (1918–2003), one of the founders of the so-called 'neo-classical synthesis' (see D'Adda 2012) and the only Italian-born Nobel Prize-winner for economics. Modigliani became an American citizen after his flight from Italy in 1939. See his autobiography, (1999). See also the papers on Modigliani presented at the 2005 *Accademia Nazionale dei Lincei* conference and collected in *Banca Nazionale del Lavoro Quarterly Review* (VV. AA. 2005).

33 Among the numerous comments to Napoleoni, see Bellofiore (1991, an intelligent defence) and Cavalieri (2006, an intelligent criticism).

34 To celebrate Sraffa's 75th birthday, in 1973, Sylos Labini edited a collected volume of papers from various authors on Sraffian topics (Sylos Labini 1973). This *Festschrift* was not openly dedicated to Sraffa owing to the latter's proverbial shyness and reserve (Roncaglia 2012b: 719).

References

Albertone, M. (1979) *Fisiocrati. Istruzione e cultura*, Torino: Fondazione Einaudi.

Alessandrini, P., Crivellini, M. (2004) 'Fuà e la scuola di economia di Ancona', in Garofalo G., Graziani A. (eds) (2004).

Allocati, A. (ed.) (1990), *Carteggio Loria-Graziani, 1888–1943*, Roma: Ministero dei beni culturali.

Amari, G., Rocchi, N. (eds) (2007) *Federico Caffè. Un economista per gli uomini comuni*, Roma: Ediesse.

Amari, G., Rocchi, N. (eds) (2009) *Federico Caffè. Un economista per il nostro tempo*, Roma: Ediesse.

Amoroso, L. (1932) 'Contributo alla teoria matematica della dinamica economica', in *Nuova collana di economisti stranieri e italiani*, vol. 5, *Dinamica economica*, Torino: Utet.

Annali dell'economia italiana (1984) *Keynes in Italia*, Roma: Istituto IPSOA.

Antonelli, G. B. (1951) [1886] *Sulla teoria matematica dell'economia politica*, reprinted in *Giornale degli economisti*, 1951, 3. English transl. (1971) 'On the Mathematical Theory of Political Economy', in Chipman, J. S., Hurwicz, L., Richter, M., Sonnenschein, K. H. F. (eds), *Preference, Utility and Demand*, New York: Harcourt Brace and Jovanovich.

Arena, R. (1998) 'Marco Fanno', in Meacci, F. (ed.) (1998).

Arias, G. (1934) [1928] 'Politica ed economia nel pensiero di Niccolò Machiavelli', in Arias, G., *Economia corporativa*, vol. I, Firenze: Cya.

Arias, G. (2009) *Antologia di scritti*, Roggi, P. (ed.), intr. by O. Ottonelli, Firenze: Le Monnier, Fondazione Spadolini – Nuova Antologia.

Artoni, R. (2012) 'Francesco Saverio Nitti', in Istituto della Enciclopedia italiana (2012): 672–9.

Asso, P. F. (1981–1982) '*La riforma monetaria* di Keynes e gli economisti italiani', *Il pensiero economico moderno*, 1981, 2–3; 1982: 1.

Asso, P. F. (ed.) (2001) *From Economists to Economists. The International Spread of Italian Economic Thought, 1750–1950*, Firenze: Polistampa.

Augello, M. M. (ed.) (1990) *Joseph Alois Schumpeter. A Reference Guide*, Berlin: Springer.

Augello, M. M. (ed.) (2012) *Dizionario degli economisti accademici italiani dell'Ottocento*, Pisa-Roma: Serra.

Augello M. M., Guidi, M. E. L. (1988) 'I "Politecnici del commercio" e la formazione della classe dirigente economica nell'Italia post-unitaria', in Augello, M. M., Bianchini, M., Gioli, G., Roggi, P. (eds) (1988).

Augello, M. M., Guidi M. E. L. (eds) (2002–2003) *La scienza economica in Parlamento, 1861–1922*, 2 vols, Milano: Angeli.

Augello, M. M., Guidi, M. E. L. (1996) 'The emergence of economic periodical literature in Italy (1750–1900)', in VV. AA. (1996).

Augello, M. M., Guidi, M. E. L. (eds) (2007) *L'economia divulgata. Stili e percorsi italiani (1840–1922)*, III, *La 'Biblioteca dell'economista' e la circolazione internazionale dei manuali*, Milano: Franco Angeli.

Augello, M. M., Guidi, M. E. L. (eds) (2009) *Riccardo Dalla Volta. Crisi della concorrenza, concentrazioni industriali e imperialismo all'alba del Novecento*, Firenze: Fondazione Spadolini – Nuova Antologia.

Augello, M. M., Michelini, L. (1997) 'Maffeo Pantaleoni (1857–1924): biografia scientifica, storiografia e bibliografia', *Il pensiero economico italiano*, 1.

Augello, M. M., Pavanelli, G. (eds) (2005) *Tra economia, politica e impegno civile: Gerolamo Boccardo e il suo tempo*, Genova: Brigati.

Augello, M. M., Bianchini, M., Gioli, G., Roggi, P. (eds) (1988) *Le cattedre di economia politica in Italia. La diffusione di una disciplina 'sospetta' (1750–1900)*, Milano: Angeli.

Augello, M. M., Bianchini, M., Guidi, M. E. L. (eds) (1996) *Le riviste di economia in Italia (1700–1900). Dai giornali scientifico-letterari ai periodici specialistici*, Milano: Franco Angeli.

Bacchi Andreoli, S. (1949) 'La teoria keynesiana in Italia', part I, *Bancaria*, Nov.

Backhaus, J. G. (ed.) (2001) *On the Frontiers of the Modern Theory of Value. Essays on Attilio da Empoli (1904–1948)*, *Journal of Economic Studies*, 3.

Badaloni, N. (1973) *La cultura*, in *Storia d'Italia*, vol. III, *Dal primo Settecento all'Unità*, Torino: Einaudi.

Baer, C. (1844a) 'Della ricchezza individuale e della ricchezza nazionale', *Il Museo*, I, vol. III.

Baer, C. (1844b) 'Dell'indole ed oggetto della economia pubblica', *Il Museo*, I, vol. IV.

Baffi, P. (1965) [1954] *Memoria sull'azione di Einaudi 1945–1948*, in Baffi, P., *Studi sulla moneta*, Milano: Giuffrè.

Bairati, P., Carrubba, S. (1990) *La trasparenza difficile. Storia di due giornali economici: Il Sole e 24 Ore*, Palermo: Sellerio.

Baker, G. R. F. (1978) *Sallustio Bandini*, Firenze: Olschki.

Bandini, S. A. (1978) [1737] *Discorso sopra la Maremma di Siena*, Conenna Bonelli, L. (ed.), appendix to Baker, G. R. F. (1978).

Baranzini, M. (forthcoming) 'La scuola di economia anglo-italiana: Cambridge e Oxford. Su alcuni programmi di ricerca più significativi', in Accademia nazionale dei Lincei, *Gli economisti italiani. Protagonisti, paradigmi, politiche*, Rome, 25–26 September 2013.

Barbagallo, F. (1984) *Nitti*, Torino: Utet.

Barbieri, L. (ed.) (1988) [1934] *Indici per autori e per materie della Nuova Antologia dal 1866 al 1930*, Roma: La Nuova Antologia.

Barca, L., Botta, F., Zevi, A. (eds) (1975) *I comunisti e l'economia italiana 1944–1974*, Bari: De Donato.

Barile, N. L. (2012) 'Usura', in Istituto della Enciclopedia italiana: 59–65.

Barone, E. (1912) 'Studi di teoria finanziaria. I redditi e la pressione tributaria', *Giornale degli economisti*: 316–53.

Barone, E. (1915) *Principii di economia politica*, Roma: Athenaeum.

Barone, E. (1936) *Le opere economiche*, vol. II, *Principi di economia politica*, Bologna: Zanichelli.

Bartoli, H. (2003) *Histoire de la pensée économique en Italie*, Paris: Publications de la Sorbonne.

Bartolozzi Batignani, S. (ed.) (1985) *Dai progetti cristiano-sociali alla Costituente. Il pensiero economico di P. E. Taviani*, Firenze: Le Monnier.

Barucci, P. (1961) 'Economia e "incivilimento" in Gian Domenico Romagnosi', *Giornale degli economisti e Annali di economia*. Reprinted in Barucci (2009).

Barucci, P. (1965) *Il pensiero economico di Melchiorre Gioja*, Milano: Giuffrè.

Barucci, P. (1969) Introduction to Saraceno (1969).

Barucci, P. (1972) 'The Spread of Marginalism in Italy (1871–1890)', *History of Political Economy*, 2.

Barucci, P. (2009) [1977] 'La "cultura economica" di Alessandro Manzoni', in Barucci (2009).

Barucci, P. (1980) *Economisti alla Costituente*, in Mori, G. (ed.), *La cultura economica nel periodo della ricostruzione*, Bologna: Il Mulino.

Barucci, P. (ed.) (2003) *Le frontiere dell'economia politica. Gli economisti stranieri in Italia: dai mercantilisti a Keynes*, Firenze: Polistampa.

Barucci, P. (ed.) (2006) *Luigi Einaudi. Considerazioni finali della Banca d'Italia*, Milano: Treves.

Barucci, P. (2009) *Sul pensiero economico italiano (1750–1900)*, Napoli: Istituto italiano per gli studi filosofici.

Barucci, P., Costabile, L., Di Matteo, M. (eds) (2008) *Gli archivi e la storia del pensiero economico*, Bologna: Il Mulino.

Bazzichi, O. (2012) *Giuseppe Toniolo. Alle origini della dottrina sociale della Chiesa*, Torino: Lindau.

Becattini, G. (1962) *Il concetto d'industria e la teoria del valore*, Torino: Boringhieri.

Becattini, G. (ed.) (1990) *Il pensiero economico: temi, problemi e scuole*, Torino: Utet.

Becattini, G. (1998) *Distretti industriali e made in Italy*, Torino: Bollati Boringhieri.

Becattini, G., Sylos Labini, P., Garegnani, P., Graziani, A. (1984) 'Relazioni sull'attività del gruppo CNR per lo studio dei problemi economici della distribuzione, del progresso tecnico e dello sviluppo', *Quaderni di storia dell'economia politica*, 3.

Beccaria C. (1958) [1769] *Elementi di economia pubblica*, in Romagnoli, S. (ed.), *Opere*, Firenze: Sansoni, vol. I.

Beccaria, C. (1970) [1764] *Dei delitti e delle pene*, Venturi, F. (ed.), Torino: Einaudi.

Bellanca, N. (1996) 'La sistemazione dell' "originalità" in Giovanni Demaria. L'economia come sistema auto-organizzato mediante fluttuazioni', in Bini, P. (ed.) (1996).

Bellanca, N. (1997) *Economia politica e marxismo in Italia. Problemi teorici e nodi storiografici*, Milano: Unicopli.

Bellanca, N., Giocoli, N. (1998) *Maffeo Pantaleoni. Il Principe degli economisti italiani*, Firenze: Polistampa.

Bellofiore, R., ed. (1986) *Tra teoria economica e grande cultura europea: Piero Sraffa*, Milano: FrancoAngeli.

Bellofiore, R. (1991) *La passione della ragione. Scienza economica e teoria critica in Claudio Napoleoni*, Milano: Unicopli.

Bellofiore, R., Beltrame G. (2004) 'L'insegnamento dell'economia politica come problema in Claudio Napoleoni', in Garofalo, G., Graziani, A. (eds) (2004): 183–267.

Belloni, G. (1803) [1757] *Dissertazione sopra il commercio*, in *Scrittori classici italiani di economia politica, parte moderna*, tomo II, Milano: Destefanis.

Benini, R. (1892) 'Sulle dottrine economiche di Antonio Serra. Appunti critici', *Giornale degli economisti*, vol. II.

Benson, L. (1950) 'Achille Loria's influence on American economic thought', *Agricultural History*, XXIV: 182–99.

Béraud, A., Faccarello, G. (eds) (1992) *Nouvelle histoire de la pensée économique, tome I, Des scolastiques aux classiques*, Paris: La Découverte.

Bernardi, E. (2012) 'Manlio Rossi-Doria', in Istituto della Enciclopedia italiana (2012): 694–9.

Bertolino, A. (1956) Preface to C. Cattaneo, *Scritti economici*, Firenze: Le Monnier.

Bianchi, G. (2007) *Come cambia una rivista. La 'Riforma sociale' di Luigi Einaudi 1900–1918*, Torino: Giappichelli.

Bianchini, M. (1996) 'La "Civiltà cattolica" e il carattere etico dell'economia politica', in Augello, M. M., Bianchini, M., Guidi, M. E. L. (eds) (1996).

Bianchini, M. (2012) 'Geminiano Montanari', in Istituto della Enciclopedia italiana: 371–4.

Bilotti, E. (ed.) (1988) *Questioni economiche e di vita accademica. La corrispondenza di D. Berardi con M. Pantaleoni*, Corigliano Calabro: Iprastah.

Bini, P. (1982) 'Il salario "corporativo" negli studi economici fra le due guerre', in Faucci, R. (ed.) (1982), vol. II.

Bini, P. (ed.) (1986) 'Gli scritti in tedesco di Costantino Bresciani Turroni', *Banca Toscana. Studi e informazioni*, suppl. to n. 4.

Bini, P. (1992) *Costantino Bresciani Turroni. Ciclo, moneta, sviluppo*, Civitanova M.: Otium.

Bini, P., ed. (1996) *Giovanni Demaria e la teoria economica dei fatti nuovi, Storia del pensiero economico*: 31–2.

Bini, P. (2007) *Maffeo Pantaleoni visto da Piero Bini*, Roma: Luiss.

Bini, P., Fusco, A. M. (eds) (2004) *Umberto Ricci (1879–1946). Economista militante e uomo combattivo*, Firenze: Polistampa.

Blanqui, A. (1882) [1837] *Histoire de l'économie politique en Europe depuis les anciens jusqu'à nos jours*, Paris: Guillaumin.

Bobbio, N. (1970) *Una filosofia militante. Studi su Carlo Cattaneo*, Torino: Einaudi.

Bobbio, N. (1971) 'L'ideologia in Pareto e in Marx', in Bobbio, N., *Saggi sulla scienza politica in Italia*, Bari: Laterza.

Boccardo, G. (1882) 'Gli eretici dell'economia e la questione sociale', in *Biblioteca dell'economista*, III, 9, part I.

Boldizzoni, F. (2012) 'Lodovico Antonio Muratori', in Istituto della Enciclopedia italiana: 375–9.

Borsari, S. (ed.) (1964) *L'opera di Benedetto Croce*, Napoli: Nella sede dell'Istituto.

Botero, G. (1997) [1589] *La ragion di Stato*, Continisio, C. (ed.), Roma: Donzelli.

Bottasso, E. (ed.) (1990) *Catalogo storico delle edizioni Pomba e Utet 1791–1990*, Torino: Utet.

Bottiglieri B. (1984) *La politica economica dell'Italia centrista (1948–1958)*, Milano: Comunità.

Brandolini, A., Gobbi, G. (1990) 'Il contributo italiano alla fondazione e allo sviluppo della "Econometric Society"', *Quaderni di storia dell'economia politica*, 2–3.

Breglia, A. (1965) *Reddito sociale*, Sylos Labini, P. (ed.), Roma: Athenaeum.

Breglia, A. (1973) [1950] 'Il problema del finanziamento del Piano del Lavoro', *Giovane Critica*, 34–35–36.

Bresciani Turroni, C. (1931) *Le vicende del marco tedesco*, 'Annali di economia', vol. VIII; English translation: *The Economics of Inflation. A Study of Currency Depreciation in Post-War Germany* (1937), London: Allen and Unwin.

Bresciani Turroni, C. (1938) 'The "multiplier" in practice: some results of recent German experience', *Review of Economic Statistics*: 76–88.

Bresciani Turroni, C. (1939) 'Osservazioni sulla teoria del moltiplicatore', *Rivista bancaria*: 639–714.

Bresciani Turroni, C. (1951) *Corso di economia politica*, vol. II, Milano: Giuffrè.

Bresciani Turroni, C. (2006) [1945] *Liberalismo e politica economica*, Bologna: Il Mulino.

Bruni, L. (1997) 'Il dialogo con Vailati e la teoria dell'azione di Pareto', *Il pensiero economico italiano*, 1.

Bruni, L. (2010) 'Il "Delle virtù e dei premi" di Giacinto Dragonetti (e una polemica di Croce)', *Storia del pensiero economico*, 1.

Bruni, L. (2012) 'Virtù civili', in Istituto della Enciclopedia Italiana: 66–72.

Busino, G. (1971) 'I fondamenti dell'economia e della sociologia nelle polemiche tra il Pareto e Croce', *Rassegna economica*: 1095–1135.

Busino, G. (1977) *Vilfredo Pareto e l'industria del ferro nel Valdarno*, Milano: Banca commerciale italiana.

Cabiati, A. (1940) 'Intorno ad alcune recenti indagini sulla teoria pura del collettivismo', *Rivista di storia economica*, 2.

Cafagna, L. (ed.) (1962) *Il Nord nella storia d'Italia*, Bari: Laterza.

Caffè, F. (1956) 'Benessere (economia del)', in Napoleoni, C. (ed.) (1956).

Caffè, F. (1966a) *Politica economica. Sistematica e tecniche di analisi*, Torino: Boringhieri.

Caffè, F. (1966b) 'Vecchi e nuovi trasferimenti anormali di capitali', in VV. AA. (1966), vol. 1.

Caffè, F. (1975a) 'Luigi Einaudi nel centenario della nascita', in VV. AA. (1975).

Caffè, F. (1975b) *Frammenti per la storia del pensiero economico*, Milano: Giuffrè.

Caffè, F. (1975c) 'La politica pubblica e i prezzi amministrati', reprinted in Amari and Rocchi (eds) (2007).

Caffè, F. (1977) *Keynes e i suoi contemporanei*, in Faucci, R. (ed.) (1977).

Caffè, F. (1978) 'Rapporti tra economisti italiani e il pensiero economico all'estero negli anni della grande crisi', in Toniolo, Gianni (ed.) (1978).

Caffè, F. (1983) Introduction to Del Vecchio, G. (1983).

Caffè, F. (1987) 'V. Marrama e gli anni difficili della ricostruzione post-bellica', in Gandolfo, G. (ed.) (1987).

Caffè, F. (2007) *Scritti quotidiani*, preface by P. Ciocca, Roma: Manifestolibri.

Caffè, F. (2013) *Contro gli incappucciati della finanza. Tutti gli scritti: Il Messaggero 1974–1986; L'Ora 1983–1987*, Amari, G. (ed.), Roma: Castelvecchi.

Camcastle, C. (2005) *The More Moderate Side of Joseph de Maistre*, Montreal-Kingston-Ithaca: McGill-Queen's University Press.

Cangiani, M., Frigato, P. (2012) 'Federico Caffè and institutional economics', in VV. AA. (2012).

Capra, C. (ed.) (1999) *Pietro Verri e il suo tempo*, vol. II, Milano: Cisalpino.

Capra, C. (2002) *I progressi della ragione. Vita di Pietro Verri*, Bologna: Il Mulino.

Caracciolo, A. (1968) *Stato e società civile. Problemi dell'unificazione italiana*, Torino: Einaudi.

Carli, G. (1993) *Cinquant'anni di vita italiana*, in collaboration with P. Peluffo, Roma-Bari: Laterza.

Cassata, F. (2008) 'A "scientific basis" for fascism: the neo-organicism of Corrado Gini', *History of economic ideas*, 3.

Cassata, F. (2009) 'La "dura fatica" dei numeri: Riccardo Bachi e la statistica economica', in Marchionatti, R. (ed.) (2009).

Cassata, F., Marchionatti, R. (2010) 'Cronache economiche di un trentennio. Lo sviluppo dell'economia italiana 1881–1913 nell'interpretazione di Luigi Einaudi e la sua scuola', *Rivista di storia economica*, 2.

Cattaneo, C. (1939) [1847] 'D'alcune istituzioni agrarie dell'Alta Italia applicabili a sollievo dell'Irlanda', in Cattaneo (1939).

Cattaneo, C. (1939) [1851, 1853] 'Su la bonificazione del piano di Magadino. Primo e secondo rapporto', in Cattaneo (1939).

Cattaneo, C. (1939) *Saggi di economia rurale*, Einaudi, L. (ed.), Torino: Einaudi.

Cattaneo, C. (1956) [1836] 'Una strada di ferro da Milano a Venezia', in *Scritti economici*, Bertolino, A. (ed.), vol. I, Firenze: Le Monnier.

Cattaneo, C. (1956) [1836–37] 'Della carità legale', in Bertolino, A. (ed.), *Scritti economici*, vol. I, Firenze: Le Monnier.

Cattaneo, C. (1957) [1861] 'La China antica e moderna', in Alessio, F. (ed.), *Scritti*, Firenze: Sansoni.

Cattaneo, C. (1972) [1843] 'Dell'economia nazionale di Federico List', in Castelnuovo Frigessi, D. (ed.), *Opere scelte*, vol. II, Torino: Einaudi.

Cavalcanti, M. L. (1984) *La politica commerciale italiana 1945–1952. Uomini e fatti*, Napoli: Edizioni scientifiche italiane.

Cavalieri, D. (2006) *Scienza economica e umanesimo positivo. Claudio Napoleoni e la critica della ragione economica*, Milano: Franco Angeli.

Cavour, C. (1855) [1852] 'Discorso sul bilancio attivo del 1852', in Cavour, C., *Opere politico-economiche del conte Camillo Benso di Cavour*, Cuneo: Galimberti.

Cavour, C. (1962) *Scritti di economia 1835–1850*. Sirugo, F. (ed.), Milano: Feltrinelli.

Cavour, C. (1962a) [1847] 'Influenza delle riforme sulle condizioni economiche dell'Italia', *Il Risorgimento*, in Cavour, C. (1962).

Cavour, C. (1962b) [1848] [Anonymous article on *Risorgimento*], in Cavour, C. (1962).

Cavour, C. (1962c) [1835] *Taxe des pauvres en Angleterre*, in Cavour, C. (1962).

Cavour, C. (1962d) [1846] 'Des chemins de fer en Italie', *Revue nouvelle*, in Cavour, C. (1962).

Cavour, C. (1962e) [1849–50] 'Corso di economia politica professato dal signor F. Ferrara', *il Risorgimento*, in Cavour, C. (1962).

Cavour, C. (1971) *Scritti inediti e rari*, Romeo, R. (ed.), Santena: Fondazione 'C. Cavour'.

Cesarano, F. (1976) 'Monetary theory in Ferdinando Galiani's "Della moneta"', *History of Political Economy*: 380–99.

Cesarano, F. (1986) 'La teoria della politica economica nei "Dialogues" di Ferdinando Galiani', *Rivista di politica economica*: 1691–1706.

Cesarano, F. (1990) 'Law and Galiani on Money and Monetary Systems', *History of Political Economy*: 321–40.

Ciasca, R. (1916) *L'origine del 'Programma per l'opinione nazionale italiana' del 1847–48*, Milano-Roma-Napoli: Albrighi e Segati.

Cinquant'anni di un editore. Le edizioni Einaudi negli anni 1933–1983 (1983) Torino: Einaudi.

Ciocca, P. (2008) *Giovanni Giolitti, vittima incolpevole degli economisti*, in Barucci, P., Costabile, L., Di Matteo, M. (eds) (2008).

Clapham, J. (1953) [1922] 'Of Empty Economic Boxes', reprinted in Boulding, K., Stigler, G. (eds), *Readings in Price Theory*, London: Allen and Unwin.

Coats, A. W. 'Bob' (1996) 'British Nineteenth Century Periodicals', in VV. AA. (1996).

Cochrane, E. W. (1961) *Tradition and Enlightenment in the Tuscan Academies, 1690–1800*, Roma: Edizioni di storia e letteratura.

Cognetti de Martiis, S. (1881) *Le forme primitive nella evoluzione economica*, Torino: Loescher.

Cognetti de Martiis, S. (1886) 'L'economia politica come scienza autonoma', *Giornale degli economisti*, 2.

Conigliani, C. A. (1903) [1899] 'L'economia capitalista nel sistema teorico del Loria', in Conigliani, C. A., *Saggi di economia politica e di scienza delle finanze*, Torino: Bocca.

Constant, B. (1822) *Commentaire sur l'ouvrage de Filangieri*, Paris: Dufart.

Corbino, E. (1972) *Racconto di una vita*, Napoli: Edizioni scientifiche italiane.

Corbino, E. (1982) [1931–38] *Annali dell'economia italiana*, 5 vols, Città di Castello: Leonardo da Vinci; reprinted by Ipsoa: Roma.

Corrado, D., Solari, S. (2009) 'Economic Justice in social Catholicism: the difficult application of natural law', *Il pensiero economico italiano*, 1.

Cosciani, C. (1977) *Scienza delle finanze*, Torino: Utet.

Cossa, L. (2000) [1880] *A Guide to the Study of Political Economy*, Backhouse, R. E. (ed.), London: Routledge.

Costabile, L. (2004) 'Il Centro di specializzazione e ricerche economico-agrarie di Portici', in Garofalo, Graziani (eds) (2004).

Costabile, L., Scazzieri, R. (2012) 'Tendenze attuali del pensiero economico italiano', in Istituto dell'enciclopedia italiana: 739–65.

Cozzi, T., Marchionatti, R. (eds) (2001) *Piero Sraffa's Political Economy. A Centenary Estimate*, London: Routledge.

Croce, B. (1923) [1908] *Filosofia della pratica. Economica ed etica*, Bari: Laterza.

Croce, B. (1932) [1924] *Conversazioni critiche*, Bari: Laterza.

Croce, B. (1945) [1927] 'Liberismo e liberalismo', in Croce, B., *Etica e politica*, Bari: Laterza.

Croce, B. (2001a) [1896] 'Le teorie storiche del prof. Loria', in Croce, B. (2001d), vol. I.

Croce, B. (2001b) [1897] 'Per la interpetrazione e la critica di alcuni concetti del marxismo', in Croce, B. (2001d), vol. I.

Croce, B. (2001c) [1899] 'Una obiezione alla legge marxistica della caduta del saggio di profitto', in Croce, B. (2001d), vol. I.

Croce, B. (2001d) [1900] *Materialismo storico ed economia marxistica*, Napoli: Bibliopolis, 2 vols.

Croce, B. (2001e) [1900] 'Sul principio economico. Due lettere al prof. V. Pareto', I, in Croce, B. (2001d), vol. I.

Croce, B. (2001f) [1900] 'Sul principio economico. Due lettere al prof. V. Pareto', II, in Croce, B. (2001d), vol. I.

Cuoco, V. (1860) [1806] *Saggio storico sulla rivoluzione di Napoli*, Preface to the second edition, Napoli: Lombardi.

Custodi, P. (ed.), *Scrittori classici italiani di economia politica* (1803–1816), 50 vols, Milano: De Stefanis/Imperial regia stamperia.

D'Adda, C. (2012) 'Franco Modigliani', in Istituto della Enciclopedia Italiana (2012): 653–9.

D'Amico, M. (1975) 'Il contributo alla teoria economica di Enrico Barone', *Giornale degli economisti e Annali di economia*: 183–211.

da Empoli, D. (2004) 'Gli studi negli USA della prima generazione', in Garofalo, G., Graziani, A. (eds) (2004).

Dal Pane, L. (1953) 'Uno storico dell'economia toscana del Settecento: Gian Francesco Pagnini', in VV. AA., *Studi in memoria di G. Borgatta*, Milano: Istituto di cultura bancaria, vol. I.

Dalla Volta, R. (2009) *Crisi della concorrenza, concentrazioni industriali e imperialismo all'alba del Novecento*, edited by Augello, M. M., Guidi, M. E. L., Firenze: Le Monnier, Fondazione Spadolini – Nuova Antologia.

Davanzati, B. (1804) [1588] *Notizia de' cambi*, in *Scrittori Classici...*, *parte antica*, vol. II: Milano, Destefanis.

De Augustinis, M. (2006) [1837] *Istituzioni di economia sociale*, Patalano, R. (ed.), Manduria: Lacaita.

De Bonis, V., Fausto, D., (eds.) (2003) *The Theory of Public Finance in Italy from the Origins to the 1940s*, special issue of *Il pensiero economico italiano*, 1.

De Cecco, M. (1968) *Saggi di politica monetaria*, Milano: Giuffrè.

De Viti de Marco, A. (1890) 'Le teorie economiche di Antonio Serra', *Memorie dell'Istituto Lombardo*, vol. XVIII.

De Viti de Marco, A. (1961) [1934] *Principii di economia finanziaria*, Torino: Boringhieri.

De Viti de Marco, A. (1980) [1901] 'Angelo Messedaglia', in Finoia, M. (ed.) (1980).

De Viti de Marco, A. (1990) [1898, 1934] *La funzione della banca*, preface by G. Parravicini, Torino: Utet.

De Viti de Marco, A. (1994) [1930] 'Al lettore', preface to *Un trentennio di lotte politiche, 1894–1922*, Fusco, A. M. (ed.), Napoli: Giannini.

Del Vecchio, G. (1925) 'I sistemi di economia teorica e l'originalità scientifica di Maffeo Pantaleoni', *Giornale degli economisti*, March.

Del Vecchio, G. (1930) *Lezioni di economia pura*, Padova: Cedam.

Del Vecchio, G. (1932) [1926] 'Il costo quale elemento della teoria economica', in Del Vecchio (1932).

Del Vecchio, G. (1932) *Vecchie e nuove teorie economiche*, in *Nuova collana di economisti stranieri e italiani*, vol. I, *Storia delle teorie*, Torino: Utet.

Del Vecchio, G. (1937) Introduction to *Nuova collana di economisti*, vol. IV, *Economia pura*, Torino: Utet.

Del Vecchio, G. [1952] *La costruzione scientifica della dinamica economica*, in Del Vecchio (1983).

Del Vecchio, G. (1956) Introduction to Id., *Capitale e interesse*, Torino: Einaudi.

Del Vecchio, G. (1977) [1925] 'L'opera scientifica di Enrico Barone', reprinted in Quadrio Curzio, A., Scazzieri, R., (eds) (1977).

Del Vecchio, G. (1983) [1952] *La costruzione scientifica della dinamica economica*, in Del Vecchio (1983).

Del Vecchio, G. (1983) *Antologia degli scritti nel centenario della nascita*, F. Caffè (ed.), Milano: Franco Angeli.

Del Vecchio, G. (1997) [1930] *Lineamenti di teoria monetaria*, Graziani, A., Realfonzo, R. (eds), preface by O. Weinberger, Torino: Utet.

Delli Gatti, D., Gallegati, M. (1991) 'Reddito, investimenti e fluttuazioni economiche: l' "economia sequenziale" di Marco Fanno', *Quaderni di storia dell'economia politica*, 1.

Demaria, G. (1934) *Le basi logiche della economia dinamica nel clima scientifico odierno*, Milano: tipografia S. Giuseppe.

Demaria, G. (1942) ' "L'ordine nuovo" e il problema industriale italiano del dopoguerra', in Demaria (1951).

Demaria, G. (1951) *Problemi economici e sociali del dopoguerra 1945–1950*, T. Bagiotti (ed.), Milano: Malfasi.

Demaria, G. *et alii* (1968–87) *Ricerche di cinematica storica*, 4 vols, Padova: Cedam.

Demaria, G. (1981) 'Those dynamic years 1930–32', *Banca Nazionale del Lavoro Quarterly Review*, March.

Demaria, G. (1995) 'La formazione intellettuale e scientifica di un economista critico', *Il pensiero economico italiano*, 1.

Demaria, G. (1998) [1932] 'Di un principio di indeterminazione in economia dinamica', *Rivista internazionale di scienze sociali e discipline ausiliarie*. English translation. 'On a principle of indetermination in economic dynamics', in Pasinetti, L. L. (ed.), *Italian economic papers*, vol. III.

di Fenizio, F. (1965) *La programmazione economica*, Torino: Utet.

Di Matteo, M., Donzelli, F. (eds) (2012) 'Alternative approaches to the building of economic dynamics in the years of high theory', *History of Economic Ideas*, 2.

Di Matteo, M., Longobardi, E. (eds) (2012) *Attilio da Empoli (1904–1948). Un economista partecipe del suo tempo*, Milano: FrancoAngeli.

Di Matteo, M., Vercelli, A. (ed.) 2005, 'Passione e impegno. Intervista a Siro Lombardini', *Il pensiero economico italiano*, 1.

Di Nardi, G. (1987) Introduction to F. Galiani, *Della moneta*, Napoli: Banco di Napoli.

Diaz, F. (1966) *Francesco Maria Gianni dalla burocrazia alla politica sotto Pietro Leopoldo di Toscana*, Milano-Napoli: Ricciardi.

Dobb, M. H. [1946] *Studies on the Development of Capitalism*, Italian translation as *Problemi di storia del capitalismo* (1958), Roma: Editori riuniti.

Dobb, M. H. (1973) *Theories of Value and Distribution since Adam Smith*, Cambridge: Cambridge University Press.

Donzelli F. (1997) 'Pareto's Mechanical Dream', *History of Economic Ideas*, 3.

Dooley, P. C. (1998) 'Enrico Barone', in Meacci, F. (ed.), (1998).

Doria, P. M. (1973) [1713?] *Massime generali e particolari colle quali di tempo in tempo hanno gli Spagnoli governato il Regno di Napoli*, V. Conti (ed.), Napoli: Guida.

Einaudi, L. (1902) *Studi sugli effetti delle imposte. Contributo allo studio dei problemi tributari municipali*, Torino: La Riforma Sociale.

Einaudi, L. (1931) 'Per la storia di un gruppo che non riuscì ad esser partito', *Riforma sociale*, 11–12.

Einaudi, L. (1932) 'Il problema dell'ozio', *La Cultura*, 1.

Einaudi, L. (1933) 'The Physiocratic theory of taxation', in VV. AA., *Economic Essays in Honour of Gustav Cassel*, London: Allen and Unwin.

Einaudi, L. (1940) 'Le premesse del ragionamento economico e la realtà storica', *Rivista di storia economica*, 3.

Einaudi, L. (1942) 'Economia di concorrenza e capitalismo storico. La terza via fra i secoli XVIII e XIX', *Rivista di storia economica*, 2.

Einaudi, L. (1950) *La guerra e l'unità europea*, Milano: Comunità.

Einaudi, L. (1953) [1933] 'Dei libri italiani posseduti da Adamo Smith, di due lettere non ricordate e della sua prima fortuna in Italia', in Einaudi (1953).

Einaudi, L. (1953) [1935] 'Di un economista e statistico piemontese non abbastanza pregiato', in Einaudi (1953).

Einaudi, L. (1953) [1938] 'Una disputa a torto dimenticata fra autarcisti e liberisti', in Einaudi (1953).

Einaudi, L. (1953) [1939] 'Di una controversia tra Scialoja e Magliani intorno ai bilanci napoletano e sardo', in Einaudi (1953).

Einaudi, L. (1953) [1945] 'Galiani economista', in Einaudi (1953).

Einaudi, L. (1953) [1951] 'Dalla leggenda al monumento', in Einaudi (1953).

Einaudi, L. (1953) *Saggi bibliografici e storici intorno alle dottrine economiche*, Roma: Edizioni di storia e letteratura.

Einaudi, L. [1956] 'Di Ezio Vanoni e del suo piano', in Einaudi (1974c) [1959].

Einaudi, L. (1956a) *Lo scrittoio del Presidente*, Torino: Einaudi.

Einaudi, L. (1956b) 'Risparmio e investimento', in Einaudi (1956a).

Einaudi, L. (1958) [1912] 'Intorno al concetto di reddito imponibile e di un sistema di imposte sul reddito consumato. Saggio di una teoria dell'imposta dedotta esclusivamente dal principio dell'uguaglianza', in Einaudi (1958) [1941].

Einaudi, L. (1958) [1919] 'Osservazioni critiche intorno alla teoria dell'ammortamento dell'imposta', in Einaudi (1958) [1941].

Einaudi, L. (1958) [1941] *Saggi sul risparmio e l'imposta*, Torino: Einaudi.

Einaudi, L. (1959) [1938] *Miti e paradossi della giustizia tributaria*, Torino: Einaudi.

Einaudi, L. (1959–66) *Cronache economiche e politiche di un trentennio 1893–1925*, 8 vols, Torino: Einaudi.

Einaudi, L. (1960) 'Rumore', in *Corriere della sera*, 1 October.

Einaudi, L. (1961) [1920] 'Come si giunse al trattato di Versailles. (Dal libro di un economista)', in Einaudi (1959–66), vol. V.

Einaudi, L. (1974a) [1924] *La terra e l'imposta*, Torino: Einaudi.

Einaudi, L. (1974b) [1956] 'L'andazzo è agli sganciamenti' in Einaudi (1974c) [1959].

Einaudi, L. (1974c) [1959] *Prediche inutili*, Torino: Einaudi.

Einaudi, L. (1980) [1950] 'La scienza economica. Reminiscenze', reprinted in Finoia, M. (ed.).

Einaudi, L. (1982) *Interventi e relazioni parlamentari*, vol. II, Torino: Fondazione Luigi Einaudi

Einaudi, L. (2006) [1928–29] 'Contribution to the quest for an optimal tax', in Einaudi, Luca, Faucci, R., Marchionatti, R. (eds) (2006).

Einaudi, L. (2006) [1933] 'My plan is not Keynes's', in Einaudi, Luca, Faucci, R., Marchionatti, R. (eds) (2006).

Einaudi, L. (2006) [1936] 'The theory of imaginary money from Charlemagne to the French revolution', in Einaudi, Luca, Faucci, R., Marchionatti, R. (eds.) (2006).

Einaudi, L. (2006) [1955] 'Know before legislating', in Einaudi, Luca, Faucci, R., Marchionatti, R. (eds.) (2006).

Einaudi, L. (2012) [1924] *Le lotte del lavoro*, postface by Marchionatti, R., Roma: Edizioni di storia e letteratura.

Einaudi, L., Rossi, E. (1988) *Carteggio (1925–1961)*, Torino: Fondazione L. Einaudi.

Einaudi, Luca, Faucci, R., Marchionatti, R. (eds) (2006) *Luigi Einaudi, Selected Economic Essays*, Basingstoke – New York: Palgrave Macmillan.

Erba, A. (2011) 'Economic Structure and national accounting: G. Ortes' contribution to economic science', *History of Economic Ideas*, 1.

Esposto, A., Tiberi, M. (eds) (1995) *Federico Caffè. Realtà e critica del capitalismo italiano*, Roma: Donzelli.

Fanfani, A. (1942) *Storia delle dottrine economiche. Il volontarismo*, 3rd edition, Milano-Messina: Principato.

Fanfani, A. (2005) [1933, 1944] *Cattolicesimo e protestantesimo nella formazione storica del capitalismo*, Editorial note to the Italian reprint of 1944 by Pagliai, L., Foreword to the appendix by Cristiano, C., Venezia: Marsilio.

Fanno, M. (1931) 'Cicli di produzione, cicli del credito e fluttuazioni industriali', *Giornale degli economisti*: 329–71; English translation, 'Production cycles, credit cycles and industrial fluctuations' (1993), *Structural Change and Economic Dynamics*, 4.

Fanno, M. (1935) *I trasferimenti anormali di capitali e le crisi*, Torino: Einaudi.

Fanno, M. (1938) *Principii di scienza economica. Introduzione alla teoria economica del corporativismo*, Padova: Cedam.

Fanno, M. (1954) [1933] 'Il punto critico della deflazione', originally in *Economic Essays in Honour of Gustav Cassel*, London: Allen and Unwin; reprinted in *Scritti vari di economia e di finanza*, Padova: Cedam.

Fanno, M. (1992) [1933] *Teoria del credito e della circolazione*, Realfonzo, R., Graziani, A. (eds), Napoli: Edizioni scientifiche italiane.

Fasiani, M. (1949) 'Contributi di Pareto alla scienza delle finanze', in VV. AA. (1949).

Fasiani, M. (1980) [1932] *La teoria della finanza pubblica in Italia*, in Finoia, M. (ed.) (1980).

Faucci, R. (ed.) (1977) *John Maynard Keynes nel pensiero e nella politica economica*, Milano: Feltrinelli.

Faucci, R. (ed.) (1982) *Gli Italiani e Bentham*, Milano: FrancoAngeli, 2 vols.

Faucci, R. (1986) *Einaudi*, Torino: Utet.

Faucci, R. (ed.) (1989) *Roberto Michels: economia, sociologia, politica*, Torino: Giappichelli.

Faucci, R. (ed.) (1990) *Il pensiero economico italiano fra le due guerre (1915–1943)*, *Quaderni di storia dell'economica politica*, 2–3.

Faucci, R. (1990) 'Materiali e ipotesi sulla cultura economica italiana fra le due guerre mondiali', in Becattini, G. (ed.) (1990).

Faucci, R. (1995) *L'economista scomodo. Vita e opere di Francesco Ferrara*, Palermo: Sellerio.

Faucci, R. (2000) *L'economia politica in Italia dal Cinquecento ai nostri giorni*, Torino: Utet.

Faucci, R. (2002) 'L'economia 'per frammenti' di Federico Caffè', *Rivista italiana degli economisti*, 3.

Faucci, R. (2010) 'Croce and Gramsci as "economists"', *Studi economici*, 100.

Faucci, R., Giocoli, N. (2001) 'Editors' introduction' to VV. AA. (2001) *Della Moneta by Ferdinando Galiani: A Quarter Millennium Assessment*, History of Economic Ideas, 3.

Faucci, R., Perri, S. (1995) 'Socialism and Marginalism in Italy, 1880–1910', in Steedman, I., (ed.) (1995).

Faucci, R., Perri, S. (2003) 'Achille Loria: his vision and economic analysis', in Samuels, W. J. (ed.) (2003).

Faucci, R., Rancan, A. (2009) 'Transforming the economy: Saint-Simon and his influence on Mazzini', *History of Economic Ideas*, 2.

Ferrara, F. (1935) [1858] *Lezioni di economia politica*, vol. II, Bologna: Zanichelli.

Ferrara, F. (1955) [1836] 'Sulla teoria della statistica secondo Romagnosi', in Rossi Ragazzi, B. (ed.), *Opere complete*, vol. I, Roma: De Luca.

Ferrara, F. (1955) [1850] 'Ragguaglio storico sulla scuola fisiocratica', in Rossi Ragazzi, B. (ed.), *Opere complete*, vol. II, Roma: De Luca.

Ferrara, F. (1955) [1854] 'Sismondi, Destutt de Tracy, Droz', in Rossi Ragazzi, B. (ed.), *Opere complete*, vol. II, Roma: De Luca.

Ferrara, F. (1955) [1855] 'G. B. Say', in Rossi Ragazzi, B. (ed.), *Opere complete*, vol. II, Roma: De Luca.

Ferrara, F. (1956) [1851] 'Bastiat, Garnier, Stuart Mill', in Rossi Ragazzi, B. (ed.) *Opere complete*, vol. III, Roma: De Luca.

Ferrara, F. (1956) [1856] 'David Ricardo', in Rossi Ragazzi, B. (ed.), *Opere complete*, vol. III, Roma: De Luca.

Ferrara, F. (1956) [1863] 'La teoria delle mercedi', in Rossi Ragazzi, B. (ed.) *Opere complete*, vol. IV, Roma: De Luca.

Ferrara, F. (1961) [1856] 'Della moneta e dei suoi surrogati', in Caffè, F. (ed.), *Opere complete*, vol. V, Roma: De Luca.

Ferrara, F. (1965) *Opere complete*, Caffè F., Sirugo F. (eds), vol. VI, Roma: De Luca.

Ferrara, F. (1972) [1874] 'Il germanismo economico in Italia', in Caffè, F. (ed.), *Opere complete*, vol. X, Roma: De Luca.

Ferrara, F. (1976) [1865] 'La tassa sul macino', in Faucci, R. (ed.), *Opere complete*, vol. VIII, Roma: De Luca.

Ferrara, F. (1976) [1875a] 'Il congresso di Milano', in Faucci, R. (ed.) *Opere complete*, vol. VIII, Roma: De Luca.

Ferrara, F. (1976) [1875b] 'L'italianità della scienza economica', in Faucci, R. (ed.) *Opere complete*, vol. VIII, Roma: De Luca.

Ferrara, F. (1976) [1884] 'Il problema ferroviario e le scuole economiche in Italia', in Faucci, R. (ed.), *Opere complete*, vol. VIII, Roma: De Luca.

Ferrara F. (1986) [1856] *Lezioni di economia politica, parte I*, in Barucci, P., Asso, P. F. (eds.), *Opere complete*, vol. XI, Roma: Bancaria.

Ferrara, F. (1992) [1858] *Lezioni di economia politica, parte II*, in Barucci, P., Asso, P. F. (eds) *Opere complete*, vol. XII, Roma: Bancaria.

Ferraris, C. F. (2007) *Scienza dell'amministrazione, critica del socialismo scientifico e teoria del decentramento, Scritti 1875–1898*, Ingravalle, F. (ed.), Torino: Claudiana.

Ferri, E. (1894) *Socialismo e scienza positiva. Darwin, Spencer, Marx*, Roma: Casa editrice italiana.

Ferri, G. (1983) 'Il pensiero monetario di Geminiano Montanari', *Note economiche*: 148–70.

Ferrone, V. (2012) *The Politics of Enlightenment. Constitutionalism, Republicanism, and the Rights of Man in Gaetano Filangieri*, London-New York-Delhi: Anthem Press.

Filangieri, G. (2004) [1780] *La scienza della legislazione*, vol. II, Venezia: Centro studi sull'Illuminismo europeo 'G. Stiffoni'.

Finoia, M. (ed.) (1980) *Il pensiero economico italiano 1850–1950*, Bologna: Cappelli.

Fiorot, D. (1983) *Il giovane Nitti (1888–1905). Una rilettura critica delle opere giovanili nittiane*, Milano: Comunità.

Firpo, L. (1976) *Vita di Giuseppe Pomba da Torino*, Torino: Utet.

Foà, B. (1990) 'Da Graziani a Keynes: un giovane economista negli anni Trenta', in Faucci, R. (ed.) (1990).

Forte, F. (1982) *Luigi Einaudi: il mercato e il buongoverno*, Torino: Einaudi.

Forte F. (2009a) 'La teoria dell'economia pubblica e le regole dell'ottima tassazione secondo R. Fubini', in Marchionatti, R. (ed.) (2009).

Forte, F. (2009b) *L'economia liberale di Luigi Einaudi. Saggi*, Firenze: Olschki.

Fossati, E. (1937) *New Deal. Il nuovo ordine economico di Franklin D. Roosevelt*, Padova: Cedam.

Francioni, G. (1990) 'Beccaria filosofo utilitarista', in VV. AA. (1990a).

Francioni, G., Romagnoli, S. (eds) (1993) *'Il Caffè' 1764–66*, Torino: Bollati Boringhieri.

Fried, F. (1933) *La fine del capitalismo*, Milano: Bompiani.

Fuà, E. (2004), *Fuga a due*, Bologna: Il Mulino.

Fuà, G. (1947) '"Momento critico" dell'inflazione', *Critica economica*, 1.

Fuà, G., Sylos Labini, P. (1963) *Idee per la programmazione economica*, Bari: Laterza.

Fuoco, F. (1969) [1825–27] *Saggi economici*, 2 vols, Roma: Bizzarri.

Gagliardi, A. (2010) *Il corporativismo fascista*, Roma-Bari: Laterza.

Galiani, F. (1958) [1770] *Dialoghi sul commercio dei grani*, Torino: Boringhieri.

Galiani, F. (1987) [1770] *Dialogues sur le commerce des bleds*, De Rosa, L. (ed.), Napoli: Banco di Napoli.

Galiani, F. (1987) [1780] *Della moneta*, Napoli: Banco di Napoli; English edition (1977) *On money*, translated by Toscano, P., Chicago: Department of Economics.

Gallegati, M. (1982) 'Formazione e distribuzione del sovrappiù nell "economia senza valore" di Antonio Graziadei (1894–1909)', in Faucci, R. (ed.) (1982), vol. II.

Gallegati, M., Faucci, R. (2010) 'Marshall in Italy', in Raffaelli, T., Becattini, G., Dardi, M. (eds.) (2010).

Gandolfo, G. (1987) 'The life and works of V. Marrama', in Gandolfo, G. (ed.) (1987) *Keynesian Theory, Planning Models and Quantitative Economics. Essays in Memory of Vittorio Marrama*, Milano: Giuffrè.

Gangemi, L. (1924) *La politica economica e finanziaria del governo fascista nel periodo dei pieni poteri*, Bologna: Zanichelli.

Garegnani, P. (1979) *Valore e domanda effettiva*, Torino: Einaudi.

Garegnani, P. (1981) *Marx e gli economisti classici*, Torino: Einaudi.

Garofalo, G. (1984) 'Un canale di penetrazione della teoria keynesiana in Italia: "L'Industria" 1945–1952', in VV. AA. (1984).

Garofalo, G., Graziani, A. (eds) (2004) *La formazione degli economisti in Italia (1950–1975)*, Bologna: il Mulino.

Gattei, G. (2012) 'Antonio Graziadei' in Istituto della Enciclopedia italiana: 632–7.

Genovesi, A. (1963) *Autobiografia e lettere*, Milano: Feltrinelli.

Genovesi, A. (1977) *Scritti*, Venturi, F. (ed.), Torino: Einaudi.

Genovesi, A. (2005) [1765] *Delle lezioni di commercio o sia di economia civile, con Elementi del commercio*, Perna, M. L. (ed.), Napoli: Istituto italiano per gli studi filosofici.

Gentilucci, C. E. (2006) *L'agitarsi del mondo in cui viviamo. L'economia politica di Enrico Barone*, Torino: Giappichelli.

Gerschenkron, A. [1962] *Economic Backwardness in Historical Perspective*; Italian translation (1965) *Il problema storico dell'arretratezza economica*, Torino: Einaudi.

Gianformaggio, L. (1982) 'Su Helvétius, Beccaria e Bentham', in Faucci, R. (ed.), vol. I.

Gigliobianco, A. (2006) *Via Nazionale*, Roma: Donzelli.

Gini, C. (1927) 'The scientific basis of Fascism', *Political Science Quarterly*, 1.

Gini, C. (1930) 'The Italian demographic problem and the Fascist policy on population', *Journal of Political Economy*, 6.

Giocoli, N. (1997) 'La teoria dell'interesse di Galiani e l'ipotesi di Bernoulli', *Il pensiero economico italiano*, 1.

Gioja, M. (1830) [1818–19] *Del merito e delle ricompense. Trattato storico e filosofico*, 2nd edition, Lugano: Ruggia.

Gioja, M. (1838) [1815–17] *Nuovo prospetto delle scienze economiche*, Lugano: Ruggia.

Gioja, M. (1962) [1798] *Saggio sopra i pregiudizi popolari*, in De Felice, R. (ed.), *I giornali giacobini italiani*, Milano: Feltrinelli.

Gioli, G. (1972) 'Gli albori dello smithianesimo in Italia', *Rivista di politica economica*: 917–62.

Gioli, G. (ed.) (1987) *Le teorie della popolazione prima di Malthus*, Milano: Angeli.

Gioli, G. (1993) 'The diffusion of the economic thought of Adam Smith in Italy', in Mizuta, H., Sugiyama, C. (eds) (1993) *Adam Smith. International Perspectives*, Basingstoke and London: Macmillan.

Gladstone, D. (ed.) (1999) *Before Beveridge: Welfare Before the Welfare State*, London: Civitas.

Glisenti, G., Elia, L. (eds) (1961) *'Cronache sociali', 1947–1951*, 2 vols, S. Giovanni Valdarno: Elia.

Goethe J. W. (1993) [1817] *Viaggio in Italia*, Milano: Mondadori.

Gordon, B. (1976) *Political Economy in Parliament, 1819–1823*, London: Macmillan.

Gramsci, A. (1994) *Scritti di economia politica*, introduction by G. Lunghini, Turin: Bollati Boringhieri.

Gramsci, A. (1996) *Lettere dal carcere*, vol. II, Palermo: Sellerio.

Granata, M. (2007) *Cultura del mercato. La Commissione parlamentare d'inchiesta sulla concorrenza (1961–1965)*, Soveria Mannelli: Rubbettino.

Graziani, A. (1979) *L'economia italiana dal 1945 a oggi*, Bologna: il Mulino.

Graziani, A. (1981) *Teoria economica. Macroeconomia*, Napoli: ESI.

Graziani, A. (1989) 'Schumpeter and Italian economic thought in the inter-war period', *Studi economici*: 41–83.

Graziani, A. (1995) 'La teoria del credito nel pensiero di Antonio De Viti de Marco' in Pedone, A. (ed.).

Graziani, A. (1998) *Lo sviluppo dell'economia italiana dalla Ricostruzione alla moneta europea*, Torino: Bollati Boringhieri.

Graziani, A. (2004) 'Moneta, banche e reddito nel pensiero di Carlo Antonio Broggia', in Broggia, C. A. [1752?] *Il banco e il monte de' pegni – Del lusso*, Napoli: La città del sole.

Graziani, A., sr. (1889) *Storia critica della teoria del valore in Italia*, Milano: Hoepli.

Graziani, A. sr. (ed.) (1913) *Economisti del Cinque e Seicento*, Bari: Laterza.

Greenfield, K. R. (1964) [1934] *Economia e liberalismo nel Risorgimento*, Bari: Laterza.

Grembi, V. (2002) 'La questione della proprietà intellettuale: il contributo degli economisti italiani al dibattito', in Augello, M. M., Guidi M. E. L. (eds) (2002), vol. I.

Grillo, M., (ed.) (1994) *Protezionismo e liberismo. Momenti del dibattito sull'economia siciliana del primo Ottocento*, Catania: C.u.e.c.m.

Grillo, M. (1996) 'Cultura economica ed economia politica nei periodici catanesi di metà Ottocento (1834–1859)', in Augello M. M., Bianchini M., Guidi M. E. L. (eds) (1996).

Griziotti, B. (1992) [1917] *The different fiscal burden of public debt and extraordinary taxation*, in Pasinetti, L. L. (ed.) (1992/1996/1998), vol. I.

Groenewegen, P. D. (1986) Introduction to *P. Verri 1771 Reflections on Political Economy*, Reprints of Economic Classics, Sydney.

Guerraggio, A., Mercurelli Salari, F. (1985) 'G. B. Antonelli nella economia matematica italiana di fine Ottocento', *Quaderni di storia dell'economia politica*, 3.

Guidi, M. E. L. (1990) 'Provvidenza, dolore, progresso. L'economia politica di Francesco Ferrara nel suo orizzonte intellettuale', in VV. AA. (1990b).

Harcourt, G. C. (1973) [1972] *La teoria del capitale. Una controversia tra le due Cambridge*, translation of *Some Cambridge Controversies in the Theory of Capital*, with a preface to the Italian edition, Milano: ISEDI.

Harcourt, G. C., Laing, N. F. (eds) (1971) *Capital and Growth*, Harmondsworth: Penguin Books.

Hayek, F. A. (ed.) (1935) *Collectivist Economic Planning*, London: Routledge.

Hutchison, T. H. (1988) *Before Adam Smith. The Emergence of Political Economy 1662–1776*, Oxford and New York: Blackwell.

Ingrao, B. (1994) 'Physical methaphors and models in Pareto's thought', *Archives internationales d'histoire des sciences*, 132.

Ingrao, B., Israel, G. (1990) *The Invisible Hand. Economic Equilibrium in the History of Science*, Cambridge: MIT Press (first Italian edition 1987).

Isabella, M. (2012) *Giuseppe Pecchio*, in Istituto della Enciclopedia italiana: 397–401.

Isnenghi, M. (1979) *Intellettuali militanti e intellettuali funzionari. Appunti sulla cultura fascista*, Torino: Einaudi.

Istituto della Enciclopedia italiana (2012) *Il contributo italiano alla storia del pensiero. Ottava appendice, Economia*, Roma.

Izzo, L., Pedone, A., Spaventa, L., Volpi, F. (1970, 1975) *Il controllo dell'economia nel breve termine*, Ministero del bilancio e della programmazione economica – ISCO, Milano: Angeli.

Jaffé, W. J. (ed.) (1965) *Correspondence of Léon Walras and Related Papers*, Amsterdam: North-Holland, 3 vols.

Jannaccone, P. (1912) 'Il paretaio', *La riforma sociale*, vol. XIX.

Jannaccone, P. (1936) *Prezzi e mercati*, Torino: Utet.

Jevons, W. S. (1970) *The Theory of Political Economy*, Black, R. D. C. (ed.), Harmondsworth: Penguin Books.

Kayaalp, O. (1988) 'Ugo Mazzola and the Italian theory of public goods', *History of Political Economy*, 1.

Keynes, J. M. (1964) [1936] *The General Theory of Employment, Interest and Money*, London: Macmillan.

Keynes, J. M. (1972) [1930] 'Economic Perspectives for our Grandchildren', in Keynes, J. M. (1972).

Keynes, J. M. (1972) [1933] *The Means to Prosperity*, in Keynes, J. M. (1972).

Keynes, J. M. (1972) *The Collected Essays of JMK*, vol. IX, *Essays in Persuasion* [with additional essays], London and Basingstoke: Macmillan.

Kirman, A. (1998) 'Vilfredo Pareto', in Meacci, F. (ed.) (1998).

Kuenne, R. E. (1968) 'Barone, Enrico', in *The International Encyclopaedia of the Social Sciences*, vol. I, London-New York: Collier-Macmillan.

Kurz, H. D., Salvadori, N. (eds) (1998) *The Elgar Companion to Classical Economics*, Cheltenham: Elgar, vol. I.

Kurz, H. D., Pasinetti, L. L., Salvadori, N. (eds) (2008) *Piero Sraffa: the Man and the Scholar. Exploring His Unpublished Papers*, Abingdon and New York: Routledge.

La Salvia, S. (1977) *Giornalismo lombardo: gli 'Annali universali di statistica'*. vol. I (1824–44), Roma: Elia.

Lanaro, S. (1992) *Storia dell'Italia repubblicana. Dalla fine della guerra agli anni novanta*, Venezia: Marsilio.

Lenti, L. (1983) *Le radici nel tempo. Passato al presente e futuro*, Milano: Angeli.

Leone, E. (1910) *L'economia edonistica*, Milano: Libreria editrice 'Avanti!'.

Leopardi, G. (1967) [1834] *Dialogo di Tristano e di un amico*, in Id., *I canti – Operette morali*, Milano: Bietti.

Levi, A. (1928) *Il positivismo politico di Carlo Cattaneo*, Bari: Laterza.

Lombardini, S. (1967) *La programmazione: idee, esperienze, problemi*, Torino, Einaudi.

Loria, A. (1890) 'La scuola austriaca nell'economia politica', *Nuova Antologia*, April.

Loria, A. (1891–92) 'The landed theory of profit', *Quarterly Journal of Economics*, VI.

Luini, L. (1995) 'Scienze naturali e scienze sociali. Le chiose matematiche di Frisi a Verri e Lloyd', in Roncaglia, A. (ed.) (1995).

Lunghini, G. (ed.) (1981) *Scelte politiche e teorie economiche in Italia 1945–1978*, Torino: Einaudi.

Lunghini, G., Targetti Lenti, R. (2004) 'Di Fenizio e l'economia politica di Keynes', in Garofalo, G., Graziani, A. (eds) (2004).

Maccabelli, T. (1996) 'La *Biblioteca italiana* e *Il conciliatore nella Milano della Restaurazione. Il dibattito economico*', in Augello, M. M., Bianchini, M., Guidi, M. E. L. (eds) (1996).

Macchioro, A. (1990) 'La "philosophia naturalis" gioiana dell'economia', *Bollettino storico piacentino*, January-December.

Maestro, M. (1976) 'Gaetano Filangieri and his Science of Legislation', *Transactions of the American Philosophical Society*, 66 (6).

Magliulo, A. (1991) *Ezio Vanoni. La giustizia sociale nell'economia di mercato*, Roma: Studium.

Magliulo, A. (1998) *Marco Fanno e la cultura economica del Novecento*, Firenze: Polistampa.

Malagola Anziani, V. (1979) 'La scuola classica in Italia: il caso di Francesco Fuoco', in Salvemini, B., Malagola Anziani, V., Di Battista, F., Barucci, P. (1979).

Mancini, O., Perillo, F., Zagari, E. (eds) (1982) *La teoria economica del corporativismo*, vol. II, Napoli: Edizioni scientifiche italiane.

Mannori, L. (1984) *Uno stato per Romagnosi*, vol. I, Milano: Giuffrè.

Manzoni, A. (1885) *Opere inedite e rare*, Bonghi, R. (ed.), Milano: Rechiedei.

Marchionatti, R. (1999) 'Achille Loria, "Italian correspondent of the Royal Economic Society"', in D'Orsi, A. (ed.) (1999), *Achille Loria, Quaderni di storia dell'Università di Torino*, 3.

Marchionatti, R. (2011) *Attilio Cabiati. Profilo di un economista liberale*, Torino: Aragno.

Marchionatti, R. (ed.) (2000) *'From Our Italian Correspondent'. Luigi Einaudi's Articles in The Economist, 1908–1946*, 2 vols, Firenze: Olschki.

Marchionatti, R. (ed.) (2009) *La scuola di economia di Torino. Co-protagonisti ed epigoni*, Firenze: Olschki.

Marcoaldi, F. (ed.) (1986) *Vent'anni di economia e politica: le carte De' Stefani 1922–1941*, Milano: Franco Angeli.

Marcuzzo, C., Rosselli, A. (eds) (2005) *Economists in Cambridge. A study through their correspondence, 1907–1946*, London: Routledge.

Marongiu, G. (1995–96) *Storia del fisco in Italia*, 2 vols, Torino: Einaudi.

Marshall, A. (1986) [1890] *Principles of economics*, 8th edition, London: Macmillan.

Marx, K. (1990) [1867] *Capital*, Book 1, London: Penguin Books.

Masci, G. (1982) [1934] 'Crisi economica ed economia corporativa', in Mancini, O., Perillo, F., Zagari, E. (eds) (1982).

Mazzini, G. (2009) [1860] *Dei doveri dell'uomo*, in *Scritti politici*, Milano: Mondadori.

Meacci, F. (ed.) (1998) *Italian Economists of the 20th Century*, Cheltenham: Elgar.

Meacci, F. (2012) 'Marco Fanno', in Istituto della Enciclopedia italiana: 592–6.

Meek, R. L. (1967) 'The Scottish contribution to Marxist sociology', in Id., *Economics and Ideology and other Essays*, London: Chapman and Hall.

Michelagnoli, G. (2010) *A. Fanfani. Dal corporativismo al neovolontarismo statunitense*, Soveria Mannelli: Rubbettino.

Michelini, L. (1998) *Marginalismo e socialismo: Maffeo Pantaleoni (1882–1904)*, Milano: FrancoAngeli.

Michelini, L., Guidi, M. E. L. (eds) (2001) *Marginalismo e socialismo nell'Italia liberale 1870–1925*, Fondazione Giangiacomo Feltrinelli, Annali, XXXV.

Minghetti, M. (1872) [1843] 'Della proprietà rurale e dei patti fra il padrone e il lavoratore', in Minghetti (1872).

Minghetti, M. (1872) [1846] *Della riforma delle leggi frumentarie in Inghilterra*, in Minghetti (1872).

Minghetti, M. (1872) *Opuscoli letterari ed economici*, Firenze: Le Monnier.

Minghetti, M. (1896) [1841] *La tendenza degli interessi materiali nel secolo presente*, in Minghetti (1896).

Minghetti, M. (1896) *Scritti vari*, Bologna: Zanichelli.

Minghetti, M. (2012) [1859] *Della economia pubblica e delle sue attinenze colla morale e col diritto*, abridged edition, Barrotta, P. L. (ed.), Ravenna: Libro aperto.

Ministero per la Costituente (1946–47) *Rapporto della Commissione Economica*, 12 vols, Roma: Istituto poligrafico dello Stato.

Modigliani, F. (1999) *Avventure di un economista*, Roma-Bari: Laterza.

Molesti, R. (1987) 'Antonio Zanon, la dinamica della popolazione e l'economia veneta del '700', in Gioli, G. (ed.).

Montanari, G. (1913) [1683] *La zecca in consulta di Stato*, reprinted in A. Graziani sr, (ed.).

Montesano, A. (2006) 'The Paretian theory of ophelimity in closed and open cycles', *History of Economic Ideas*, 3.

Montesano, A. (forthcoming) 'Pantaleoni, Pareto e le loro scuole' in Accademia nazionale dei Lincei, *Gli economisti italiani. Protagonisti, paradigmi, politiche*, Rome, 25–26 September 2013.

Morandi, R. (1975) [1960] *Democrazia diretta e riforme di struttura*, Torino: Einaudi.

Mori R. (1951) *Le riforme leopoldine nel pensiero degli economisti toscani del '700'* Firenze: Sansoni.

Mornati, F. (1997) 'Le corporatisme italien vu par les économistes français des années trente', *Il pensiero economico italiano*, 1.

Mornati, F. (2012) 'Enrico Barone', in Istituto della Enciclopedia italiana: 539–46.

Mortara, G. (1937) [book review of Barone, E., *Opere economiche*], *Giornale degli economisti*: 886.

Myrdal, G. (1958) *Value in Social Theory*, New York: Harper; Italian translation (1966) *Il valore nella teoria sociale*, Torino: Einaudi.

Naldi, N. (2008) 'Piero Sraffa: emigration and scientific activity (1921–45)', in Kurz, H. D., Pasinetti, L. L., Salvadori, N. (eds) (2008).

Napoleoni, C. (ed.) (1956) *Dizionario di economia politica*, Milano: Comunità.

Napoleoni, C. (1992) [1983] 'Il capitale e il pensiero economico di Marx', in Napoleoni, C. (1992).

Napoleoni, C. (1992) [1986] 'Critica ai critici', in Napoleoni, C. (1992).

Napoleoni, C. (1992) *Dalla scienza all'utopia*, Vaccarino, G. L. (ed.) Torino: Boringhieri.

Negri Zamagni, V. (2012) 'Giuseppe Toniolo', in Istituto della Enciclopedia italiana: 725–8.

Nitti, F. S. (1971) [1891] *Scritti di economia e finanza*, vol. I, Dal Pane, L. (ed.), Bari: Laterza.

Nuccio, O. (1984–87) *Il pensiero economico italiano 1050–1450*, 3 vols, Sassari: Gallizzi.

Nuccio, O. (2009) *La storia del pensiero economico come storia della genesi dello spirito capitalistico*, Roma: Luiss University Press.

Oldrini, G. (1973) *La cultura filosofica napoletana dell'Ottocento*, Roma-Bari: Laterza.

Ortes, G. (1999) [1772] *Errori popolari intorno all'economia nazionale e al governo delle nazioni*, Longoni, F. (ed.), Milano-Napoli: Ricciardi.

Osculati, F., (ed.) (2007) *La figura e l'opera di Benvenuto Griziotti*, Milano: Cisalpino.

Padoa Schioppa, T. (1997) *Il governo dell'economia*, Bologna: Il Mulino.

Pagliai, L. (2009) *Per il bene comune: poteri pubblici ed economia nel pensiero di Giorgio La Pira*, Firenze: Polistampa.

Pallini, L. (1988) 'Tra politica e scienza: le vicende della cattedra di economia politica all'Università di Torino, 1800–1858', in Augello, M. M., Bianchini, M., Gioli, G., Roggi, P. (eds).

Palmieri, G. (1991) [1787] *Riflessioni sulla pubblica felicità relativamente al regno di Napoli*, Fusco, A. M. (ed.), Roma-Bari: Laterza.

Palmerio, G. (1995) 'Il contributo di F. Caffè alla teoria della politica economica', in Esposto, A., Tiberi, M. (eds).

Palomba, G. (1966) 'Il pensiero scientifico di Luigi Amoroso', *Rivista di politica economica*, April.

Panizza, G., Costa, B. (eds) (1997, 2000) *L'archivio Verri*, 2 vols, Milano: Fondazione R. Mattioli per la storia del pensiero economico.

Pantaleoni, M. (1891) 'Imposta e debito in riguardo alla loro pressione', English translation 'The burden of taxation and debt' in Pasinetti, L. L. (ed.) (1992), vol. I.

Pantaleoni, M. (1919) [1911] 'Considerazioni su un sistema di prezzi politici', *Giornale degli economisti*, January-February, in Pantaleoni.

Pantaleoni, M. (1919) *La fine provvisoria di un'epopea*, Bari: Laterza.

Pantaleoni, M. (1925) [1897] 'Del carattere delle divergenze d'opinione esistenti tra economisti' in Pantaleoni, vol. I.

Pantaleoni, M. (1925) [1898] 'An attempt to analyze the concepts of "strong and weak" in their economic connexion', *The Economic Journal*, June; Italian translation in Pantaleoni, vol. I.

Pantaleoni, M. (1925) [1898] 'Dei criteri che devono informare la storia delle dottrine economiche' in Pantaleoni, vol. I.

Pantaleoni, M. (1925) [1913] 'L'atto economico', in Pantaleoni, vol. I.

Pantaleoni, M. (1925) *Erotemi di economia*, 2 vols, Bari: Laterza.

Pantaleoni, M. (1931) [1889] *Principii di economia pura*, Milano: Treves.

Pantaleoni, M. (1936) [1895] 'La caduta della Società di credito mobiliare italiano', in Pantaleoni.

Pantaleoni, M. (1936) [1915] 'Istituti di credito mobiliare italiani o esteri', reprinted in Pantaleoni; originally in Preziosi, G.

Pantaleoni, M. (1936) [1924] 'Le casse di risparmio e gli istituti bancari', reprinted in Pantaleoni.

Pantaleoni, M. (1936) *Studi storici di economia*, Bologna: Zanichelli.

Pantaleoni, M. (1938) [1910] 'L'identità di pressione teorica di qualunque imposta a parità di ammontare e la sua semiotica', reprinted in Pantaleoni.

Pantaleoni, M. (1938) *Studi di finanza e di statistica*, Bologna: Zanichelli.

Papi, G. U. (1933) *Escape from Stagnation. An Essay on Business Fluctuations*, London: P. S. King and Sons.

Papi, G. U. (1943) *Lezioni di economia politica corporativa*, vol. III, *Teoria delle fluttuazioni economiche – L'ordinamento corporativo italiano*, Padova: Cedam.

Papini, G. (1929) Introduction to Verri, P., *Discorso sull'indole del piacere e del dolore*, Lanciano: Carabba.

Parente, L. (1973) 'Ideologia politica e realtà sociale nell'attività pubblicistica di M. De Augustinis', *Archivio storico per le province napoletane*, vol. XI.

Pareto, V. (1894) [1893] Introduction to Marx, K., *Il capitale*, P. Lafargue (ed.), Palermo: Sandron.

Pareto, V. (1949) [1896–97] *Corso di economia politica*, vol. I, Torino: Einaudi.

Pareto, V. (1952) [1900] 'Sul fenomeno economico. Lettera a Benedetto Croce', in Pareto.

Pareto, V. (1952) [1901] 'Le nuove teorie economiche. Appunti', in Pareto.

Pareto V. (1952) *Scritti teorici*, G. Demaria (ed.), Milano: Malfasi.

Pareto, V. (1960) *Lettere a Maffeo Pantaleoni*, 3 vols, De Rosa, G. (ed.), Roma: Banca nazionale del lavoro.

Pareto, V. (1965a) *Écrits sur la courbe de la répartition de la richesse*, Busino, G. (ed.), Genève: Droz.

Pareto, V. (1965b) *Cronache italiane*, Mongardini C. (ed.), Brescia: Morcelliana.

Pareto, V. (1966) [1907] 'L'economia e la sociologia dal punto di vista scientifico', in Pareto.

Pareto, V. (1966) [1911] 'Rentiers et spéculateurs', in Pareto.

Pareto, V. (1966) [1913] 'Il massimo di utilità per una collettività in sociologia', in Pareto. English translation 'The community's utility maximum in sociology', in Pasinetti, L. L. (ed.) (1992), vol. I.

Pareto, V. (1966) *Scritti sociologici*, Busino, G. (ed.), Torino: Utet.

Pareto, V. (1973) *Epistolario 1890–1923*, Busino, G. (ed.), vol. II, Roma: Accademia dei Lincei.

Pareto, V. (2006) [1906, 1909] *Manuale di economia politica*, Montesano, A., Zanni, A., Bruni, L. (eds), Milano: Egea.

Pareto, V. (2007) [1892–93] *Considerations on the Fundamental Principles of Pure Political Economy*, Marchionatti, R., Mornati, F. (eds), London: Routledge.

Pareto, V. (2009) [1896] 'The curve of the distribution of wealth', in Chipman, J. S. (ed.) 'Some papers of Pareto from the French and German', *History of economic ideas*, 1.

Pascal, R. (1938) 'Property and Society: the Scottish Historical School of the Eighteenth Century', *Modern Quarterly*, March.

Pasinetti, L. L. (1977) *Lectures on the Theory of Production*, New York: Columbia University Press.

Pasinetti, L. L. (1985) 'Piero Sraffa, economista italiano a Cambridge', *Economia politica*, 3. English translation, 'Piero Sraffa: an Italian economist at Cambridge', in Pasinetti (ed.) (1998).

Pasinetti, L. L. (ed.) (1992/1996/1998) *Italian Economic Papers*, 3 vols, Bologna: Il Mulino/Oxford University Press.

Pavanelli, G. (ed.) (1989) 'Finanziamento della guerra e circuito dei capitali in alcune memorie inedite', *Storia del pensiero economico*, 18.

Pavanelli, G. (1993) 'Stabilità interna e vincolo estero nel dibattito economico italiano (1919–1939)', *Il pensiero economico italiano*, 2.

Pecchio, G. (1826) *L'anno mille ottocento ventisei dell'Inghilterra*, Lugano: Vanelli.

Pecchio, G. (1849) [1829] 'Dell'influenza che gli economisti esercitarono sulle riforme introdotte ne' diversi stati d'Italia nel secolo XVIII', appendix to *Storia dell'economia pubblica in Italia ossia epilogo critico degli economisti italiani preceduto da un'introduzione di G. P.*, 3rd edition, Lugano: Tip. della Svizzera italiana.

Pecchio, G. (1976) [1831] *Osservazioni semiserie di un esule sull'Inghilterra*, Milano: Longanesi.

Pecora, G. (2007) *Il pensiero politico di Gaetano Filangieri. Una analisi critica*, Soveria Mannelli: Rubbettino.

Pecorari, P. (1983) *Luigi Luzzatti e le origini dello 'statalismo' economico nell'età della Destra storica*, Padova: Signum.

Pedone A. (ed.) (1995) *Antonio De Viti de Marco*, Roma-Bari: Laterza.

Pellanda, A. (2003) 'Angelo Messedaglia', in Samuels W. J. (ed.).

Perri, S. (1998) 'Classical Economics in Italy', in Kurz, H. D., Salvadori, N. (eds), vol. I.

Perri, S. (2012) 'Achille Loria', in Istituto della Enciclopedia italiana: 643–8.

Perrotta, C. (2012) 'Bernardo Davanzati', in Istituto della Enciclopedia italiana: 319–25.

Persky, J. (1992) 'Retrospectives: Pareto's Law', *The Journal of Economic Perspectives*, 2.

Pesciarelli, E. (1978) 'The Italian contribution to the four-stage theory', *History of Political Economy*, 4.

Pesenti, A. (1946) 'Una caratteristica dell'imperialismo: la moneta manovrata', *Critica economica*, 4.

Pesenti, A. (1972) *La cattedra e il bugliolo*, Milano: La Pietra.

Petitti di Roreto, C. I. (1969) [1841] *Del lavoro dei fanciulli nelle manifatture*, in Petitti di Roreto, vol. I.

Petitti di Roreto C. I. (1969) [1845] *Delle strade ferrate italiane e del migliore ordinamento di esse*, in Petitti di Roreto (1969), vol. II.

Petitti di Roreto, C. I. (1969) *Opere scelte*, Bravo, G. M. (ed.), 2 vols, Fondazione Luigi Einaudi, Torino.

Petretto, A. (1982) 'Enrico Barone e i fondamenti della teoria dell'allocazione delle risorse', in Faucci, R. (ed.), vol. II.

Piscitelli, E. (1975) *Da Parri a De Gasperi. Storia del dopoguerra 1945–48*, Milano: Feltrinelli.

Pivetti, M. (ed.) (2000) *Piero Sraffa*, Roma: Carocci.

Pomini, M. (2012) 'From steady state to dynamic equilibrium: the perspective in the inter-war period', in Di Matteo, M., Donzelli, F. (eds).

Pomini, M., Tusset G. (2009) 'Habits and expectations: dynamic and general equilibrium in the Italian Paretian school', *History of Political Economy*, 2.

Porta, P. L. (1993) 'A note on Italian economics in the early Nineteenth century from Restoration to Risorgimento', *History of Economic Ideas*, 1.

Porta, P. L., Scazzieri, R. (1999) 'Il contributo di Pietro Verri alla teoria economica. Società commerciale, società civile e governo dell'economia', in Capra, C. (ed.), vol. II.

Porta, P. L., Scazzieri, R. (2000) 'Pietro Verri's political economy: commercial society, civil society, and the science of the legislator', *History of Political Economy*, 1.

Potier, J.-P. (1998) 'Léon Walras et l'école lombarde-venitienne' à travers sa correspondence (1874–1886)', in *L'économie, une science pour l'homme et la société. Mélanges en l'honneur d'Henri Bartoli*, Paris.

Preziosi, G. (1915) *La Germania alla conquista dell'Italia*, Firenze: Libreria della Voce.

Puviani, A. (1973) [1903] *Teoria dell'illusione finanziaria*, Volpi, F. (ed.), Milano: Isedi.

Pyke, F., Becattini, G., Sengenberger, W. (eds) (1991) *Distretti industriali e cooperazione fra imprese in Italia, Studi e informazioni*, Quaderni 34.

Quadrio Curzio, A., Scazzieri, R. (eds) (1977) *Protagonisti del pensiero economico*, vol. II, Bologna: il Mulino.

Rabbeno, U. (1891) 'The present condition of political economy in Italy', *Political science quarterly*.

Raffaelli, T. (1990) 'Il problema dell'indeterminazione nell'epistemologia di G. Demaria', in Faucci, R. (ed.).

Raffaelli, T. (2012) 'Carlo Cattaneo', in Istituto della Enciclopedia italiana: 304–8.

Raffaelli, T., Becattini, G., Dardi, M. (eds) (2010) *The Impact of Alfred Marshall's Ideas. The Global Diffusion of His Work*, Cheltenham: Elgar.

Rancan, A. (2006) 'Democrazia e mercato. I limiti del discorso economico secondo Mazzini', *Annali della Fondazione Luigi Einaudi*, XL.

Realfonzo, R. (1990) 'Un interprete italiano di Schumpeter: Luigi Lugli', in Faucci, R. (ed.).

Realfonzo, R. (1995) 'La teoria della banca come "organo dei pagamenti a credito'', in Pedone A. (ed.).

Reinert, S. A. (2007) 'Emulazione e traduzione: la genealogia occulta della storia del commercio', in VV. AA. (2007).

Reinert S. A. (2012) 'Girolamo Belloni', in Istituto della Enciclopedia italiana: 271–4.

Ricci, U. (1919) *Politica ed economia*, Roma: La Voce.

Ricci, U. (1939) [1925] 'Pareto e l'economia pura', in Id., *Tre economisti italiani: Pantaleoni, Pareto, Loria*, Bari: Laterza.

Ricci, U. (1980) [1918] 'Sull'opportunità di una storia dell'economia politica italiana', in Finoia, M. (ed.).

Ricci, U. (1999) *Saggi sul risparmio*, Lanciano: Carabba.

Ricossa, S. and Tuccimei, E. (eds) (1992) *La Banca d'Italia e il risanamento postbellico 1945–48*, in *Collana storica della Banca d'Italia, Documenti*, Roma-Bari: Laterza.

Ridolfi, C. (2008) *Scritti scelti*, Faucci, R. (ed.), Firenze: Le Monnier, Fondazione Spadolini – Nuova Antologia.

Roggi, P. (2010) *Amintore Fanfani imprenditore della politica*, Firenze: Regione Toscana.

Romagnosi, G. (1829) 'Del pauperismo britannico', in Sestan, E. (ed.) (1957).

Romagnosi, G. (1839) [1827] *Questioni sull'ordinamento delle statistiche* in Id., *Collezione degli articoli di economia politica e statistica civile*, Prato: Guasti.

Romagnosi, G. (1932) [1827] 'Della libera universal concorrenza nell'ordine sociale delle ricchezze', in Garino-Canina, A. (ed.), *Nuova collana di economisti stranieri e italiani*, vol. II, *Economisti italiani del Risorgimento*, Torino: Utet.

Romani, M. A. (ed.) (2012) *Luigi Einaudi e il 'Corriere della sera' 1894–1925*, 2 vols, Milano: Fondazione Corriere della sera.

Romani, R. (1994) *L'economia politica del Risorgimento italiano*, Torino: Bollati Boringhieri.

Roncaglia, A. (1990) 'Le scuole sraffiane', in Becattini, G. (ed.).

Roncaglia, A. (ed.) (1995) *Alle origini del pensiero economico in Italia. Moneta e sviluppo negli economisti napoletani dei secoli XVII–XVIII*, Bologna: Il Mulino.

Roncaglia, A. (1999) 'Antonio Serra', *Rivista italiana degli economisti*, 3: 421–38.

Roncaglia A. (2000) *Piero Sraffa's Political Economy. His Life, Thought and Cultural Heritage*, London: Routledge.

Roncaglia, A. (2007) 'The history of a journal: *Banca Nazionale del Lavoro Quarterly Review*, 1947–2007', *Banca Nazionale del Lavoro Quarterly Review*, vol. 60.

Roncaglia, A. (2012a) 'Antonio Serra', in Istituto della Enciclopedia italiana: 412–19.

Roncaglia, A. (2012b) 'Paolo Sylos Labini', in Istituto della Enciclopedia italiana: 718–24.

Roncaglia, A. (2012c) 'Piero Sraffa', in Istituto della Enciclopedia italiana: 710–17.

Rosselli, A. (2000) 'Early Views on Monetary Policy: The Neapolitan debate on the Theory of Exchange', *History of political economy*, 1: 61–82.

Rosselli, A. (2001) 'The role of the precious metals on *Della Moneta* by Ferdinando Galiani', in Faucci, R., Giocoli, N. (eds) (2001).

Rosselli, C. (1973) *Socialismo liberale*, J. Rosselli (ed.), Torino: Einaudi.

Rossi, E. (1953) *Lo Stato industriale*, Bari: Laterza.

Rossi-Doria, M. (1963) *Rapporto sulla Federconsorzi*, Bari: Laterza.

Rota, D. (ed.) (1989) *Pietro Custodi tra rivoluzione e restaurazione*, 2 vols, Lecco: Cattaneo.

Rotondi, C. (2006) 'Avalutatività e responsabilità nel liberalismo economico di Bresciani Turroni', introduction to Bresciani Turroni, C. (2006) [1945].

Ruffolo, G. (1973) *Rapporto sulla programmazione*, Roma-Bari: Laterza.

Sacco, P. L., Zamagni, S. (eds) (2002) *Complessità relazionale e comportamento economico*, Bologna: Il Mulino.

Salvadori, N. (ed.) (1998) *Omaggio a Piero Sraffa (1898–1983). Storia teoria documenti*, *Il pensiero economico italiano*, I.

Salvati, M. (1982) *Stato e industria nella ricostruzione. Alle origini del potere democristiano*, Milano: Feltrinelli.

Salvatorelli, L. (1935) *Il pensiero politico italiano dal 1700 al 1870*, Torino: Einaudi.

Salvemini, B. (1980) *Economia politica e arretratezza meridionale nell'età del Risorgimento. L. de Samuele Cagnazzi e la diffusione dello smithianesimo nel regno di Napoli*, Lecce: Milella.

Salvemini, B., Malagola Anziani, V., Di Battista, F., Barucci, P. (1979) *Sul classicismo economico in Italia: il 'caso' Francesco Fuoco*, Università di Firenze: Facoltà di economia e commercio.

Samuels, W. J. (ed.) (2003) *European Economists of Early 20th Century*, vol. II, Cheltenham: Elgar.

Samuelson, P. A. (1947) *Foundations of Economic Analysis*, Harvard: Harvard University Press. Italian translation (1973), *Fondamenti di analisi economica* Gay, A. (ed.), Milano: Il Saggiatore.

Samuelson, P. A. (1997) [Review of Steedman 1995], *The European Journal of the History of Economic Thought*, 4: 179–87.

Santarelli, E. (1982) 'Calcolo edonistico e sfruttamento del lavoro nel marxismo "microeconomico" di Enrico Leone (1898–1916)', in Faucci, R. (ed.) (1982), vol. II.

Santarelli, E. (1984) 'L'influsso dell'analisi schumpeteriana della funzione imprenditoriale e del credito nel pensiero italiano fra le due guerre', *Giornale degli economisti e Annali di economia*: 507–29.

Saraceno, P. (1969) [1948] *Elementi per un piano economico 1949–1952*, in Id., Barucci, P. (ed.), *Ricostruzione e pianificazione 1943/1948*, Bari: Laterza.

Saraceno, P. (1992) *Studi sulla questione meridionale 1965–75*, Bologna: il Mulino.

Say, J. B. (1827) 'Sur l'objet et l'utilité des statistiques', *Revue encyclopédique*, Septembre.

Say, J.-B. (1832) *Cours complet d'économie politique pratique*, Bruxelles: Dumont.

Say, J.-B. (1840) *Cours complet d'économie politique pratique*, IIe édition, Bruxelles: Société de librairie belge.

Scapparone, P. (2006) 'The Paretian theory of ophelimity in closed and open cycles: a commentary', *History of Economic Ideas*, 3.

Schumpeter, J. A. (1994) [1942] *Capitalism, Socialism and Democracy*, London: Routledge.

Schumpeter, J. A. (1994) [1954] *History of Economic Analysis*, London: Routledge.

Schumpeter, J. A. (1997) [1949] 'Vilfredo Pareto 1848–1923', in Id., *Ten Great Economists from Marx to Keynes*, London: Routledge.

Scialoja, A. (2006a) *Opere*, vol. I, Gioli, G. (ed.), Milano: Franco Angeli.

Scialoja, A. (2006b) *Opere*, vol. II, Magliulo, A. (ed.), Milano: FrancoAngeli.

Scialoja, A. (2006c) *Opere*, vol. III, Pesciarelli, E., Gallifante, M. F., Perri, S., Romani, R. (eds), Milano: Franco Angeli.

Scialoja, A. (2013) [1857] *I bilanci di Napoli e degli stati sardi*, in Scialoja (2013).

Scialoja, A. (2013) *Opere*, vol. IV, Bientinesi, F., Gioli, G. (eds), Milano: Franco Angeli.

Sensales, A. (2011) *Fedele Lampertico. Economia, popolo e Stato nell'Italia liberale*, Lecce: Manni.

Serra, A. (2011) [1613] *Short Treatise on the Causes that Can Make Kingdoms Abound in Gold and Silver even in Absence of Mines*, edited and with an introduction by Reinert, S. A. London: Anthem Press (Italian text in the appendix).

Sestan, E. (ed.) (1957) *Opere di Giandomenico Romagnosi, Carlo Cattaneo, Giuseppe Ferrari*, Milano-Napoli: Ricciardi.

Shackle, G. L. S. (1984) [1967] *The Years of High Theory*; Italian translation, *Gli anni dell'alta teoria*, Roma: Istituto della Enciclopedia italiana.

Silvestri, P. (2008) *Il liberalismo di Luigi Einaudi o del Buongoverno*, Soveria Mannelli: Rubbettino.

Simon, F. (2011) 'An economic approach to the study of law in the eighteenth century: Gaetano Filangieri and *La scienza della legislazione*', *Journal of the History of Economic Thought*, 2.

Skidelski, R. (1992) *John Maynard Keynes, II, The Economists as Saviour, 1920–1937*, London and Basingstoke: Macmillan. Italian translation, *JMK. L'economista come salvatore* (1996), Torino: Bollati Boringhieri.

Smith, A. (1978) [1763–64] *Lectures on Jurisprudence*, Meek, R. L., Raphael, D. D., Stein, P. G. (eds), Oxford: Clarendon Press.

Smith, A. (1979) [1776] *An Inquiry into the Nature and Causes of the Wealth of Nations*, Campbell, R. H., Skinner, A. S., Todd, W. B. (eds), vol. I, Indianapolis: Liberty Classics.

Soddu, P. (2008) *Ugo La Malfa. Il riformista moderno*, Roma: Carocci.

Soresina, M. (2001) *Conoscere per amministrare: Luigi Bodio. Statistica, economia e pubblica amministrazione*, Milano: Franco Angeli.

Spicciani, A. (1990) *Giuseppe Toniolo tra economia e storia*, Napoli: Guida.

Spicciani, A. (1997) *Per un nuovo diritto del lavoro. Il pensiero e l'opera di Giuseppe Toniolo*, Pisa: ETS.

Spiegel, H. W. (ed.) (1952) *The Development of Economic Thought. Great Economists in Perspective*, New York and London: Wiley.

Spirito, U. (1970) *Il corporativismo*, Firenze: Sansoni.

Spoto, L. (1988) 'Le cattedre di economia in Sicilia nel periodo 1779–1860', in Augello, M. M., Bianchini, M., Gioli, G., Roggi, P. (eds) (1988).

Sraffa, P. (1922) 'The Bank crisis in Italy', *The Economic Journal*: 178–97.

Sraffa, P. (1953) [1926] 'The laws of return under competitive conditions', reprinted in *Readings in Price Theory*, edited by the American Economic Association, London: Allen and Unwin.

Sraffa, P. (1960) *Production of Commodities by Means of Commodities*, Cambridge: Cambridge University Press; Italian edition, *Produzione di merci a mezzo di merci*, Torino: Einaudi.

Sraffa, P. (1998) [1925] 'Sulle relazioni fra costo e quantità prodotta', *Annali di economia*; English translation, 'On the relations between costs and quantity produced', in *Italian economic papers*, Pasinetti, L. L. (ed.), vol. III.

Sraffa, P. (1994) [1920] *L'inflazione monetaria durante e dopo la guerra*, Milano: Tipografia salesiana; new edition with an introduction by M. De Cecco, *Economia politica*, 2.

Steedman, I. (ed.) (1995) *Socialism and Marginalism in Economics, 1870–1930*, London and New York: Routledge.

Steve, S. (1976) *Lezioni di scienza delle finanze*, Padova: Cedam.

Sturzo, L. (1995) *Contro lo statalismo*, Dalu, L. (ed.), preface by Antiseri, D., Soveria Mannelli: Rubbettino.

Sullo, F. (1960) 'Il dibattito politico sulla programmazione economica in Italia dal 1945 al 1960', in VV. AA. (1960).

Suriani, V. (2005) 'La Scuola di scienze corporative di Pisa e la studio dell'economia programmatica negli anni trenta', in *Il pensiero economico italiano*, 1.

Sylos Labini, P. (1946) *Disoccupazione e opere pubbliche*, in *Ministero per la Costituente, Atti della commissione per lo studio dei problemi del lavoro*, III, Roma: U.E.S.I.S.A.

Sylos Labini, P. (1964) [1956] *Oligopolio e progresso tecnico*, Torino: Einaudi. English translation, Cambridge, Mass.: Harvard University Press, 1969.

Sylos Labini, P. (1966) [1950] 'I keynesiani (lettera a un amico dall'America)', appendix to Breglia, A. (1966) *L'economia dal punto di vista monetario*, Roma: Ateneo.

Sylos Labini, P. (1970) [1954] 'Il problema dello sviluppo economico in Marx', reprinted in Sylos Labini, P., *Problemi dello sviluppo economico*, Bari: Laterza.

Sylos Labini, P. (ed.) (1973) *Prezzi relativi e distribuzione del reddito*, Boringhieri, Torino.

Sylos Labini, P. (1986) *Le classi sociali negli anni '80*, Roma-Bari: Laterza.

Sylos Labini, P. (2000) *Sottosviluppo. Una strategia di riforme*, Bari-Roma: Laterza.

Sylos Labini, P. (2003) *Berlusconi e gli anticorpi. Diario di un cittadino indignato*, Roma-Bari: Laterza.

Sylos Labini, P. (2006) *Ahi serva Italia. Un appello ai miei concittadini*, Petrini, R. (ed.), Roma-Bari, Laterza.

Tagliacozzo, G. (ed.) (1937) *Economisti napoletani dei secoli XVII e XVIII*, Bologna: Cappelli.

Tagliacozzo, G. (1945) 'Croce and the nature of economic science', *Quarterly Journal of Economics*, 59.

Taparelli d'Azeglio, L. (1845) *Saggio teoretico di diritto naturale appoggiato sul fatto*, Livorno: Mansi.

Tiran, A. (1993) 'Pietro Verri, aux origines de la théorie de la valeur e de la loi des débouchés de Jean-Baptiste Say', *Revue d'économie politique*: 445–71.

Toniolo, G. (1915) *Trattato di economia sociale. Introduzione*, Firenze: Libreria editrice fiorentina.

Toniolo, Gianni (ed.) (1978) *Industria e banca nella grande crisi 1929–1934*, Milano: Etas libri.

Travagliante, P. (ed.) (1994) *Sui privilegi in materia di industria. Il concorso di economia del 1841 nell'università degli studi di Catania*, Catania: Cuecm.

Travagliante, P. (1996) 'Cultura economica e dibattito politico nei periodici palermitani degli anni trenta e quaranta', in Augello, M. M., Bianchini, M., Guidi, M. E. L. (eds) (1996).

Tusset, G. (2004) *La teoria dinamica nel pensiero economico italiano (1890–1940)*, Firenze: Polistampa.

Tusset, G. (2012) 'Individual and market inertia in Luigi Amoroso's cycle model', *History of Economic Ideas*, 2.

Università degli studi di Torino (1993) *Materiali per una storia del Laboratorio di economia politica, Torino 1893–1993* (Torino: no publisher given).

Urbinati, N. (1990) *Le civili libertà. Positivismo e liberalismo nell'Italia liberale*, Venezia: Marsilio.

Valenti, G. (1891) *Le idee economiche di Giandomenico Romagnosi*, Roma: Loescher.

Valenti, G. (1901) *La proprietà della terra e la costituzione economica. Saggi critici sul sistema di Achille Loria*, Bologna: Zanichelli.

Vasco G. (1989) *Opere*, Perna, M. L. (ed.), Torino: Fondazione Luigi Einaudi.

Venturi, F. (1969) *Settecento riformatore. Da Muratori a Beccaria*, Torino: Einaudi.

Venturi, F. (1977) *Le vite incrociate di Henry Lloyd e Pietro Verri*, Torino: Tirrena Stampatori.

Verri, A. (1993) [1765–66] 'Alcune idee sulla filosofia morale', in Francioni, G., Romagnoli, S. (eds) (1993).

Verri, P. (1964a) *Del piacere e del dolore ed altri scritti*, De Felice, R. (ed.), Milano: Feltrinelli.

Verri, P. (1964b) [1763] *Meditazioni sulla felicità*, in Verri, P. (1964a).

Verri, P. (1964c) [1773] *Discorso sull'indole del piacere e del dolore*, in Verri, P. (1964a).

Verri, P. (1984) 'Lettere al fattore di Biassono', Pino Pongolini, F. (ed.), *Rivista milanese di economia*, 10.

Verri, P. (2002) [1781] *Discorsi*, Milano: Fondazione Giangiacomo Feltrinelli.

Verri, P. (2006) *Scritti di economia finanza e amministrazione*, Bognetti, G., Moioli, A., Porta, P. L., Tonelli, G. (eds), Roma: Edizioni di storia e letteratura.

Vianello, C. A. (ed.) (1939) *La riforma monetaria in Lombardia nella seconda metà del '700'*, Milano: Università Bocconi.

Vianello, C. A. (ed.) (1942) *Economisti minori del Settecento lombardo*, Milano: Giuffrè.

Vianello, C. A. (ed.) (1943) *Le consulte amministrative inedite di Cesare Beccaria*, Milano: Giuffrè.

Villari, L. (1959) *Il pensiero economico di Antonio Genovesi*, Firenze: Le Monnier.

Villari, L. (ed.) (1972) *Il capitalismo italiano del Novecento*, Roma-Bari: Laterza.

Vistalli, F. (1954) *Giuseppe Toniolo*, Roma: Comitato G. Toniolo.

Vito, F. (1934) 'Il risparmio forzato e la teoria dei cicli economici', *Rivista internazionale di scienze sociali*, 1.

VV. AA. (1933) *L'economia programmatica*, Firenze: Sansoni.

VV. AA. (1946) *Pianificazione economica collettivistica. Studi critici sulle possibilità del socialismo*, no place [but Torino]: Einaudi.

VV. AA. (1949) *Vilfredo Pareto. L'economista e il sociologo*, Milano: Malfasi.

VV. AA. (1955) *La lotta contro i monopoli*, Bari: Laterza.

VV. AA. (1956a) *Giacobini italiani*, vol. I, Cantimori, D. (ed.) Bari: Laterza.

VV. AA. (1956b) *Studi in onore di A. Genovesi nel bicentenario della istituzione della cattedra di economia*, Demarco, D. (ed.) Napoli: l'Arte Tipografica.

VV. AA. (1960) *I piani di sviluppo in Italia dal 1945 al 1960*, Milano: Giuffrè.

VV. AA. (1966) *Studi in onore di Marco Fanno*, vol. 1, Padova: Cedam.

VV. AA. (1968) *Il Mezzogiorno nelle ricerche della SVIMEZ: 1946–67*, Milano: Giuffrè.

VV. AA. (1975) *Commemorazione di Luigi Einaudi nel centenario della nascita (1874–1974)*, Torino: Fondazione L. Einaudi.

VV. AA. (1978) *Il Piano del Lavoro della CGIL*, Milano: Feltrinelli.

VV. AA. (1981) *Banca e industria fra le due guerre. L'economia e il pensiero economico*, Bologna: Banco di Roma/il Mulino.

VV. AA. (1983) *Keynes in Italia, Catalogo bibliografico*, Banca Toscana, Studi e informazioni, Quaderni 7.

VV. AA. (1984) *Dal corporativismo allo sviluppo. 50 anni di politica economica in Italia. L'azione di Ugo La Malfa*, Roma: Edizioni della Voce.

VV. AA. (1986) *Donato Menichella. Testimonianze e studi raccolti dalla Banca d'Italia*, Roma-Bari.

VV. AA. (1988) *Il mestiere di economista*, Torino: Einaudi.

VV. AA. (1990a) *Cesare Beccaria tra Milano e l'Europa*, Bari: Cariplo-Laterza.

VV. AA., (1990b) *Francesco Ferrara e il suo tempo*, Roma: Associazione bancaria italiana.

VV. AA. (1993a) 'Sulla storiografia del pensiero economico italiano fra Settecento e Novecento', *Il pensiero economico italiano*, 1.

VV. AA. (1993b) *Tensioni e prospettive economico-monetarie nel XVII secolo: Geminiano Montanari*, Modena: Mucchi.

VV. AA. (1995) *Il ministero per la Costituente. L'elaborazione dei principi della Carta costituzionale*, Firenze: La Nuova Italia.

VV. AA. (1996) *Political economy in European periodicals, 1700–1900*, *History of Economic Ideas*, 3.

VV. AA. (1999) *Manlio Rossi-Doria e le trasformazioni nel Mezzogiorno d'Italia*, Manduria: Lacaita.

VV. AA. (2000) *Una rivista all'avanguardia. La 'Riforma sociale' 1894–1935*, Malandrino, C. (ed.), Firenze: Olschki.

VV. AA. (2001) *Della Moneta by Ferdinando Galiani: A Quarter Millennium Assessment*, Faucci, R., Giocoli, N. (eds), *History of Economic Ideas*, 3.

VV. AA. (2004a) 'I novant'anni della *Rivista di politica economica* (1911–2000)', Bini, P. (ed.), *Rivista di politica economica*.

VV. AA. (2004b) *Piero Sraffa, Convegno internazionale*, Roma: Accademia nazionale dei Lincei.VV. AA. (2007), *Genovesi economista*, Napoli: Nella sede dell'Istituto italiano per gli studi filosofici.

VV. AA. (2005) 'Franco Modigliani between economic theory and social commitment', *Banca Nazionale del Lavoro Quarterly Review*, vol. LVIII: 233–4.

VV. AA. (2009) *La scuola di economia di Torino. Co-protagonisti ed epigoni*, Marchionatti, R. (ed.), Firenze: Olschki.

VV. AA. (2011a) *Angelo Messedaglia e il suo tempo*, Gioia, V., Noto S. (eds.), Macerata: Eum.

VV. AA. (2011b) *Francesco Saverio Nitti. Atti del convegno nazionale di studi*, F. Barbagallo and P. Barucci (eds), Napoli: Istituto italiano per gli studi filosofici.

VV. AA. (2011c) *L'identità culturale della Sicilia risorgimentale. Atti del convegno per il bicentenario della nascita di Emerico Amari e Francesco Ferrara*, F. Simon (ed.), *Storia e politica*, 2.

VV. AA. (2011d) *Studi su Jean-Charles-Léonard Sismonde de Sismondi*, Faucci R., Jacoponi, L. (eds), *Il pensiero economico italiano*, 2.

VV. AA. (2011e) *Antonio Pesenti a cento anni dalla nascita, Il pensiero economico italiano*, 1.

VV. AA. (2012) *Symposium on Federico Caffè: Public Policy and Economic Thought*, *History of Economic Ideas*, 1.

Weintraub, E. R. (1997) 'Why so Many Italian Economists?', *Rivista di storia economica*, 2.

Whitaker, J. K. (ed.) (1996) *The Correspondence of Alfred Marshall, Economist*, vol. I, Cambridge-New York-Melbourne: Cambridge University Press.

Winch, D. (1978) *Adam Smith's Politics. An Essay in Historiographic Revision*, Cambridge: Cambridge University Press; Italian translation (1991) *La politica di Adam Smith*, Civitanova M.: Otium.

Zagari, E. (ed.) (1975) *Marxismo e revisionismo. Bernstein Sorel Graziadei Leone*, Napoli: Guida.

Zamagni, S. (2010) 'Perché ritornare a Giacinto Dragonetti', Università di Bologna: AICCON.

Zamagni, S. (2012) 'Bene comune e fraternità', in Istituto della Enciclopedia italiana: 17–26.

Zanni A. (1977) 'Mortara e Del Vecchio nel 1938', *Note economiche*, 5–6.

Zanni, A. (1983) 'Gustavo Del Vecchio. Teoria e storia in un mediatore di cultura', *Revue internationale d'histoire de la banque*.

Zanni, A. (1985) 'Sulla mancata apparizione della "Teoria generale" di Keynes in una seconda serie della "Nuova collana degli economisti" (con corrispondenza inedita)', *Quaderni di storia dell'economia politica*, 3.

Zanni, A. (1996) 'Demaria negli anni Trenta attraverso un epistolario (giugno 1930–febbraio 1939)', in Bini (ed.).

Index

For Product Safety Concerns and Information please contact our EU
representative GPSR@taylorandfrancis.com Taylor & Francis Verlag GmbH,
Kaufingerstraße 24, 80331 München, Germany

Printed and bound by CPI Group (UK) Ltd, Croydon, CR0 4YY
01/05/2025
01858357-0002